THE ANCIENT RÉGIME

"LES ORIGINES
DE LA FRANCE CONTEMPORAINE"

THE ANCIENT RÉGIME

By Hippolyte A. Taine

TRANSLATED BY JOHN DURAND

BOOKS FOR LIBRARIES PRESS
FREEPORT, NEW YORK

First Published 1881
Reprinted 1972

INTERNATIONAL STANDARD BOOK NUMBER:
0-8369-6785-2

LIBRARY OF CONGRESS CATALOG CARD NUMBER:
79-38368

PRINTED IN THE UNITED STATES OF AMERICA
BY
NEW WORLD BOOK MANUFACTURING CO., INC.
HALLANDALE, FLORIDA 33009

NOTE BY THE TRANSLATOR.

The reader of the following pages will find certain words spelt in a different mode from that which prevails in England; also words used according to a different standard of expression. In explanation of these differences, for which the translator has to claim the indulgence of the English reader, it is proper to state that the translation was made specially for the public of the United States, where the author is less read in the original than in England; and again, that the edition is printed from American stereotype plates, in which the necessary alterations are impracticable. Taking into account these conditions of publication, it is hoped that the peculiarities referred to will not be found serious blemishes in the English rendering of the author's ideas.

                                                              J. D.

South Orange, New Jersey :
    March 11, 1876.

PREFACE.

In 1849, being twenty one years of age, I was an elector and was very much perplexed; for I had to write out a list of fifteen or twenty deputies, and, moreover, according to French practice, not only to select men but to discriminate between theories. I was required to be royalist or republican, democrat or conservative, socialist or Bonapartist; I was neither, nor even anything at all, and, at times, I envied all these men of conviction who had the good fortune to be something. After hearing the various doctrines I felt there was undoubtedly some void in my mind. Motives valid for others were not so for me; I could not understand how, in politics, one could make up his mind according to his predilections. My positive friends constructed a constitution as if it were a house, according to the most attractive, the newest and the simplest plan; and there was no lack of models : the mansion of the marquis, the domicile of the bourgeois, the working-man's lodging, barracks for soldiers, the communist philanstery, and even the gipsy's encampment. Each one asserted of his model: " This is the true abode of man, the only one a man of sense can dwell in." In my opinion, the argument was weak; personal fancies did not strike me as authorities. It seemed to me that a house should not be built for the architect, nor for itself, but for the owner and occupant. To ask the opinion of the owner, to submit plans to the French people of its future dwelling, was too evidently a parade or a deception : in such cases the question is tantamount to the answer, and besides, had this answer been unconditional, France was scarcely more at liberty to give it than I was; ten million ignorant men cannot constitute a wise one. A people, on being consulted, may, indeed, tell the form of government they like, but not the form they need; this is possible only through experience; time is required to ascertain if the political dwelling is convenient, durable, proof against inclemencies, suited to the occupant's habits, pursuits, character, peculiarities and caprices. Now, as proof of this, we have never been content with our own; within eighty years we have pulled it down thirteen times in order to rebuild it, and this we have done in vain, not having yet found one that suits us. If other people have been more fortunate, if, in other countries, many political institutions are durable and last indefinitely, it is because they have been organized in a peculiar manner, around a primitive and massive nucleus, supported on some old central edifice, many times repaired but always preserved, enlarged by degrees, adapted and modified according to the wants of the inhabitants. None of them were built at one stroke, on a new pattern, and according to the provisions of reason alone. We must, perhaps, admit that there is no other way of building permanently, and that the sudden concoction of a new constitution, suitable and durable, is an undertaking surpassing the forces of the human mind. In any event, I came to the conclusion that if we should ever discover the one we need it will not be by the means in practice. The point is to *discover* it, if it exists, and not to put it to vote. In this respect, our preferences would be fruitless; nature and history have chosen for us in advance; it is for us to adapt ourselves to them, as it is certain they will not accommodate themselves to us. The social and political mould into which a nation may enter and *remain* is not subject to its will, but determined by its character and its past. It is essential that, even in its least traits, it should be shaped on the living traits to which it is applied; otherwise it will burst and fall to pieces. Hence, if we should succeed in finding ours, it will only be through a study of ourselves, while the more we understand exactly what we are, the more certainly shall we distinguish what best suits us. We ought, therefore, to reverse the ordinary methods, and form some conception of the nation before formulating its constitution. Doubtless the first operation is much more tedious and difficult than the second. How much time, how much study, how many observations rectified one by the other, how many researches in the past and the present, over all the domains of thought and of action, what manifold and age-long labors to acquire an accurate and complete idea of a great people which has lived a people's age, and which still lives! But it is the only means of building well after having reasoned unsoundly, and I promised myself that, for my own part, if I should some day undertake to form a political opinion, it would be only after having studied France.

What is contemporary France? To answer this question we must know how this France is formed, or, what is still better, to act as spectator at its formation. At the end of the last century, like a moulting insect, it underwent a metamorphosis. Its ancient organization is dissolved ; it tears away its most precious tissues and falls into convulsions which seem mortal. Then, after multiplied throes and a painful lethargy, it re-establishes itself. But its organization is no longer the same : by silent interior travail a new being is substituted for the old. In 1808, its leading characteristics are decreed and defined : departments, *arondissements*, cantons and communes, no change has since taken place in its exterior divisions and functions ; Concordat, Code, Tribunals, University, Institute, Préfets, Council of State. Taxes, Collectors, Cours des Comptes, a uniform and centralized administration, its principal organs, are still the same ; nobility, commoners, artisans, peasants, each class has henceforth the position, the sentiments, the traditions which we see at the present day. Thus the new creature is at once stable and complete ; consequently its structure, its instincts and its faculties mark in advance the circle within which its thought and its action will be stimulated. Around it, other nations, some precocious, others backward, all with greater cautiousness, some with better success, operate in like manner the transformation which transfers them from the feudal to the modern order of things; the gestation is universal and all but simultaneous. But, beneath the new forms as beneath the ancient, the weak is always the prey of the strong. Woe to those whose too lingering evolution surrenders them to the neighbor suddenly emancipated from his chrysalis state, and the first to go forth fully armed! Woe likewise to him whose too violent and too abrupt evolution has badly balanced his internal economy, and who, through the exaggeration of his governing forces, through the deterioration of his deep-seated organs, through the gradual impoverishment of his vital tissues is doomed to inconsiderate acts, to debility, to impotency, amidst sounder and better balanced neighbors! In the organization which France effected for herself at the beginning of the century, all the general lines of her contemporary history were traced,— political revolutions, social Utopias, division of classes, policy of the church, conduct of the nobility, of the commonalty, and of the people, the development, the direction, or deviation of philosophy, of letters and of the arts. Hence, when we wish to understand our present condition our attention always reverts to the terrible and fruitful crisis by which the ancient régime produced the Revolution, and the Revolution the new régime.

Ancient régime, Revolution, new régime, I am going to try to describe these three conditions with exactness. I presume to declare here that I have no other object in view. A historian may be allowed to act as a naturalist: I have confronted my subject as I would the metamorphosis of an insect. Moreover, the event is so interesting in itself it is worth the trouble of being observed for itself alone, and no effort is required to exclude mental reservations. Partiality being set aside, curiosity becomes scientific and is wholly centred in the secret forces which guide the marvellous process. These forces are the situation, the passions, the ideas, the wills of each group, and we are able to distinguish them, almost to measure them. They lie under our eyes; we are not reduced to conjectures about them, to uncertain divinations, to vague indications. By singular good fortune we perceive the men themselves, their exterior and their interior. The French of the ancient régime are still within range of our observation. Each of us, in our youth, has been able to associate with some of the survivors of this vanished society. Many of their mansions still remain with their apartments and furniture intact. By means of their pictures and engravings we follow them in their domestic life, we see their costumes, their attitudes and their gestures. With their literature, their philosophy, their sciences, their gazettes, and their correspondences, we can repro- duce all their thoughts, and even their familiar conversation. A multitude of memoirs, issuing for the past thirty years from public and private archives, lead us from one drawing-room to another as if we were introduced into them. The letters and journals of travellers from other countries control and complete, by their independent delineations, the portraits which this society has traced of itself. It has set forth everything pertaining to itself except what it regarded as commonplace and familiar to its contemporaries, what appeared technical, tiresome and vulgar, what affected the province, the commonalty, the peasant, the artisan, the administration and the household. I was desirous of supplying these omissions, and, outside the small circle of learned and cultured Frenchmen, of comprehending France. Owing to the kindness of M. Maury and the precious indications of M. Boutaric, I have examined a mass of manuscript documents, the correspondence of a large number of intendants, directors of excise, farmers-general, magistrates, employés, and private persons of every kind and of every degree during the thirty last years of the ancient régime, the reports and memorials of the various departments of the royal household, the *procès-verbaux* and *cahiers* of the States-General, in one hundred and seventy-six volumes, the correspondence of the military officers in 1789 and 1790, the letters, memoirs and statistical details contained in the hundred *cartons* of the ecclesiastical committee, the correspondence in

ninety-four files of the departmental and municipal administrations with the ministers from 1790 to 1799, the reports of the
councillors of State on their mission at the end of 1801, the
correspondence of préfets under the Consulate, the Empire, and
under the Restoration up to 1823, and a number of documents
so unknown and so instructive that, indeed, the history of the
Revolution seems still unpublished.   At least, we have but these
documents to show us living figures, the petty nobles, curates,
monks and nuns of the provinces, lawyers, aldermen and bourgeoisie of the towns, the rural attorneys and village syndics, the
laborers and artisans, officers and soldiers.   These only enable us
to see, nearly in detail, the condition of men, the interior of a
parsonage, of a convent, of a town council, the wages of a
workman, the produce of a field, the taxes imposed on a peasant,
the occupation of a collector, the outlay of a noble or of a
prelate, the budget, the retinue and ceremonial of a court.
Owing to these we can give precise figures, and know, hour by
hour, the occupation of a day, and, better still, tell the order of
a bill of fare, and recompose an ostentatious toilet.   We have,
again, marked out on paper and classed by dates the varieties of
dress worn by the queen, Marie Antoinette, and, on the other
hand, we can picture to ourselves the attire of a peasant, describe
his bread, state the kinds of flour composing it, and give in *sous*
and *deniers* how much it cost him a pound.   With such resources
one becomes almost the contemporary of the men whose history
one writes, and, more than once, at the Archives, in tracing their
handwriting on the yellow paper, I was tempted to speak to
them aloud.

August, 1875.

CONTENTS.

BOOK SECOND.

HABITS AND CHARACTERS.

BOOK THIRD.

THE SPIRIT AND THE DOCTRINE.

BOOK FOURTH.

THE PROPAGATION OF THE DOCTRINE.

BOOK FIFTH.

THE PEOPLE.

THE ANCIENT RÉGIME.

BOOK FIRST.

The Structure of Society.

CHAPTER I.

THE ORIGIN OF PRIVILEGES.—I. Services and Recompenses of the Clergy. —II. Services and Recompenses of the Nobles.—III. Services and Recompenses of the King.

In 1789 three classes of persons, the Clergy, the Nobles, and the King, occupied the most prominent position in the State, with all the advantages pertaining thereto; namely, authority, property, honors, or, at the very least, privileges, immunities, favors, pensions, preferences, and the like. If they occupied this position for so long a time, it is because for so long a time they had deserved it. They had, in short, through an immense and secular effort, constructed by degrees the three principal foundations of modern society.

I.

Of these three superadded foundations the most ancient and deepest was the work of the clergy. For twelve hundred years and more they had labored upon it, both as architects and workmen, at first alone and then almost alone. In the beginning, during the first four centuries, they constituted religion and the church. Let us ponder over these two words, in order to weigh them well. On the one hand, in a society founded on conquest, hard and cold like a machine of brass, forced by its very struct-

ure to destroy among its subjects all courage to act and all desire to live, they had proclaimed the "glad tidings," held forth
the "kingdom of God," preached loving resignation in the hands
of a Heavenly Father, inspired patience, gentleness, humility,
self-abnegation, and charity, and opened the only issues by which
man stifling in the Roman 'ergastulum' could again breathe and
see daylight—and this is religion.   On the other hand, in a State
gradually undergoing depopulation, crumbling away, and fatally
becoming a prey, they had formed a living society governed by
laws and discipline, rallying around a common object and a
common doctrine, sustained by the devotion of chiefs and by
the obedience of believers, alone capable of subsisting beneath
the flood of barbarians which the empire in ruin suffered to pour
in through its breaches—and this is the church.

It continues to build on these two first foundations, and after
the invasion, for over five hundred years, it saves what it can
still save of human culture.   It marches in the van of the barbarians or converts them directly after their entrance, which is a
wonderful advantage.   Let us judge of it by a single fact: In
Great Britain, which like Gaul had become Latin, but whereof
the conquerors remained pagan during a century and a half, arts,
industries, society, language, all were destroyed; nothing remained of an entire people, either massacred or fugitive, but
slaves.   We have still to divine their traces; reduced to the condition of beasts of burden, they disappear from history.   Such
might have been the fate of Europe if the clergy had not
promptly tamed the fierce brutes to which it belonged.   Before
the bishop in his gilded cope, before the monk, "emaciated, clad
in skins," wan, "dirtier and more spotted than a chameleon,"[1]
the converted German stood fear-stricken as before a sorcerer.
In his calm moments, after the chase or inebriety, the vague divination of a mysterious and grandiose future, the dim conception
of an unknown tribunal, the rudiment of conscience which he
already had in his forests beyond the Rhine, arouses in him
through sudden alarms half-formed, menacing visions.   At the
moment of violating a sanctuary he asks himself whether he
may not fall on its threshold with vertigo and a broken neck.[2]

---

[1] "Les Moines d'Occident," by Montalembert, I. 277; St. Lupicin before the Burgun-
dian King Chilperic, II. 416; St. Karileff before King Childebert; cf. *passim*, Gregory of
Tours and the Bollandist collection.

[2] No legend is more frequently encountered; we find it as late as the twelfth century.

Convicted through his own perplexity, he stops and spares the farm, the village, and the town which live under the priest's protection. If the animal impulse of rage, or of primitive lusts, leads him to murder or to rob, later, after satiety, in times of sickness or of misfortune, taking the advice of his concubine or of his wife, he repents and makes restitution twofold, tenfold, a hundredfold, unstinted in his gifts and immunities.[1] Thus, over the whole territory the clergy maintain and enlarge their asylums for the oppressed and the vanquished. On the other hand, among the warrior chiefs with long hair, by the side of kings clad in furs, the mitred bishop and abbot, with shaven brows, take seats in the assemblies; they alone know how to use the pen and how to discuss. Secretaries, councillors, theologians, they participate in all edicts; they have their hand in the government; they strive through its agency to bring a little order out of immense disorder; to render the law more rational and more humane, to re-establish or preserve piety, instruction, justice, property, and especially marriage. To their ascendency is certainly due the police system, such as it was, intermittent and incomplete, which prevented Europe from falling into a Mongolian anarchy. If, down to the end of the twelfth century, the clergy bears heavily on the princes, it is especially to repress in them and beneath them the brutal appetites, the rebellions of flesh and blood, the outbursts and relapses of irresistible ferocity which are undermining the social fabric. Meanwhile, in its churches and in its convents, it preserves the ancient acquisitions of humanity, the Latin tongue, Christian literature and theology, a portion of pagan literature and science, architecture, sculpture, painting, the arts and industries which aid worship, the more valuable industries which provide man with bread, clothing, and shelter, and especially the greatest of all human acquisitions, and the most opposed to the vagabond humor of the idle and plundering barbarian, the habit and taste for labor. In the districts depopulated through Roman exactions, through the revolt of the Bagaudes, through the invasion of the Germans, and the raids of brigands, the Benedictine monk built his cabin of boughs amid briers and brambles;[2] large areas around him, formerly culti-

---

[1] Chilperic, for example, acting under the advice of Fredegonde after the death of their children.

[2] Montalembert, *ibid*, II. book 8; and especially " Les Forêts de la France dans l'antiquité et au Moyen Age," by Alfred Maury. *Spinæ et repres* is a phrase constantly recurring in the lives of the saints.

vated, are nothing but abandoned thickets. Along with his associates he clears the ground and erects buildings; he domesticates half-tamed animals; he establishes a farm, a mill, a forge, an oven, and shops for shoes and clothing. According to the rules of his order, he reads daily for two hours; he gives seven hours to manual labor, and he neither eats nor drinks more than is absolutely essential. Through his intelligent, voluntary labor, conscientiously performed and with a view to the future, he produces more than the layman. Through his temperate, judicious, economical system he consumes less than the layman. Hence it is that where the layman had failed he sustains himself and even prospers.[1] He welcomes the unfortunate, feeds them, sets them to work, and unites them in matrimony; beggars, vagabonds, and fugitive peasants gather around the sanctuary. Their camp gradually becomes a village and next a small town; man ploughs as soon as he can be sure of his crops, and becomes the father of a family as soon as he considers himself able to provide for his offspring. In this way new centres of agriculture and industry are formed, which likewise become new centres of population.[2]

To food for the body add food for the soul, not less essential; for, along with aliments, it was still necessary to furnish man with inducements to live, or, at the very least, with the resignation which makes life endurable; also with the affecting or poetic reverie which supplies the place of absent felicity. Down to the middle of the thirteenth century the clergy stands almost alone in furnishing this. Through its innumerable legends of saints, through its cathedrals and their construction, through its statues and their expression, through its services and their still transparent meaning, it rendered visible "the kingdom of God," and set up an ideal world at the end of the actual world, like a magnificent golden pavilion at the end of a miry morass.[3] The

---

[1] We find the same thing to-day with the colonies of Trappists in Algiers.

[2] "Polyptique d'Irminon," by Guérard. In this work we see the prosperity of the domain belonging to the Abbey of St. Germain des Près at the end of the eighth century. According to M. Guérard's statistics, the peasantry of Paliseau were about as prosperous in the time of Charlemagne as at the present day.

[3] There are twenty-five thousand lives of the saints, between the sixth and tenth centuries, collected by the Bollandists. The last that are truly inspired are those of St. Francis of Assisi and his companions at the beginning of the fourteenth century. The same vivid sentiment extends down to the end of the fifteenth century in the works of Fra Angelico and Hans Memling. The Sainte Chapelle in Paris, the upper church at Assisi, Dante's

saddened heart, athirst for tenderness and serenity, takes refuge in this divine and gentle world. Persecutors there, about
to strike, are arrested by an invisible hand; wild beasts become
docile; the stags of the forest come of their own accord every
morning to draw the chariots of the saints; the country blooms
for them like a new Paradise; they die only when it pleases
them. Meanwhile they comfort mankind; goodness, piety, for-
giveness flows from their lips with ineffable sweetness; with eyes
upturned to heaven, they see God, and without effort, as in a
dream, they ascend into the light and seat themselves at His
right hand. How divine the legend, how inestimable in value,
when, under the universal reign of brute force, to endure this life
it was necessary to imagine another, and to render the second as
visible to the spiritual eye as the first was to the physical eye.
The clergy thus nourished men for more than twelve centuries,
and in the grandeur of its recompense we can estimate the depth
of their gratitude. Its popes, for two hundred years, were the
dictators of Europe. It organized crusades, dethroned monarchs, and distributed kingdoms. Its bishops and abbots became
here, sovereign princes, and there, veritable founders of dynasties.
It held in its grasp a third of the territory, one-half of the revenue, and two-thirds of the capital of Europe. Let us not believe that man counterfeits gratitude, or that he gives without a
valid motive; he is too egotistical and too envious for that.
Whatever may be the institution, ecclesiastic or secular, whatever
may be the clergy, Buddhist or Christian, the contemporaries
who observe it for forty generations are not bad judges; they
surrender to it their will and their possessions, just in proportion
to its services, and the excess of their devotion may measure the
immensity of its benefaction.

II.

Up to this point no aid is found against the power of the
sword and the battle-axe except in persuasion and in patience.
Those States which, imitating the old empire, attempted to rise
up into compact organizations, and to interpose a barrier against
constant invasion, obtained no hold on the shifting soil; after

---

Paradise, and the Fioretti, furnish an idea of these visions. As regards modern literature, the state of a believer's soul in the middle ages is perfectly described in the
" Pélerinage à Kevlaar," by Heine, and in " Les Reliques vivantes," by Tourgueneff.

Charlemagne everything melts away. There are no more soldiers after the battle of Fontanet; during half a century bands
of four or five hundred brigands sweep over the country, killing,
burning, and devastating with impunity. But, by way of compensation, the dissolution of the State raises up at this very time a
military generation. Each petty chieftain has planted his feet
firmly on the domain he occupies, or which he withholds; he no
longer keeps it in trust, or for use, but as property, and an inheritance. It is his own manor, his own village, his own earldom;
it no longer belongs to the king; he contends for it in his own
right. The benefactor, the conservator at this time is the man
capable of fighting, of defending others, and such really is the
character of the newly established class. The noble, in the language of the day, is the man of war, the *soldier* (miles), and it is
he who lays the second foundation of modern society.

In the tenth century his extraction is of little consequence.
He is oftentimes a Carlovingian count, a beneficiary of the king,
the sturdy proprietor of one of the last of the Frank estates.
In one place he is a martial bishop or a valiant abbot; in another
a converted pagan, a retired bandit, a prosperous adventurer, a
rude huntsman, who long supported himself by the chase and
on wild fruits.[1] The ancestors of Robert the Strong are unknown, and later the story runs that the Capets are descended
from a Parisian butcher. In any event the noble of that epoch
is the brave, the powerful man, expert in the use of arms, who,
at the head of a troop, instead of flying or paying ransom, offers
his breast, stands firm, and protects a patch of the soil with his
sword. To perform this service he has no need of ancestors;
all that he requires is courage, for he is himself an ancestor;
security for the present, which he insures, is too acceptable to
permit any quibbling about his title.

Finally, after so many centuries, we find each canton possessing its armed men, a settled body of troops capable of
resisting nomadic invasion; the community is no longer a prey
to strangers; at the end of a century this Europe, which had
been sacked by flotillas of two-masted vessels, is to throw two
hundred thousand armed men into Asia, and henceforth, both
north and south, in the face of Mussulmans and of pagans,

---

[1] As, for example, Tertulle, founder of the Plantagenet family, Rollo, Duke of Normandy, Hugues, Abbot of St. Martin, of Tours and of St. Denis.

instead of being conquered it is to conquer. For the second time an ideal figure becomes apparent after that of the saint,[1] the hero; and the new-born sentiment, as efficacious as the old one, thus groups men together into a stable society. This consists of a resident corps of gendarmes, in which, from father to son, one is always a gendarme. Each individual is born into it with his hereditary rank, his local post, his pay in landed property, with the certainty of never being abandoned by his chieftain, and with the obligation of giving his life for his chieftain in time of need. In this epoch of perpetual warfare only one regimen is suitable, that of a body of men confronting the enemy, and such is the feudal system; we can judge by this trait alone of the perils which it wards off, and of the service which it enjoins. "In those days," says the Spanish general-chronicle, "kings, counts, nobles, and knights, in order to be ready at all hours, kept their horses in the rooms in which they slept with their wives." The viscount in his tower defending the entrance to a valley or the passage of a ford, the marquis thrown as a forlorn hope on the burning frontier, sleeps with his hand on his weapon, like an American lieutenant among the Sioux behind a western stockade. His dwelling is simply a camp and a refuge; straw and heaps of leaves overspread the pavement of the great hall; here he rests with his cavaliers, taking off a spur if he has a chance to sleep; the loopholes in the wall scarcely allow daylight to enter; the main thing is not to be shot with arrows. Every taste, every sentiment is subordinated to military service; there are certain places on the European frontier where a child of fourteen is required to march, and where the widow up to sixty is required to remarry. Men to fill up the ranks, men to mount guard, is the call which at this moment proceeds from all institutions like the summons of a brazen horn.

Thanks to these braves, the peasant *(villanus)* enjoys protection. He is no longer to be slaughtered, no longer to be led captive with his family, in herds, with his neck in the yoke. He ventures to plough and to sow, and to rely upon his crops; in case of danger he knows that he can find an asylum for himself, and for his grain and cattle, in the circle of palisades at

---

[1] See the "Cantilenes" of the tenth century in which the "Chansons de Geste" are foreshadowed.

the base of the fortress. By degrees necessity establishes a tacit contract between the military chieftain of the donjon and the early settlers of the open country, and this becomes a recognized custom. They work for him, cultivate his ground, do his carting, pay him quittances, so much for house, so much per head for cattle, so much to inherit or to sell; he is compelled to support his troop. But when these rights are discharged he errs if, through pride or greediness, he takes more than his due. As to the vagabonds, the wretched, who, in the universal disorder and devastation, seek refuge under his guardianship, their condition is harder; the soil belongs to him, because without him it would be uninhabitable; if he assigns them a plot of ground, if he perm.its them merely to encamp on it, if he sets them to work or furnishes them with seeds, it is on conditions which he prescribes. They are to become his serfs, his mortmains; wherever they may go he is to have the right of fetching them back, and from father to son they are his born domestics, assignable to any pursuit he pleases, taxable and workable at his discretion, and not allowed to transmit anything to a child unless the latter, "living from their pot," can, after their death, continue their service. "Not to be killed," says Stendhal, "and to have a good sheepskin coat in winter, was, for many people in the tenth century, the height of felicity"; let us add, for a woman, that of not being violated by a whole band. When we clearly represent to ourselves the condition of humanity in those days, we can comprehend how men readily accepted the most obnoxious of feudal rights, even that of the *droit du seigneur.* The risks to which they were daily subject were even worse.[1] The proof of it is that the people flocked to the feudal structure as soon as it was completed. In Normandy, for instance, when Rollo had divided off the lands with a line, and hung the robbers, the inhabitants of the neighboring provinces rushed in to establish themselves. The slightest security sufficed to repopulate a country.

People accordingly lived, or rather began to live, under the rude, iron-gloved hand which used them roughly, but which afforded them protection. The seignior, sovereign and proprie-

---

[1] See in the "Voyages de Caillaud," in Nubia and Abyssinia, the raids for slaves made by the Pacha's armies; Europe presented about the same spectacle between the years 800 and 900.

tor, maintains for himself under this double title, the moors, the river, the forest, all the game; it is no great evil, since the country is nearly a desert, and he devotes his leisure to exterminating large wild beasts.   He alone possessing the resources, is the only one that is able to construct the mill, the oven, and the wine-press; to establish the ferry, the bridge, or the highway, to dike in a marsh, and to raise or purchase a bull; and to indemnify himself he taxes for these, or forces their use.   If he is intelligent and a good manager of men, if he seeks to derive the greatest profit from his ground, he gradually relaxes, or allows to become relaxed, the meshes of the net in which his villeins and serfs work unprofitably because they are too tightly drawn. Habit, necessity, a voluntary or forced conformity, have their effect; seigniors, villeins, serfs, and bourgeois, in the end adapted to their condition, bound together by a common interest, form together a society, a veritable corporation.   The seigniory, the county, the duchy becomes a patrimony which is loved through a blind instinct, and to which all are devoted.   It is confounded with the seignior and his family; in this relation people are proud of him; they narrate his feats of arms; they cheer him as his cavalcade passes along the street; they rejoice in his magnificence through sympathy.[1]   If he becomes a widower and has no children, they send deputations to him to entreat him to remarry, in order that at his death the country may not fall into a war of succession or be given up to the encroachments of neighbors.   Thus there is a revival, after a thousand years, of the most powerful and the most vivacious of the sentiments that support human society. This one is the more precious because it is capable of expanding: for the small feudal patrimony to become the great national patrimony, it now suffices for all the seigniories to be combined in the hands of a single seignior, and that the king, chief of the nobles, should overlay the work of the nobles with the third foundation of France.

III.

The King built the whole of this foundation, one stone after another.   Hugues Capet laid the first one.   Before him royalty

---

[1] See the zeal of subjects for their lords in the historians of the middle ages; Gaston Phœbus, Comte de Foix, and Guy, Comte de Flandres in Froissart; Raymond de Béziers and Raymond de Toulouse, in the chronicle of Toulouse.   This profound sentiment of small local patrimonies is apparent at each provincial assembly in Normandy, Brittany, Franche-Comté, etc.

conferred on the King no right to a province, not even Laon; it is
he who added his domain to the title.   During eight hundred
years, through conquest, craft, inheritance, the work of acquisition
goes on; even under Louis XV. France is augmented by the acquisition of Lorraine and Corsica.   Starting from nothing, the
King is the maker of a compact State, containing a population of
twenty-six millions, and then the most powerful in Europe.
Throughout this interval he is at the head of the public defence;
the liberator of the country against foreigners, against the Pope
in the fourteenth century, against the English in the fifteenth,
against the Spaniards in the sixteenth.   In the interior, from the
twelfth century onward, with the helmet on his brow, and always
on the road, he is the great justiciary, demolishing the towers of
the feudal brigands, repressing the excesses of the powerful, protecting the oppressed;[1] he puts an end to private warfare; he
establishes order and tranquillity;—an immense accomplishment,
which, from Louis le Gros to St. Louis, from Philippe le Bel to
Charles VII., and to Louis XI., from Henry IV. to Louis XIII.
and Louis XIV., continues uninterruptedly up to the middle of
the eighteenth century in the edict against duels and in the
"Grands Jours."[2]   Meanwhile all useful projects carried out under his orders, or developed under his patronage, roads, harbors,
canals, asylums, universities, academies, institutions of piety, of
refuge, of education, of science, of industry, and of commerce,
bear his imprint and proclaim the public benefactor.   Services of
this character challenge a proportionate recompense; it is allowed
that from father to son he is wedded to France; that she acts only
through him; that he acts only for her; while every souvenir of
the past and every present interest combine to sanction this union.
The Church consecrates it at Rheims by a sort of eighth sacrament,
accompanied with legends and miracles; he is the anointed of
God.[3]   The nobles, through an old instinct of military fealty, consider themselves his body-guard, and down to August 10, 1789,
rush forward to die for him on his staircase; he is their general by
birth.   The people, down to 1789, regard him as the redresser
of abuses, the guardian of the right, the protector of the weak,

---

[1] Suger, Life of Louis VI.

[2] "Les Grands Jours d'Auvergne," by Fléchier, ed. Chéruel.   The last feudal brigand,
the Baron of Plumartin, in Poitou, was taken, tried, and executed under Louis XV. in
1756.

[3] As late as Louis XV. a *procès-verbal* is made of the number of cures of the King's evil.

the great almoner, the universal refuge. At the beginning of the reign of Louis XVI. "the shouts of *Vive le roi*, which began at six o'clock in the morning, continued scarcely interrupted until after sunset."[1] When the Dauphin was born the joy of France was that of a whole family. "People stopped each other in the streets, spoke together without any acquaintance, and everybody embraced everybody he knew."[2] Every one, through vague tradition, through immemorial respect, feels that France is a vessel constructed by his hands and the hands of his ancestors; that, in this sense, the structure is his property; that his right in it is that of each passenger to his private goods; and that his whole duty consists in being expert and vigilant in the conduct of the magnificent ship over the sea whereon the public welfare floats beneath his banner.

Under the ascendency of such an idea he was allowed to do everything. By fair means or foul, he so reduced ancient authorities as to make them a mere ruin, a semblance, a souvenir. The nobles are simply his officials or his courtiers. Since the Concordat he nominates the dignitaries of the Church. The States-General were not convoked for a hundred and seventy-five years; the provincial assemblies which continue to subsist do nothing but apportion the taxes; the parliaments are exiled when they risk a remonstrance. Through his council, his intendants, his sub-delegates, he interposes in the most trifling of local matters. He enjoys a revenue of four hundred and seventy-seven millions.[3] He disburses one-half of that of the Clergy. In short, he is absolute master, and he so declares himself.[4] Possessions, freedom from taxation, the satisfactions of vanity, a few remnants of local jurisdiction and authority, are consequently all that is left to his ancient rivals; in exchange for these they enjoy his favors and marks of preference.

---

[1] "Mémoires of Madame Campan," I. 89; II. 215.

[2] In 1785 an Englishman visiting France boasts of the political liberty enjoyed in his country. As an offset to this the French reproach the English for having decapitated Charles I., and "glory in having always maintained an inviolable attachment to their own king; a fidelity, a respect which no excess or severity on his part has ever shaken." ("A Comparative View of the French and of the English Nation," by John Andrews, p. 257.)

[3] Memoirs of D'Augeard, private secretary of the Queen, and a former farmer-general.

[4] The following is the reply of Louis XV. to the Parliament of Paris, March 3, 1766, in a *lit'de justice:* "The sovereign authority is vested in my person. . . . The legislative power, without dependence and without division, exists in myself alone. Public security emanates wholly from myself; I am its supreme custodian. My people are one only with me ; nationalrights and interests, of which an attempt is made to form a body separatefrom those of the monarch, are necessarily combined with my own, and rest only in my hands."

Such, in brief, is the history of the privileged classes, the Clergy, the Nobles, and the King. It must be kept in mind to comprehend their situation at the moment of their fall ; having created France, they enjoy it. Let us see clearly what becomes of them at the end of the eighteenth century ; what portion of their advantages they preserved; what services they still render, and what services they do not render.

CHAPTER II.

I.

THE privileged classes number about 270,000 persons, comprising of the nobility 140,000 and of the clergy 130,000.[1] This
makes from 25,000 to 30,000 noble families; 23,000 monks in
2,500 monasteries, and 37,000 nuns in 1,500 convents, and 60,000
curates and vicars in as many churches and chapels. Should the
reader desire a more distinct impression of them, he may imagine
on each square league of territory, and to each thousand of inhabitants, one noble family in its weathercock mansion, in each
village a curate and his church, and, every six or seven leagues,
a conventual body of men or of women. We have here the ancient chieftains and founders of France; thus entitled, they still
enjoy many possessions and many rights.

II.

Let us always keep in mind what they were, in order to
comprehend what they are. Great as their advantages may
be, these are merely the remains of still greater advantages.
This or that bishop or abbot, this or that count or duke,
whose successors make their bows at Versailles, were formerly
the equals of the Carlovingians and the first Capets. A Sire
de Montlhéry held King Philippe I. in check.[2] The abbey
of St. Germain des Prés possessed four hundred and thirty thousand *hectares* of land (about 900,000 acres), almost the extent

---

[1] See note 1 at the end of the volume.
[2] Suger "Vie de Louis VI.," chap. viii. Philippe I. became master of the Chateau de
Montlhéry only by marrying one of his sons to the heiress of the fief. He thus addressed his
successor: "My child, take good care to keep this tower of which the annoyances have made
me grow old, and whose frauds and treasons have given me no peace nor rest."

of an entire department. We need not be surprised that they remained powerful, and, especially, rich; no stability is greater than that of an associative body. After eight hundred years, in spite of so many strokes of the royal axe, and the immense change in the culture of society, the old feudal root lasts and still vegetates. We remark it first in the distribution of property.[1] A fifth of the soil belongs to the crown and the communes, a fifth to the third estate, a fifth to the rural population, a fifth to the nobles and a fifth to the clergy. Accordingly, if we deduct the public lands, the privileged classes own one-half of the kingdom. This large portion, moreover, is at the same time the richest, for it comprises almost all the large and imposing buildings, the palaces, castles, convents, and cathedrals, and almost all the valuable movable property, such as furniture, plate, objects of art, the accumulated masterpieces of centuries. We can judge of it by an estimate of the portion belonging to the clergy. Its possessions, capitalized, amount to nearly 4,000,000,000 francs;[2] the income from this amounts to 80 or 100 millions, to which must be added the *dime*, or tithes, 123 millions per annum, in all 200 millions, a sum which must be doubled to show its equivalent at the present day; and to this must be added the chance contributions and the usual church collections.[3] To fully realize the breadth of this golden stream

---

[1] Léonce de Lavergne, "Les Assemblées Provinciales," p. 19. Consult the official statement of the provincial assemblies, and especially the chapters treating of the *vingtièmes* (an old tax of one-twentieth on incomes.—Tr.)

[2] A report made by Treilhard in the name of the ecclesiastic committee, (Moniteur, 19th December, 1789) : The religious establishments for sale in Paris alone were valued at 150 millions. Later (in the session of the 13th February, 1791), Amelot estimates the property sold and to be sold, not including forests, at 3,700 millions. M. de Bouillé estimates the revenue of the clergy at 180 millions. (Mémoires, p. 44). [French currency is so well known to readers in general it is not deemed necessary to reduce statements of this kind to the English or American standard, except in special cases.—Tr.]

[3] A report by Chasset on Tithes, April, 1790. Out of 123 millions 23 go for the costs of collection ; but, in estimating the revenue of an individual the sums he pays to his intendants, overseers and cashiers are not deducted.

Talleyrand (October 10, 1789) estimates the revenue of real property at 70 millions and its value at 2,100 millions. On examination however both capital and revenue are found considerably larger than at first supposed. (Reports of Treilhard and Chasset). Moreover, in his valuation, Talleyrand left out habitations and their enclosures as well as a reservation of one-fourth of the forests. Besides this there must be included in the revenue before 1789 the seigniorial rights enjoyed by the Church. Finally, according to Arthur Young, the rents which the French proprietor received were not two and a half per cent. as nowadays but three and a half.

The necessity of doubling the figures to obtain a present money valuation is supported by innumerable facts, and among others the price of a day's labor, which at that time was nineteen *sous*. (Arthur Young).

let us look at some of its affluents.   Three hundred and ninety-nine monks at Prémontré estimate their revenue at more than 1,000,000 livres, and their capital at 45,000,000.   The Provincial of the Dominicans of Toulouse admits, for his two hundred and thirty-six monks, "more than 200,000 livres net revenue, not including the convent and its enclosure; also, in the colonies, real estate, negroes and other effects, valued at several millions."   The Benedictines of Cluny, numbering two hundred and thirty-eight, enjoy a revenue of 1,800,000 livres.   Those of Saint-Maur, numbering sixteen hundred and seventy-two, estimate the movable property of their churches and houses at 24,000,000, and their net revenue at 8,000,000, "without including that which accrues to Messieurs the abbots and priors commendatory," which means as much and perhaps more.   Dom Rocourt, abbot of Clairvaux, has from 300,000 to 400,000 livres income; the Cardinal de Rohan, archbishop of Strasbourg, more than 1,000,000.[1] In Franche-Comté, Alsace and Roussillon the clergy own one-half of the territory; in Hainaut and Artois, three-quarters; in Cambrésis fourteen hundred plough-areas out of seventeen hundred.[2]   Almost the whole of Le Velay belongs to the Bishop of Puy, the abbot of La Chaise-Dieu, the noble chapter of Brionde, and to the seigniors of Polignac.   The canons of St. Claude, in the Jura, are the proprietors of twelve thousand serfs or ' mainmorts.' [3]

Through fortunes of the first class we can imagine those of the second.   As along with the noble it comprises the ennobled, and as the magistrates for two centuries, and the financiers for one century had acquired or purchased nobility, it is clear that here are to be found almost all the great fortunes of France, old or new, transmitted by inheritance, obtained through court favors, or acquired in business; when a class reaches the summit it is recruited out of those who are mounting or clambering up. Here, too, there is colossal wealth.   It has been calculated that the appanages of the princes of the royal family, the Comtes of Artois and of Provence, the Ducs d'Orléans and de Penthièvre

---

[1] National archives, among the papers of the ecclesiastical committee, sections 10, 11, 13, 25. Beugnot's Memoirs, I. 49, 79 ; Delbos, "L'Eglise de France," I. 399; Duc de Lévis, "Souvenirs et Portraits," p. 156.

[2] Léonce de Lavergne, "Economie Rurale en France," p. 24. Perin, "La Jeunesse de Robespierre," (Memorial of grievances in Artois), p. 317.

[3] Boiteau, "Etat de la France en 1789," p. 47. Voltaire, "Politique et Legislation," the petition of the serfs of St. Claude.

then covered one-seventh of the territory.[1] The princes of the blood have together a revenue of from 24,000,000 to 25,000,000; the Duc d'Orléans alone has a rental of 11,500,000.[2]

These are the vestiges of the feudal régime. Similar vestiges are found in England, in Austria, in Germany and in Russia. Proprietorship, indeed, a long time survives the circumstances on which it is founded. Sovereignty had constituted property ; divorced from sovereignty it has remained in the hands formerly sovereign. In the bishop, the abbot and the count, the king respected the proprietor while overthrowing the rival, and, in the existing proprietor a hundred traits still indicate the annihilated or modified sovereign.

III.

Such is the total or partial exemption from taxation. The tax-collectors halt in their presence because the king well knows that feudal property has the same origin as his own; if royalty is one privilege seigniory is another ; the king himself is simply the most privileged among the privileged. The most absolute, the most infatuated with his rights, Louis XIV., entertained scruples when extreme necessity compelled him to enforce on everybody the tax of the tenth.[3] Treaties, precedents, immemorial custom, reminiscences of ancient rights again restrain the fiscal hand. The clearer the resemblance of the proprietor to the ancient

---

1 Necker, "De l'Administration des Finances," II. 272.

2 De Bouillé, "Mémoires," p. 41. It must not be forgotten that these figures must be doubled to show corresponding sums of the present day.   10,000 livres (francs) rental in 1766 equal in value 20,000 in 1825. (Madame de Genlis, "Memoirs," chap. IX.)

Arthur Young, visiting a chateau in Seine-et-Marne, writes : "I have been sifting Madame de Guerchy on the expenses of living . . . and I learn that to live in a chateau like this with six men servants, five maids, eight horses, a garden and a regular table, with company, but never go to Paris, might be done for 1,000 louis per annum. It would in England cost 2,000.   At the present day in France 24,000 francs would be 50,000 and more." Arthur Young adds : "There are gentlemen (noblesse) that live in this country on 6,000 or 8000 livres, that keep two men, two maids, three horses and a cabriolet." To do this nowadays would require from 20,000 to 25,000.

Living in the provinces, especially, is dearer through the effect of rail-road communication. "According to my friends du Rouergue," he says again, "I could live at Milhau with my family in the greatest abundance on 100 louis (2,000 francs) ; there are noble families supporting themselves on revenues of fifty and even twenty-five louis." At Milhau, to-day, prices are triple and even quadruple. In Paris, a house in the Rue St. Honoré which was rented for 6,000 francs in 1787 is now rented for 16,000 francs.

3 "Rapports de l'Agence du clergé de 1780 à 1785." In relation to the feudal rights the abolition of which is demanded in Boncerf's work, the Chancellor Séguier said in 1775: "Our Kings have themselves declared that they are, fortunately, impotent to make any attack on property."

independent sovereign the greater his immunity. At one time he is guaranteed by a recent treaty, by his position as a stranger, by his almost royal extraction. " In Alsace foreign princes in possession, with the Teutonic order and the order of Malta, enjoy exemption from all real and personal contributions." " In Lorraine the chapter of Remiremont has the privilege of assessing itself in all state impositions." [1] Again, he is protected by the maintenance of the provincial Assemblies, and through the incorporation of the nobility with the soil : in Languedoc and in Brittany the plebeian estate alone paid the *taille*.[2] Everywhere else his quality preserved him from it, him, his chateau and the chateau's dependences ; the *taille* reaches him only through his farmers. And better still, it is sufficient that he himself should work, or a steward, to communicate to the land his original independence ; so soon as he touches the soil, either personally or through his agent, he exempts four ploughing-areas (*quatre charrues*), three hundred arpents,[3] which in other hands, would pay two thousand francs tax, and besides this, " the woods, the meadows, the vines, the ponds and the enclosed land belonging to the chateau, of whatever extent it may be." Consequently, in Limousin and elsewhere, in regions principally devoted to pasturage or to vineyards, he takes care to manage himself, or to have managed, a certain portion of his domain ; in this way he exempts it from the tax collector.[4] There is yet more. In Alsace, through an express covenant he does not pay a cent of tax. Thus, after the assaults of four hundred and fifty years, taxation, the first of fiscal-instrumentalities, the most burdensome of all, leaves feudal property almost intact.[5] For a century back, two new instrumentalities, the capitation-tax and the *vingtièmes*, seem more efficacious, and yet are but little more so.

---

[1] Léonce de Lavergne, "Les Assemblées provinciales," p. 296. Report of M. Schwendt on Alsace in 1787. Warroquier, "Etat de la France en 1789," I. 541. Necker, "De l'Administration des Finances," I. 19, 102. Turgot, (collection of economists), "Réponse aux observations du garde des sceaux sur la suppression des corvées," I. 559.

[2] This term embraces various taxes originating in feudal times, and rendered particularly burdensome to the peasantry through the management of the privileged classes.—TR.

[3] The *arpent* measures between one and one and a half acres.

[4] De Tocqueville, "L'Ancien Régime et la Révolution," p. 406. "The inhabitants of Montbazen had subjected to taxation the stewards of the duchy which belonged to the Prince de Rohan. This prince caused this abuse to be stopped and succeeded in recovering the sum of 5,344 livres which he had been made to pay unlawfully under this right."

[5] Necker, "Administration des Finances:" ordinary taxation produced 91,000,000; let es, 76,500,000; the capitation-tax, 41,500,000.

C

At first, through a master-stroke of ecclesiastical diplomacy, the clergy diverts or weakens the blow. Forming a body, and holding assemblies, it is able to negotiate with the king, to buy itself off, to avoid being taxed by others, to tax itself, to have it understood that its payments are not compulsory contributions, but a "free gift," to obtain in exchange a mass of concessions, to diminish this gift, sometimes not to make it, in any event to reduce it to sixteen millions every five years, that is to say to a little more than three millions per annum; in 1788 it is only 1,800,000 livres, and in 1789 it is refused altogether.[1] And still better: as it borrows to provide for this tax, and as the *décimes* which it raises on its property do not suffice to reduce the capital and meet the interest on its debt, it has the adroitness to secure, besides, a grant from the king out of the royal treasury, each year, of 2,500,000 livres, so that, instead of paying, it receives; in 1787 it receives in this way 1,500,000 livres. In relation to the nobles, they, unable to combine together, to have representatives, to act in a public way, operate in a private way, confronting ministers, intendants, sub-delegates, farmer-generals, and all others clothed with authority, their quality securing attentions, consideration and favors. In the first place, this quality exempts themselves, their dependants, and the dependants of their dependants, from drafting in the militia, from lodging soldiers, from *(la corvée)* laboring on the highways. Next, the capitation being fixed according to the tax system, they pay little, because their taxation is of little account. Moreover, each one brings all his credit to bear against assessments ; " your sympathetic heart," writes one of them to the intendant, "will never allow a father of my condition to be taxed for the *vingtièmes* rigidly like a father of low birth." On the other hand, as the tax-payer pays the capitation-tax at his actual residence, often far away from his estates, and no one having any knowledge of his personal income, he may pay whatever seems to him proper. There are no proceedings against him, if he is a noble; the greatest circumspection is

---

[1] Raudot, "La France avant la Révolution," p. 51. De Bouillé, "Mémoires," p. 44. Necker, "De l'Administration des Finances," v. II. p. 181. The above relates to what was called the clergy of France, (116 dioceses). The clergy called foreign, consisted of that of the three bishoprics and of the countries acquired after Louis XIV.; it had a separate régime and paid somewhat like the nobles. The *décimes* which the clergy of France levied on its property amounted to a sum of 10,500,000 livres.

used towards persons of high rank; "in the provinces," says Turgot, "the capitation-tax of the privileged classes has been successively reduced to an exceedingly small matter, whilst the capitation-tax of those who are liable to the *taille* is almost equal to the aggregate of that tax." And finally, "the collectors think that they are obliged to act towards them with marked consideration" even when they owe; "the result of which," says Necker, "is that very ancient, and much too large amounts, of their capitation-tax remain unpaid." Accordingly, not having been able to repel the assault of the fisc in front they evaded it or diminished it until it became almost unobjectionable. In Champagne, "on nearly 1,500,000 livres provided by the capitation-tax, they paid in only 14,000 livres," that is to say, "2 sous and 2 deniers for the same purpose which costs 12 sous per livre to those chargeable with the *taille*." According to Calonne, "if concessions and privileges had been suppressed the *vingtièmes* would have furnished double the amount." In this respect the most opulent were the most skilful in protecting themselves. "With the intendants," said the Duc d'Orléans, "I settle matters, and pay about what I please," and he calculated that the provincial administration, rigorously taxing him, would cause him to lose 300,000 livres rental. It has been proved that the princes of the blood paid, for their two-twentieths, 188,000 instead of 2,400,000 livres. In the main, in this régime, exception from taxation is the last remnant of sovereignty or, at least, of independence. The privileged person avoids or repels taxation, not merely because it despoils him, but because it belittles him; it is a mark of plebeian condition, that is to say, of former servitude, and he resists the fisc as much through pride as through interest.

IV.

Let us follow him home to his own domain. A bishop, an abbé, a chapter of the clergy, an abbess, each has one like a lay seignior; for, in former times, the monastery and the church were small governments like the county and the duchy.

Intact on the other bank of the Rhine, almost ruined in France, the feudal structure everywhere discloses the same plan. In certain places, better protected or less attacked, it has preserved all its ancient externals. At Cahors, the bishop-count of the town had the right, on solemnly officiating, "to place his casque, cuirass, gauntlets and sword on the altar." [1]   At Besançon, the archbishop-prince has six high officers, who owe him homage for their fiefs, and who attend at his coronation and at his obsequies.   At Mende,[2] the bishop, seignior-suzerain for Gévaudan since the eleventh century, appoints "the courts, ordinary judges and judges of appeal, the commissaries and syndics of the country," disposes of all the places, "municipal and judiciary," and, entreated to appear in the assembly of the three orders of the province, "replies that his place, his possessions and his rank exalting him above every individual in his diocese, he cannot sit under the presidency of any person; that, being seignior-suzerain of all estates and particularly of the baronies, he cannot give way to his vassals," in brief that he is king, or but little short of it, in his own province.   At Remiremont, the noble chapter of canonesses has, "inferior, superior, and ordinary judicature in fifty-two bans of seigniories," the gift of seventy-five curacies and of ten male canonships, appointing the municipal officers of the town, and, besides this, three lower and higher courts, and everywhere the officials in the jurisdiction over woods and forests.   Thirty-two bishops, without counting the chapters, are thus temporal seigniors, in whole or in part, of their episcopal town, sometimes of the surrounding district, and sometimes, like the bishop of St. Claude, of the entire country.   Here the feudal tower has been preserved.   Elsewhere it is plastered over anew, and more particularly in the appanages.   In these domains, comprising more than twelve of our departments, the princes of the blood appoint to all offices in the judiciary and to all clerical livings.   Being substitutes of the king they enjoy his serviceable and honorary rights.   They are almost delegated kings, and for life; for they not only receive all that the king would receive as seignior, but again a portion of that which he would receive as monarch.   For example, the house of Orleans collects the excises,[3] that is to say the duty on liquors, on works in gold or silver, on manufactures of iron, on steel, on cards,

---

[1] See "La France ecclésiastique, 1788," for these details.

[2] Official statements and manuscript reports of the States-General of 1789.   "Archives nationales," vol. LXXXVIII. pp. 23, 85, 121, 122, 152. Procès-verbal of January 12, 1789

[3] Necker, "De l'Administration des Finances," v. II. pp. 271, 272.   "The house of Orleans, he says, is in possession of the excises."   He values this tax at 51,000,000 for the entire kingdom.

on paper and starch, in short, on the entire sum-total of one of the most onerous indirect imposts.   It is not surprising, if, approximating to the sovereign condition, they have, like sovereigns themselves, a council, a chancellor, an organized debt, a court,[1] a domestic ceremonial system, and that the feudal edifice in their hands should put on the luxurious and formal trappings which it had assumed in the hands of the king.

Let us turn to its inferior personages, to a seignior of medium rank, on his square league of ground, amidst the thousand inhabitants who were formerly his villeins or his serfs, within reach of the monastery, or chapter, or bishop whose rights intermingle with his rights.   Whatever may have been done to abase him his position is still very high.   He is yet, as the intendants say, "the first inhabitant;" a prince whom they have half despoiled of his public functions and consigned to his honorary and available rights, but who nevertheless remains a prince.[2]   He has his bench in the church, and his right of sepulture in the choir ; the tapestry bears his coat of arms ; they bestow on him incense, "holy water by distinction."   Often, having founded the church, he is its patron, choosing the curate and claiming to control him ; in the rural districts we see him advancing or retarding the hour of the parochial mass according to his fancy. If he bears a title he is supreme judge, and there are entire provinces, Maine and Anjou, for example, where there is no fief without the judge.   In this case he appoints the bailiff, the registrar, and other legal and judicial officers, attorneys, notaries, seigniorial sergeants, constabulary on foot or mounted, who draw up documents or decide in his name in civil and criminal cases on the first trial.   He appoints, moreover, a forest-warden, or decides forest offences, and enforces the penalties which this officer inflicts.   He has his prison for delinquents of various kinds, and sometimes his forked gibbets.   On the other hand, as

---

[1] Beugnot, "Mémoires," v. I. p. 77.   Observe the ceremonial system with the Duc de Penthièvre, chapters I., III.   The Duc d'Orléans organizes a chapter and bands of canonesses.   The post of chancellor to the Duc d'Orléans is worth 100,000 livres per annum, ("Gustave III. et la cour de France," by Geffroy, I. 410.)

[2] De Tocqueville, *ibid.* p. 40.   Renauldon, advocate in the bailiwick of Issoudun, "Traité historique et pratique des droits seigneuriaux, 1765," pp. 8, 10, 81 and *passim.*   Memorial of a magistrate of the Chatelet on seigniorial judgments, 1789.   Duvergier, "Collection des Lois," Decrees of the 15–28 March, 1790, on the abolition of the feudal régime, Merlin of Douai, reporter, I. 114   Decrees of 19–23 July, 1790, I. 293.   Decrees of the 13–20 April, 1791, I 295.

compensation for his judicial costs, he obtains the property of the man condemned to death and the confiscation of his estate ; he succeeds to the bastard born and dying in his seigniory without leaving a testament or legitimate children ; he inherits from the possessor, legitimately born, dying intestate in his house without apparent heirs ; he appropriates to himself movable objects, animate or inanimate, which are found astray and of which the owner is unknown ; he claims one-half or one-third of treasure-trove, and, on the coast, he takes for himself the waif of wrecks ; and finally, what is more fruitful, in these times of misery, he becomes the possessor of abandoned lands that have remained untilled for ten years.   Other advantages demonstrate still more clearly that he formerly possessed the government of the canton. Such are, in Auvergne, in Flanders, in Hainaut, in Artois, in Picardy, Alsace, and Lorraine, the dues *de poursoin ou de sauvement* (care or safety within the walls of a town), paid to him for his general protection ; those *de guet et de garde* (watch and guard), claimed by him for military protection ; of *afforage*, exacted of those who sell beer, wine and other beverages, wholesale or retail ; of *fouage*, dues on fires, in money or grain, which, according to many common-law systems, he levies on each fire-side, house or family ; of *pulvérage*, quite common in Dauphiny and Provence, on passing flocks of sheep ; the *lods et ventes* (lord's due), an almost universal tax, consisting of the deduction of a sixth, often of a fifth or even a fourth, of the price of every piece of ground sold, and of every lease exceeding nine years ; the dues for redemption or relief, equivalent to one year's income, and which he receives from collateral heirs, and often from direct heirs ; and finally, a rarer due, but the most burdensome of all, that of *acapte ou de plait-a-merci*, which is a double rent, or a year's yield of fruits, payable as well on the death of the seignior as on that of the copyholder.   These are veritable taxes, on land, on movables, personal, for licenses, for traffic, for mutations, for successions, established formerly on the condition of performing a public service which he is no longer obliged to perform.

Other dues are also ancient imposts, but he still performs the service for which they are a quittance.   The king, in fact, suppresses many of the tolls, twelve hundred in 1724, and the suppression is kept up ; but a good many remain to the profit of the seignior,—on bridges, on highways, on fords, on boats ascending or descending, he being at the expense of keeping up bridge, road, ford and tow-path, several being very lucrative, one of them producing 90,000 livres.[1] In like manner, on condition of maintaining the market-place and of providing scales and weights gratis, he levies a tax on provisions and on merchandise brought to his fair or to his market;—at Angoulême a forty-eighth of the grain sold, at Combourg near Saint-Malo, so much per head of cattle, elsewhere so much on wine, eatables and fish.[2] Having formerly built the oven, the wine-press, the mill and the slaughter-house, he obliges the inhabitants to use these or pay for their support, and he demolishes all constructions which might enter into competition with him.[3] These, again, are evidently monopolies and *octrois* going back to the time when he was in possession of public authority.

Not only did he then possess the public authority but he possessed the soil and the men on it. Proprietor of men, he is so still, at least in many respects and in many provinces. "In Champagne proper, in the Sénonais, in la Marche, in the Bourbonnais, in the Nivernais, in Burgundy, in Franche-Comté, there are none, or very few domains, no signs remaining of ancient servitude. . . . A good many personal serfs, or so constituted through their own gratitude, or that of their progenitors, are still found."[4] There, man is a serf, sometimes by virtue of his

---

[1] National archives, G, 300, (1787). "M. de Boullongne, seignior of Montereau, possesses a toll-right consisting of 2 deniers (farthings) per ox, cow, calf or pig; 1 per sheep; 2 for a laden animal; 1 sou and 8 deniers for each four-wheeled vehicle; 5 deniers for a two-wheeled vehicle, and 10 deniers for a vehicle drawn by three, four, or five horses; besides a tax of 10 deniers for each barge, boat or skiff ascending the river; the same tax for each team of horses dragging the boats up; 1 denier for each empty cask going up." Analogous taxes are enforced at Varennes for the benefit of the Duc de Chatelet, seignior of Varennes.

[2] National archives, K, 1453, No. 1448: A letter by M. de Meulan, dated June 12, 1789. This tax on grain belonged at that time to the Comte d'Artois. Chateaubriand, "Mémoires," I. 73.

[3] Renauldon, *ibid*. 249, 258. "There are few seignioral towns which do not have the lord's slaughter-houses. The butcher must obtain special permission from the seignior." The tax on grinding was an average of a sixteenth. In many provinces, Anjou, Berry, Maine, Brittany, there was a lord's mill for cloths and barks.

[4] Renauldon, *ibid*. pp. 181, 200, 203; observe that he wrote this in 1765. Louis XVI. suppressed villeinage on the royal domains in 1778; and many of the seigniors, especially in Franche-Comté, followed his example.

Beugnot, "Mémoires," v. I. p. 142. Voltaire, "Mémoire au roi sur les serfs du Jura." "Mémoires de Bailly," II. 214, according to an official report of the Nat. Ass., August 7, 1789. I rely on this report and on the book of M. Clerget, curate of Onans in Franche-Comté, who is mentioned in it. M. Clerget says that there are still at this time (1789) 1,500,000 subjects of the king in a state of servitude but he brings forward no proofs to support these figures. Nevertheless it is certain that the number of serfs and mortmains is still

birth, and again through a territorial condition. Whether in servitude, or as mortmains, or as cotters, one way or another, fifteen hundred thousand individuals, it is said, wore about their necks a remnant of the feudal collar; this is not surprising since, on the other side of the Rhine, almost all the peasantry still wear it. The seignior, formerly master and proprietor of all their goods and chattels and of all their labor, can still exact of them from ten to twelve *corvées* per annum and a fixed annual tax. In the barony of Choiseul near Chaumont in Champagne, "the inhabitants are required to plough his lands, to sow and reap them for his account and to put the products into his barns; each plot of ground, each house, every head of cattle pays a quit-claim; children may inherit from their parents only on con- dition of remaining with them; if absent at the time of their decease he is the inheritor." This is what was styled in the language of the day an estate "with excellent dues." Elsewhere the seignior inherits from collaterals, brothers or nephews, if they were not in community with the defunct at the moment of his death, which community is only valid through his consent. In the Jura and the Nivernais, he may pursue fugitive serfs, and demand, at their death, not only the property left by them on his domain, but, again, the pittance acquired by them elsewhere. At Saint-Claude he acquires this right over any person that passes a year and a day in a house belonging to the seigniory. As to ownership of the soil we see still more clearly that he once had entire possession of it. In the district subject to his juris- diction the public domain remains his private domain; roads, streets and open squares form a part of it; he has the right to plant trees in them and to take trees up. In many provinces, through a pasturage rent, he obliges the inhabitants to pay for permits to pasture their cattle in the fields after the crop, and in the open common lands, *(les terres vaines et vagues)*. Unnavigable streams belong to him, as well as islets and accumulations formed in them and the fish that are found in them. He has the right of the chase over the whole extent of his jurisdiction, this

---

very great.   National archives, H, 723, memorials on mortmains in Franche-Comté in 1788; H, 200, memorials by Amelot on Burgundy in 1785.   " In the sub-delegation of Charolles the inhabitants seem a century behind the age; being subject to feudal tenures, such as mort- main, neither mind nor body have any play.   The redemption of mortmain, of which the king himself has set the example, has been put at such an exorbitant price by laymen, the unfortunate sufferers cannot, and will not be able to secure it."

or that plebeian being sometimes compelled to throw open to him his park enclosed by walls.

One more trait serves to complete the picture. This head of the State, a proprietor of man and of the soil, was once a resident cultivator on his own small farm amidst others of the same class, and, by this title, he reserved to himself certain working privileges which he always retained. Such is the right of *banvin*, still widely diffused, consisting of the privilege of selling his own wine, to the exclusion of all others, during thirty or forty days after gathering the crop. Such is, in Touraine, the right of *préage*, which is the right to send his horses, cows and oxen " to browse under guard in his subjects' meadows." Such is, finally, the monopoly of the great dove-cot, from which thousands of pigeons issue to feed at all times and seasons and on all grounds, without any one daring to kill or take them. Through another effect of the same qualification he imposes quit-claims on property on which he has formerly given perpetual leases, and, under the terms *cens, censives* (quit-rents), *carpot* (share in wine), *champart* (share in grain), *agrier* (a cash commission on general produce), *terrage parciere* (share of fruits), all these collections, in money or in kind, are as various as the local situations, accidents and transactions could possibly be. In the Bourbonnais he has one-quarter of the crop; in Berry twelve sheaves out of a hundred. Occasionally his debtor or tenant is a community : one deputy in the National Assembly owned a fief of two hundred casks of wine on three thousand pieces of private property.[1] Besides, through the *retrait censuel* (a species of right of redemption), he can " retain for his own account all property sold on the condition of remunerating the purchaser, but previously deducting for his benefit the lord's dues *(lods et ventes)*." The reader, finally, must take note that all these restrictions on property constitute, for the seignior, a privileged credit as well on the product as on the price of the ground, and, for the copyholders, an unprescriptive, indivisible and irredeemable debt.

Such are the feudal rights. To form an idea of them in their totality we must always imagine the count, bishop or abbot of the tenth century as sovereign and proprietor in his own canton. The form which human society then takes grows out of the

---

[1] Boiteau, *ibid.* p. 25, (April, 1790). Beugnot, "Mémoires," I. 142.

exigencies of near and constant danger with a view to local defence, by subordinating all interests to the necessities of living, in such a way as to protect the soil by fixing on the soil, through property and its enjoyment, a troop of brave men under the leadership of a brave chieftain. The danger having passed away the structure became dilapidated. For a pecuniary compensation the seigniors allowed the economical and tenacious peasant to pick off it a good many stones. Through constraint they suffered the king to appropriate to himself the public portion. The primitive foundation remains, property as organized in ancient times, the fettered or exhausted land supporting a social conformation that has melted away, in short, an order of privileges and of thraldom of which the cause and the purpose have disappeared.[1]

V.

All this does not suffice to render this order detrimental or even useless. In reality, the local chief who no longer performs his ancient service may perform a new one in exchange for it Instituted for war when life was militant, he may serve in quiet times when the régime is pacific, while the advantage to the nation is great in which this transformation is accomplished; for, retaining its chiefs, it is relieved of the uncertain and perilous operation which consists in creating others. There is nothing more difficult to establish than a government, that is to say, a stable government: this involves the command of some and the obedience of all, which is against nature. That a man in his cabinet, often a feeble old person, should dispose of the lives and property of twenty or thirty thousand men, most of whom he has never seen; that he should order them to pay away a tenth or a fifth of their income and they should do it; that he should order them to go and slaughter or be slaughtered and that they should go; that they should thus continue for ten years, twenty years, through every kind of trial, defeat, misery and invasion, as with the French under Louis XIV., the English under Pitt, the Prussians under Frederick II., without either sedition or internal disturbances, is certainly a marvellous thing, and, for a people to remain free it is essential that they should

---

[1] See note 2 at the end of the volume.

be ready to do this always.   Neither this fidelity nor this concord is due to sober reflection *(la raison raisonnante);* reason is too vacillating and too feeble to bring about such a universal and energetic result.   Abandoned to itself and suddenly restored to a natural condition, the human flock is capable only of agitation, of mutual strife until pure force at length predominates, as in barbarous times, and until, amidst the dust and outcry, some military leader rises up who is, generally, a butcher.   Historically considered it is better to continue so than to begin over again.   Hence, especially when the majority is uncultivated, it is beneficial to have chiefs designated beforehand through the hereditary custom by which people follow them, and through the special education by which they are qualified.   In this case the public has no need to seek for them to obtain them.   They are already at hand, in each canton, visible, accepted beforehand ; they are known by their names, their title, their fortune, their way of living ; deference to their authority is established.   They are almost always deserving of this authority ; born and brought up to exercise it they find in tradition, in family example and in family pride, powerful ties that nourish public spirit in them; there is some probability of their comprehending the duties with which their prerogative endows them.

Such is the renovation which the feudal régime admits of. The ancient chieftain can still guarantee his pre-eminence by his services, and remain popular without ceasing to be privileged. Once a captain in his district and a permanent gendarme, he is to become the resident and beneficent proprietor, the voluntary promoter of useful undertakings, obligatory guardian of the poor, the gratuitous administrator and judge of the canton, the unsalaried deputy of the king, that is to say, a leader and protector as formerly, through a new system of patronage accommodated to new circumstances.   Local magistrate and central representative, these are his two principal functions, and, if we extend our observation beyond France we find that he exercises either one or the other, or both together.

CHAPTER III.

I.

LET us consider the first one, local government. There are countries at the gates of France in which feudal subjection, more burdensome than in France, seems lighter because, in the other scale, the benefits counterbalance disadvantages. At Munster, in 1809, Beugnot finds a sovereign bishop, a town of convents and a large seigniorial mansion, a few merchants for indispensable trade, a small bourgeoisie, and, all around, a peasantry composed of either *colons* or serfs. The seignior deducts a portion of all their crops in provisions or in cattle, and, at their deaths, a portion of their inheritances; if they go away their property reverts to him. His servants are chastised like Russian moujiks, and in each outhouse is a trestle for this purpose "without prejudice to graver penalties," probably the bastinado and the like. But "never did the culprit entertain the slightest idea of complaint or appeal." For if the seignior whips them as the father of a family he protects them "as the father of a family, ever coming to their assistance when misfortune befalls them, and taking care of them in their illness;" he provides an asylum for them in old age; he looks after their widows, and rejoices when they have plenty of children ; he is bound to them by common sympathies they are neither miserable nor uneasy; they know that, in every extreme or unforeseen necessity, he will be their refuge.[1] In the Prussian states, and according to the code of Frederick the Great, a still more rigorous servitude is atoned for by similar obligations. The peasantry, without their seignior's permission, cannot alienate a field, mortgage it, cultivate it differently, change their occupation or marry. If they leave the seigniory he can pursue them in every direction and bring them back by force. He has the right of surveillance over their private life, and he chastises them if drunk or lazy. When young they serve for years as servants in his mansion; as cultivators they owe him *corvées* and, in certain places, three times a week. But, according to both law and custom, he is obliged "to see that they are educated, to succor them in indigence, and, as far as possible, to provide them with the means of support." Accordingly he is charged with the duties of the government of which he enjoys the advantages, and, under the heavy hand which curbs them, but which sustains them, we do not find his subjects recalcitrant. In England, the upper class attain to the same result by other ways. There also the soil still pays the ecclesiastic tithe, strictly the tenth, which is much more than in France.[2] The squire, the nobleman, possesses a still larger portion of the soil than his French neighbor and, in truth, exercises greater authority in his canton. But his tenants, the lessees and the farmers, are no longer his serfs, nor even his vassals; they are free. If he governs it is through influence and not by virtue of a command. Proprietor and patron, he is held in respect; lord-lieutenant, officer in the militia, administrator, justice, he is visibly useful. And, above all, he lives at home, from father to son ; he belongs to the district; he is in hereditary and constant relation with the local public, through his occupations and through his pleasures, through the chase and caring for the poor, through his farmers whom he admits at his table, and through his neighbors whom he meets in committee or in the vestry. This shows how the old hierarchies are main-

---

[1] Beugnot, "Mémoires," v. I. p. 292.   De Tocqueville, "L'Ancien Régime et la Révolution."

[2] Arthur Young, "Travels in France," II. 456.   In France, he says, it is from the eleventh to the thirty-second. "But nothing is known like the enormities committed in England where the tenth is really taken."

tained : it is necessary, and it suffices, that they should change their military into a civil order of things and find modern employment for the chieftain of feudal times.

II.

If we go back a little way in our history we find here and there similar nobles.[1] Such was the Duc de Saint-Simon, father of the writer, a real sovereign in his government of Blaye, and respected by the king himself. Such was the grandfather of Mirabeau, in his chateau of Mirabeau in Provence, the haughtiest, most absolute, most intractable of men, "demanding that the officers whom he appointed in his regiment should be favorably received by the king and by his ministers," tolerating the inspectors only as a matter of form, but heroic, generous, faithful, distributing the pension offered to himself among six wounded captains under his command, mediating for poor litigants in the mountain, driving off his grounds the wandering attorneys who come to practise their chicanery, "the natural protector of man," even against ministers and the king. A party of tobacco inspectors having searched his curate's house, he pursues them so energetically on horseback that they hardly escape him by fording the Durance, whereupon, "he wrote to demand the dismissal of the officers, declaring that unless this was done every person employed in the Excise should be driven into the Rhine or the sea; some of them were dismissed and the director himself came to give him satisfaction." Finding his canton sterile and the settlers on it idle he organizes them into companies, men, women and children, and, in the foulest weather, puts himself at their head, with his twenty severe wounds and his neck supported by a piece of silver; he pays them to work, making them clear off the lands, which he gives them on leases of a hundred years, and he makes them enclose a mountain of rocks with high walls and plant it with olive trees. "No one, under any pretext could be excused from working unless he was ill,

---

[1] Saint-Simon, "Mémoires," ed. Chéruel, vol. I. Lucas de Montigny, "Mémoires de Mirabeau," I. 53–182. Marshal Marmont, "Mémoires," I. 9, 11. Chateaubriand, "Mémoires," I. 17. De Montlosier, "Mémoires," 2 vol. *passim.* Mme. de Larochejacquelein, "Souvenirs," *passim.* Many details concerning the types of the old nobility will be found in these passages. They are truly and forcibly depicted in two novels by Balzac, in "Béatrix," the Baron de Guénic, and in the "Cabinet des Antiques," the Marquis d'Esgrignon.

and in this case under treatment, or occupied on his own property, a point in which my father could not be deceived, and nobody would have dared to do it." These are the last offshoots of the old, knotty, savage trunk, but still capable of affording shelter. Others could still be found in remote cantons, in Brittany and in Auvergne, veritable district commanders, and I am sure that in time of need the peasants would obey them as much out of respect as from fear. Vigor of heart and of body justifies its own ascendency, while the superabundance of energy which begins in violence ends in beneficence.

Less independent and less harsh a paternal government subsists elsewhere, if not in the law at least through custom. In Brittany, near Tréguier and Lannion, says the bailiff of Mirabeau,[1] "the entire staff of the coast-guard is composed of people of quality and of races of a thousand years. I have not seen one of them get irritated with a peasant-soldier, while, at the same time, I have seen on the part of the latter an air of filial respect for them. . . . It is a terrestrial paradise with respect to patriarchal manners, simplicity and true grandeur: the attitude of the peasants towards the seigniors is that of an affectionate son with his father; and the seigniors in talking with the peasants use their rude and coarse language, and speak only in a kind and genial way. We see mutual regard between masters and servants." Farther south, in the *Bocage*, a wholly agricultural region, and with no roads, where ladies are obliged to travel on horseback and in ox-carts, where the seignior has no farmers, but only twenty-five or thirty *métayers* who work for him on shares, the supremacy of the great is no offence to their inferiors. People live together harmoniously when living together from birth to death, familiarly, and with the same interests, occupations and pleasures; like soldiers with their officers, on campaigns and under tents, in subordination although in companionship, familiarity never endangering respect. "The seignior often visits them on their small farms,[2] talks with them about their affairs, about taking care of their cattle, sharing in the accidents and mishaps which likewise seriously affect him. He attends their

---

[1] A letter of the bailiff of Mirabeau, 1760, published by M. de Loménie in the "Correspondant," v. XLXIX. p. 132.

[2] Mme. de Larochejacquelein, *ibid.* I. 84. "As M. de Marigny had some knowledge of the veterinary art the peasants of the canton came after him when they ' ad sick animals."

children's weddings and drinks with the guests. On Sunday there are dances in the chateau court, and the ladies take part in them." When he is about to hunt wolves or boars the curate gives notice of it in the sermon ; the peasants, with their guns, gaily assemble at the rendezvous, finding the seignior who assigns them their posts, and strictly observing the directions he gives them. Here are soldiers and a captain ready made. A little later, and of their own accord, they will choose him for commandant in the national guard, mayor of the commune, chief of the insurrection, and, in 1792, the marksmen of the parish are to march under him against " the blues " as, at this epoch, against the wolves. Such are the remnants of the good feudal spirit, like the scattered remnants of a submerged continent. Before Louis XIV., the spectacle was similar throughout France. "The rural nobility of former days," says the Marquis de Mirabeau, " spent too much time over their cups, slept on old chairs or pallets, mounted and started off to hunt before daybreak, met together on St. Hubert's, and did not part until after the octave of St. Martin's. . . . These nobles led a gay and hard life, voluntarily, costing the State very little, and producing more for it by staying at home and utilizing manure-heaps than we of to-day with our tastes, our researches, our cholics and our vapors. . . . The custom, and it may be said, the passion of constantly making presents to the seigniors, is well known. I have, in my time, seen this custom everywhere disappear, and properly. . . . The seigniors are no longer of any consequence to them ; it is quite natural that they should be forgotten by them as they forget. . . . The seignior being no longer known on his estates, everybody pillages him, which is right."[1] Everywhere, except in remote corners, the affection and unity of the two classes has disappeared ; the shepherd is separated from his flock, and the pastors of the people end in being considered its parasites.

Let us first follow them into the provinces. We here find only the minor class of nobles and a portion of those of medium rank ; the rest are in Paris.[2] There is the same line of separation in the church : abbés-commendatory, bishops and archbishops very seldom live at home ; the grand-vicars and canons live in

---

[1] Marquis de Mirabeau, " Traité de la Population," p. 57.

[2] De Tocqueville, *ibid.* p. 180. This is proved by the registers of the capitation-tax which was paid at the actual domicile.

the large towns; only priors and curates dwell in the rural districts; ordinarily the entire ecclesiastic or lay staff is absent; residents are furnished only by the secondary or inferior grades. What are their relations with the peasant? One point is certain, and that is that they are not usually hard, nor even indifferent, to him. Separated by rank they are not so by distance; neighborhood is of itself a bond among men. I have read in vain, but I have not found them the rural tyrants which the declaimers of the Revolution portray them. Haughty with the bourgeois they are generally kind to the villager. "Let any one travel through the provinces," says a contemporary advocate, "over the estates occupied by the seigniors; out of a hundred one may be found where they tyrannize over their dependants; all the others patiently share the misery of those subject to their jurisdiction. . . . They give their debtors time, remit sums due, and afford them every facility for settlement. They mollify and temper the sometimes over-rigorous proceedings of the *fermiers*, stewards and other men of business."[1] An Englishwoman, who observes them in Provence just after the Revolution, says that, detested at Aix, they are much beloved on their estates. "Whilst they pass the first citizens with their heads erect and an air of disdain, they salute peasants with extreme courtesy and affability." One of them distributes among the women, children and the aged on his domain wool and flax to spin during the bad season, and, at the end of the year, he offers a prize of one hundred livres for the two best pieces of cloth. In numerous instances the peasant-purchasers of their land voluntarily restore it for the purchase money. Around Paris, near Romainville, after the terrible storm of 1788 there is prodigal alms-giving; "a very wealthy man immediately distributes forty thousand francs among the surrounding unfortunates;" during the winter, in Alsace and in Paris, everybody is giving; "in front of each hotel belonging to a well-known family a big log is burning to which, night and day, the poor can come and warm themselves." In the way of charity, the monks who remain on their premises and witness the public misery continue faithful to the spirit of their institution. On

---

[1] Renauldon, *ibid.*, Preface p. 5. Anne Plumptre, "A narrative of three years residence in France from 1802 to 1805," II. 357. Baroness Oberkirk, "Mémoires," II. 389. "De l'état religieux," by the abbés Bonnefoi and Bernard, 1784, p. 295. Mme. Vigée-Lebrun, "Souvenirs," p. 171.

D

the birth of the Dauphin the Augustins of Montmorillon in Poitou pay out of their own resources the *tailles* and *corvées* of nineteen poor families. In 1781, in Provence, the Dominicans of Saint Maximin support the population of their district in which the tempest had destroyed the vines and the olive trees. "The Carthusians of Paris furnish the poor with eighteen hundred pounds of bread per week. During the winter of 1784 there is an increase of alms-giving in all the religious establishments; their farmers distribute aid among the poor people of the country, and, to provide for these extra necessities, many of the communities increase the rigor of their abstinences." When, at the end of 1789, their suppression is in question, I find a number of protests in their favor, written by municipal officers, by prominent individuals, by a crowd of inhabitants, workmen and peasants, and these columns of rustic signatures are truly eloquent. Seven hundred families of Cateau-Cambrésis[1] send in a petition to retain "the worthy abbés and monks of the Abbey of St. Andrew, their common fathers and benefactors, who fed them during the tempest." The inhabitants of St. Savin, in the Pyrenees, "portray with tears of grief their consternation" at the prospect of suppressing their abbey of Benedictines, the sole charitable organization in this poor country. At Sierk, near Thionville, "the Chartreuse," say the leading citizens, "is, for us, in every respect, the Ark of the Lord; it is the main support of from more than twelve to fifteen hundred persons who come to it every day in the week. This year the monks have distributed amongst them their own store of grain at sixteen livres less than the current price." The regular canons of Domièvre, in Lorraine, feed sixty poor persons twice a week; it is essential to retain them, says the petition, "out of pity and compassion for the poor beings whose misery cannot be imagined; where there are no regular convents and canons in their dependency, the poor cry with misery."[2] At Moutiers-Saint-John, near Sémur in Burgundy, the Benedictines of Saint-Maur support the entire village

---

[1] Archives nationales, D, XIX. portfolios 14, 15, 25. Five bundles of papers are filled with these petitions.

[2] *Ibid.* D, XIX. portfolio 11. An admirable letter by Joseph of Saintignon, abbé of Domièvre, general of the regular canons of Saint-Sauveur and a resident. He has 23,000 livres income, of which 6,066 livres is a pension from the government, in recompense for his services. His personal expenditure not being over 5,000 livres "he is in a situation to distribute among the poor and the workmen, in the space of eleven years, more than 250,000 livres."

and supply it this year with food during the famine. Near Morley in Barrois, the abbey of Auvey, of the Cistercian order, "was always, for every village in the neighborhood, a bureau of charity." At Airvault, in Poitou, the municipal officers, the colonel of the national guard, and numbers of "rustics and inhabitants" demand the conservation of the regular canons of St. Augustin. "Their existence," says the petition, "is absolutely essential, as well for our town as for the country, and we should suffer an irreparable loss in their suppression." The municipality and permanent council of Soissons write that the establishment of Saint-Jean des Vignes "has always earnestly claimed its share of the public charges. This is the institution which, in times of calamity, welcomes shelterless citizens and provides them with subsistence. It alone bears the expenses of the assembly of the bailiwick at the time of the election of deputies to the National Assembly. A company of the regiment of Armagnac is actually lodged under its roof. This institution is always found wherever sacrifices are to be made." In scores of places declarations are made that the monks are "the fathers of the poor." In the diocese of Auxerre, during the summer of 1789, the Bernardines of Rigny "stripped themselves of all they possessed in favor of the inhabitants of neighboring villages: bread, grain, money and other supplies, have all been lavished on about twelve hundred persons who, for more than six weeks, never failed to present themselves at their door daily. . . . Loans, advances made on farms, credit with the purveyors of the house, all has contributed to facilitating their means for relieving the people." I omit many other traits equally forcible; we see that the ecclesiastical and lay seigniors are not simple egoists when they live at home. Man is compassionate of ills of which he is a witness; absence is necessary to deaden their vivid impression; the heart is moved by them when the eye contemplates them. Familiarity, moreover, engenders sympathy; one cannot remain insensible to the trials of a poor man to whom, for over twenty years, one says good-morning every day on passing him, with whose life one is acquainted, who is not an abstract unit in the imagination, a statistical cipher, but a sorrowing soul and a suffering body. And so much the more because, since the writings of Rousseau and the economists, a spirit of humanity, daily growing stronger, more penetrating and more universal, has arisen to soften the heart. Henceforth the poor are thought of, and it is esteemed an honor to think of them. We have only to read the memorials of the States-General[1] to see that the spirit of philanthropy spreads from Paris even to the chateaux and abbeys of the provinces. I am satisfied that, excepting scattered country squires, either huntsmen or drinkers, carried away by the need of physical exercise, and confined through their rusticity to an animal life, most of the resident seigniors resembled, in fact or in intention, the gentry whom Marmontel, in his moral tales, then brought on the stage; for fashion took this direction, and people in France always follow the fashion. There is nothing feudal in their characters; they are "sensible" folks, mild, very courteous, tolerably cultivated, fond of generalities, and easily and quickly roused, and very much in earnest, like that amiable logician the Marquis de Ferrières, an old light-horseman, deputy from Saumur in the National Assembly, author of an article on Theism, a moral romance and genial memoirs of no great importance; nothing could be more remote from the ancient harsh and despotic temperament. They would be glad to relieve the people, and they try to favor them as much as they can.[2] They are found detrimental, but they are not wicked; the evil is in their situation and not in their character. It is their situation, in fact, which, allowing them rights without exacting services, debars them from the public offices, the beneficial influence, the effective patronage by which they might justify their advantages and attach the peasantry to them.

But on this ground the central government occupies their place. For a long time they are very feeble against the intendant, utterly powerless to protect their parish. Twenty gentlemen cannot assemble and deliberate without the king's special permission.[3] If those of Franche-Comté happen to dine together and hear a mass once a year, it is through tolerance, and even then this harmless coterie may assemble only in the presence of the intendant. Separated from his equals, the seignior, again, is sep-

---

[1] On the conduct and sentiments of lay and ecclesiastical seigniors cf. Léonce de La-vergne, "Les Assemblées provinciales," 1 vol. Legrand, "L'intendance du Hainaut," 1 vol. Hippeau, "Le Gouvernement de Normandie," 9 vols.

[2] "The most active sympathy filled their breasts; that which an opulent man most dreaded was to be regarded as insensible." Lacretelle, vol. V. p. 2.

[3] Floquet, "Histoire du Parlement de Normandie," vol. VI. p. 696. In 1772 twenty-five gentlemen are imprisoned or exiled for having signed a protest against the orders of the court.

arated from his inferiors.   The administration of a village is of
no concern to him; he has not even its superintendence.   The
apportionment of taxes, the militia contingent, the repairs of the
church, the summoning and presiding over a parish assembly,
the making of roads, the establishment of charity workshops, all
this is the intendant's business or that of the communal officers
whom the intendant appoints or directs.[1]   Except through his
justiciary rights, so much curtailed, the seignior is an idler in
public matters.[2]   If, by chance, he should desire to act in an
official capacity, to make some reclamation for the community,
the bureaux of administration would soon close his mouth.
Since Louis XIV., the clerks have things their own way; all legislation and the entire administrative system operate against the
local seignior to deprive him of his functional efficacy and to
confine him to his naked title.   Through this separation of functions and title his pride increases as he becomes less useful.   His
self-love, deprived of its broad pasture-ground, falls back on a
small one; henceforth he seeks distinctions and not influence;
he thinks only of precedence and not of government.[3]   In
short, the local government, in the hands of clowns brutalized
by men of the pen, is a plebeian, scribbling affair which seems
to him offensive.   " His pride would be wounded if he were
asked to attend to it.   Raising taxes, levying the militia, regulating the *corvées*, are servile acts, the works of a syndic."   He accordingly abstains, remains isolated on his manor and leaves to
others a task from which he is excluded and which he disdains.
Far from protecting his peasantry he is scarcely able to protect
himself, to preserve his immunities, to have his poll-tax and
vingtièmes reduced, to obtain exemption from the militia for his
domestics, and to keep his own person, dwelling, dependants, and
hunting and fishing rights from the universal usurpation which
places all possessions and all privileges in the hands of " Monseigneur l'intendant" and Messieurs the sub-delegates.   And

---

[1] De Tocqueville, *ibid.* pp. 39, 56, 75, 119, 184.   He has developed this point with admirable force and insight.

[2] De Tocqueville, *ibid.* p. 376.   Complaints of the provincial assembly of Haute-Guyenne.
"People complain daily that there is no police in the rural districts.   How could there be
one?   *The noble takes no interest in anything*, excepting a few just and benevolent
seigniors who take advantage of their influence with their vassals to prevent affrays."

[3] Records of the States-General of 1789.   Many of the memorials of the noblesse consist
of the requests by nobles, men and women, of some honorary distinctive mark, for instance
a cross or a ribbon which will make them recognizable.

the more so because he is often poor. Bouillé estimates that
all the old families, save two or three hundred, are ruined.[1] In
Rouergue several of them live on an income of fifty and even
twenty-five louis, (1000 and 500 francs). In Limousin, says an intendant at the beginning of the century, out of several thousands
there are not fifteen who have twenty thousand livres income. In
Berry, towards 1754, "three-fourths of them die of hunger." In
Franche-Comté the fraternity to which we have alluded appears
in a humorous light, "after the mass each one returning to his
domicile, some on foot and others on their Rosinantes." In
Brittany "there is a crowd of gentlemen cellar-rats on the farms
in the lowest occupations." One M. de la Morandais becomes
the overseer of an estate. A certain family with nothing but a
small farm "attests its nobility only by the dove-cote ; it lives
like the peasants, eating nothing but brown bread." Another
gentleman, a widower, "passes his time in drinking, living licen-
tiously with his servants, and covering butter-pots with the handsomest title-deeds of his lineage." All the chevaliers de Chateaubriand," says the father, "were drunkards and beaters of
hares." He himself just makes shift to live in a miserable
way, with five domestics, a hound and two old mares "in a
chateau capable of accommodating a hundred seigniors with
their suites." Here and there in the various memoirs we see these
strange superannuated figures passing before the eye, for instance, in Burgundy, "gentlemen huntsmen wearing gaiters and
hob-nailed shoes, carrying an old rusty sword under their arms,
dying with hunger and refusing to work ;"[2] elsewhere, "M. de
Pérignan, with his red garments, perruque and visage, having dry stone walls built on his domain, and getting intoxicated
with the blacksmith of the place ;" related to Cardinal Fleury, he
is made the first Duc de Fleury.

Everything contributes to this downfall, the law, habits and
customs, and, above all, the right of primogeniture. Instituted
for the purpose of maintaining undivided sovereignty and patronage it ruins the nobles since sovereignty and patronage have

---

[1] De Bouillé, "Mémoires," p. 50. De Tocqueville, *ibid.* pp. 118, 119. De Loménie,
"Les Mirabeau," p. 132. A letter of the bailiff of Mirabeau, 1760. De Chateaubriand,
"Mémoires," I. 14, 15, 29, 76, 80, 125. Lucas de Montigny, "Mémoires de Mirabeau," I.
160. Reports of the Société du Berry, "Bourges en 1753 et 1754," according to a diary (in
the national archives), written by one of the exiled parliamentarians, p. 273.

[2] "La vie de mon père," by Rétif de la Bretonne, I. 146.

no material to work on. "In Brittany," says Chateaubriand, "the elder sons of the nobles swept away two-thirds of the property, while the younger sons shared in one-third of the paternal heritage."[1] Consequently, "the younger sons of younger sons soon come to the sharing of a pigeon, rabbit, hound and fowling-piece. The entire fortune of my grandfather did not exceed five thousand livres income, of which his elder son had two-thirds, three thousand three hundred livres, leaving one thousand six hundred and sixty-six livres for the three younger ones, upon which sum the elder still had a *préciput* claim."[2] This fortune, which crumbles away and dies out, they neither know how, nor are they disposed, to restore by commerce, manufactures or proper administration of it; it would be derogatory. "High and mighty seigniors of dove-cote, frog-pond and rabbit-warren," the more substance they lack the more value they set on the name. Add to all this the winter sojourn in town, the ceremonial and expenses comportable with vanity and social requirements, and the visits to the governor and the intendant: a man must be either a German or an Englishman to be able to pass three gloomy, rainy months in a castle or on a farm, alone, in companionship with rustics, at the risk of becoming as awkward and as fantastic as they.[3] They accordingly run in debt, become involved, sell one piece of ground and then another piece: a good many alienate the whole, excepting their small manor and their seigniorial dues, the *cens* and the *lods et ventes*, and their hunting and justiciary rights on the territory of which they were formerly proprietors.[4] Since they must support themselves on these privileges they must necessarily enforce them, even when the privilege is burdensome, and even when the debtor is a poor man. How could they

---

[1] The rule is analogous with the other *coutumes* (common-law rules), of other places and especially in Paris. (Renauldon, *ibid.* p. 134.)

[2] A sort of dower right.

[3] Mme. d'Oberkirk, "Mémoires," I. 395.

[4] De Bouillé, "Mémoires," p. 50. According to him, "all the noble old families, excepting two or three hundred, were ruined. A larger portion of the great titled estates had become the appanage of financiers, merchants and their descendants. The fiefs, for the most part, were in the hands of the bourgeoisie of the towns." Léonce de Lavergne, "Economie rurale en France," p. 26. "The greatest number vegetated in poverty in small country fiefs often not worth more than 2,000 or 3,000 francs a year." In the apportionment of the indemnity in 1825, many received less than 1,000 francs. The greater number of indemnities do not exceed 50,000 francs. "The throne," says Mirabeau, "is surrounded only by ruined nobles."

remit dues in grain and in wine when these constitute their
bread and wine for the entire year? How could they dispense
with the fifth and the fifth of the fifth *(du quint et du requint)*
when this is the only coin they obtain? why, being needy,
should they not be exacting? Accordingly, in relation to the
peasant, they are simply his creditors; and to this end comes
the feudal régime transformed by the monarchy. Around the
chateau I see sympathies declining, envy raising its head, and
hatreds on the increase. Set aside in public matters, freed
from taxation, the seignior remains isolated and a stranger
among his vassals ; his extinct authority with his unimpaired
privileges form for him an existence apart. When he emerges
fiom it, it is to forcibly add to the public misery. From this soil,
ruined by the fisc, he takes a portion of its product, so much in
sheaves of wheat and so many measures of wine. His pigeons
and his game eat up the crops. People are obliged to grind in
his mill, and to leave with him a sixteenth of the flour. The
sale of a field for the sum of six hundred livres puts one hundred livres into his pocket. A brother's inheritance reaches
a brother only after he has gnawed out of it a year's income.
A score of other dues, formerly of public benefit, no longer
serve but to support a useless private individual. The peasant,
then as at the present day, eager for gain, determined and
accustomed to do and to suffer everything to save or gain a
crown, ends by bestowing side glances of anger on the turret in
which are preserved the archives, the rent-roll, the detested parchments by means of which a man of another species, favored to
the detriment of the rest, a universal creditor and paid to do
nothing, grazes over all the ground and feeds on all the products.
Let the opportunity come to enkindle all this covetousness, and
the rent-roll will burn, and with it the turret, and with the turret,
the chateau.

III.

The spectacle becomes still more gloomy, on passing from the
estates on which the seigniors reside to those on which they are
non-residents. Noble or ennobled, lay and ecclesiastic, the latter
are privileged among the privileged, and form an aristocracy
inside of an aristocracy. Almost all the powerful and accredited
families belong to it whatever may be their origin and their

date.[1] Through their habitual or frequent residence near the
court, through their alliances or mutual visits, through their
habits and their luxuries, through the influence which they
exercise and the enmities which they provoke, they form a
group apart, and are those who possess the most extensive
estates, the leading suzerainties, and the completest and most
comprehensive jurisdictions. Of the court nobility and of the
higher clergy, they number, perhaps, a thousand in each order,
while their small number only brings out in higher relief the
enormity of their advantages. We have seen that the appanages
of the princes of the blood comprise a seventh of the territory;
Necker estimates the revenue of the estates enjoyed by the
king's two brothers at two millions.[2] The domains of the Ducs
de Bouillon, d'Aiguillon, and some others cover entire leagues,
and, in immensity and continuity, remind one of those which
the Duke of Sutherland and the Duke of Bedford now possess
in England. With nothing else than his forests and his canal,
the Duke of Orleans, before marrying his wife, as rich as himself,
obtains an income of a million. A certain seigniory, le Clermontois, belonging to the Prince de Condé, contains forty
thousand inhabitants, which is the extent of a German princIpality; "moreover all the taxes or subsidies occurring in le Clermontois are imposed for the benefit of His Serene Highness,
the king receiving absolutely nothing."[3] Naturally authority
and wealth go together, and, the more an estate yields, the more
its owner resembles a sovereign. The archbishop of Cambray,
Duc de Cambray, Comte de Cambrésis, possesses the suzerainty
over all the fiefs of a region which numbers over seventy-
five thousand inhabitants; he appoints one-half of the aldermen of Cambray and the whole of the administrators of Ca-
teau ; he has the nomination to two great abbeys, and pre-

---

[1] De Bouillé, "Mémoires," p. 50. Cherin, "Abrégé chronologique des édits" (1788).
"Of this innumerable multitude composing the privileged order scarcely a twentieth part of
it can really pretend to nobility of an immemorial and ancient date." 4,070 financial, administrative, and judicial offices conferred nobility. Turgot, "Collection des Economistes,"
II. 276. "Through the facilities for acquiring nobility by means of money there is no rich
man who does not at once become noble." D'Argenson, "Mémoires," III. 402.
[2] Necker, "De l'Administration des Finances," II. 271. Legrand, "L'Intendance de
Hainaut," pp. 104, 118, 152, 412.
[3] Even after the exchange of 1784, the prince retains for himself "all personal impositions
as well as subventions on the inhabitants," except a sum of 6,000 livres for roads. Archives
nationales, G, 192, a memorial of April 14th, 1781, on the state of things in the Clermontois.
Report of the provincial assembly of the Three Bishoprics (1787), p. 380.

sides over the provincial assemblies and the permanent bureau
which succeeds them; in short, under the intendant, or at his
side, he maintains a pre-eminence, and better still, an influence,
somewhat like that to-day maintained over his domain by a
grand-duke incorporated into the new German empire. Near
him, in Hainaut, the abbé of Saint-Amand possesses seven-
eighths of the territory of the provostship while levying on
the other eighth the seigniorial taxes of the *corvées* and the
dime; and more besides, he nominates the provost of the aldermen, so that, in the words of the grievances, "he composes
the entire State, or rather he is himself the State."[1]   I should
never end if I were to specify all these big prizes.   Let us select
only those of the prelacy, and but one particular side, that
of money.   In the "Almanach Royal," and in "La France Ecclésiastique" for 1788, we may read their admitted revenues; but
the veritable revenue is one-half more for the bishoprics, and
double and triple for the abbeys; and we must again double
the veritable revenue in order to estimate its value in the money
of to-day.[2]   The one hundred and thirty-one bishops and archbishops possess in the aggregate 5,600,000 livres of episcopal income and 1,200,000 livres in abbeys, averaging 50,000 livres per
head as in the printed record, and in reality 100,000; a bishop
thus, in the eyes of his contemporaries, according to the statement of spectators cognizant of the actual truth, was "a grand
seignior, with an income of 100,000 livres."[3]   Some of the most
important sees are magnificently endowed.   That of Sens brings
in 70,000 livres; Verdun, 74,000; Tours, 82,000; Beauvais,
Toulouse and Bayeux, 90,000; Rouen, 100,000; Auch, Metz
and Albi, 120,000; Narbonne, 160,000; Paris and Cambray,
200,000 according to official reports, and probably half as much
more in sums actually collected.   Other sees, less lucrative, are,
proportionately, still better provided.   Imagine a small provincial
town, oftentimes not even a petty sub-prefecture of our times,—
Conserans, Mirepoix, Lavaur, Rieux, Lombez, Saint-Papoul,
Comminges, Luçon, Sarlat, Mende, Fréjus, Lescar, Belley, Saint-
Malo, Tréguier, Embrun, Saint-Claude,—and, in the neighborhood, less than two hundred, one hundred, and sometimes even

---

[1] The town of St. Amand, alone, contains to-day 10,210 inhabitants.
[2] See note 3 at the end of the volume.
[3] De Ferrières, "Mémoires," II. 57. "All had 100,000, some 200, 300, and even 800,000."

less than fifty parishes, and, as recompense for this slight ecclesiastical surveillance, a prelate receiving from 25,000 to 70,000 livres, according to official statements ; from 37,000 to 105,000 livres in actual receipts ; and from 74,000 to 210,000 livres in the money of to-day. As to the abbeys, I count thirty-three of them producing to the abbé from 25,000 to 120,000 livres, and twenty-seven which bring from 20,000 to 100,000 livres to the abbess ; weigh these sums taken from the Almanach, and bear in mind that they must be doubled, and more, to obtain the real revenue, and be quadrupled, and more, to obtain the actual value. It is evident, that, with such revenues, coupled with the feudal rights, police, justiciary and administrative, which accompany them, an ecclesiastic or lay grand seignior is, in fact, a sort of prince in his district ; that he bears too close a resemblance to the ancient sovereign to be entitled to live as an ordinary individual ; that his private advantages impose on him a public character ; that his rank, and his enormous profits, make it incumbent on him to perform proportionate services, and that, even under the sway of the intendant, he owes to his vassals, to his tenants, to his feudatories the support of his mediation, of his patronage and of his gains.

This requires a home residence, but, generally, he is an absentee. For a hundred and fifty years a kind of all-powerful attraction diverts the grandees from the provinces and impels them towards the capital ; and the movement is irresistible, for it is the effect of two forces, the greatest and most universal that influence mankind, one, a social position, and the other the national character. A tree is not to be severed from its roots with impunity. An aristocracy, organized to rule, becomes detached from the soil when it no longer rules ; and it ceases to rule the moment when, through increasing and constant encroachments, almost the entire justiciary, the entire administration, the entire police, each detail of the local or general government, the power of initiating, of collaboration, of control regarding taxation, elections, roads, public works and charities, passes over into the hands of the intendant or of the sub-delegate, under the supreme direction of the comptroller-general or of the king's council.[1]   Clerks, gentry " of the robe and the quill,"

---

[1] De Tocqueville, *ibid.* book 2, chap. 2. p. 182. Letter of the bailiff of Mirabeau, August 23, 1770. " This feudal order was merely vigorous, and they have pronounced it barbarous

plebeians enjoying no consideration, perform the work; there is no way to prevent it. Even with the king's delegates, a provincial governor, were he hereditary, a prince of the blood, like the Condés in Burgundy, must efface himself before the intendant; he holds no effective office; his public duties consist of self-parade and in giving entertainments. And yet he would badly perform others; the administrative machine, with its thousands of hard, creaking and dirty wheels, as Richelieu and Louis XIV. fashioned it, can work only in the hands of workmen removable at pleasure, unscrupulous and prompt to give way to the judgment of the State. It is impossible to commit oneself with rogues of that description. He accordingly abstains, and abandons public affairs to them. Unemployed, enervated, what could he now do on his domain, where he no longer reigns, and where dulness overpowers him? He betakes himself to the city, and especially to the court. After all, this is the only career open to him; to be successful he has to become a courtier. It is the will of the king, one must frequent his apartments to obtain his favors; otherwise, on the first application for them the answer will be, "Who is he? He is a man that I never see." In his eyes there is no excuse for absence, even when the cause is a conversion, with penitence for a motive; God is preferred to him and it is desertion. The ministers write to the intendants to ascertain if the gentlemen of their province "like to stay at home," and if they "refuse to appear and perform their duties to the king." Imagine the grandeur of a trait like this; governments, commands, bishoprics, benefices, court-offices, survivorships, pensions, credit, favors of every kind and degree for self and family, all that a State of twenty or twenty-five millions of men can offer that is desirable to ambition, to vanity, to interest, is found here collected as in a reservoir. They rush to it and draw from it. And the more readily because it is an agreeable place, arranged just as they would have it, and purposely to suit the

---

because France, which had the vices of strength has only those of feebleness, and because the flock which was formerly devoured by wolves is now eaten up with lice. . . . Three or four kicks or blows with a stick were not half so injurious to a poor man's family, nor to himself, as being devoured by six rolls of handwriting." "The nobility," says St. Simon, in his day, "has become another people with no choice left it but to crouch down in mortal and ruinous indolence, which renders it a charge and contemptible, or to go and be killed in warfare; subject to the insults of clerks, secretaries of the state and the secretaries of intendants." Such are the complaints of feudal spirits. The details which follow are all derived from Saint Simon, Dangeau, de Luynes, d'Argenson and other court historians.

social aptitudes of the French character. The court is a vast permanent drawing-room to which " access is easy and free to the king's subjects;" where they live with him, "in gentle and virtuous society in spite of the almost infinite distance of rank and power;" where the monarch prides himself on being the perfect master of a household.[1]   In fact, no drawing-room was ever so well kept up, nor so well calculated to retain its guests by every kind of enjoyment, by the beauty, the dignity and the charm of its decoration, by the selection of its company and by the interest of the spectacle.   Versailles is the only place to show oneself off, to make a figure, to push one's way, to be amused, to converse or gossip at the head-quarters of news, of activity and of public matters, with the *élite* of the kingdom and the arbiters of fashion, elegance and taste. "Sire," said M. de Vardes to Louis XIV., "away from Your Majesty one not only feels miserable but ridiculous."   None remain in the provinces except the poor rural nobility; to live there one must be behind the age, disheartened or in exile.   The king's banishment of a seignior to his estates is the highest disgrace; to the humiliation of this fall is added the insupportable weight of ennui.   The finest chateau on the most beautiful site is a frightful " desert"; nobody is seen there save the grotesques of a small town or the village rustics.[2]   " Exile alone," says Arthur Young, " forces the French nobility to do what the English prefer to do, and that is to live on their estates and embellish them."   Saint-Simon and other court historians, on mentioning a ceremony, repeatedly state that "all France was there"; in fact, every one of consequence in France is there, and each recognizes the other by this sign. Paris and the court become, accordingly, the necessary sojourn of all fine people.   In such a situation departure begets departure; the more a province is forsaken the more they forsake it. "There is not in the kingdom," says the Marquis de Mirabeau, " a single estate of any size of which the proprietor is not in Paris and who, consequently, neglects his buildings and chateaux."[3]

---

[1] Works of Louis XIV. and his own words. Mme Vigée-Lebrun, " Souvenirs," I. 71 : " I have seen the queen (Marie Antoinette), obliging Madame to dine, then six years of age, with a little peasant girl whom she was taking care of, and insisting that this little one should be served first, saying to her daughter : ' You must do the honors.' "

[2] Molière, " Misanthrope." This is the " desert " in which Célimène refuses to be buried with Alceste. See also in " Tartuffe " the picture which Dorine draws of a smal. town. Arthur Young, " Voyages en France," I. 78.

[3] ' Traité de la Population," p. 108, (1756).

The lay grand seigniors have their hotels in the capital, their *en tresol* at Versailles, and their pleasure-house within a circuit of twenty leagues; if they visit their estates at long intervals, it is to hunt. The fifteen hundred commendatory abbés and priors enjoy their benefices as if they were so many remote farms. The two thousand seven hundred vicars and canons visit each other and dine out. With the exception of a few apostolic characters the one hundred and thirty-one bishops stay at home as little as they can; nearly all of them being nobles, all of them men of society, what could they do out of the world, confined to a provincial town ? Can we imagine a grand seignior, once a gay and gallant abbé and now a bishop with a hundred thousand livres income, voluntarily burying himself for the entire year at Mende, at Comminges, in a paltry cloister? The interval has become too great between the refined, varied and literary life of the great centre, and the monotonous, inert, practical life of the provinces. Hence it is that the grand seignior who withdraws from the former cannot enter into the latter, and he remains an absentee, at least in feeling.

A country in which the heart ceases to impel the blood through its veins presents a sombre aspect. Arthur Young, who travelled over France between 1787 and 1789, is surprised to find at once such a vital centre and such dead extremities. Between Paris and Versailles the double file of vehicles going and coming extends uninterruptedly for five leagues from morning till night.[1] The contrast on other roads is very great. Leaving Paris by the Orleans road, says Arthur Young, " we met not one stage or diligence for ten miles; only two messageries and very few chaises, not a tenth of what would have been met had we been leaving London at the same hour." On the highroad near Narbonne, "for thirty-six miles," he says, "I came across but one cabriolet, half a dozen carts and a few women leading asses." Elsewhere, near St. Girons, he notices that in two hundred and fifty miles he encountered in all, "two cabriolets and three miserable things similar to our old one-horse post chaise, and not one gentleman." Throughout this country the inns are execrable; it is impossible to hire a wagon, while in England, even in a town of fifteen hundred or two thousand inhabitants,

---

[1] I have this from old people who witnessed it before 1789.

there are comfortable hotels and every means of transport. This proves that in France "there is no circulation." It is only in very large towns that there is any civilization and comfort. At Nantes there is a superb theatre "twice as large as Drury-Lane and five times as magnificent. *Mon Dieu !* I cried to myself, do all these wastes, the deserts, the heath, ling, furze, broom, and bog, that I have passed for 300 miles lead to this spectacle? . . . You pass at once from beggary to profusion, . . . the country deserted, or if a gentleman in it, you find him in some wretched hole to save that money which is lavished with profusion in the luxuries of a capital." "A coach," says M. de Montlosier, "set out weekly from the principal towns in the provinces for Paris and was not always full, which represents the activity in business. There was a single journal called the *Gazette de France*, appearing twice a week, which represents the activity of minds."[1] Some of the magistrates of Paris in exile at Bourges in 1753 and 1754, give the following picture of that place. "A town in which no one can be found with whom you can talk at your ease on any topic whatever, reasonably or sensibly; nobles, three-fourths of them dying of hunger, rotting with pride of birth, keeping apart from men of the robe and of finance, and finding it strange that the daughter of a tax-collector, married to a counsellor of the parliament of Paris, should presume to be intelligent and entertain company; citizens of the grossest ignorance, the sole support of this species of lethargy in which the minds of most of the inhabitants are plunged; women, bigoted and pretentious, and much given to play and to gallantry;"[2] in this impoverished and benumbed society, among these Messieurs Thibaudeau the counsellor and Harpin the tax-collector, among these vicomtes de Sotenville and Countesses d'Escarbagnas, lives the Archbishop, Cardinal de Larochefoucauld, grand almoner to the king, provided with four great abbeys, possessing five hundred thousand livres income, a man of the world, generally an absentee, and when at home, finding amusement in the embellishing of his gardens and palace, in short, the golden pheasant of an aviary in a poultry yard of geese.[3] Naturally there is an entire absence of political thought.

---

[1] "Mémoires de M. de Montlosier," I. p. 161.
[2] Reports of the Société de Berry, "Bourges en 1753 et 1754," p. 273.
[3] *Ibid.* p. 271. One day the cardinal, showing his guests over his palace just completed, led them to the bottom of a corridor where he had placed water closets, at that time a

"You cannot imagine," says the manuscript, "a person more in-different to all public matters." At a later period, in the very midst of events of the gravest character, and which most nearly concern them, there is the same apathy. At Chateau-Thierry, on the 4th of July, 1789,[1] there is not a café in which a news-paper can be found; there is but one at Dijon; at Moulins, the 7th of August, "in the best café in the town, where I found near twenty tables set for company, but as for a newspaper I might as well have demanded an elephant." Between Stras-bourg and Besançon there is not a gazette. At Besançon there is "nothing but the *Gazette de France*, for which, at this period, a man of common sense would not give one *sol*, . . . and the *Courier de l'Europe* a fortnight old; and well-dressed people are now talking of the news of two or three weeks past, and plainly by their discourse know nothing of what is passing." At Clermont "I dined, or supped, five times at the table d'hôte with from twenty to thirty merchants, trades-men, officers, etc., and it is not easy for me to express the insig-nificance,—the inanity of their conversation. Scarcely any pol-itics at a moment when every bosom ought to beat with none but political sensations. The ignorance or the stupidity of these people must be absolutely incredible; not a week passes with-out their country abounding with events that are analyzed and debated by the carpenters and blacksmiths of England." The cause of this inertia is manifest; interrogated on their opinions, all reply: "We are of the provinces and we must wait to know what is going on in Paris." Never having acted, they do not know how to act. But, thanks to this inertia, they let them-selves be driven. The provinces form an immense stagnant pond, which, by a terrible inundation, may be emptied exclu-sively on one side, and suddenly; the fault lies with the engi-neers who failed to provide it with either dikes or outlets.

Such is the languor or, rather, the prostration, into which local life falls when the local chiefs deprive it of their presence, action,

---

novelty.   M. Boutin de la Coulommière, the son of a receiver-general of the finances, made an exclamation at the sight of the ingenious mechanism which it pleased him to keep moving, and, turning towards the abbé de Canillac, he says: "That is really admirable, but what seems to me still more admirable is that His Eminence, being above all human weak-ness, should condescend to make use of it."   This anecdote is valuable, as it serves to illustrate the rank and position of a grand-seignior prelate in the provinces.
[1] Arthur Young, v. II. p. 230 and the following pages.

or sympathy. I find only three or four grand seigniors taking a part in it, practical philanthropists following the example of English noblemen; the Duc d'Harcourt, who settles the law-suits of his peasants; the Duc de Larochefoucauld-Liancourt who establishes a model farm on his domain, and a school of industrial pursuits for the children of poor soldiers; and the Comte de Brienne, whose thirty villages are to demand liberty of the Convention.[1] The rest, for the most part liberals, content themselves with discussions on public affairs and on political economy. In fact, the difference in manners, the separation of interests, the remoteness of ideas are so great that contact between those most exempt from haughtiness and their immediate tenantry is rare, and at long intervals. Arthur Young, needing some information at the house of the Duc de Larochefoucauld himself, the steward is sent for. " At an English nobleman's, there would have been three or four farmers asked to meet me, who would have dined with the family amongst the ladies of the first rank. I do not exaggerate when I say that I have had this at least an hundred times in the first houses of our islands. It is, however, a thing that in the present style of manners in France would not be met with from Calais to Bayonne except, by chance, in the house of some great lord that had been much in England, and then not unless it was asked for. The nobility in France have no more idea of practising agriculture, and making it a subject of conversation, except on the mere theory, as they would speak of a loom or a bowsprit, than of any other object the most remote from their habits and pursuits." Through tradition, fashion and deliberation, they are, and wish only to be, people of society; their sole concern is to talk and to hunt. Never have the leaders of men so unlearned the art of leading men ; the art which consists of marching along the same pathway with them, but at the head, and directing their labor by sharing in it. Our Englishman, an eye-witness and competent, again writes: " Thus it is whenever you stumble on a grand seignior, even one

---

[1] De Loménie, "Les Mirabeau," p. 134. A letter of the bailiff, September 25, 1760: " I am at Harcourt, where I admire the master's honest, benevolent greatness. You cannot imagine my pleasure on fête days at seeing the people everywhere around the chateau, and the good little peasant boys and girls looking right in the face of their good landlord and almost pulling his watch off to examine the trinkets on the chain, and all with a fraternal air, without familiarity. The good duke does not allow his vassals to go to law; he listens to them and decides for them, humoring them with admirable patience." Lacretelle, " Dix ans d'épreuve," p. 58.

E

that was worth millions, you are sure to find his property desert. Those of the Duc de Bouillon and of the Prince de Soubise are two of the greatest properties in France; and all the signs I have yet seen of their greatness are wastes, landes, deserts, fern, ling. Go to their residence, wherever it may be, and you would probably find them in the midst of a forest very well peopled with deer, wild boars and wolves." "The great proprietors," says another contemporary,[1] "attracted to and kept in our cities by luxurious enjoyments know nothing of their estates," save "of their agents whom they harass for the support of a ruinous ostentation. How can ameliorations be looked for from those who even refuse to keep things up and make indispensable repairs?" A sure proof that their absence is the cause of the evil is found in the visible difference between the domain worked under an absent abbé-commendatory and a domain superintended by monks living on the spot. "The intelligent traveller recognizes it" at first sight by the state of cultivation. "If he finds fields well enclosed by ditches, carefully planted, and covered with rich crops, these fields, he says to himself, belong to the monks. Almost always, alongside of these fertile plains, is an area of ground badly tilled and almost barren, presenting a painful contrast; and yet the soil is the same, being two portions of the same domain; he sees that the latter is the portion of the abbé-commendatory." "The abbatial manse," said Lefranc de Pompignan, "frequently looks like the patrimony of a spendthrift; the monastic manse is like a patrimony whereon nothing is neglected for its amelioration," to such an extent that "the two-thirds" which the abbé enjoys bring him less than the third reserved by his monks.—The ruin or impoverishment of agriculture is, again, one of the effects of absenteeism; there was, perhaps, one-third of the soil in France, which, deserted as in Ireland, was as badly tilled, as little productive as in Ireland in the hands of the rich absentees, the English bishops, deans and nobles.

Doing nothing for the soil, how could they do anything for men? Now and then, undoubtedly, especially with farms that pay no rent, the steward writes a letter, alleging the misery of the farmer. There is no doubt, also, that, especially for thirty years back, they desire to be humane; they descant among themselves

---

[1] "De l'état religieux," by the abbés de Bonnefoi et Bernard, 1784, pp. 287, 291.

about the rights of man; the sight of the pale face of a hungry peasant would give them pain. But they never see him; does it ever occur to them to fancy what it is like under the awkward and complimentary phrases of their agent? Moreover, do they know what hunger is? Who amongst them has had any rural experiences? And how could they picture to themselves the misery of this forlorn being? They are too remote from him to do that, too ignorant of his mode of life. The portrait they conceive of him is imaginary; never was there a falser representation of the peasant; accordingly the awakening is to be terrible. They view him as the amiable swain, gentle, humble and grateful, simple-hearted and right-minded, easily led, being conceived according to Rousseau and the idyls performed at this very epoch in all private drawing-rooms.[1] Lacking a knowledge of him they overlook him; they read the steward's letter and immediately the whirl of high life again seizes them and, after a sigh bestowed on the distress of the poor, they make up their minds that their income for the year will be short. A disposition of this kind is not favorable to charity. Accordingly, complaints arise, not against the residents but against the absentees.[2] "The possessions of the Church, says a memorial, serve only to nourish the passions of their holders." "According to the canons, says another memorial, every beneficiary must give a quarter of his income to the poor; nevertheless in our parish there is a revenue of more than twelve thousand livres, and none of it is given to the poor unless it is some small matter at the hands of the curate." "The abbé de Conches gets one-half of the tithes and contributes nothing to the relief of the parish." Elsewhere, "the chapter of Écouis, which owns the benefice of the tithes is of no advantage to the poor, and only seeks to augment its income." Near by, the abbé of Croix-Leu-froy, "a heavy tithe-owner, and the abbé de Bernay, who gets fifty-seven thousand livres from his benefice, and who is a non-resident, keep all and scarcely give enough to their officiating curates to keep them alive." "I have in my parish, says a curate of Berry,[3] six simple benefices of which the titularies are al-

---

[1] See on this subject "La partie de chasse de Henri IV.," by Collé. Cf. Berquin, Florian, Marmontel, etc., and likewise the engravings of that day.

[2] Boivin-Champeaux, "Notice historique sur la Révolution dans le département de l'Eure," pp. 63, 61.

[3] Archives nationales, Reports of the States-General of 1789, T, XXXIX., p. 111. Letter

ways absent, and they enjoy together an income of nine thousand livres; I sent them in writing the most urgent entreaties during the calamity of the past year; I received from one of them two louis only, and most of them did not even answer me." Stronger is the reason for a conviction that in ordinary times they will make no remission of their dues. Moreover, these dues, the *censives*, the *lods et ventes*, tithes, and the like, are in the hands of a steward, and he is a good steward who returns a large amount of money. He has no right to be generous at his master's expense, and he is tempted to turn the subjects of his master to his own profit. In vain might the soft seignorial hand be disposed to be easy or paternal; the hard hand of the proxy bears down on the peasants with all its weight, and the cautiousness of a chief gives place to the exactions of a clerk.—How is it then when, instead of a clerk on the domain, a *fermier* is found, an adjudicator who, for an annual sum, purchases of the seignior the management and product of his dues? In the *election* of Mayenne,[1] and certainly also in many others, the principal domains are rented in this way. Moreover there are a number of dues, like the tolls, the market-place tax, that on the flock apart, the monopoly of the oven and of the mill which can scarcely be managed otherwise; the seignior must necessarily employ an adjudicator who spares him the disputes and the trouble of collecting.[2] In this case, so frequent, the pressure and the rapacity of the contractor, who is determined to gain or, at least, not to lose, falls on the peasantry: "He is a ravenous wolf," says Renauldon, "let loose on the estate, who draws upon it to the last sou, who crushes the subjects, reduces them to beggary, forces the cultivators to desert, and renders odious the master who finds himself obliged to tolerate his exactions to be able to profit by them." Imagine, if you can, the evil which a country usurer exercises, armed against them with such burdensome rights; it is the feudal seigniory in the hands of Harpagon, or rather of old Grandet. When, indeed, a tax becomes insupportable we see, by the local complaints, that it is nearly

---

of the 6th March, 1789, from the curate of St. Pierre de Ponsigny, in Berry.   D'Argenson, 6th July, 1756. "The late cardinal de Soubise had three millions in cash and he gave nothing to the poor."

[1] De Tocqueville, *ibid.* 405.   Renauldon, *ibid.* 628.

[2] The example is set by the king who sells to the farmer-generals, for an annual sum, the management and product of the principal indirect taxes.

always a *fermier* who enforces it : [1] it is one of these, acting for a body of canons, who claims Jeanne Mermet's paternal inheritance on the pretence that she had passed her wedding night at her husband's house.   It would be difficult to find parallel exactions in the Ireland of 1830, on those estates where, the farmer-general renting to sub-farmers, and the latter to others still below them, the poor tenant at the foot of the ladder himself bore the full weight of it, so much the more crushed because his creditor, crushed himself, measured the requirements he exacted by those he had to submit to.

Suppose that, seeing this abuse of his name, the seignior is desirous of withdrawing the administration of his domains from these mercenary hands; in most cases he is unable to do it : he is too deeply in debt, having appropriated to his creditors a certain portion of his land, a certain branch of his income.   For centuries, the nobles are involved through their luxuriousness, their prodigality, their carelessness, and through that false sense of honor which consists in looking upon attention to accounts as the occupation of an accountant.   They take pride in their negligence, regarding it, as they say, living nobly.[2]   "Monsieur the archbishop," said Louis XVI. to M. de Dillon, "they say that you are in debt, and even largely."   "Sire," replied the prelate, with the irony of a grand seignior, "I will ask my intendant and inform Your Majesty."   Marshal de Soubise has five hundred thousand livres income, which is not sufficient for him. We know the debts of the Cardinal de Rohan and of the Comte d'Artois; their millions of income were vainly thrown into this gulf.   The Prince de Guéménée happens to become bankrupt on thirty-five millions.   The Duke of Orleans, the richest proprietor in the kingdom, owed at his death seventy-four millions.   When it became necessary to pay the creditors of the emigrants out of the proceeds of their possessions, it was proved that most of the

---

[1] Voltaire, "Politique et Législation, La voix du Curé," (in relation to the serfs of St. Claude).   A speech of the Duke d'Aiguillon, August 4th, 1789, in the National Assembly : "The proprietors of fiefs, of seigniorial estates, are rarely guilty of the excesses of which their vassals complain; but their agents are often pitiless."

[2] Beugnot, "Mémoires," v. I. p. 136.   Duc de Lévis, "Souvenirs et portraits," p. 156. "Moniteur," the session of November 22, 1872, M. Bocher says : "According to the statement drawn up by order of the Convention the Duke of Orleans's fortune consisted of 74,000,000 of indebtedness and 140,000,000 of assets.   On the 8th January, 1792, he had assigned to his creditors 38,000,000 to obtain his discharge."

large fortunes were eaten up with mortgages.[1] Readers of the
various memoirs know that, for two hundred years, the deficiencies had to be supplied by marriages for money and by the
favors of the king. This explains why, following the king's example, the nobles converted everything into money, and especially the places at their disposition, and, in relaxing authority
for profit, why they alienated the last fragment of government
remaining in their hands. Everywhere they thus laid aside the
venerated character of a chief to put on the odious character of
a trafficker. "Not only," says a contemporary,[2] "do they give
no pay to their officers of justice, or take them at a discount,
but, what is worse, the greater portion of them make a sale of
these offices." In spite of the edict of 1693, the judges thus appointed take no steps to be admitted into the royal courts and
they take no oaths. "What is the result? Justice, too often
administered by knaves, degenerates into brigandage or into a
frightful impunity."—Ordinarily the seignior who sells the office
on a financial basis, deducts, in addition, the hundredth, the fif-
tieth, the tenth of the price, when it passes into other hands;
and at other times he disposes of the survivorship. He creates
these offices and survivorships purposely to sell them. "All the
seigniorial courts, say the memorials, are infested with a crowd
of officials of every description, seigniorial sergeants, mounted
and unmounted officers, keepers of the provostship of the funds,
guards of the constabulary; it is by no means rare to find as
many as ten in an arrondissement which could hardly maintain
two if they confined themselves within the limits of their duties."
Also "they are at the same time judges, attorneys, fiscal-attor-
neys, registrars, notaries," each in a different place, each practising in several seigniories under various titles, all perambulat-
ing, all in league like thieves at a fair, and assembling together
in the taverns to plan, prosecute and decide. Sometimes the
seignior, to economize, confers the title on one of his own dependants: "At Hautemont, in Hainaut, the fiscal-attorney is a
domestic." More frequently he intrusts it to some starveling
advocate of a petty village in the neighborhood on wages which

---

[1] In 1785, the Duke de Choiseul in his testament estimated his property at fourteen
millions and his debts at ten millions. Comte de Tilly, "Mémoires," II. 215.

[2] Renauldon, *ibid.* 45, 52, 628. Duvergier, "Collection des Lois," II. 391; law of August
31; October 18, 1792. Memorial of a magistrate of the Chatelet on seigniorial courts
(1789), p. 69. Legrand, "l'Intendance du Hainaut," p. 119.

"would not suffice to keep him alive a week." He indemnifies himself out of the peasants. Processes of chicanery, delays and wilful complications in the proceedings, sittings at three livres the hour for the advocate, and three livres the hour for the bailiff: the black brood of judicial leeches suck so much the more eagerly, because the more numerous, a still more meagre prey, having paid for the privilege of sucking it.[1] The arbitrariness, the corruption, the laxity of such a régime can be divined. "Impunity," says Renauldon, "is nowhere greater than in the seigniorial tribunals. . . . The foulest crimes obtain no consideration there," for the seignior dreads supplying the means for a criminal trial, while his judges or prosecuting attorneys fear that they will not be paid for their proceedings. Moreover, his jail is often a cellar under the chateau ; "there is not one tribunal out of a hundred in conformity with the law in respect of prisons ;" their keepers shut their eyes or stretch out their hands. Hence it is that "his estates become the refuge of all the scoundrels in the canton." The effect of his indifference is terrible and it is to react against him : to-morrow, at the club, the attorneys whom he has multiplied will demand his head, and the bandits whom he has tolerated will place it on the end of a pike.

One point remains, the chase, wherein the noble's jurisdiction is still active and severe, and it is just the point which is found the most offensive. Formerly, when one-half of the canton consisted of forest, or waste land, while the other half was being ravaged by wild beasts, he was justified in reserving the right to hunt them ; it entered into his function as local captain. He was the hereditary gendarme, always armed, always on horseback, as well against wild boars and wolves as against rovers and brigands. Now that nothing is left to him of the gendarme but the title and the epaulettes he maintains his privilege through tradition, thus converting a service into an annoyance. Hunt he must, and he alone must hunt ; it is a physical necessity and, at the same time, a sign of his blood. A Rohan, a Dillon, chases the stag although belonging to the church, in spite of edicts

---

[1] Archives nationales, H, 614 ("Mémoire" by René de Hauteville, advocate to the Parliament, Saint-Brieuc, October 5, 1776.) In Brittany the number of seigniorial courts is immense, the pleaders being obliged to pass through four or five jurisdictions before reaching the Parliament. "Where is justice rendered ? In the cabaret, in the tavern, where, in the bosom of intoxication and debauchery, the judge sells justice to whoever pays the most for it."

and in spite of the canons. "You hunt too much," said Louis
XV.,[1] to the latter; "I know something about it. How can you
prohibit your curates from hunting if you pass your life in setting
them such an example?—Sire, for my curates the chase is a
fault, for myself it is the fault of my ancestors." When the self-
love of caste thus mounts guard over a right it is with obstinate
vigilance. Accordingly, their captains of the chase, their game-
keepers, their wood-rangers, their forest-wardens protect brutes as
if they were men, and men as if they were brutes. In the bailiwick of Pont-l'Evêque in 1789 four instances are cited "of recent
assassinations committed by the game-keepers of Mme. d'A——,
Mme. N——, a prelate and a marshal of France, on plebeians caught breaking the game laws or carrying guns. All
four publicly escape punishment." In Artois, a parish makes
declaration that "on the lands of the chattellany the game de-
vours all the *avêtis* (pine saplings) and that the growers of them
will be obliged to abandon their business." Not far off, at
Rumancourt, at Bellone, "the hares, rabbits and partridges entirely devour them, Count d'Oisy never hunting nor having
hunts." In twenty villages in the neighborhood around Oisy
where he hunts it is on horseback and across the crops. "His
game-keepers, always armed, have killed several persons under
the pretence of watching over their master's rights. . . . The
game, which greatly exceeds that of the royal captainries, consumes annually all prospects of a crop, twenty thousand *razières*
of wheat and as many of other grains." In the bailiwick of
Evreux "the game has just destroyed everything up to the very
houses. . . . On account of the game the citizen is not free to
pull up the weeds in summer which clog the grain and injure the
seed sown. . . . How many women are there without husbands,
and children without fathers, on account of a poor hare or rabbit!" The game-keepers of the forest of Gouffray in Normandy "are so terrible that they maltreat, insult and kill men.
. . . I know of farmers who, having pleaded against the lady to
be indemnified for the loss of their wheat, not only lost their
time but their crops and the expenses of the trial. . . . Stags
and deer are seen roving around our houses in open daylight."
In the bailiwick of Domfront, "the inhabitants of more than ten
parishes are obliged to watch all night for more than six months

---

[1] Beugnot, "Mémoires," vol. I. p. 35.

of the year to secure their crops.[1]—This is the effect of the right of the chase in the provinces. It is, however, in the Ile-de-France, where captainries abound, and become more extensive, that the spectacle is most lamentable. A *procès-verbal* shows that in the single parish of Vaux, near Meulan, the rabbits of warrens in the vicinity ravage eight hundred cultivated *arpents* of ground and destroy the crops of two thousand four hundred *setiers* (three acres each), that is to say, the annual supplies of eight hundred persons. Near that place, at la Rochette, herds of deer and of stags devour everything in the fields during the day, and, at night, they even invade the small gardens of the inhabitants to consume vegetables and to break down young trees. It is found impossible in a territory subjected to a captainry to retain vegetables safe in gardens, enclosed by high walls. At Farcy, of five hundred peach trees planted in a vineyard and browsed on by stags, only twenty remain at the end of three years. Over the whole territory of Fontainebleau, the communities, to save their vines, are obliged to maintain, with the assent always of the captainry, a gang of watchmen who, with licensed dogs, keep watch and make a hubbub all night from the first of May to the middle of October. At Chartrettes the deer cross the Seine, approach the doors of the Comtesse de Larochefoucauld and destroy entire plantations of poplars. A domain rented for two thousand livres brings in only four hundred after the establishment of the captainry of Versailles. In short, eleven regiments of an enemy's cavalry, quartered on the eleven captainries near the capital, and starting out daily to forage, could not do more mischief. We need not be surprised if, in the neighborhood of these lairs, the people become weary of cultivating.[2] Near Fontainebleau and Melun, at Bois-le-Roi, three-

---

[1] Boivin-Champeaux, *ibid.* 48. Renauldon, 26, 416. Manuscript reports of the States-General (Archives nationales) t. CXXXII. pp. 896 and 901. Hippeau, "Le Gouvernement de Normandie," VII. 61, 74. Périn, "La Jeunesse de Robespierre," pp. 314-324. "Essai sur les capitaineries royales et autres," (1789) *passim.* De Loménie, "Beaumarchais et son temps," I. 125. Beaumarchais having purchased the office of lieutenant-general of the chase in the bailiwicks of the Louvre warren (twelve to fifteen leagues in circumference) tries delinquents under this title. July 15th, 1766, he sentences Ragondet, a farmer, to a fine of one hundred livres together with the demolition of the walls around an enclosure, also of his shed newly built without license, as tending to restrict the pleasures of the king.

[2] D'Argenson, "Mémoires," ed. Rathery, January 21, 1757. "The sieur de Montmorin, captain of the game-preserves of Fontainebleau, derives from his office enormous sums, and behaves himself like a brigand. The population of more than a hundred villages around no longer sow their land, the fruits and grain being eaten by deer, stags and other game.

quarters of the ground remains waste; almost all the houses in
Brolle are in ruins, only half-crumbling gables being visible; at
Coutilles and at Chapelle-Rablay, five farms are abandoned;
at Arbonne, numerous fields are neglected; at Villiers, and at
Dame-Marie, where there were four farming companies and a
number of special cultures, eight hundred *arpents* remain untilled.   Strange to say, as the century becomes more polished
the system of the chase becomes more imperious.   The officers
of the captainry are zealous because they labor under the eye
and for the "pleasures" of their master.   In 1789, eight hundred preserves had just been planted in one single canton of the
captainry of Fontainebleau, and in spite of the proprietors of
the soil.   According to the regulations of 1762 every private individual domiciled on the reservation of a captainry is interdicted from enclosing his homestead or any ground whatever
with hedges or ditches, or walls without a special permit.   In
case of a permit being given he must leave a wide, open, and
continuous space in order to let the huntsmen easily pass
through.   He is not allowed to keep any ferret, any fire-arm,
any instrument adapted to the chase, nor to be followed by any
dog even if not adapted to it, except the dog be held by a leash
or clog fastened around its neck.   And better still.   He is forbidden to reap his meadow or his luzerne before St. John's day,
to enter his own field between the first of May and the twenty-
fourth of June, to visit any island in the Seine, to cut grass on it
or osiers, even if the grass and osiers belong to him.   The reason is, that now the partridge is hatching and the legislator
protects it; he would take less pains for a woman in confine-
ment; the old chroniclers would say of him, as with William
Rufus, that his bowels are paternal only for animals.   Now, in
France, four hundred square leagues of territory are subject to
the control of the captainries, and, over all France, game, large
or small, is the tyrant of the peasant.   The conclusion is—
rather, listen to the people's conclusion.   "Every time," says M.
Montlosier, in 1789, "that I chanced to encounter herds of deer

---

They keep only a few vines which they preserve six months of the year by mounting guard
day and night with drums, making a general turmoil to frighten off the destructive animals."
January 23, 1753.—"M. le Prince de Conti has established a captainry of eleven leagues
around Ile-Adam and where everybody is vexed at it."   September 23, 1753.—"Since
M. le Duc d'Orléans came to Villers-Cotterets, he has revived the captainry; there are more
than sixty places for sale on account of these princely annoyances"

or does on my road my guides immediately shouted, There goes the nobility! alluding to the ravages committed by these animals on their grounds." Accordingly, in the eyes of their subjects, they are wild animals.

This shows to what privileges lead when divorced from services. It is thus that an obligation to protect degenerates into a right of devastation; thus do humane and rational beings act, unconsciously, like irrational and inhuman beings. Divorced from the people they misuse them; nominal chiefs, they have unlearned the function of an effective chief; having lost all public character they abate nothing of their private advantages. So much the worse for the canton, and so much the worse for themselves! The thirty or forty poachers whom they prosecute to-day on their estates will march to-morrow to attack their chateaux at the head of an insurrection. The absence of the masters, the apathy of the provinces, the bad state of cultivation, the exactions of agents, the corruption of the tribunals, the vexations of the captainries, indolence, the indebtedness and exigencies of the seignior, desertion, misery, the brutality and hostility of vassals, all proceeds from the same cause and terminates in the same effect. When sovereignty becomes transformed into a sinecure it becomes burdensome without being useful, and on becoming burdensome without being useful it is overthrown.

CHAPTER IV.

I.

USELESS in the canton, they might have been useful at the
centre of the State, and, without taking part in the local government, they might have served in the general government.   Thus
does a lord, a baronet, a squire act in England, even when not a
"justice" of his county or a committee-man in his parish.   Elected
a member of the lower house, a hereditary member of the upper
house, he holds the strings of the public purse and prevents the
sovereign from spending too freely.   Such is the régime in countries where the feudal seigniors, instead of allowing the sovereign
to ally himself with the people against them, allied themselves
with the people against the sovereign.   To protect their own interests better they secured protection for the interests of others,
and, after having served as the representatives of their com-
peers they became the representatives of the nation.   Nothing
of this kind takes place in France.   The States-General are
fallen into desuetude, and the king may with truth declare himself the sole representative of the country.   Like trees rendered

lifeless under the shadow of a gigantic oak, other public powers perish through his growth; whatever still remains of these encumbers the ground, and forms around him a circle of clambering briers or of decaying trunks. One of them, the Parliament, an offshoot simply of the great oak, sometimes imagined itself in possession of a root of its own; but its sap was too evidently derivative for it to stand by itself and provide the people with an independent shelter. Other bodies, surviving, although stunted, the assembly of the clergy and the provincial assemblies, still protect an order, and four or five provinces; but this protection extends only to the order itself or to the province, and, if it protects a special interest it is commonly at the expense of the general interest.

II.

Let us observe the most vigorous and the best-rooted of these bodies, the assembly of the clergy. It meets every five years, and, during the interval, two agents, selected by it, watch over the interests of the order. Convoked by the government, subject to its guidance, retained or dismissed when necessary, always in its hands, used by it for political ends, it nevertheless continues to be a refuge for the clergy, which it represents. But it is an asylum solely for that body, and, in the series of transactions by which it defends itself against fiscal demands, it eases its own shoulders of the load only to make it heavier on the shoulders of others. We have seen how its diplomacy saved clerical immunities, how it bought off the body from the poll-tax and the *vingtièmes*, how it converted its portion of taxation into a "free gift," how this gift is annually applied to refunding the capital which it has borrowed to obtain this exemption, by which delicate art it succeeds, not only in not contributing to the treasury, but in withdrawing from it every year about 1,500,000 livres, all of which is so much the better for the church but so much the worse for the people. Now run through the file of folios in which from one period of five years to another the reports of its agents follow each other,—so many clever men thus preparing themselves for the highest positions in the church, the abbés de Boisgelin, de Périgord, de Barral, de Montesquiou; at each moment, owing to their solicitations with judges and the council, owing to the authority which the discontent of the powerful or-

der felt to be behind them gives to their complaints, some ecclesiastical matter is decided in an ecclesiastical sense; some
feudal right is maintained in favor of a chapter or of a bishop;
some public demand is thrown out.[1] In 1781, notwithstanding a
decision of the Parliament of Rennes, the canons of St. Malo
are sustained in their monopoly of the district oven, to the detriment of the bakers who prefer to bake at their own domiciles,
as well as of the inhabitants who would have to pay less for bread
made by the bakers. In 1773, Guénin, a schoolmaster, discharged by the bishop of Langres, and supported in vain by the
inhabitants, is compelled to hand his place over to a successor
appointed by the bishop. In 1770, Rastel, a Protestant, having
opened a public school at Saint-Affrique, is prosecuted at the demand of the bishop and of clerical agents; his school is closed
and he is imprisoned. When an organized body keeps the
purse-strings in its own hands it secures many favors; these are
the equivalent for the money it grants. The commanding tone
of the king and the submissive air of the clergy effect no fundamental change; with both of them it is a bargain,[2] giving and·
taking on both sides, this or that law against the Protestants
going for one or two millions added to the free gift. In this
way the revocation of the Edict of Nantes is gradually brought
about, article by article, one turn of the rack after another turn,
each fresh persecution purchased by a fresh largess, the clergy
helping the State on condition that the State becomes an executioner. Throughout the eighteenth century the church sees that
this operation continues.[3] In 1717, an assemblage of seventy-
four persons having been surprised at Andure the men are sent
to the galleys and the women are imprisoned. In 1724, an edict
declares that all who are present at any meeting, or who shall
have any intercourse, direct or indirect, with preachers, shall be
condemned to the confiscation of their property, the women to
have their heads shaved and be shut up for life, and the men to be
sent to the galleys for life. In 1745 and 1746, in Dauphiny, two

---

[1] "Rapport de l'agence du clergé," from 1775 to 1780, pp. 31-34. *Ibid.* from 1780 to 1785,
p. 237.

[2] Lanfrey, " L'Eglise et les philosophes," *passim.*

[3] Boiteau, "Etat de la France en 1789," pp. 205, 207. D'Argenson, "Mémoires," May
5, 1752, pp. 3, 22; September 25, 1753; October 17, 1753, and October 26, 1775. Prud-
'homme, "Résumé général des cahiers des Etats-Généraux," 1789, (Memorials of the
Clergy). "Histoire des églises du désert," par Charles Coquerel, I. 151 and those following.

hundred and seventy-seven Protestants are condemned to the galleys, and numbers of women are whipped. Between 1744 and 1752, in the east and in the south, six hundred Protestants are imprisoned and eight hundred condemned to various penalties. In 1774, the two children of Roux, a Calvinist of Nimes, are carried off. Up to nearly the beginning of the Revolution, in Languedoc, ministers are hung, while dragoons are despatched against congregations assembled to worship God in deserted places; the mother of M. Guizot here received shots in the skirts of her dress; this is owing to the fact that, in Languedoc, through the provincial States-Assembly "the bishops control temporal affairs more than elsewhere, their disposition being always to dragoon and make converts at the point of the bayonet." In 1775, at the coronation of the king, archbishop Loménie of Brienne, a well-known unbeliever, addresses the young king: "You will disapprove of the culpable systems of toleration. . . . Complete the work undertaken by Louis the Great. To you is reserved the privilege of giving the final blow to Calvinism in your kingdom." In 1780, the assembly of the clergy declares "that the altar and the throne would equally be in danger if heresy were allowed to throw off its shackles." Even in 1789, the clergy in its memorials, while consenting to the toleration of non-Catholics, finds the edict of 1788 too liberal; they desire that they should be excluded from judicial offices, that they should never be allowed to worship in public, and that mixed marriages should be interdicted; and much more than this; they demand preliminary censure of all works issued by the book-sellers, an ecclesiastical committee to act as informers, and igno-minious punishment to be awarded to the authors of irreligious books; and lastly they claim for their body the direction of public schools and the oversight of private schools. There is nothing strange in this intolerance and selfishness. A collective body, as with an individual, thinks of itself first of all and above all. If, now and then, it sacrifices some one of its privileges it is for the purpose of securing the alliance of some other body. In that case, which is that of England, all these privileges, which compound with each other and afford each other mutual support, form, through their combination, the public liberties. In this case, only one body being represented, its deputies are neither directed nor tempted to make concession to others; the interest of the body is their sole guide; they subordinate the common interest to it and serve it at any cost, even to criminal attacks on the public welfare.

III.

Thus do public bodies work when, instead of being associated together, they are separate. The same spectacle is apparent on contemplating castes and coteries; their isolation is the cause of their egoism. From the top to the bottom of the scale the legal and moral powers which should represent the nation represent themselves only, while each one is busy in its own behalf at the expense of the nation. The nobility, in default of the right to meet together and to vote, exercises its influence, and, to know how it uses this, it is sufficient to read over the edicts and the Almanach. A regulation imposed on Marshal de Ségur[1] has just restored the old barrier which excluded plebeians from military rank, and thenceforward, to be a captain, it is necessary to prove four degrees of nobility. In like manner, in late days, one must be a noble to be a master of requests, and it is secretly determined that in future "all ecclesiastical property, from the humblest priory to the richest abbeys, shall be reserved to the nobility." In fact, all the high places, ecclesiastic or laic, are theirs; all the sinecures, ecclesiastic or laic, are theirs, or for their relations, adherents, proteges, and servitors. France is like a vast stable in which the blood-horses obtain double and triple rations for doing nothing, or for only half-work, whilst the draft-horses perform full service on half a ration, and that often not supplied. Again, it must be noted, that among these blood-horses is a privileged set which, born near the manger, keeps its fellows away and feeds bountifully, fat, shining, with their skins polished, and up to their bellies in litter, and with no other occupation than that of appropriating everything to themselves. These are the court nobles, who live within reach of favors, brought up from infancy to ask for them, to obtain and to ask again, solely attentive to royal condescension and frowns, for whom the *Œil de bœuf*[2] forms the universe, "in-

---

[1] De Ségur, "Mémoires," vol. I. pp. 16, 41. De Bouillé, "Mémoires," p. 54. Mme. Campan, "Mémoires," v. I. p. 237, proofs in detail.

[2] An antechamber in the palace of Versailles in which there was a round or bull's-eye window, where courtiers assembled to await the opening of the door into the king's apartment.—TR.

different to the affairs of the State as to their own affairs, allowing one to be governed by provincial intendants as they allowed the other to be governed by their own intendants."

Let us contemplate them at work on the budget. We know how large that of the church is; I estimate that they absorb at least one-half of it. Nineteen chapters of male nobles, twenty-five chapters of female nobles, two hundred and sixty commanderies of Malta belong to them by institution. They occupy, by favor, all the archbishoprics, and, except five, all the bishoprics.[1] They furnish three out of four abbés-commendatory and vicars-general. If, among the abbeys of females royally nominated, we set apart those bringing in twenty thousand livres and more, we find that they all have ladies of rank for abbesses. One fact alone shows the extent of these favors: I have counted eighty-three abbeys of men possessed by the almoners, chaplains, preceptors or readers to the king, queen, princes, and princesses; one of them, the abbé de Vermont, has 80,000 livres income in benefices. In short, large or small, the fifteen hundred ecclesiastical sinecures under royal appointment constitute a currency for the service of the great, whether they pour it out in golden rain to recompense the assiduity of their intimates and followers, or keep it in large reservoirs to maintain the dignity of their rank. Besides, according to the fashion of giving more to those who have already enough, the richest prelates possess, above their episcopal revenues, the wealthiest abbeys. According to the Almanach, M. d'Argentré, bishop of Séez,[2] thus enjoys an extra income of 34,000 livres; M. de Suffren, bishop of Sisteron, 36,000; M. de Girac, bishop of Rennes, 40,000; M. de Bourdeille, bishop of Soissons, 42,000; M. d'Agout de Bonneval, bishop of Pamiers, 45,000; M. de Marbœuf, bishop of Autun, 50,000; M. de Rohan, bishop of Strasbourg, 60,000; M. de Cicé, archbishop of Bordeaux, 63,000; M. de Luynes, archbishop of Sens, 82,000; M. de Bernis, archbishop of Alby, 100,000; M. de Brienne, archbishop of Toulouse, 106,000; M. de Dillon, archbishop of Narbonne, 120,000; M. de Larochefoucauld, archbishop of Rouen, 130,000; that is to say, double and sometimes triple the sums stated, and quadruple, and often six times as much, according to the present standard. M. de

---

[1] "La France ecclésiastique," 1788.
[2] Granier de Cassagnac, "Des causes de la Révolution Française," III. 58.

F

Rohan derived from his abbeys, not 60,000 livres but 400,000, and M. de Brienne, the most opulent of all, next to M. de Ro han, the 24th of August, 1788, at the time of leaving the ministry,[1] sent to withdraw from the treasury " the 20,000 livres of his month's salary which had not yet fallen due, a punctuality the more remarkable that, without taking into account the salary of his place, with the 6,000 livres pension attached to his blue ribbon, he possessed, in benefices, 678,000 livres income, and that, still quite recently, a cutting of wood on one of his abbey domains yielded him a million."

Let us pass on to the lay budget; here also are prolific sinecures, and almost all belong to the nobles. Of this class there are in the provinces the thirty-seven great governments-general, the seven small governments-general, the sixty-six lieutenancies-general, the four hundred and seven special governments, the thirteen governorships of royal palaces, and a number of others, all of them for ostentation and empty honors, all in the hands of the nobles, all lucrative, not only through salaries paid by the treasury, but also through local profits. Here, again, the nobility allowed itself to evade the authority, the activity and the usefulness of its charge on the condition of retaining its title, pomp and money.[2] The intendant is really the governor; "the titular governor, exercising a function with special letters of command," is only there to give dinners; and again he must have permission to do that, "the permission to go and reside at his place of government." The place, however, yields fruit: the government-general of Berry is worth 35,000 livres income, that of Guyenne 120,000, that of Languedoc 160,000; a small special government, like that of Havre, brings in 35,000 livres, besides the accessories; a medium lieutenancy-general, like that of Rous-

1 Marmontel, "Mémoires," v. II. book xiii. p. 221.
2 Boiteau, " Etat de la France en 1789," pp. 55, 248. D'Argenson, " Considérations sur le gouvernement de la France," p. 177. De Luynes, "Journal," XIII. 226, XIV. 287, XIII. 33, 158, 162, 118, 233, 237, XV. 268, XVI. 304. The government of Ham is worth 11,250 livres, that of Auxerre 12,000, that of Briançon 12,000, that of the islands of Ste. Marguerite 16,000, that of Schelestadt 15,000, that of Brisach from 15 to 16,000, that of Gravelines 18,000. The ordinance of 1776 had reduced these various places as follows: (Warroquier, II. 467). 18 general governments to 60,000 livres, 21 to 30,000; 114 special governments; 25 to 12,000 livres, 25 to 10,000 and 64 to 8,000; 176 lieutenants and commandants of towns, places, etc., of which 35 were reduced to 16,600 and 141 from 2,000 to 6,000. The ordinance of 1788 established, besides these, 17 commands in chief with from 20,000 to 30,000 livres fixed salary and from 4,000 to 6,000 a month for residence, and commands of a secondary grade.

sillon, 13,000 to 14,000 livres; one special government from 12,000 to 18,000 livres; and observe that, in the Isle of France alone, there are thirty-four, at Vervins, Senlis, Melun, Fontaine-bleau, Dourdan, Sens, Limours, Etampes, Dreux, Houdan and other towns as insignificant as they are pacific; it is the staff of the Valois dynasty which, since the time of Richelieu, has ceased to perform any service, but which the treasury continues to pay.

Consider these sinecures in one province alone, in Languedoc, a country of provincial assemblies—where it seems as if the tax-payer's purse ought to be better protected. There are three sub-commandants at Tournon, Alais, and Montpelier, " each one paid 16,000 livres, although without any functions since their places were established at the time of the religious wars and troubles, to keep down the Protestants." Twelve royal lieuten-ants are equally useless, and only for parade. The same with three lieutenants-general, each one "receiving in his turn, every three years, a gratuity of 30,000 livres, for services rendered in the said province, which are vain and chimerical, and which are not specified ;" because none of them reside there, and, if they are paid, it is to secure their support at the court. " Thus the Comte de Caraman, who has more than 600,000 livres income as proprietor of the Languedoc canal, receives 30,000 livres every three years, without legitimate cause, and independently of frequent and ample gifts which the province awards to him for repairs on his canal." The province likewise gives to the commandant, Comte de Périgord, a gratuity of 12,000 livres in addition to his salary, and to his wife another gratuity of 12,000 livres on her honoring the states for the first time with her pres-ence. It again pays, for the same commandant, forty guards, " of which twenty-four only serve during his short appearance at the Assembly," and who, with their captain, annually cost 15,000 livres. It pays likewise for the Governor from eighty to one hundred guards, "who each receive 300 or 400 livres, besides many exemptions, and who are never on service, since the Governor is a non-resident." The expense of these lazy subalterns is about 24,000 livres, besides 5,000 to 6,000 for their captain, to which must be added 7,500 for gubernatorial secretaries, besides 60,000 livres salaries, and untold profits for the Governor himself. I find everywhere secondary idlers swarming in the shadow of idlers in chief, and deriving their vigor from the public purse

which is the common nurse. All these people parade and
drink and eat copiously, in grand style: it is their principal
service, and they attend to it conscientiously. The sessions
of the Assembly are junketings of six weeks' duration, in which
the intendant expends 25,000 livres in dinners and receptions.[1]

Equally lucrative and useless are the court offices[2]—so many
domestic sinecures, the profits and accessories of which largely
exceed the emoluments. I find in the printed register 295
cooks, without counting the table-waiters of the king and his
people, while "the head butler obtains 84,000 livres a year in
billets and supplies," without counting his salary and the "grand
liveries" which he receives in money. The head chambermaids
to the queen, inscribed in the Almanach for 150 livres and paid
12,000 francs, make in reality 50,000 francs by the sale of the
candles lighted during the day. Augeard, private secretary, and
whose place is set down at 900 livres a year, confesses that it is
worth to him 200,000. The head huntsman at Fontainebleau
sells for his own benefit each year 20,000 francs worth of
rabbits. "On each journey to the king's country residences the
ladies of the bedchamber gain eighty per cent. on the expenses
of moving; it is said that the coffee and bread for each of these
ladies costs 2,000 francs a year, and so on with other things."
"Mme. de Tallard made 115,000 livres income out of her place
of governess to the children of France, because her salary was
increased 35,000 livres for each child." The Duc de Penthièvre,
as grand admiral, received an anchorage due on all vessels "entering the ports and rivers of France," which produced annually
91,484 francs. Mme. de Lamballe, superintendent of the
queen's household, inscribed for 6,000 francs, gets 150,000.[3]
The Duc de Gèvres gets 50,000 crowns by one show of fire-
works out of the fragments and scaffolding which belong to him
by virtue of his office.[4]—Grand officers of the palace, governors

[1] Archives nationales, H, 944, April 25, and September 20, 1780. Letters and Memoirs
of Furgole, advocate at Toulouse.
[2] Archives nationales, O, 738 (Reports made to the bureau-general of the king's household, March, 1780, by M. Mesnard de Chousy). Augeard, "Mémoires," 97. Mme.
Campan, "Mémoires," I. 291. D'Argenson, "Mémoires," February 10, December 9, 1751,
"Essai sur les Capitaineries royales et autres" (1789), p. 80. Warroquier, "Etat de la
France en 1789," I. 266.
[3] "Marie Antoinette," by D'Arneth and Geffroy, II. 377.
[4] Mme. Campan, "Mémoires," I. 296, 298, 300, 301; III. 78. Hippeau, "Le Gouvernement de Normandie," IV. 171 (Letter from Paris, December 13, 1780). D'Argenson,
"Mémoires," September 5, 1755. Bachaumont, January 19, 1758. "Mémoire sur l'impo-
sition territoriale," by M. de Calonne (1787), p. 54.

of royal establishments, captains of captainries, chamberlains, equerries, gentlemen in waiting, gentlemen in ordinary, pages, governors, almoners, chaplains, ladies of honor, ladies of the bed-chamber, ladies in waiting on the King, the Queen, on Monsieur, on Madame, on the Comte D'Artois, on the Comtesse D'Artois, on Mesdames, on Madame Royale, on Madame Elisabeth, in each princely establishment and elsewhere—hundreds of places pro-vided with salaries and accessories are without any service to per-form, or simply answer a decorative purpose. " Mme. de Laborde has just been appointed keeper of the queen's bed, with 12,000 francs pension out of the king's privy purse ; nothing is known of the duties of this position, as there has been no place of this kind since Anne of Austria." The eldest son of M. de Machault is appointed intendant of the classes. "This is one of the employ-ments called complimentary : it is worth 18,000 livres income to sign one's name twice a year." And likewise with the post of secretary-general of the Swiss guards, worth 30,000 livres a year and assigned to the Abbé Barthélemy; and the same with the post of secretary-general of the dragoons, worth 20,000 livres a year, held in turn by Gentil Bernard and by Laujon, two small pocket poets.? It would be simpler to give the money without the place. There is, indeed, no end to them. On reading various memoirs day after day it seems as if the treasury was open to plunder. The courtiers, unremitting in their attentions to the king, force him to sympathize with their troubles. They are his intimates, the guests of his drawing-room ; men of the same stamp as himself, his natural clients, the only ones with whom he can converse, and whom it is necessary to make contented; he cannot avoid helping them. He must necessarily contribute to the dowries of their children since he has signed their marriage contracts ; he must necessarily enrich them since their profusion serves for the embellishment of his court. Nobility being one of the glories of the throne, the occupant of the throne is obliged to regild it as often as is necessary.[1] In this connection a few figures and anecdotes among a thousand speak most eloquently.[2]

---

[1] D'Argenson, "Mémoires," December 9, 1751. "The expense to courtiers of two new and magnificent coats, each for two fête days, ordered by the king, completely ruins them."

[2] De Luynes, "Journal," XIV. pp. 147–295, XV. 36, 119. D'Argenson, "Mémoires," April 8, 1752, March 30 and July 28, 1753, July 2, 1735, June 23, 1756. Hippeau, *ibid.* IV. p. 153 (Letter of May 15, 1780). Necker, "De l'Administration des Finances," II. pp. 265, 269, 270, 271, 228. Augeard, "Mémoires," p 249.

"The Prince de Pons had a pension of 25,000 livres, out of the king's bounty, on which his Majesty was pleased to give 6,000 to Mme. de Marsan, his daughter, Canoness of Remiremont. The family represented to the king the bad state of the Prince de Pons's affairs, and his Majesty was pleased to grant to his son, Prince Camille, 15,000 livres of the pension vacated by the death of his father, and 5,000 livres increase to Mme. de Marsan." M. de Conflans espouses Mlle. Portail. " In honor of this marriage the king was pleased to order that out of the pension of 10,000 livres granted to Mme. la Presidente Portail, 6,000 of it should pass to M. de Conflans after the death of Mme. Portail." M. de Séchelles, a retiring minister, "had 12,000 livres on an old pension which the king continued; he has, besides this, 20,000 livres pension as minister; and the king gives him in addition to all this a pension of 40,000 livres." The motives which prompt these favors are often remarkable. M. de Rouillé has to be consoled for not having participated in the treaty of Vienna; this explains why "a pension of 6,000 livres is given to his niece, Mme. de Castellane, and another of 10,000 to his daughter, Mme. de Beuvron, who is very rich." "M. de Puisieux enjoys about 76,000 or 77,000 livres income from the bounty of the king; it is true that he has considerable property, but the revenue of this property is uncertain, being for the most part in vines." "A pension of 10,000 livres has just been awarded to the Marquise de Lède because she is disagreeable to Mme. Infante, and to secure her resignation." The most opulent stretch out their hands and take accordingly. "It is estimated that last week 128,000 livres in pensions were bestowed on ladies of the court, while for the past two years the officers have not received the slightest pension: eight thousand livres to the Duchesse de Chevreuse, whose husband has an income of 500,000 livres; 12,000 livres to Mme. de Luynes, that she may not be jealous; 10,000 to the Duchesse de Brancas; 10,000 to the dowager Duchesse de Brancas, mother of the preceding," etc. At the head of these leeches come the princes of the blood. "The king has just given 1,500,000 livres to M. le Prince de Conti to pay his debts, 1,000,000 of which is under the pretext of indemnifying him for the injury done him by the sale of Orange, and 500,000 livres as a gratuity." "The Duc d'Orléans formerly had 50,000 crowns pension, as a poor man, and awaiting his father's inheritance. This event making him rich, with an income of more than 3,000,000 livres, he gave up his pension. But having since represented to the king that his expenditure exceeded his income, the king gave him back his 50,000 crowns." Twenty years later, in 1780, when Louis XVI., desirous of relieving the treasury, signs "the great reformation of the table, 600,000 livres are given to Mesdames for their tables." This is what the dinners, cut down, of three old ladies, cost the public! For the king's two brothers, 8,300,000 livres, besides 2,000,000 income in appanages; for the Dauphin, Madame Royale, Madame Elisabeth, and Mesdames 3,500,000 livres; for the queen, 4,000,000 ;—such is the statement of Necker in 1784. Add to this the casual donations, admitted or concealed ; 200,000 francs to M. de Sartines, to aid him in paying his debts ; 200,000 to M. Lamoignon, keeper of the seals; 100,000 to M. de Miromesnil for expenses in establishing himself; 166,000 to the widow of M. de Maurepas; 400,000 to the Prince de Salm ; 1,200,000 to the Duc de Polignac for the pledge of the county of Fenestranges; 754,337 to Mesdames to pay for Bellevue.[1] "M. de Calonne," says Augeard, a reliable witness,[2] "scarcely entered on his duties, raised a loan of 100,000,000 livres, one-quarter of which did not find its way into the royal treasury ; the rest was eaten up by people at the court; his donations to the Comte d'Artois are estimated at 56,000,000 ; the portion of Monsieur is 25,000,000 ; he gave to the Prince de Condé, in exchange for 300,000 livres income, 12,000,000 paid down and 600,000 livres annuity, and he causes the most burdensome acquisition to be made for the State, in exchanges of which the damage is more than five to one." We must not forget that in actual rates all these donations, pensions, and salaries are worth double the amount.

Such is the use of the great in relation to the central power;

---

[1] Nicolardot, "Journal de Louis XVI.," p. 228. Appropriations in the Red Book of 1774 to 1789: 227,985,716 livres, of which 80,000,000 are in acquisitions and gifts to the royal family. Among others there are 14,600,000 to the Comte d'Artois and 14,450,000 to Monsieur; 7,726,253 are given to the Queen for Saint-Cloud: 8,700,000 for the acquisition of Ile-Adam.

[2] Cf. "Compte général des revenus et dépenses fixes au 1er Mai, 1789" (Imprimerie royale, 1789, in 4to). Estate of Ile-Dieu, acquired in 1783 of the Duc de Mortemart, 1,000,000 ; estate of Viviers, acquired of the Prince de Soubise in 1784, 1,500,000; estates of St. Priest and of St. Etienne, acquired in 1787 of M. Gilbert des Voisins, 1,335,935; the forests of Camors and of Floranges, acquired of the Duc de Liancourt in 1785, 1,200,000; the county of Montgommery, acquired of M. Clement de Basville in 1785, 3,306,604.

instead of constituting themselves representatives of the people, they aimed to be the favorites of the sovereign, and they shear the flock which they ought to preserve.

IV.

The excoriated flock is to discover finally what is done with its wool. "Sooner or later," says a parliament of 1764,[1] "the people will learn that the remnants of our finances continue to be wasted in donations which are frequently undeserved; in excessive and multiplied pensions for the same persons; in dowries and promises of dowry, and in useless offices and salaries." Sooner or later they will thrust back "these greedy hands which are always open and never full; that insatiable crowd which seems to be born only to seize all and possess nothing, and as pitiless as it is shameless." And when this day arrives the extortioners will find that they stand alone. For the characteristic of an aristocracy which cares only for itself is to lapse into a coterie. Having forgotten the public, it additionally neglects its subordinates; after being separated from the nation it separates itself from its own adherents. Like a set of staff-officers on furlough, it indulges in sports without giving itself further concern about inferior officers ; when the hour of battle comes nobody will march under its orders, and chieftains are sought elsewhere. Such is the isolation of the seigniors of the court, and of the prelates among the lower grades of the nobility and the clergy; they appropriate to themselves too large a share, and give nothing, or almost nothing, to the people who are not of their society. For a century a steady murmur against them is rising, and goes on expanding until it becomes an uproar, in which the old and the new spirit, feudal ideas and philosophic ideas, threaten in unison. "I see," said the bailiff of Mirabeau,[2] "that the nobility is demeaning itself and becoming a wreck. It is extended to all those children of bloodsuckers, the vagabonds of finance, introduced by La Pompadour, herself the off-

---

[1] "Le President des Brosses," by Foisset.   (Remonstrances to the king by the Parliament of Dijon, Jan. 19, 1764).

[2] Lucas de Montigny, "Mémoires de Mirabeau." Letter of the bail'ff, May 26, 1781. D'Argenson, "Mémoires," IV. 156, 157, 160, 76; VI. p. 320. Marshal Marmont, "Mémoires," I. 9. De Ferrières, "Mémoires," preface. See, on the difficulty in succeeding, the Memoirs of Dumourier. Chateaubriand's father is likewise one of the discontented, "a political *frondeur*, and very inimical to the court " (I. 206). Records of the States-General of 1789, a general summary by Prud'homme, II. *passim.*

spring of this foulness.   One portion of it demeans itself in its servility to the court ; the other portion is amalgamated with that quill-driving rabble who are converting the blood of the king's subjects into ink ; another perishes stifled beneath vile robes, the ignoble atoms of cabinet-dust which an office drags up out of the mire ; " and all, parvenus of the old or of the new race, form a band called the court. "The court!" exclaims D'Argenson. "The entire evil is found in this word.   The court has become the senate of the nation ; the least of the valets at Versailles is a senator ; chambermaids take part in the government, if not to legislate, at least to impede laws and regulations ; and by dint of hindrance there are no longer either laws, or rules, or law-makers. . . . Under Henry IV. courtiers remained each one at home ; they had not entered into ruinous expenditure to belong to the court ; favors were not thus *due* to them as at the present day. . . . The court is the sepulchre of the nation." Many noble officers, finding that high grades are only for courtiers, abandon the service, and betake themselves with their discontent to their estates.   Others, who have not left their domains, brood there in discomfort, idleness, and *ennui*, their ambition embittered by their powerlessness.   In 1789, says the Marquis de Ferrières, most of them "are so weary of the court and of the ministers, they are almost democrats." At least, "they want to withdraw the government from the ministerial oligarchy in whose hands it is concentrated ; " there are no grand seigniors for deputies ; they set them aside and "absolutely reject them, saying that they would traffic with the interests of the nobles ; " they themselves, in their memorials, insist that there be no more court nobility.

The same sentiments prevail among the lower clergy, and still more actively ; for they are excluded from the high offices, not only as inferiors, but again as plebeian.[1]   Already, in 1766, the Marquis de Mirabeau writes : "It would be an insult to most of our pretentious ecclesiastics to offer them a curacy.   Revenues and honors are for the abbés-commendatory, for tonsured beneficiaries not in orders, for the numerous chapters." On the contrary, "the true pastors of souls, the collaborators in the

---

[1] "Ephémérides du citoyen," II. 202, 203.   Voltaire, "Dictionnaire philosophique," article "Curé de Campagne." Abbé Guettée, "Histoire de l'Eglise de France," XII. 130.

holy ministry, scarcely obtain a subsistence." The first class "drawn from the nobility and from the best of the bourgeoisie have pretensions only, without being of the true ministry. The other, only having duties to fulfil without expectations and almost without income . . . can be recruited only from the lowest ranks of civil society," while the parasites who despoil the laborers "affect to subjugate them and to degrade them more and more." "I pity," said Voltaire, "the lot of a country curate, obliged to contend for a sheaf of wheat with his unfortunate parishioner, to plead against him, to exact the tithe of peas and lentils, to waste his miserable existence in constant strife. . . . I pity still more the curate with a fixed allowance to whom monks, called *gros décimateurs*,[1] dare offer a salary of forty ducats, to go about during the year, two or three miles from his home, day and night, in sunshine and in rain, in the snow and in the ice, exercising the most trying and most disagreeable functions." Attempts are made for thirty years to secure their salaries and raise them a little; in case of their inadequacy the beneficiary, collator or tithe-owner of the parish is required to add to them until the *curé* obtains 500 livres (1768), then 700 livres (1785), the vicar 200 livres (1768), then 250 (1778), and finally 350 (1785). Strictly, at the prices at which things are, a man may support himself on that.[2] But he must live among the destitute to whom he owes alms, and he cherishes at the bottom of his heart a secret bitterness towards the indolent Dives who, with full pockets, despatches him, with empty pockets, on a mission of charity. At Saint-Pierre de Barjouville, in the Toulousain, the archbishop of Toulouse appropriates to himself one-half of the tithes and gives away eight livres a year in alms; at Bretx, the chapter of Isle Jourdain, which retains one-half of certain tithes and three-quarters of others, gives ten livres; at Croix Falgarde, the Benedictines, to whom a half of the tithes belong, give ten livres per annum.[3] At Sainte-Croix de Bernay in Normandy,[4] the non-resident abbé, who receives

---

[1] Those entitled to tithes in cereals.—Tr.

[2] A *curé's* salary at the present day is, at the minimum, 900 francs with a house and perquisites.

[3] Théron de Montaugé, "L'agriculture et les classes rurales dans le pays Toulousain," p. 86.

[4] Périn, "la Jeunesse de Robespierre," complains of the rural parishes of Artois, p. 320. Boivin-Champeaux, *ibid.* pp. 65, 68. Hippeau, *ibid.* VI. p. 79, et VII. 177. Letter of M.

57,000 livres gives 1,050 livres to the curate without a parsonage, whose parish contains 4,000 communicants.   At Saint-Aubin-sur-Gaillon, the abbé, a *gros décimateur*, gives 350 livres to the vicar, who is obliged to go into the village and obtain contributions of flour, bread and apples.   At Plessis Hébert, " the substitute *déportuaire*,[1] not having enough to live on is obliged to get his meals in the houses of neighbouring curates."   In Artois, where the tithes are often seven and a half and eight per cent. on the product of the soil, a number of curates have a fixed rate and no parsonage ; their church goes to ruin and the beneficiary gives nothing to the poor.   " At Saint-Laurent, in Normandy, the curacy is worth not more than 400 livres, which the curate shares with an *obitier*,[2] and there are 500 inhabitants, three-quarters of whom receive alms."   As the repairs on a parsonage or on a church are usually at the expense of a seignior or of a beneficiary often far off, and in debt or indifferent, it sometimes happens that the priest does not know where to lodge, or to say mass.   " I arrived," says a curate of the Touraine, "in the month of June, 1788. . . . The parsonage would resemble a hideous cave were it not open to all the winds and the frosts ; below there are two rooms with stone floors, without doors or windows, and five feet high ; a third room six feet high, paved with stone, serves as parlor, hall, kitchen, wash-house, bakery, and sink for the water of the court and garden ; above are three similar rooms, the whole cracking and tumbling in ruins, absolutely threatening to fall, without either doors and windows that hold," and, in 1790, the repairs are not yet made.   See, by way of contrast, the luxury of the prelates possessing half a million income, the pomp of their palaces, the hunting equipment of M. de Dillon, bishop of Evreux, the confessionals lined with satin of M. de Barral, bishop of Troyes, and the innumerable culinary utensils in massive silver of M. de Rohan, bishop of Strasbourg.

Such is the lot of curates at the established rates, and there are "a great many" who do not get the established rates, withheld from them through the ill-will of the higher clergy; who, with

---

Sergent, curate of Vallers, January 27, 1790.   (Archives nationales, DXIX. portfolio 24.) Letter of M. Briscard, curate of Beaumont-la-Roger, diocese of Evreux, December 19, 1789. (*Ibid.* DXIX. portfolio 6.)   " Tableau moral du clergé de France" (1789), p. 2.

[1] He who has the right of receiving the first year's income of a parish church after a vacancy caused by death.—TR.

[2] One who performs masses for the dead at fixed epochs.—TR.

their perquisites, get only from 400 to 500 livres, and who
vainly ask for the meagre pittance to which they are entitled by
the late edict. "Should not such a request," says a curate, " be
willingly granted by Messieurs of the upper clergy who suffer
monks to enjoy from five to six thousand livres income each
person, whilst they see curates, who are at least as necessary,
reduced to the lighter portion, as little for themselves as for their
parish ? "—And they yet gnaw on this slight pittance to pay the
free gift. In this, as in the rest, the poor are charged to discharge
the rich. In the diocese of Clermont, " the curates, even with
the simple fixed rates, are subject to a tax of 60, 80, 100, 120
livres and even more ; the vicars, who live only by the sweat of
their brows, are taxed 22 livres." The prelates, on the contrary,
pay but little, and "it is still a custom to present bishops on
New-Year's day with a receipt for their taxes." [1]—There is no
escape for the curates. Save two or three small bishoprics of
"lackeys," all the dignities of the church are reserved to the
nobles; "to be a bishop nowadays," says one of them, "a man
must be a gentleman." I regard them as sergeants who, like
their fellows in the army, have lost all hope of becoming officers.
Hence there are some whose anger bursts its bounds: "We,
unfortunate curates at fixed rates; we, commonly assigned to
the largest parishes, like my own which, for two leagues in the
woods, includes hamlets that would form another; we, whose
lot makes even the stones and beams of our miserable dwellings
cry aloud," we have to endure prelates "who would still, through
their forest-keepers, prosecute a poor curate for cutting a stick
in their forests, his sole support on his long journeys over the
road." On their passing, the poor man "is obliged to jump close
against a slope to protect himself from the feet and the spat-
terings of the horses, as likewise from the wheels and, perhaps,
the whip of an insolent coachman," and then, "begrimed with
dirt, with his stick in one hand and his hat, such as it is, in the
other, he must salute, humbly and quickly, through the door of
the close, gilded carriage, the counterfeit hierophant who is snor-
ing on the wool of the flock the poor curate is feeding, and
of which he merely leaves him the dung and the grease." The
whole letter is one long cry of rage; it is rancor of this stamp
which is to fashion Joseph Lebons and Fouchés. In this situa-

[1] Complaints on the additional burdens which the Third-Estate have to support, by Gautier
de Bianzat (1788), p. 237.

tion and with these sentiments it is evident that the lower clergy will treat its chiefs as the provincial nobility treated theirs.[1] They will not select "for representatives those who swim in opulence and who have always regarded their sufferings with tranquillity." The curates, on all sides "will confederate together" to send only curates to the States-General, and to exclude "not only canons, abbés, priors and other beneficiaries, but again the principal superiors, the heads of the hierarchy," that is to say, the bishops. In fact, in the States-General, out of three hundred clerical deputies we count two hundred and eight curates, and, like the provincial nobles, these bring along with them the distrust and the ill-will which they have so long entertained against their chiefs. Events are soon to prove this. If the first two orders are constrained to combine against the communes it is at the critical moment when the curates withdraw. If the institution of an upper chamber is rejected it is owing to the commonalty of the gentry *(la plèbe des gentilshommes)* being unwilling to allow the great families a prerogative which they have abused.

V.

One privilege remains, the most considerable of all, that of the king ; for, in this staff of hereditary nobles he is the hereditary general. His office, indeed, is not a sinecure, like their rank ; but it involves quite as grave disadvantages and worse temptations. Two things are pernicious to man, the lack of occupation and the lack of restraint ; neither inactivity nor omnipotence are comportable with his nature; the absolute prince who is all-powerful, like the listless aristocracy with nothing to do, ending in becoming useless and mischievous. In grasping all powers the king insensibly took upon himself all functions,— an immense undertaking and one surpassing human strength. For it is the Monarchy, and not the Revolution, which endowed France with administrative centralization.[2] Three functionaries, one above the other, manage all public business under the direction of the king's council; the comptroller-general at the

---

[1] Hippeau, *ibid.* VI. 164. (Letter of the curate of Marolles and of thirteen others. Letter of the bishop of Evreux, March 20, 1789. Letter of the abbé d'Osmond, April 2, 1789). Archives nationales, manuscript documents *(procès-verbaux)* of the States-General, V. 148. pp. 245-247. Memorials of the curates of Toulouse, t. 150, p. 282, in the representations of the Dijon chapter.

[2] De Tocqueville, book II. This capital truth has been established by M. de Tocqueville with superior discernment.

centre, the intendant in each generalship,[1] the sub-delegate in
each election, fixing, apportioning and levying taxes and the
militia, laying out and building highways, employing the national
police force, distributing succor, regulating cultivation, imposing
their tutelage on the parishes, and treating municipal magistrates
as valets. "A village," says Turgot,[2] "is simply an assemblage
of houses and huts, and of inhabitants equally passive. . . . Your
Majesty is obliged to decide wholly by yourself or through your
mandataries. . . . Each awaits your special instructions to contribute to the public good, to respect the rights of others, and
even sometimes to exercise his own." Consequently, adds
Necker, "the government of France is carried on in the bureaux.
. . . The clerks, relishing their influence, never fail to persuade
the minister that he cannot separate himself from command in a
single detail." Bureaucratic at the centre, arbitrariness, ex-
ceptions and favors everywhere, such is a summary of the
system. "Sub-delegates, officers of elections, receivers and comptrollers of the *vingtièmes*, commissaries and collectors of the
tailles, officers of the salt-tax, process-servers, *voituriers-buralistes*,
overseers of the *corvées*, clerks of the excise, of the registry, and
of dues reserved, all these men belonging to the tax-service, each
according to his disposition, subject to their petty authority,
and overwhelm with their fiscal knowledge, the ignorant and
inexperienced tax-payers incapable of recognizing when they are
cheated." [3] A rude species of centralization, with no control over
it, with no publicity, without uniformity, thus installs over the
whole country an army of petty pachas who, as judges, decide
causes in which they are themselves the contestants, ruling by
delegation, and, to sanction their stealings or their insolence,
always having on their lips the name of the king, who is obliged
to let them do as they please. In short, the machine, through

---

[1] A term indicating a certain division of the kingdom of France to facilitate the collection
of taxes. Each generalship was subdivided into *elections*, in which there was a tribunal
called the bureau of finances.

[2] Remonstrances of Malesherbes; Memorials by Turgot and Necker to the king, (Laboulaye, "De l'administration française sous Louis XVI.," Revue des cours litteraires, IV.
423, 759, 814.)

[3] Financiers have been known to tell citizens: "The *ferme* (revenue-agency), ought to
grant you favors, you ought to be forced to come and ask for them. He who pays never
knows what he owes. The *fermier* is sovereign legislator in matters relating to his personal
interest. Every petition, in which the interests of a province, or those of the whole nation are concerned, is regarded as penal temerity if it is signed by a person in his private
capacity, and as illicit association if it be signed by several." Malesherbes, *ibid.*

its complexity, irregularity, and dimensions, escapes from his grasp. A Frederick II., who rises at four o'clock in the morning, a Napoleon who dictates half the night in his bath, and who works eighteen hours a day, would scarcely suffice for its needs. Such a régime cannot operate without constant strain, without indefatigable energy, without infallible discernment, without military rigidity, without superior genius; on these conditions alone can one convert twenty-five millions of men into automatons and substitute his own will, lucid throughout, coherent throughout and everywhere present, for the wills of those he abolishes. Louis XV. lets "the good machine" work by itself, while he settles down into apathy. "They would have it so, they thought it all for the best," [1] is his manner of speaking when ministerial measures prove unsuccessful. "If I were a lieutenant of the police," he would say again, "I would prohibit cabs." In vain is he aware of the machine being dislocated, for he can do nothing and he causes nothing to be done. In the event of misfortune he has a private reserve, his purse apart. "The king," said Mme. de Pompadour, "would sign away a million without thinking of it, but he would scarcely bestow a hundred louis out of his own little treasury." Louis XVI. strives for some time to remove some of the wheels, to introduce better ones and to reduce the friction of the rest; but the pieces are too rusty, and too weighty; he cannot adjust them, or harmonize them and keep them in their places; his hand falls by his side wearied and powerless. He is content to practise economy himself; he records in his journal the mending of his watch, and allows the public vehicle in the hands of Calonne to be loaded with fresh abuses that it may revert back to the old rut from which it is to issue only by breaking down.

Undoubtedly the wrong they do, or which is done in their name, dissatisfies and chagrins them, but, at bottom, their conscience is not disturbed. They may feel compassion for the people, but they do not feel themselves culpable; they are its sovereigns and not its patrons. France, to them, is as a domain to its seignior, while a seignior is not deprived of honor in being prodigal and neglectful. He merely gambles away his own property, and nobody has a right to call him to account. Founded on feudal

---

[1] Mme. Campan, "Mémoires," v. I. p. 13. Mme. du Hausset, "Mémoires," p. 114.

seigniory royalty is like an estate, an inheritance, and it would be
infidelity, almost treachery in a prince, in any event weak and
base, to allow any portion of the trust received by him intact
from his ancestors for transmission to his children, to pass into the
hands of his subjects. Not only according to mediæval traditions
is he proprietor-commandant of the French and of France, but
again, according to the theory of the legists, he is, like Cæsar, the
sole and perpetual representative of the nation, and, according to
the theological doctrine, like David, the sacred and special dele-
gate of God himself. It would be astonishing, if, with all these
titles, he did not consider the public revenue as his personal revenue, and if, in many cases, he did not act accordingly. Our
point of view, in this matter, is so essentially opposed to his, we
can scarcely put ourselves in his place; but at that time his point
of view was everybody's point of view. It seemed, then, as
strange to meddle with the king's business as to meddle with that
of a private person. Only at the end of the year 1788[1] the famous *salon* of the Palais-Royal " with boldness and unimaginable
folly, asserts that in a true monarchy the revenues of the State
should not be at the sovereign's disposition; that he should be
granted merely a sum sufficient to defray the expenses of his
establishment, of his donations, and for favors to his servants as
well as for his pleasures, while the surplus should be deposited in
the royal treasury to be devoted only to purposes sanctioned by
the National Assembly." To reduce the sovereign to a civil list,
to seize nine-tenths of his income, to forbid him cash acquittances,
what an outrage ! The surprise would be no greater if at the
present day it were proposed to divide the income of each mill-
ionaire into two portions, the smallest to go for the owner's support, and the largest to be placed in the hands of the government
to be expended in works of public utility. An old farmer-general, an intellectual and unprejudiced man, gravely attempts to
justify the purchase of Saint-Cloud by calling it " a ring for the
queen's finger." The ring cost, indeed, 7,700,000 francs, but
" the king of France then had an income of 477,000,000. What
could be said of any private individual who, with 477,000 livres
income, should, for once in his life, give his wife diamonds worth

---

[1] " Gustave III. et la cour de France," by Geffroy, II. 474. ("Archives de Dresde,"
French correspondence, November 20, 1788.)

7,000 or 8,000 livres?"[1]   People would say that the gift is moderate, and that the husband is reasonable.

To properly understand the history of our kings, let the fundamental principle be always recognized that France is their territory, a farm transmitted from father to son, at first small, then slowly enlarged, and, at last, prodigiously enlarged, because the proprietor, always on the watch, has found means to make favorable additions to it at the expense of his neighbors; at the end of eight hundred years it comprises about 27,000 square leagues of territory.   His interests and his self-love certainly harmonize at certain points with the public welfare; in the aggregate, he is not a poor administrator, and, since he has always aggrandized himself, he has done better than many others.   Moreover, around him, a number of expert individuals, old family councillors, withdrawn from business and devoted to the domain, with good heads and gray beards, respectfully remonstrate with him when he spends too freely; they often interest him in public improvements, in roads, canals, hotels for invalids, military schools, scientific institutions and charity workshops; in the limitation of mainmorts, in the toleration of heretics, in the postponement of monastic vows to the age of twenty-one, in provincial assemblies, and in other reforms by which a feudal domain becomes transformed into a modern domain.   Nevertheless, the domain, feudal or modern, remains his property which he can abuse as well as use; now, whoever uses with full sway ends by abusing with full license.   If, in his ordinary conduct, personal motives do not prevail over public motives, he might be a saint like Louis IX., a stoic like Marcus Aurelius, while remaining a seignior, a man of the world like the people of his court, yet more badly brought up, worse surrounded, more solicited, more tempted and more blindfolded.   At the very least he has, like them, his own self-love, his own tastes, his own kindred, his mistress, his wife, his friends, all intimate and influential solicitors who must first be satisfied, while the nation only comes after them.   The result is, that, for a hundred years, from 1672 to 1774, whenever he makes war it is through pique, through vanity, through family interest, through calculation of private advantages, or to gratify a woman.   Louis XV. maintains his wars yet worse than in undertaking them;[2]

---

[1] Augeard, "Mémoires," p. 135.

[2] " Mme. de Pompadour, writing to Marshal d'Estrées, in the army, about the campaign

G

while Louis XVI., during the whole of his foreign policy, finds a
trammel in the conjugal netting. Domestically, he lives like other
seigniors, but more grandly, because he is the greatest seignior in
France; I shall describe his course presently, and farther on we
shall see by what exactions this pomp is supported. In the meantime, let us note two or three details. According to authentic
statements, Louis XV. expended on Mme. de Pompadour thirty-
six millions of livres, which is at least seventy-two millions nowadays.[1] According to d'Argenson,[2] in 1751, he has four thousand horses in his stable, and we are assured that his household
alone, or his personalty, "cost this year 68,000,000," almost a quarter of the public revenue. Why be astonished if we look upon
the sovereign in the manner of the day, that is to say, as a cas-
tellan in the enjoyment of his hereditary property? He constructs, he entertains, he gives festivals, he hunts, he spends
money according to his station. Moreover, being the master of
his own funds, he gives to whomsoever he pleases, and all his
selections are favors. "Your Majesty knows better than myself,"
writes the abbé de Vermond to the empress Maria Theresa,[3]
"that, according to immemorial custom, three-fourths of the
places, honors and pensions are awarded not on account of services but out of favor and through influence. This favor was
originally prompted by birth, alliance, and fortune; it rarely has
any other basis than patronage and intrigue. This course of
things, so well established, is respected as a sort of justice even
by those who suffer the most from it; a man of worth not able to
dazzle by his court alliances, nor through a bewildering expenditure, would not dare to demand a regiment, however ancient and
illustrious his services, or his birth. Twenty years ago, the
sons of dukes and of ministers, of people attached to the court,
the relations and protégés of mistresses, became colonels at the
age of sixteen; M. de Choiseul excited loud complaints on ex-

operations, and tracing for him a sort of plan, had marked on the paper with *mouches* (face-
patches), the different places which she advised him to attack or defend." Mme. de Genlis,
"Souvenirs de Félicie," p. 329. Narrative by Mme. de Puisieux, the mother-in-law of
Marshal d'Estrées.

[1] According to the manuscript register of Mme. de Pompadour's expenses, in the archives
of the préfecture of Versailles, she had expended 36,327,268 livres. Granier de Cassagnac,
I. 91.

[2] D'Argenson, "Mémoires," VI. 398 (April 24, 1751). "M. du Barry declared openly
that he had consumed 18,000,000 belonging to the State." (Correspondence by Métra, I. 27.)

[3] "Marie Antoinette," by d'Arneth and Geffroy, vol. II. p. 168 (June 5, 1774).

tending this age to twenty-three years; but to compensate favoritism and absolutism he assigned to the pure grace of the king, or rather to that of his ministers, the appointment to the lieutenant-colonelcies and to the majorities which, until that time, belonged of right to priority of services in the government; also the commands of provinces and of towns. You are aware that these places have been largely multiplied, and that they are bestowed through favor and credit, like the regiments. The *cordon bleu* and the *cordon rouge* are in the like position, and even sometimes the cross of St. Louis. Bishoprics and abbeys are still more constantly subject to the régime of influence. As to positions in the finances, I dare not allude to them. Appointments in the judiciary are the most conditioned by services rendered; and yet how much do not credit and recommendation influence the nomination of intendants, first presidents"—and others? Necker, entering on his duties, finds twenty-eight millions in pensions paid from the royal treasury, and, at his fall, there is an outflow of money showered by millions on the people of the court. Even during his term of office the king allows himself to make the fortunes of his wife's friends of both sexes; the Countess de Polignac obtains 400,000 francs to pay her debts, 800,000 francs dowry for her daughter, and, besides, for herself, the promise of an estate of 35,000 livres income, and, for her lover, the Count de Vaudreil, a pension of 30,000 livres; the Princess de Lamballe obtains 100,000 crowns per annum, as much for the post of superintendent of the queen's household, which is revived in her behalf, as for a position for her brother.[1] But it is under Calonne that prodigality reaches insanity. The king is reproached for his parsimony; why should he be sparing of his purse? Started on a course not his own, he gives, buys, builds, and exchanges; he assists those belonging to his own society, doing everything in a style becoming to a grand seignior, that is to say, throwing money away by handfuls. One instance enables us to judge of this: in order to assist the bankrupts Guéménée, he purchases of them three estates for about 12,500,000 livres, which they had just purchased for 4,000,000; moreover, in exchange for two domains in Brittany, which produce 33,758 livres income, he

---

[1] "Marie Antoinette," *ibid.* vol. II. p. 377; vol. III. p. 391.

makes over to them the principality of Dombes which produces nearly 70,000 livres income.[1] When we come to read the Red Book further on we shall find 700,000 livres of pensions for the Polignac family, most of them reversionary from one member to another, and nearly 2,000,000 of annual benefactions to the Noailles family. The king has forgotten that his favors are mortal blows, "the courtier who obtains 6,000 livres pension, receiving the *taille* of six villages."[2] Each largess of the monarch, considering the state of the taxes, is based on the privation of the peasants, the sovereign, through his clerks, taking bread from the poor to give coaches to the rich. The centre of the government, in short, is the centre of the evil; all the wrongs and all the miseries start from it as from a centre of pain and inflammation; here it is that the public abscess comes to a head, and here will it break.

VI.

Such is the just and fatal effect of privileges turned to selfish purposes instead of being exercised for the advantage of others. To him who utters the word, sire or seignior means " the protector who feeds, the ancient who leads;"[3] with this title and for this purpose too much cannot be granted to him, for there is no more difficult nor more exalted function. But he must fulfil its duties; otherwise in the day of peril he will be left to himself. Already, and long before the day arrives, his flock is no longer his own; if it marches onward it is through routine; it is simply a multitude of persons, but no longer an organized body. Whilst in Germany and in England the feudal régime, retained or transformed, still composes a living society, in France its mechanical framework encloses only so many human particles. We still find the material order, but we no longer find the moral order of things. A lingering, deep-seated revolution has destroyed the close hierarchical union of recognized supremacies and of voluntary deferences. It is like an army in which the sentiments that form its chiefs and those that form its subordinates have disappeared; grades are indicated by uniforms, but they have no hold

---

[1] Archives nationales, H, 1456, Memoir for M. Bouret de Vezelay, syndic for the creditors.
[2] Marquis de Mirabeau, " Traité de la population," p. 81.
[3] *Lord,* in Old Saxon, signifies "he who provides food;" *seignior,* in the Latin of the middle ages, signifies "the ancient," the head or chief of the flock.

on consciences; all that constitutes a well-founded army, the legitimate ascendency of officers, the justified trust of soldiers, the daily interchange of mutual obligations, the conviction of each being useful to all, and that the chiefs are the most useful of all, is wanting to it. How could we encounter this conviction in an army whose staff-officers have no other occupation but to dine out, to display their epaulettes and to receive double pay ? Long before the final crash France is in a state of dissolution, and she is in a state of dissolution because the privileged classes had forgotten their characters as *public men.*

BOOK SECOND.

Habits and Characters.

***

CHAPTER I.

THE PRINCIPLE OF SOCIAL HABITS UNDER THE ANCIENT REGIME.—The Court and a life of pomp and parade.—I. The physical aspect and the moral character of Versailles.—II. The king's household.—Its officials and expenses.—His military family, his stable, kennel, chapel, attendants, table, chamber, wardrobe, outhouses, furniture, journeys.—III. The society of the king.—Officers of the household.—Invited guests.—IV. The king's occupations.—Rising in the morning, mass, dinner, walks, hunting, supper, play, evening receptions.—He is always on parade and in company.—V. Diversions of the royal family and of the court.—Louis XV.— Louis XVI.—VI. Other similar lives.—Princes and princesses.—Seigniors of the court.—Financiers and parvenus.—Ambassadors, ministers, governors, general officers.—VII. Prelates, seigniors and minor provincial nobles. —The feudal aristocracy transformed into a drawing-room group.

A MILITARY staff on furlough for a century and more, around a commander-in-chief who gives fashionable entertainments, is the principle and summary of the habits of society under the ancient régime. Hence, if we seek to comprehend them, we must first study them at their centre and their source, that is to say, in the court itself. Like the whole ancient régime the court is the empty form, the surviving adornment of a military institution, the causes of which have disappeared while the effects remain, custom surviving utility. Formerly, in the early times of feudalism, in the companionship and simplicity of the camp and the castle, the nobles served the king with their own hands, one providing for his house, another bringing a dish to his table, another disrobing him at night, and another looking after his falcons and horses.

Still later, under Richelieu and during the Fronde,[1] amid the sudden attacks and the rude exigencies of constant danger they constitute the garrison of his hotel, forming an armed escort for him, and a retinue of ever-ready swordsmen. Now as formerly they are equally assiduous around his person, wearing · their swords, awaiting a word, and eager to do his bidding, while those of highest rank seemingly perform domestic service in his household. Pompous parade, however, has been substituted for efficient service; they are elegant adornments only, and no longer useful instrumentalities; they act along with the king who is himself an actor, their persons serving as royal decoration.

I.

It must be admitted that the decoration is successful, and, that since the fêtes of the Italian Renaissance, more magnificent displays have not been seen. Let us follow the file of carriages which, from Paris to Versailles, rolls steadily along like a river. Certain horses called "*des enragés,*" fed in a particular way, go and come in three hours.[2] One feels, at the first glance, as if he were in a city of a particular stamp, suddenly erected and at one stroke, like a prize-medal for a special purpose, of which only one is made, its form being a thing apart, as well as its origin and use. In vain is it one of the largest cities of the kingdom, with its population of eighty thousand souls;[3] it is filled, peopled, and occupied by the life of a single man; it is simply a royal residence, arranged entirely to provide for the wants, the pleasures, the service, the guardianship, the society, the display of a king. Here and there, in corners and around it, are inns, stalls, taverns, hovels for laborers and for drudges, for dilapidated soldiers and accessory menials; these tenements necessarily exist, since mechanicians are essential to the most magnificent apotheosis.

---

[1] "Mémoires de Laporte" (1632). "M. d'Epernon came to Bordeaux, where he found His Eminence very ill. He visited him regularly every morning, having two hundred guards to accompany him to the door of his chamber." "Mémoires de Retz." "We came to the audience, M. de Beaufort and myself, with a corps of nobles which might number three hundred gentlemen; MM. the princes had with them nearly a thousand gentlemen." All the memoirs of the time show on every page that these escorts were necessary to make or repel sudden attacks.

[2] Mercier, "Tableau de Paris," IX. 3.

[3] Leroi, "Histoire de Versailles," II. 21. (70,000 fixed population and 10,000 floating population according to the registers of the mayoralty.)

The rest, however, consists of sumptuous hotels and edifices, sculptured façades, cornices and balustrades, monumental stairways, seigniorial architecture, regularly spaced and disposed, as in a procession, around the vast and grandiose palace where all this terminates. Here are the fixed abodes of the noblest families; to the right of the palace are the hôtels de Bourbon, d'Ecquervilly, de la Trémoille, de Condé, de Maurepas, de Bouillon, d'Eu, de Noailles, de Penthièvre, de Livry, du Comte de la Marche, de Broglie, du Prince de Tingry, d'Orléans, de Chatillon, de Villerry, d'Harcourt, de Monaco; on the left are the pavilions d'Orléans, d'Harcourt, the hôtels de Chevreuse, de Babelle, de l'Hôpital, d'Antin, de Dangeau, de Pontchartrain—no end to their enumeration. Add to these those of Paris, all those which, ten leagues around, at Sceaux, at Génevilliers, at Brunoy, at Ile-Adam, at Rancy, at Saint-Ouen, at Colombes, at Saint-Germain, at Marly, at Bellevue, in countless places, form a crown of architectural flowers, from which daily issue as many gilded wasps to shine and buzz about Versailles, the centre of all lustre and affluence. About a hundred of these are "presented" each year, men and women, which makes about two or three thousand in all;[1] this forms the king's society, the ladies who courtesy before him, and the seigniors who accompany him in his carriage; their hotels are near by, or within reach, ready to fill his drawing-room or his antechamber at all hours.

A drawing-room like this calls for proportionate dependencies; the hotels and buildings at Versailles devoted to the private service of the king and his attendants count by hundreds. No human existence since that of the Cæsars has so spread itself out in the sunshine. In the Rue des Reservoirs we have the old hotel and the new one of the governor of Versailles, the hotel of the tutor to the children of the Comte d'Artois, the wardrobe of the crown, the building for the dressing-rooms and green-rooms of the actors who perform at the palace, with the stables belonging to Monsieur. In the Rue des Bon-Enfants are the hotel of the keeper of the wardrobe, the lodgings for the fountain-men, the hotel of the officers of the Comtesse de Provence. In the Rue de la Pompe, the hotel of the grand-provost, the Duke of Orleans's stables, the hotel of the Comte d'Artois's

---

[1] Warroquier, "Etat de la France" (1789). The list of persons presented at court between 1779 and 1789, contains 463 men and 414 women. Vol. II. p. 515.

guardsmen, the queen's stables, the pavilion des Sources.   In the Rue Satory the Comtesse d'Artois's stables, Monsieur's English garden, the king's ice-houses, the riding-hall of the king's light-horseguards, the garden belonging to the hotel of the treasurers of the buildings.   Judge of other streets by these four.   One cannot take a hundred steps without encountering some accessory of the palace,—the hotel of the staff of the body-guard, the hotel of the staff of light-horseguards, the immense hotel of the body-guard itself, the hotel of the gendarmes of the guard, the hotel of the grand wolf-huntsman, of the grand falconer, of the grand huntsman, of the grand-master, of the commandant of the canal, of the comptroller-general, of the superintendent of the buildings, and of the chancellor ; buildings devoted to falconry, and the *vol de cabinet*, to boar-hunting, to the grand kennel, to the dauphin kennel, to the kennel for untrained dogs, to the court carriages, to shops and storehouses connected with amusements, to the great stable and the little stables, to other stables in the Rue de Limoges, in the Rue Royale, and in the Avenue Saint-Cloud ; to the king's vegetable garden, comprising twenty-nine gardens and four terraces ; to the great dwelling occupied by two thousand persons, with other tenements called " Louises" in which the king assigned temporary or permanent lodgings, —words on paper render no physical impression of the physical enormity.

At the present day nothing remains of this old Versailles, mutilated and appropriated to other uses, but fragments, which nevertheless, go and see.   Observe those three avenues meeting in the great square, two hundred and forty feet broad and twenty-four hundred long, and not too large for the gathering crowds, the display, the blinding velocity of the escorts in full speed and of the carriages running "at death's door;"[1] observe the two stables facing the chateau with their railings one hundred and ninety-two feet long, costing, in 1682, three millions, that is to say, fifteen millions to-day; so ample and beautiful that, even under Louis XIV. himself, they sometimes served as a cavalcade circus for the princes, sometimes as a theatre, and sometimes as a ball-room ; then let the eye follow the development of the gigantic semi-circular square which, from railing to railing and

---

[1] People were run over almost every day in Paris by the fashionable vehicles, it being the habit of the great to ride very fast.

from court to court, ascends and slowly decreases, at first between the hotels of the ministers and then between the two
colossal wings, terminating in the ostentatious frame of the marble court where pilasters, statues, pediments, and multiplied and
accumulated ornaments, story above story, carry the majestic regularity of their lines and the overcharged mass of their decoration up to the sky.   According to a bound manuscript bearing
the arms of Mansart, the palace cost 153,000,000, that is to say,
about 750,000,000 francs of to-day:[1] when a king aims at imposing display this is the cost of his lodging.   Now turn the eye
to the other side, towards the gardens, and this self-display becomes the more impressive.   The parterres and the park are,
again, a drawing-room in the open air; there is nothing natural
of nature here; she is put in order and rectified wholly with
a view to society; this is no place to be alone and to relax
oneself, but a place for promenades and the exchange of polite
salutations.   Those formal groves are walls and hangings; those
shaven yews are vases and lyres.   The parterres are flowering
carpets.   In those straight, rectilinear avenues the king, with his
cane in his hand, groups around him his entire retinue.   Sixty
ladies in brocade dresses, expanding into skirts measuring twenty-
four feet in circumference, easily find room on the steps of the
staircases.[2]   Those verdant cabinets afford shade for a princely
collation.   Under that circular portico, all the seigniors enjoying
the privilege of entering it witness together the play of a new
jet d'eau.   Their counterparts greet them even in the marble
and bronze figures which people the paths and basins, in the
dignified face of an Apollo, in the theatrical air of a Jupiter, in
the worldly ease or studied nonchalance of a Diana or a Venus.
The stamp of the court, deepened through the joint efforts of
society for a century, is so strong that it is graven on each detail
as on the whole, and on material objects as on matters of the
intellect.

---

[1] 153,282,827 livres, 10 sous, 3 deniers. "Souvenirs d'un page de la cour de Louis XVI.,"
by the Count d'Hézecques, p. 142. In 1690, before the chapel and theatre were constructed,
it had already cost 100,000,000, (St. Simon, XII. 514. Memoirs of Marinier, clerk of the
king's buildings.)

[2] Museum of Engravings, National Library. "Histoire de France par estampes," *passim*,
and particularly the plans and views of Versailles, by Aveline; also, "the drawing of a collation given by M. le Prince in the Labyrinth of Chantilly," Aug. 29, 1687.

II.

The foregoing is but the framework; before 1789 it was completely filled up. " You have seen nothing," says Chateaubriand, " if you have not seen the pomp of Versailles, even after the disbanding of the king's household; Louis XIV. was always there." [1] It is a swarm of liveries, uniforms, costumes and equipages as brilliant and as varied as in a picture. I should be glad to have lived eight days in this society. It was made expressly to be painted, being specially designed for the pleasure of the eye, like an operatic scene. But how can we of to-day imagine people for whom life was wholly operatic ? At that time a grandee was obliged to live in great state; his retinue and his trappings formed a part of his personality; he fails in doing himself justice if these are not as ample and as splendid as he can make them; he would be as much mortified at any blank in his household as we with a hole in our coats. Should he make any curtailment he would decline in reputation; on Louis XVI. undertaking reforms the court says that he acts like a bourgeois. When a prince or princess becomes of age a household is formed for them ; when a prince marries, a household is formed for his wife ; and by a household it must be understood that it is a pompous display of fifteen or twenty distinct services,—stables, a hunting-train, a chapel, a surgery, the bedchamber and the wardrobe, a chamber for accounts, a table, pantry, kitchen, and wine-cellars, a fruitery, a *fourrière*, a common kitchen, a cabinet, a council ; [2] she would feel that she was not a princess without all this. There are 274 appointments in the household of the Duc d'Orléans, 210 in that of Mesdames, 68 in that of Madame Elisabeth, 239 in that of the Comtesse d'Artois, 256 in that of the Comtesse de Provence, and 496 in that of the Queen. When the formation of a household for Madame Royale, one month old, is necessary, " the queen," writes the Austrian ambassador, " desires to suppress a baneful indolence, a useless affluence of attendants, and every practice tending to give birth to sentiments of pride   In spite of the said retrenchment the household of the young princess is to consist of nearly eighty persons destined to the sole

---

[1] Memoirs, I. 221.   He was presented at court February 19, 1787.

[2] For these details cf. Warroquier, vol. I. *passim*.   Archives impériales, O, 710 *bis*, the king's household, expenditure of 1771.   D'Argenson, February 25, 1752.   In 1771 three millions are expended on the installation of the Count d'Artois.   A suite of rooms for Mme. Adelaide cost 800,000 livres.

service of her Royal Highness."[1]   The civil household of Monsieur comprises 420 appointments, his military household, 179; that of the Comte d'Artois 237 and his civil household 456. Three-fourths of them are for display; with their embroideries and laces, their unembarrassed and polite expression, their attentive and discreet air, their easy way of saluting, walking and smiling, they appear well in an antechamber, placed in lines, or scattered in groups in a gallery; I should have liked to contemplate even the stable and kitchen array, the figures filling up the background of the picture.   By these stars of inferior magnitude we may judge of the splendor of the royal sun.

The king must have guards, infantry, cavalry, body-guards, French guardsmen, Swiss guardsmen, *Cent Suisses*, light-horse-guards, gendarmes of the guard, gate-guardsmen, in all, 9,050 men,[2] costing annually 7,681,000 livres.   Four companies of the French guard, and two of the Swiss guard, parade every day in the court of the ministers between the two railings, and when the king issues in his carriage to go to Paris or Fontainebleau the spectacle is magnificent.   Four trumpeters in front and four behind, the Swiss guards on one side and the French guards on the other, form a line as far as it can reach.[3]   The *Cent Suisses* march ahead of the horsemen in the costume of the sixteenth century, wearing the halberd, ruff, plumed hat, and the ample parti-colored striped doublet; alongside of these are the provost-guard with scarlet facings and gold frogs, and companies of yeomanry bristling with gold and silver.   The officers of the various corps, the trumpeters and the musicians, covered with gold and silver lace, are dazzling to look at; the kettledrum suspended at the saddle-bow, overcharged with painted and gilded ornaments, is a curiosity for a glass case; the negro cymbal-player of the French guards resembles the sultan of a fairy-tale.   Behind the carriage and alongside of it trot the body-guards, with sword and carbine, wearing red breeches, high black boots, and a blue coat sewn with white embroidery, all of

---

[1] Marie Antoinette, "Correspondance secrète," by d'Arneth and Geffroy, III. 292.   Letter of Mercy, January 25, 1779.   Warroquier, in 1789, mentions only fifteen places in the household of Madame Royale.   This, along with other indications, shows the inadequacy of official statements.

[2] The number ascertainable after the reductions of 1775 and 1776, and before those of 1787. See Warroquier, vol. I.   Necker, "Administration des Finances," II. 119.

[3] "La Maison du Roi en 1786," colored engravings in the Museum of Engravings.

them unquestionable gentlemen; there were twelve hundred of these selected among the nobles and according to size; among them are the guards *de la manche,* still more intimate, who at church and on ceremonial occasions, in white doublets starred with silver and gold spangles,. holding their damascene partisans in their hands, always remain standing and turned towards the king " so as to see his person from all sides. " Thus is his protection ensured. Being a gentleman the king is a cavalier, and he must have a suitable stable,[1] 1,857 horses, 217 vehicles, 1,458 men whom he clothes, the liveries costing 540,000 francs a year; besides these there were 20 tutors and sub-tutors, almoners, professors, cooks, and valets to govern, educate and serve the pages; and again about thirty physicians, apothecaries, nurses for the sick, intendants, treasurers, workmen, and licensed and paid merchants for the accessories of the service; in all more than 1,500 men. Horses to the amount of 250,000 francs are purchased yearly, and there are stock-stables in Limousin and in Normandy to draw on for supplies. 287 horses are exercised daily in the two riding-halls; there are 443 saddle-horses in the small stable, 437 in the large one, and these are not sufficient for the " vivacity of the service." The whole cost 4,600,000 livres in 1775, which sum reaches 6,200,000 livres in 1787.[2] Still another spectacle should be seen with one's own eyes,— the pages,[3] the grooms, the laced pupils, the silver-button pupils, the boys of the little livery in silk, the instrumentalists and the mounted messengers of the stable. The use of the horse is a feudal art; no luxury is more natural to a man of quality. Think of the stables at Chantilly, which are palaces. To convey an idea of a well-educated and genteel man he was then called

---

[1] Archives nationales, O¹, 738. Report by M. Tessier (1780), on the large and small stables. The queen's stables comprise 75 vehicles and 330 horses. These are the veritable figures taken from secret manuscript reports, showing the inadequacy of official statements. The Versailles Almanach of 1775, for instance, states that there were only 335 men in the stables while we see that in reality the number was four or five times as many. " Previous to all the reforms, says a witness, I believe that the number of the king's horses amounted to 3,000." (D'Hézecques, "Souvenirs d'un page de Louis XVI.," p. 121.)

[2] " La Maison du Roi justifiée par un soldat citoyen," (1786) according to statements published by the government. " La future maison du roi" (1790). "The two stables cost in 1786, the larger one 4,207,606 livres, and the smaller 3,509,402 livres, a total of 7,717,058 livres, of which 486,546 livres were for the purchase of horses."

[3] " On my arrival at Versailles (1786), there were 150 pages, not including those of the princes of the blood who lived at Paris. A page's coat cost 1,500 livres, (crimson velvet embroidered with gold on all the seams, and a hat with feather and Spanish point lace.)" D'Hézecques, *ibid.* 112.

" an accomplished cavalier ; " in fact his importance was fully
manifest only when he was in the saddle, on a blood-horse like
himself. Another genteel taste, an effect of the preceding, is
the chase. It costs the king from 1,100,000 to 1,200,000 livres a
year, and requires 280 horses besides those of the two stables. A
more varied or more complete equipment could not be imagined,
—a pack of hounds for the boar, another for the wolf, another
for the roe-buck, a cast (of hawks) for the crow, a cast for the
magpie, a cast for merlins, a cast for hares, a cast for the fields.
In 1783, 179,194 livres are expended for feeding horses, and
53,412 livres for feeding dogs.[1] The entire territory, ten leagues
around Paris, is a game-preserve ; " not a gun could be fired there ; [2]
accordingly the plains are seen covered with partridges accustomed to man, quietly picking up the grain and never stirring as
he passes." Add to this the princes' captainries, extending as far
as Villers-Cotterets and Orleans ; these form an almost continuous circle around Paris, thirty leagues in circumference, where
game, protected, replaced and multiplied, swarms for the pleasure
of the king. The park of Versailles alone forms an enclosure of
more than ten leagues. The forest of Rambouillet embraces 25,000
arpents (30,000 acres). Herds of seventy-five and eighty stags
are encountered around Fontainebleau. No true hunter could
read the minute-book of the chase without feeling an impulse of
envy. The wolf-hounds run twice a week, and they take forty
wolves a year. Between 1743 and 1744 Louis XV. runs down
6,400 stags. Louis XVI. writes, August 30th, 1781 : " Killed 460
head to-day." In 1780 he brings down 20,534 head; in 1781,
20,291 ; in fourteen years, 189,251 head, besides 1,254 stags,
while boars and bucks are proportionate ; and it must be noted
that this is all done by his own hand, since his parks approach
his houses.

Such, in fine, is the character of a " well-appointed household,
that is to say, provided with its dependencies and services.
Everything is within reach ; it is a complete world in itself, and
self-sufficient. One exalted being attaches to and gathers around
it, with universal foresight and minuteness of detail, every ap-

---

[1] Archives nationales, O¹, 778. Memorial on the hunting-train between 1760 and
1792 and especially the report of 1786.
[2] Mercier, "Tableau de Paris," vol. I. p. 11; v. p. 62. D'Hézecques, *ibid.* 253.
[3] Journal de Louis XVI." published by Nicolardot, *passim.*

purtenance it employs or can possibly employ. Thus, each prince, each princess has a professional surgery and a chapel;[1] it would not answer for the almoner who says mass or the doctor who looks after their health to be obtained outside. So much stronger is the reason that the king should have ministrants of this stamp; his chapel embraces seventy-five almoners, chaplains, confessors, masters of the oratory, clerks, announcers, carpet-bearers, choristers, copyists, and composers of sacred music; his faculty is composed of forty-eight physicians, surgeons, apothecaries, oculists, operators, bone-setters, distillers, chiropodists and spagyrists (a species of alchemists). We must still note his department of profane music, consisting of one hundred and twenty-eight vocalists, dancers, instrumentalists, directors and superintendents; his library corps of forty-three keepers, readers, interpreters, engravers, medallists, geographers, binders and printers; the staff of ceremonial display, sixty-two heralds, sword-bearers, ushers and musicians; the staff of housekeepers, consisting of sixty-eight marshals, guides and commissaries. I omit other services in haste to reach the most important,—that of the table; a fine house and good housekeeping being known by the table.

There are three sections of the table service;[2] the first for the king and his younger children; the second, called the little ordinary, for the table of the grand-master, the grand-chamberlain and the princes and princesses living with the king; the third, called the great ordinary, for the grand-master's second table, that of the butlers of the king's household, the almoners, the gentlemen in waiting, and that of the *valets-de-chambre*, in all three hundred and eighty-three officers of the table and one hundred and three waiters, at an expense of 2,177,771 livres; besides this there are 389,173 livres appropriated to the table of Madame Elisabeth, and 1,093,547 livres for that of Mesdames, the total being 3,660,491 livres for the table. The wine-merchant furnished wine to the amount of 300,000 francs per annum, and

---

[1] Warroquier, vol. I. *passim.* Household of the Queen: for the chapel 22 persons, the faculty 6. That of Monsieur, the chapel 22, the faculty 21. That of Madame, the chapel 20, the faculty 9. That of the Comte d'Artois, the chapel 20, the faculty 28. That of the Comtesse d'Artois, the chapel 19, the faculty 17. That of the Duc d'Orléans, the chapel 6, the faculty 19.

[2] Archives nationales, O¹, 738. Report by M. Mesnard de Choisy, (March, 1780). They cause a reform (August 17, 1780). "La Maison du roi justifiée" (1789), p. 24. In 1788 the expenses of the table are reduced to 2,870,999 livres, of which 600,000 livres are appropriated to Mesdames for their table.

the purveyor game, meat and fish at a cost of 1,000,000 livres. Only to fetch water from Ville-d'Avray, and to convey servants, waiters and provisions, required fifty horses hired at the rate of 70,591 francs per annum. The privilege of the royal princes and princesses " to send to the bureau for fish on fast days when not residing regularly at the court," amounts in 1778 to 175,116 livres. On reading in the Almanach the titles of these officials we see a Gargantua's feast spread out before us, the formal hierarchy of the kitchens, so many grand officials of the table,—the butlers, comptrollers and comptroller-pupils, the clerks and gentlemen of the pantry, the cup-bearers and carvers, the officers and equerries of the kitchen, the chiefs, assistants and head-cooks, the ordinary scullions, turnspits and cellarers, the common gardeners and salad gardeners, laundry servants, pastry-cooks, plate-changers, table-setters, crockery-keepers, and broach-bearers, the butler of the table of the head-butler,—an entire procession of broad-braided backs and imposing round bellies, with grave countenances, which, with order and conviction, exercise their functions before the saucepans and around the buffets.

One step more and we enter the sanctuary, the king's apartment. Two principal dignitaries preside over this, and each has under him about a hundred subordinates. On one side is the grand chamberlain with his first gentlemen of the bedchamber, the pages of the bedchamber, their governors and instructors, the ushers of the antechamber, with the four first *valets-de-chambre* in ordinary, sixteen special valets serving in turn, his regular and special cloak-bearers, his barbers, upholsterers, watch-menders, waiters and porters; on the other hand is the grand-master of the wardrobe, with the masters of the wardrobe and the valets of the wardrobe regular and special, the ordinary trunk-carriers, mall-bearers, tailors, laundry servants, starchers, and common waiters, with the gentlemen, officers and secretaries in ordinary of the cabinet, in all 198 persons for domestic service, like so many domestic utensils for every personal want, or as sumptuous pieces of furniture for the decoration of the apartment. Some of them fetch the mall and the balls, others hold the mantle and cane, others comb the king's hair and dry him off after a bath, others drive the mules which transport his bed, others watch his pet greyhounds in his room, others fold, put on

and tie his cravat, and others fetch and carry off his easy chair [1]
Some there are whose sole business it is to fill a corner which
must not be left empty. Certainly, with respect to ease of
deportment and appearance these are the most conspicuous of
all; being so close to the master they are under obligation to
appear well; in such proximity their bearing must not create a
discord.

Such is the king's household, and I have only described one
of his residences. He has a dozen of them besides Versailles,
great and small,—Marly, the two Trianons, la Muette, Meudon,
Choisy, Saint-Hubert, Saint-Germain, Fontainebleau, Compiègne,
Saint-Cloud, Rambouillet,[2] without counting the Louvre, the
Tuileries and Chambord, with their parks and hunting-grounds,
their governors, inspectors, comptrollers, concierges, fountain-
tenders, gardeners, sweepers, scrubbers, mole-catchers, wood-
rangers, mounted and foot-guards, in all more than a thousand
persons. Naturally he entertains, plans and builds, and, in this
way expends three or four millions per annum.[3] Naturally, also,
he repairs and renews his furniture; in 1778, which is an
average year, this costs him 1,936,853 livres. Naturally, also,
he takes his guests along with him and defrays their expenses,
they and their attendants; at Choisy, in 1780, there are sixteen
tables with three hundred and forty-five seats besides the dis-
tributions; at Saint-Cloud, in 1785, there are twenty-six tables;
"an excursion to Marly of twenty-one days is a matter of 120, 000
livres extra expense;" the excursion to Fontainebleau has cost
as much as 400,000 and 500,000 livres. His removals, on the
average, cost half a million and more per annum.[4] To complete
our idea of this immense paraphernalia it must be borne in

---

[1] D'Hézecques, *ibid.* 212. Under Louis XVI. there were two chair-carriers to the king,
who came every morning, in velvet coats and with swords by their sides, to inspect and
empty the object of their functions; this post was worth to each one 20,000 livres per
annum.

[2] In 1787, Louis XVI. either demolishes or orders to be sold, Madrid, la Muette and Choisy;
his acquisitions, however, Saint-Cloud, Ile-Adam and Rambouillet, greatly surpassing his
reforms.

[3] Necker, "Compte-rendu," II. 452. Archives nationales, O¹, 736. "La Maison du roi
justifiée" (1789). Constructions in 1775, 3,924,400, in 1786, 4,000,000, in 1788, 3,077,000
livres. Furniture in 1788, 1,700,000 livres.

[4] Here are some of the casual expenses. (Archives nationales, O¹, 2805). On the birth
of the Duc de Bourgogne in 1751, 604,477 livres. For the Dauphin's marriage in 1770,
1,267,770 livres. For the marriage of the Comte d'Artois in 1773, 2,016,221 livres. For the
coronation in 1775, 835,862 livres. For plays, concerts and balls in 1778, 481,744 livres, and
in 1779, 382,986 livres.

mind that the artisans and merchants belonging to these various official bodies are obliged, through the privileges they enjoy, to follow the court "on its journeys that it may be provided
on the spot with apothecaries, armorers, gunsmiths, sellers of
silken and woollen hosiery, butchers, bakers, embroiderers, publi-
cans, cobblers, belt-makers, candle-makers, hatters, pork-dealers,
surgeons, shoemakers, curriers, cooks, pinkers, gilders and engravers, spur-makers, sweetmeat-dealers, furbishers, old-clothes
brokers, glove-perfumers, watchmakers, booksellers, linen-drapers,
wholesale and retail wine-dealers, carpenters, coarse-jewelry
haberdashers, jewellers, parchment-makers, dealers in trimmings,
chicken-roasters, fish-dealers, purveyors of hay, straw and oats,
hardware-sellers, saddlers, tailors, gingerbread and starch-dealers,
fruiterers, dealers in glass and in violins."[1]   One might call it
an oriental court which, to be set in motion, moves an entire
world: "when it begins to move one has to take the post in
advance to go anywhere."   The total is near 4,000 persons for the
king's civil household, 9,000 to 10,000 for his military household,
at least 2,000 for those of his kindred, in all 15,000 individuals,
at an expense of forty and fifty million livres, which would
be equal to double the amount to-day, and which, at that time,
constituted one-tenth of the public revenue.[2]   We have here the
central figure of the monarchical show.   However grand and
costly it may be, it is only proportionate to its purpose, since the
court is a public institution, and the aristocracy, with nothing to
do, devotes itself to filling up the king's drawing-room.

III.

Two causes maintain this affluence, one the feudal form still
preserved, and the other the new centralization just introduced;

---

[1] Warroquier, vol. I. *ibid.* "Marie Antoinette," by d'Arneth and Geffroy. Letter of
Mercy, Sept. 16, 1773. "The multitude of people of various occupations following the
king on his travels resembles the progress of an army."
[2] The civil households of the king, queen, and Mme. Elisabeth, of Mesdames, and Mme.
Royale, 25,700,000. To the king's brothers and sisters-in-law, 8,040,000. The king's
military household, 7,681,000, (Necker, "Compte-rendu," II. 119). From 1774 to 1788 the
expenditure on the households of the king and his family varies from 32 to 36 millions, not
including the military household, ("La Maison du roi justifiée"). In 1789 the households of
the king, queen, Dauphin, royal children and of Mesdames, cost 25,000,000. Those of
Monsieur and Madame, 3,656,000; those of the Count and Countess d'Artois, 3,656,000;
those of the Dukes de Berri and d'Angoulême, 700,000; salaries continued to persons formerly in the princes' service, 228,000. The total is 33,240,000. To this must be added the
king's military household and two millions in the princes' appanages. (A general account
of fixed incomes and expenditure on the first of May, 1789, rendered by the minister of
finances to the committee on finances of the National Assembly.)

one placing the royal service in the hands of the nobles, and the other converting the nobles into place-hunters.

Through the duties of the palace the highest nobility live with the king, residing under his roof; the grand-almoner is M. de Montmorency-Laval, bishop of Metz; the first almoner is M. de Bussuéjouls, bishop of Senlis; the grand-master of France is the Prince de Condé; the first royal butler is the Comte d'Escars; the second is the Marquis de Montdragon; the master of the pantry is the Duke de Brissac; the chief cup-bearer is the Marquis de Verneuil; the chief carver is the Marquis de la Chesnaye; the first gentlemen of the bedchamber are the Ducs de Richelieu, de Durfort, de Villequier, and de Fleury; the grand-master of the wardrobe is the Duc de la Roche-foucauld-Liancourt; the masters of the wardrobe are the Comte de Boisgelin and the Marquis de Chauvelin; the captain of the falconry is the Chevalier du Forget; the captain of the boar-hunt is the Marquis d'Ecquevilly; the superintendent of edifices is the Comte d'Angevillier; the grand-equerry is the Prince de Lambesc; the master of the hounds is the Duc de Penthièvre; the grand-master of ceremonies is the Marquis de Brèze; the grand-master of the household is the Marquis de la Suze; the captains of the guards are the Ducs d'Agen, de Villery, de Brissac, d'Aguillon, and de Biron, the Princes de Poix, de Luxembourg and de Soubise; the provost of the hotel is the Marquis de Tourzel; the governors of the residences and captains of the chase are the Duc de Noailles, Marquis de Champcenetz, Baron de Champlost, Duc de Coigny, Comte de Modena, Comte de Montmorin, Duc de Laval, Comte de Brienne, Duc d'Orléans, and the Duc de Gèvres.[1] All these seigniors are the king's necessary intimates, his permanent guests and generally hereditary, dwelling under his roof, in close and daily intercourse with him, for they are "his folks" *(gens)*[2] and perform domestic service about his person. Add to these their equals, as noble and nearly as numerous, dwelling with the queen, with Mesdames, with Mme. Elisabeth, with the Comte and Comtesse de Provence and the Comte and Comtesse d'Artois. And these are only the heads of the service; if, below them in rank and

---

[1] Warroquier, *ibid.* (1789) vol. I., *passim.*

[2] An expression of the Comte d'Artois on introducing the officers of his household to his wife.

office, I count the titular nobles, I find, among others, 68 almoners or chaplains, 170 gentlemen of the bedchamber or in
waiting, 117 gentlemen of the stable or of the hunting-train,
148 pages, 114 titled ladies in waiting, besides all the officers,
even to the lowest of the military household, without counting
1,400 ordinary guards who, verified by the genealogist, are admitted by virtue of their title to pay their court.[1] Such is the
fixed body of recruits for the royal receptions ; the distinctive
trait of this régime is the conversion of its servants into guests,
the drawing-room being filled from the anteroom.

Not that the drawing-room needs to be filled in this manner.
Being the source of all preferment and of every favor, it is natural that it should overflow ; in our levelling society, that of an
insignificant deputy, or of a mediocre journalist, or of a fashionable woman, is full of courtiers under the name of friends and
visitors.   Moreover, here, to be present is an obligation ; it might
be called a continuation of ancient feudal homage ; the staff of
nobles is maintained as the retinue of its born general.   In the
language of the day, it is called "paying one's duty to the king."
Absence, in the sovereign's eyes, would be a sign of independence
as well as of indifference, while submission as well as assiduity is
his due.   In this respect we must study the institution from the
beginning.   The eyes of Louis XIV. go their rounds at every
moment, "on arising or retiring, on passing into his apartments, in his gardens, . . . nobody escapes, even those who
hoped they were not seen ; it was a demerit with some, and the
most distinguished, not to make the court their ordinary sojourn,
to others to come to it but seldom, and certain disgrace to those
who never, or nearly never, came."[2]   Henceforth, the main
thing, for the first personages in the kingdom, men and women,
ecclesiastics and laymen, the grand affair, the first duty in life, the
true occupation, is to be at all hours and in every place under the
king's eye, within reach of his voice and of his glance.   "Whoever," says La Bruyère, "considers that the king's countenance
is the courtier's supreme felicity, that he passes his life looking on

---

[1] The number of light-horsemen and of gendarmes was reduced in 1775 and in 1776; both
bodies were suppressed in 1787.

[2] Saint-Simon, "Mémoires," XVI. 456.   This need of being always surrounded continues
up to the last moment; in 1791, the queen exclaimed bitterly, speaking of the nobility,
"when any proceeding of ours displeases them they are sulky; no one comes to my table;
the king retires alone; we have to suffer for our misfortunes." Mme. Campan, II. 177.

it and within sight of it, will comprehend to some extent how to see God constitutes the glory and happiness of the saints." There were at this time prodigies of voluntary assiduity and subjection. The Duc de Fronsac, every morning at seven o'clock, in winter and in summer, stationed himself, at his father's command, at the foot of the small stairway leading to the chapel, solely to shake hands with Mme. de Maintenon on her leaving for St. Cyr.[1] "Pardon me, Madame," writes the Duc de Richelieu to her, "the great liberty I take in presuming to send you the letter which I have written to the king, begging him on my knees that he will occasionally allow me to pay my court to him at Ruel, for *I would rather die than pass two months without seeing him.*" The true courtier follows the prince as a shadow follows its body; such, under Louis XIV., was the Duc de la Rochefoucauld, the master of the hounds. "He never missed the king's rising or retiring, both changes of dress every day, the hunts and the promenades, likewise every day, for ten years in succession, never sleeping away from the place where the king rested, and yet on a footing to demand leave,—but not to stay away all night, for he had not slept out of Paris once in forty years,—but to go and dine away from the court, and not be present on the promenade." If, later, and under less exacting masters, and in the general laxity of the eighteenth century, this discipline is relaxed, the institution nevertheless subsists;[2] in default of obedience, tradition, interest and *amour-propre* suffice for the people of the court. To approach the king, to be a domestic in his household, an usher, a cloak-bearer, a valet, is a privilege that is purchased, even in 1789, for thirty, forty, and a hundred thousand livres; so much greater the reason why it is a privilege to form a part of his society, the most honorable, the most useful, and the most coveted of all. In the first place, it is a proof of race. A man, to follow the king in the chase, and a woman, to be presented to the queen, must previously satisfy the genealogist, and by authentic documents, that his or her nobility goes back to the year 1400. In the next place, it ensures good fortune. This drawing-room is the only place within reach

---

[1] Duc de Lévis, "Souvenirs et Portraits," 29.   Mme. de Maintenon, "Correspondance."
[2] M. de V—— who was promised a king's lieutenancy or command, yields it to one of Mme. de Pompadour's protégés, obtaining in lieu of it the part of *exempt* in "Tartuffe," played by the seigniors before the king in the small cabinet. (Mme. de Hausset, 168). " M. de V—— thanked Madame as if she had made him a duke."

of royal favors; accordingly, up to 1789, the great families never stir away from Versailles, and day and night they lie in ambush. The valet of the Marshal de Noailles says to him one night on closing his curtains, "At what hour will Monseigneur be awakened?" "At ten o'clock, if no one dies during the night."[1] Old courtiers are again found who, "eighty years of age, have passed forty-five on their feet in the antechambers of the king, of the princes, and of the ministers. . . . You have only three things to do," says one of them to a debutant, "speak well of everybody, ask for every vacancy, and sit down when you can." Hence, the king always has a crowd around him. The Comtesse du Barry says, on presenting her niece at court, the first of August, 1773, "the crowd is so great at a presentation, one can scarcely get through the antechambers."[2] In December, 1774, at Fontainebleau, when the queen plays at her own table every evening, "the apartment, though vast, is never empty. . . . The crowd is so great that one can talk only to the two or three persons with whom one is playing." The fourteen apartments, at the receptions of ambassadors are full to overflowing with seigniors and richly dressed women. On the first of January, 1775, the queen "counted over two hundred ladies presented to her to pay their court." In 1780, at Choisy, a table for thirty persons is spread every day for the king, another with thirty places for the seigniors, another with forty places for the officers of the guard and the equerries, and one with fifty for the officers of the bedchamber. According to my estimate, the king, on getting up and on retiring, on his walks, on his hunts, at play, has always around him at least forty or fifty seigniors and generally a hundred, with as many ladies, besides his attendants on duty; at Fontainebleau, in 1756, although "there were neither fêtes nor ballets this year, one hundred and six ladies were counted." When the king holds a "*grand appartement*," when play or dancing takes place in the gallery of mirrors, four or five hundred guests, the elect of the nobles and of the fashion,

[1] "Paris, Versailles et les provinces au dix-huitième siècle," II. 160, 168. Mercier, "Tableau de Paris," IV. 150. De Ségur, "Mémoires," I. 16.

[2] "Marie Antoinette," by D'Arneth and Geffroy, II. 27, 255, 281. "Gustave III." by Geffroy, November, 1786, bulletin of Mme. de Staël. D'Hézecques, *ibid.* 231. Archives nationales, O¹, 736, a letter by M. Amelot, September 23, 1780. De Luynes, XV. 260, 367; XVI. 248. 163 ladies, of which 42 are in service, appear and courtesy to the king. 160 men and more than 100 ladies pay their respects to the Dauphin and Dauphine.

range themselves on the benches or gather around the card and *cavagnole* tables.[1] This is a spectacle to be seen, not by the imagination, or through imperfect records, but with our own eyes and on the spot, to comprehend the spirit, the effect and the triumph of monarchical culture. In an elegantly furnished house, the drawing-room is the principal room ; and never was one more dazzling than this. Suspended from the sculptured ceiling peopled with sporting cupids, descend, by garlands of flowers and foliage, blazing chandeliers, whose splendour is enhanced by the tall mirrors ; the light streams down in floods on gildings, diamonds, and beaming, arch physiognomies, on fine busts, and on the capacious, sparkling and garlanded dresses. The skirts of the ladies ranged in a circle, or in tiers on the benches, " form a rich *espalier* covered with pearls, gold, silver, jewels, spangles, flowers and fruits, with their artificial blossoms, gooseberries, cherries, and strawberries," a gigantic animated bouquet of which the eye can scarcely support the brilliancy. There are no black coats, as nowadays, to disturb the harmony. With the hair powdered and dressed, with buckles and knots, with cravats and ruffles of lace, in silk coats and vests of the hues of fallen leaves, or of a delicate rose tint, or of celestial blue, embellished with gold braid and embroidery, the men are as elegant as the women. Men and women, each is a selection ; they all are of the accomplished class, gifted with every grace which race, education, fortune, leisure and custom can bestow ; they are perfect of their kind. There is no toilet, no carriage of the head, no tone of the voice, no expression in language which is not a masterpiece of worldly culture, the distilled quintessence of all that is exquisitely elaborated by social art. Polished as the society of Paris may be, it does not approach this ;[2] compared with the court, it seems provincial. It is said that a hundred thousand roses are required to make an ounce of the unique perfume used by Persian kings ; such is this drawing-room, the frail vial of crystal and gold containing the substance of a human vegetation. To fill it, a great aristocracy had to be transplanted to a hot-house and become sterile in fruit and

---

[1] Cochin. Engravings of a masked ball, of a dress ball, of the king and queen at play, of the interior of a theatre (1745). Costumes of Moreau (1777). Mme. de Genlis, "Dictionnaire des etiquettes," the article *parure.*

[2] " The difference between the tone and language of the court and the town was about as perceptible as that between Paris and the provinces." (De Tilly, "Mémoires," I. 153.)

flowers, and then, in the royal alembic, its pure sap is concentrated into a few drops of aroma. The price is excessive, but only at this price can the most delicate perfumes be manufactured.

IV.

An operation of this kind absorbs him who undertakes it as well as those who undergo it. A nobility for useful purposes is not transformed with impunity into a nobility for ornament;[1] one falls himself into the ostentation which is substituted for action. The king has a court which he is compelled to maintain. So much the worse if it absorbs all his time, his intellect, his soul, the most valuable portion of his active forces and the forces of the State. To be the master of a house is not an easy task, especially when five hundred persons are to be entertained; one must necessarily pass his life in public and be on exhibition. Strictly speaking it is the life of an actor who is on the stage the entire day. To support this load, and work besides, required the temperament of Louis XIV., the vigor of his body, the extraordinary firmness of his nerves, the strength of his digestion, and the regularity of his habits; his successors who come after him grow weary or stagger under the same load. But they cannot throw it off; an incessant, daily performance is inseparable from their position and it is imposed on them like a heavy, gilded, ceremonial coat. The king is expected to keep the entire aristocracy busy, consequently to make a display of himself, to pay back with his own person, at all hours, even the most private, even on getting out of bed, and even in his bed. In the morning, at the hour named by himself beforehand,[2] the head

---

[1] The following is an example of the compulsory inactivity of the nobles—a dinner of Queen Marie Leczinska at Fontainebleau: "I was introduced into a superb saloon where I found about a dozen courtiers promenading about and a table set for as many persons, which was nevertheless prepared for but one person. . . . The queen sat down while the twelve courtiers took their positions in a semi-circle ten steps from the table; I stood alongside of them imitating their deferential silence. Her Majesty began to eat very fast, keeping her eyes fixed on the plate. Finding one of the dishes to her taste she returned to it, and then, running her eye around the circle, she said: "Monsieur de Lowenthal?" On hearing this name a fine-looking man advanced, bowing, and he replied, "Madame?" "I find that this ragout is fricassé chicken." "I believe it is, Madame." On making this answer, in the gravest manner, the marshal, retiring backwards, resumed his position, while the queen finished her dinner, never uttering another word and going back to her room the same way as she came." (Memoirs of Casenova.)

[2] "Under Louis XVI., who arose at seven or eight o'clock, the *lever* took place at half-past eleven unless hunting or ceremonies required it earlier." There is the same ceremonial at eleven, again in the evening on retiring, and also during the day, when he changes his boots. (D'Hézecque, 161.)

valet awakens him ; five series of persons enter in turn to perform their duty, and, " although very large, there are days when the waiting-rooms can hardly contain the crowd of courtiers." The first admittance is "*l'entrée familière*," consisting of the children of France, the princes and princesses of the blood, and, besides these, the chief physician, the chief surgeon and other serviceable persons.[1] Next, comes the "*grande entrée*," which comprises the grand-chamberlain, the grand-master and master of the wardrobe, the first gentlemen of the bedchamber, the Ducs d'Orleans and de Penthièvre, some other highly favored seigniors, the ladies of honor and in waiting of the queen, Mesdames and other princesses, without enumerating barbers tailors and various descriptions of valets. Meanwhile spirits of wine are poured on the king's hands from a service of plate, and he is then handed the basin of holy water; he crosses himself and repeats a prayer. Then he gets out of bed before all these people and puts on his slippers. The grand-chamberlain and the first gentleman hand him his dressing-gown; he puts this on and seats himself in the chair in which he is to put on his clothes. At this moment the door opens and a third group enters, which is the "*entrée des brevets ;* " the seigniors who compose this enjoy, in addition, the precious privilege of assisting at the "*petite coucher*," while, at the same moment there enters a detachment of attendants, consisting of the physicians and surgeons in ordinary, the intendants of the amusements, readers and others, and among the latter those who preside over physical requirements; the publicity of a royal life is so great that none of its functions can be exercised without witnesses. At the moment of the approach of the officers of the wardrobe to dress him the first gentleman, notified by an usher, advances to read to the king the names of the grandees who are waiting at the door : this is the fourth entry called "*la chambre*," and larger than those preceding it; for, not to mention the cloak-bearers, gun-bearers, rug-bearers and other valets it comprises most of the superior officials, the grand-almoner, the almoners on duty, the chaplain, the master of the oratory, the captain and major of the body-guard, the colonel-general and major of the French guards, the colonel of the king's regiment, the captain of the *Cent Suisses*,

---

[1] Warroquier, I. 94. Compare corresponding details under Louis XVI. in St. Simon. XIII. 88.

the grand-huntsman, the grand wolf-huntsman, the grand-provost, the grand-master and master of ceremonies, the first butler, the grand-master of the pantry, the foreign ambassadors, the ministers and secretaries of state, the marshals of France and most of the seigniors and prelates of distinction. Ushers place the ranks in order and, if necessary, impose silence. Meanwhile the king washes his hands and begins his toilet. Two pages remove his slippers; the grand-master of the wardrobe draws off his night-shirt by the right arm, and the first valet of the wardrobe by the left arm, and both of them hand it to an officer of the wardrobe, whilst a valet of the wardrobe fetches the shirt wrapped up in white taffeta. Things have now reached the solemn point, the culmination of the ceremony; the fifth entry has been introduced, and, in a few moments, after the king has put his shirt on, all that is left of those who are known, with other household officers waiting in the gallery, complete the influx. There is quite a formality in regard to this shirt. The honor of handing it is reserved to the sons and grandsons of France; in default of these to the princes of the blood or those legitimised; in their default to the grand-chamberlain or to the first gentleman of the bedchamber;—the latter case, it must be observed, being very rare, the princes being obliged to be present at the king's *lever*, as were the princesses at that of the queen.[1]   At last the shirt is presented and a valet carries off the old one; the first valet of the wardrobe and the first *valet-de-chambre* hold the fresh one, each by a right and left arm respectively,[2] while two other valets, during this operation, extend his dressing-gown in front of him to serve as a screen. The shirt is now on his back and the toilet commences.   A *valet-de-chambre* supports a mirror before the king while two others on the two sides light it up, if occasion requires, with flambeaux. Valets of the wardrobe fetch the rest of the attire; the grand-master of the wardrobe puts the vest on and the doublet, attaches the blue ribbon, and clasps his sword around him; then a valet assigned to the cravats brings several of these in a basket, while the master of the wardrobe arranges around the king's neck that which the king selects. After this a valet assigned to the handkerchiefs brings three of

---

[1] "Marie Antoinette," by d'Arneth and Geffroy, II. 217.

[2] In all changes of the coat the left arm of the king is appropriated to the wardrobe and the right arm to the "chambre."

these on a silver salver, while the grand-master of the wardrobe offers the salver to the king, who chooses one. Finally the master of the wardrobe hands to the king his hat, his gloves and his cane. The king then steps to the side of the bed, kneels on a cushion and says his prayers, whilst an almoner in a low voice recites the orison *Quæsumus, deus omnipotens.* This done, the king announces the order of the day, and passes with the leading persons of his court into his cabinet, where he sometimes gives audience. Meanwhile the rest of the company await him in the gallery in order to accompany him to mass when he comes out.

Such is the *lever*, a piece in five acts. Nothing could be con- trived better calculated to fill up the void of an aristocratic life ; a hundred or thereabouts of notable seigniors dispose of a couple of hours in coming, in waiting, in entering, in defiling, in taking positions, in standing on their feet, in maintaining an air of respect and of ease suitable to a superior class of walking gen- tlemen, while those best qualified are about to do the same thing over in the queen's apartment.[1] The king, however, as a set- off, suffers the same torture and the same inaction as he imposes. He also is playing a part ; all his steps and all his gestures have been determined beforehand ; he has been obliged to arrange his physiognomy and his voice, never to depart from an affable and dignified air, to award judiciously his glances and his nods, to keep silent or to speak only of the chase, and to suppress his own thoughts, if he has any. One cannot indulge in reverie, meditate or be absent-minded when one is before the footlights ; the part must have due attention. Besides, in a drawing-room there is only drawing-room conversation, and the master's thoughts, instead of being directed in a profitable channel, must be scattered about like the holy water of the court. All hours of the day are thus occupied, except three or four in the morning, during which he is at the council or in his private room ; it must

[1] The queen breakfasts in bed, and "there are ten or twelve persons present at this recep- tion," . ... the grand receptions taking place at the dressing hour. "This reception com- prised the princes of the blood, the captains of the guards and most of the grand-officers." The same ceremony occurs with the chemise as with the king's shirt. One winter day Mme. Campan offers the chemise to the queen, when a lady of honor enters, removes her gloves and takes the chemise in her hands. A movement at the door and the Duchess of Orleans comes in, takes off her gloves, and receives the chemise. Another movement and it is the Comtesse d'Artois whose privilege it is to hand the chemise. Meanwhile the queen sits there shivering with her arms crossed on her breast and muttering, "It is dread- ful, what importunity! " (Mme. Campan, II. 217; III. 309-316).

be noted, too, that on the days after his hunts, on returning home from Rambouillet at three o'clock in the morning, he must sleep the few hours he has left to him.   The ambassador Mercy,[1] never-theless, a man of close application, seems to think it sufficient; he, at least, thinks that " Louis XVI. is a man of order, losing no time in useless things;" his predecessor, indeed, worked much less, scarcely an hour a day.   Three-quarters of his time is thus given up to show.   The same retinue surrounds him when he puts on his boots, when he takes them off, when he changes his clothes to mount his horse, when he returns home to dress for the evening, and when he goes to his room at night to retire. " Every evening for six years, says a page,[2] either myself or one of my comrades has seen Louis XVI. get into bed in public," with the ceremonial just described.   " It was not omitted ten times to my knowledge, and then accidentally or through indisposition." The attendance is yet more numerous when he dines and takes supper; for, besides men there are women present, duchesses seated on the folding-chairs, also others standing around the table. It is needless to state that in the evening when he plays, or gives a ball, or a concert, the crowd rushes in and overflows.   When he hunts, besides the ladies on horses and in vehicles, besides officers of the hunt, of the guards, the equerry, the cloak-bearer, gun-bearer, surgeon, bone-setter, lunch-bearer and I know not how many others, all the gentlemen who accompany him are his permanent guests.   And do not imagine that this suite is a small one;[3] the day M. de Chateaubriand is presented there are four fresh additions, and " with the utmost punctuality" all the young men of high rank join the king's retinue two or three times a week.   Not only the eight or ten scenes which compose each of these days, but again the short intervals between the scenes are besieged and carried.   People watch for him, walk by his side and speak with him on his way from his cabinet to the chapel, between his apartment and his carriage, between his carriage and his apartment, between his cabinet and his dining-room.   And still more, his life behind the scenes belongs to the public.   If he is indisposed and broth is brought to him, if he

1 " Marie Antoinette," by d'Arneth and Geffroy, II. 223 (August 15, 1774).
2 D'Hézecques, *ibid*, p. 7.
3 Duc de Lauzun, " Mémoires," 51.   Mme. de Genlis, " Mémoires," ch. XII.   " Our husbands, regularly on that day (Saturday) slept at Versailles to hunt the next day with the king."

is ill and medicine is handed to him, "a servant immediately summons the '*grande entrée.*'"   Verily, the king resembles an oak
stifled by the innumerable creepers which, from top to bottom,
cling to its trunk.   Under a régime of this stamp there is a want
of air; some opening has to be found; Louis XV. availed himself of the chase and of suppers; Louis XVI. of the chase and
of lock-making.   And I have not mentioned the infinite detail
of etiquette, the extraordinary ceremonial of the state dinner,
the fifteen, twenty and thirty beings busy around the king's
plates and glasses, the sacramental utterances of the occasion,
the procession of the retinue, the arrival of "*la nef,*" "*l'essai des
plats,*" all as if in a Byzantine or Chinese court.[1]   On Sundays
the entire public, the public in general, is admitted, and this is
called the "*grand couvert,*" as complex and as solemn as a high
mass.   Accordingly to eat, to drink, to get up, to go to bed, is
to a descendant of Louis XIV., to officiate.[2]   Frederick II., on
hearing an explanation of this etiquette, declared that if he were
king of France his first edict would be to appoint another king
to hold court in his place.   In effect, if there are idlers to salute
there must be an idler to be saluted.   Only one way was possible by which the monarch could have been set free, and that was
to have recast and transformed the French nobles, according to
the Prussian system, into a hard-working regiment of serviceable
functionaries.   But, so long as the court remains what it is, that
is to say, a pompous parade and a drawing-room decoration, the
king himself must likewise form a showy decoration, of little use,
or of none at all.

V.

In short, what is the occupation of a well-qualified master of
a house ?   He amuses himself and he amuses his guests; under
his roof a new pleasure-party comes off daily.   Let us enumerate those of a week.   "Yesterday, Sunday," says the Duc de
Luynes, "I met the king going to hunt on the plain of St.

---

[1] The state dinner takes place every Sunday. *La nef* is a piece of plate at the centre of
the table containing between scented cushions the napkins used by the king.   The *essai* is
the tasting of each dish by the gentlemen servants and officers of the table before the king
partakes of it.   And the same with the beverages.   It requires four persons to serve the
king with a glass of wine and water.

[2] When the ladies of the king's court, and especially the princesses, pass before the king's
bed they have to make an obeisance ; the palace officials salute the *nef* on passing that.   A
priest or sacristan does the same thing on passing before the altar.

Denis, having slept at la Muette, where he intends to remain shooting to-day and to-morrow, and to return here on Tuesday or Wednesday morning, to run down a stag the same day, Wednesday."[1] Two months after this, "the king," again says M. de Luynes, "has been hunting every day of the past and of the present week, except to-day and on Sundays, killing, since the beginning, three thousand five hundred partridges." He is always on the road, or hunting, or passing from one residence to another, from Versailles to Fontainebleau, to Choisy, to Marly, to la Muette, to Compiègne, to Trianon, to Saint-Hubert, to Bellevue, to Rambouillet, and, generally, with his entire court.[2] At Choisy, especially, and at Fontainebleau this company all lead a merry life. At Fontainebleau "Sunday and Friday, play; Monday and Wednesday, a concert in the queen's apartments; Tuesday and Thursday, the French comedians; and Saturday it is the Italians;" there is something for every day in the week. At Choisy, writes the Dauphine,[3] "from one o'clock (in the afternoon) when we dine, to one o'clock at night we remain out. . . . After dining we play until six o'clock, after which we go to the theatre, which lasts until half-past nine o'clock, and next, to supper; after this, play again, until one, and sometimes half-past one, o'clock." At Versailles things are more moderate; there are but two theatrical entertainments and one ball a week; but every evening there is play and a reception in the king's apartment, in his daughters', in his mistress's, in his daughter-in-law's, besides hunts and three petty excursions a week. Records show that, in a certain year, Louis XV. slept only fifty-two nights at Versailles, while the Austrian Ambassador well says that " his mode of living leaves him not an hour in the day for attention to important matters." As to Louis XVI., we have seen that he reserves a few hours of the morning; but the machine is wound up, and go it must. How can he withdraw himself from his guests and not do

---

[1] De Luynes, IX, 75, 79, 105 (August, 1748, October, 1748).

[2] The king is at Marly, and here is a list of the excursions he is to make before going to Compiègne (De Luynes, XIV, 163, May, 1755): " Sunday, June 1st, to Choisy until Monday evening. Tuesday, the 3d, to Trianon, until Wednesday. Thursday, the 5th, return to Trianon where he will remain until after supper on Saturday. Monday, the 9th, to Crécy, until Friday, 13th. Return to Crécy the 16th, until the 21st. July 1st to la Muette, the 2d, to Compiègne."

[3] " Marie Antoinette," by d'Arneth and Geffroy, I. 19 (July 12, 1770). I. 265 (January 23, 1771). I. III. (October 18, 1770).

the honors of his house ?   Moreover, propriety and custom are despotic; a third despotism must be added, still more absolute, the imperious vivacity of a frolicsome young queen who cannot endure an hour's reading.   At Versailles, three theatrical entertainments and two balls a week, two grand suppers Tuesday and Thursday, and from time to time, the opera in Paris.[1]   At Fontainebleau, the theatre three times a week, and on other days, play and suppers.   During the following winter the queen gives a masked ball each week, in which "the contrivance of the costumes, the quadrilles arranged in ballets, and the daily rehearsals, take so much time as to consume the entire week."   During the carnival of 1777 the queen, besides her own fêtes, attends the balls of the Palais-Royal and the masked balls of the opera; a little later, I find another ball at the abode of the Comtesse Diana de Polignac, which she attends with the whole royal family, except Mesdames, and which lasts from half-past eleven o'clock at night until eleven o'clock the next morning.   Meanwhile, on ordinary days, there is the rage of faro; in her drawing-room "there is no limit to the play; in one evening the Duc de Chartres loses eight thousand louis. It really resembles an Italian carnival; there is nothing lacking, neither masks nor the comedy of private life; they play, they laugh, they dance, they dine, they listen to music, they don costumes, they get up picnics (fêtes-champêtres), they indulge in gossip and gallantries."   "The newest song,"[2] says a cultivated, earnest lady of the bedchamber, "the current witticism and little scandalous stories, formed the sole subjects of conversation in the queen's circle of intimates."   As to the king, who is rather dull and who requires physical exercise, the chase is his most important occupation.   Between 1755 and 1789,[3] he himself, on recapitulating what he had accomplished, finds "one hundred and forty boar-hunts, one hundred and thirty stag-hunts, two hundred and sixty-six of bucks, thirty-three with hounds, and one thousand and twenty-five shootings," in all fifteen hundred and sixty-two hunting-days, averaging at least one hunt every three days; besides this there are a hundred and

---

[1] "Marie Antoinette," by d'Arneth and Geffroy, II. 270 (October 18, 1774).   II. 395 (November 15, 1775).   II. 295 (February 20, 1775).   III. 25 (February 11, 1777).   IIL 119 (October 17, 1777).   III. 409 (March 18, 1780).

[2] Mme. Campan, I. 147.

[3] Nicolardot, "Journal de Louis XVI.," 129.

forty-nine excursions without hunts, and two hundred and twenty-three promenades on horseback or in carriages. "During four months of the year he goes to Rambouillet twice a week and returns after having supped, that is to say, at three o'clock in the morning."[1] This inveterate habit ends in becoming a mania, and even in something worse. "The supineness," writes Arthur Young, June 26, 1789, "and even stupidity of the court, is without example; the moment demands the greatest decision,—and yesterday, while it was actually a question whether he should be a doge of Venice or a king of France, the king went a hunting!" His journal is like that of a whipper-in. On reading it at the most important dates one is amazed at its records. He writes *nothing* on the days not devoted to hunting, which means that to him these days are of no account. "July 11, 1789, *nothing;* M. Necker leaves.—12th, vespers and benediction; Messieurs de Montmorin, de Saint-Priest and de la Luzerne leave.—13th, *nothing.*—14th, *nothing.*—29th, *nothing;* M. Necker returns.—August 4th, stag-hunt in the forest at Marly; took one; go and come on horseback.—13th, audience of the States in the gallery; Te Deum during the mass below; one stag taken in the hunt at Marly. . . . 25th, complimentary audience of the States; high mass with the *cordons bleus;* M. Bailly sworn in; vespers and benediction; state dinner. . . . October 5th, shooting near Chatillon; killed eighty-one head; interrupted by events; go and come on horseback.—October 6th, leave for Paris at half-past twelve; visit the Hotel-de-Ville; sup and rest at the Tuileries.—October 7th, *nothing;* my aunts come and dine.—8th, *nothing.* . . . 12th, *nothing;* the stag hunted at Port Royal." Shut up in Paris, the captive of the masses, his heart is always with the hounds. Twenty times in 1790 we read in his journal of a stag-hunt occurring in this or that place; he regrets not being on hand. No privation is more intolerable to him; we encounter traces of his chagrin even in the formal protest he draws up before leaving for Varennes; transported to Paris, stationary in the Tuileries, "where, far from finding conveniences to which he is accustomed, he has not even enjoyed the advantages common to persons in easy circumstances," his crown to him having apparently lost its brightest jewel.

---

[1] D'Hézecques, *ibid.* 253. Arthur Young, I. 215.

VI.

As is the general so is his staff; the grandees imitate their monarch. Like some costly colossal effigy in marble, erected in the centre of France, and of which reduced copies are scattered by thousands throughout the provinces, thus does royal life repeat itself, in minor proportions, even among the remotest gentry. The object is to make a parade and to receive; to make a figure and to pass away time in good society. I find, first, around the court, about a dozen princely courts; each prince or princess of the blood royal, like the king, has his house fitted up, paid for, in whole or in part, out of the treasury, its service divided into special departments, with gentlemen, pages, and ladies in waiting, in brief, fifty, one hundred, two hundred, and even five hundred appointments. There is a household of this kind for the queen, one for Madame Victoire, one for Madame Elisabeth, one for Monsieur, one for Madame, one for the Comte d'Artois, one for the Comtesse d'Artois; there will be one for Madame Royale, one for the little Dauphin, one for the Duc de Normandie, all three children of the king, one for the Duc d'Angoulême, one for the Duc de Berry, both sons of the Comte d'Artois : children six or seven years of age receive and make a parade of themselves. On referring to a particular date, in 1771,[1] I find still another for the Duc d'Orléans, one for the Duc de Bourbon, one for the Duchesse, one for the Prince de Condé, one for the Comte de Clermont, one for the Princess dowager de Conti, one for the Prince de Conti, one for the Comte de la Marche, one for the Duc de Penthièvre. Each personage, besides his or her apartment under the king's roof has his or her chateau and palace with his or her own circle, the queen at Trianon and at Saint Cloud, Mesdames at Bellevue, Monsieur at the Luxembourg and at Brunoy, the Comte d'Artois at Meudon and at Bagatelle, the Duc d'Orléans at the Palais-Royal, at Monceaux, at Rancy and at Villers-Cotterets, the Prince de Conti at the Temple and at Ile-Adam, the Condés at the Palais-Bourbon and at Chantilly, the Duc de

---

[1] List of pensions paid to members of the royal family in 1771. Duc d'Orléans, 150,000, Prince de Condé, 100,000; Comte de Clermont, 70,000; Duc de Bourbon, 60,000; Prince de Conti, 60,000; Comte de la Marche, 60,000; Dowager-Countess de Conti, 50,000; Duc de Penthièvre, 50,000; Princess de Lamballe, 50,000; Duchess of Bourbon, 50,000; (Archives nationales. O¹, 710, *bis*)

I

Penthièvre at Sceaux, Anet and Chateauvilain. I omit one-half of these residences. At the Palais-Royal those who are presented may come to the supper on opera days. At Chateauvilain all those who come to pay court are invited to dinner, the nobles at the duke's table and the rest at the table of his first gentleman. At the Temple one hundred and fifty guests attend the Monday suppers. Forty or fifty persons, said the Duchesse de Maine, constitute "a prince's private company."[1] The princes' train is so inseparable from their persons that it follows them even into camp. "The Prince de Condé," says M. de Luynes, "sets out for the army to-morrow with a large suite: he has two hundred and twenty-five horses, and the Comte de la Marche one hundred. M. le duc d'Orléans leaves on Monday; he has three hundred and fifty horses for himself and suite."[2] Below the rank of the king's relatives all the grandees who figure at the court figure as well in their own residences, at their hotels at Paris or at Versailles, also in their chateaux a few leagues away from Paris. On all sides, in the memoirs, we obtain a foreshortened view of some one of these seignorial existences. Such is that of the Duc de Gèvres, first gentleman of the bedchamber, governor of Paris, and of the Ile-de-France, possessing besides this the special governorships of Laon, Soissons, Noyon, Crespy and Valois, the captainry of Mousseaux, also a pension of twenty thousand livres, a veritable man of the court, a sort of sample in high relief of the people of his class, and who, through his appointments, his airs, his luxury, his debts, the consideration he enjoys, his tastes, his occupations and his turn of mind presents to us an abridgment of the fashionable world.[3] His memory for relationships and genealogies is surprising; he is an adept in the precious science of etiquette, and on these two grounds he is an oracle and much consulted. "He greatly increased the beauty of his house and gardens at Saint-Ouen. At the moment of his death," says the Duc de Luynes, "he had just added twenty-five *arpents* to it which he had begun to enclose with a covered

---

[1] Beugnot, I. 77. Mme. de Genlis, "Mémoires," ch. xvii. De Goncourt, "La Femme au dix-huitième siècle," 52. Champfort, "Caractères et Anecdotes."

[2] De Luynes, XVI. 57 (May, 1757). In the army of Westphalia the Count d'Estrées, commander-in-chief, had twenty-seven secretaries, and Gremin was the twenty-eighth. When the Duc de Richelieu set out for his government of Guyenne he was obliged to have relays of a hundred horses along the entire road.

[3] De Luynes, XVI. 186 (October, 1757).

terrace. . . . He had quite a large household of gentlemen, pages, and domestic of various kinds, and his expenditure was enormous. . . . He gave a grand dinner every day. . . . He gave special audiences almost daily. There was no one at the court, nor in the city, who did not pay his respects to him. The ministers, the royal princes themselves did so. He received company whilst still in bed. He wrote and dictated amidst a large assemblage. . . . His house at Paris and his apartment at Versailles were never empty from the time he arose till the time he retired." Two or three hundred households at Paris, at Versailles and in their environs, offer a similar spectacle. Never is there solitude. It is the custom in France, says Horace Walpole, to burn your candle down to its snuff in public. The mansion of the Duchesse de Gramont is besieged at daybreak by the noblest seigniors and the noblest ladies. Five times a week, under the Duc de Choiseul's roof, the butler enters the drawing-room at ten o'clock in the evening to bestow a glance on the immense crowded gallery and decide if he shall lay the cloth for fifty, sixty or eighty persons;[1] with this example before them all the rich establishments soon glory in providing an open table for all comers. Naturally the parvenus, the financiers who have purchased or taken the name of an estate, all those traffickers and sons of traffickers who, since Law, associate with the nobility, imitate their ways. And I do not allude to the Bourets, the Beaujons, the St. Jameses and other financial wretches whose paraphernalia effaces that of the princes; but take a plain *associé des fermes*, M. d'Epinay, whose modest and refined wife refuses such excessive display.[2] He had just completed his domestic arrangements, and was anxious that his wife should take a second maid; but she resisted; nevertheless, in this curtailed household, "the officers, women and valets, amounted to sixteen. . . . When M. d'Epinay gets up his valet enters on his duties. Two lackeys stand by awaiting his orders. The first secretary enters for the purpose of giving an account of the letters received by him and which he has to open; but he is interrupted two hundred times in this business by all sorts of people imaginable. Now it is a horse-jockey with the finest horses to sell. . . . Again some scrapegrace who calls to screech

---

[1] De Goncourt, *ibid.* 73, 75.

[2] Mme. d'Epinay, "Mémoires." Ed. Boiteau, I. 306 (1751).

out a piece of music, and in whose behalf some influence has
been exerted to get him into the opera, after giving him a few
lessons in good taste and teaching him what is proper in French
music. Again a young lady who is made to wait to ascertain if
I am still at home. . . . I get up and go out. Two lackeys
open the folding doors to let me pass, I who could pass through
the eye of a needle, while two servants bawl out in the antechamber, 'Madame, gentlemen, Madame!' All form a line, the
gentlemen consisting of dealers in stuffs, in instruments, jewellers,
hawkers, lackeys, shoeblacks, creditors, in short everything imaginable that is most ridiculous and annoying. The clock strikes
twelve or one before this toilet matter is over, and the secretary,
who, doubtless, knows by experience the impossibility of rendering a detailed statement of his business, hands to his master a
small memorandum informing him what he must say in the assembly of *fermiers.*" Indolence, disorder, debts, ceremony, the
tone and ways of the patron, all seems a parody of the real
thing. We are beholding the last stages of aristocracy. And
yet the court of M. d'Epinay is a miniature resemblance of that
of the king.

So much more essential is it that the ambassadors, ministers
and general officers who represent the king should display themselves in a grandiose manner. No circumstance rendered the
ancient régime so brilliant and more oppressive; in this, as in
all the rest, Louis XIV. is the principal author of evil as of good.
The policy which fashioned the court prescribed ostentation.
" A display of dress, table, equipages, buildings and play was
made purposely to please; these afforded opportunities for entering into conversation with him. The contagion had spread from
the court into the provinces and to the armies, where people of
any position were esteemed only in proportion to their table and
magnificence."[1] During the year passed by the Marshal de Belle-
Isle at Frankfort, on account of the election of Charles VI., he
expended 750,000 livres in journeys, transportations, festivals and

---

[1] St. Simon, XII. 457, and Dangeau, VI. 408. The Marshal de Boufflers at the camp of
Compiègne (September, 1698) had every night and morning two tables for twenty and
twenty-five persons, besides extra tables; 72 cooks, 340 domestics, 400 dozens of napkins,
80 dozens of silver plates, 6 dozens of porcelain plates. Fourteen relays of horses brought
fruits and liquors daily from Paris; every day an express brought fish, poultry and game
from Ghent, Brussels, Dunkirk, Dieppe and Calais. Fifty dozens of wine were drunk on
ordinary days and eighty dozens during the visits of the king and the princes.

dinners, in constructing a kitchen and dining-hall, and besides all this, 150,000 livres in snuff-boxes, watches and other presents; by order of Cardinal Fleury, so economical, he had in his kitchens one hundred and one officials.[1] At Vienna, in 1772, the ambassador, the Prince de Rohan, had two carriages costing together 40,000 livres, forty horses, seven noble pages, six gentlemen, five secretaries, ten musicians, twelve footmen, and four grooms whose gorgeous liveries each cost 4,000 livres, and the rest in proportion.[2] We are familiar with the profusion, the good taste, the exquisite dinners, the admirable ceremonial display of the Cardinal de Bernis in Rome. " He was called the king of Rome, and indeed he was such through his magnificence and in the consideration he enjoyed. . . . His table afforded an idea of what is possible. . . . In festivities, ceremonies and illuminations he was always beyond comparison." He himself remarked, smiling, " I keep a French inn on the cross-roads of Europe." [3] Accordingly their salaries and indemnities are two or three times more ample than at the present day. "The king gives 50,000 crowns to the great embassies. The Duc de Duras received even 200,000 livres per annum for that of Madrid, also, besides this, 100,000 crowns gratuity, 50,000 livres for secret service; and he had the loan of furniture and effects valued at 400,000 and 500,000 livres, of which he kept one-half." [4] The outlays and salaries of the ministers are similar. In 1789, the Chancellor gets 120,080 livres salary and the Keeper of the Seals 135,000. " M. de Villedeuil, as Secretary of State, was to have had 180,670 livres, but as he represented that this sum would not cover his expenses, his salary was raised to 226,000 livres, everything included." [5] Moreover, the rule is, that on retiring from office the king awards them a pension of 20,000 livres and gives a dowry of 200,000 livres to their daughters. This is not excessive considering the way they live. " They are obliged to maintain such state in their households, for

---

[1] De Luynes, XIV. 149.

[2] Abbé Georgel, " Mémoires," 216.

[3] Sainte-Beuve, " Causeries du lundi," VIII. 63, the texts of two witnesses, MM. de Genlis and Roland.

[4] De Luynes, XV. 455, and XVI. 219 (1757). "The Marshal de Belle-Isle contracted an indebtedness amounting to 1,200,000 livres, one-quarter of it for pleasure-houses and the rest in the king's service. The king, to indemnify him, gives him 400,000 livres on the salt revenue, and 80,000 livres income on the company privileged to refine the precious metals."

[5] Report of fixed incomes and expenditures, May 1st, 1789, p. 633. These figures, it must be noted, must be doubled to have their actual equivalent.

they cannot enrich themselves by their places. All keep open
table at Paris three days in the week, and at Fontainebleau every
day."[1] M. de Lamoignon being appointed Chancellor with a
salary of 100,000 livres, people at once declare that he will be
ruined;[2] "for he has taken all the officials of M. d'Aguesseau's
kitchen, whose table alone cost 80,000 livres. The banquet he
gave at Versailles to the first council held by him cost 6,000
livres, and he must always have seats at table, at Versailles and
at Paris, for twenty persons." At Chambord,[3] Marshal de Saxe
always has two tables, one for sixty, and the other for eighty
persons; also four hundred horses in his stables, a civil list of
more than 100,000 crowns, a regiment of Uhlans for his guard,
and a theatre costing over 600,000 livres, while the life he leads,
or which is maintained around him, resembles one of Rubens's
bacchanalian scenes. As to the special and general provincial
governors we have seen that, when they reside on the spot, they
fulfil no other duty than to entertain; alongside of them the intendant, who alone attends to business, likewise receives, and
magnificently, especially for the country of a States-General.
Commandants, lieutenants-general, the envoys of the central
government throughout, are equally induced by habit and propriety, as well as by their own lack of occupation, to maintain a drawing-room; they bring along with them the elegancies and hospitality of Versailles. If the wife follows them she becomes weary
and "vegetates in the midst of about fifty companions, talking
nothing but commonplace, knitting or playing loto, and sitting
three hours at the dinner table." But "all the military men, all
the neighboring gentry and all the ladies in the town," eagerly
crowd to her balls and delight in commending "her grace, her
politeness, her equality."[4] These sumptuous habits prevail even
among people of secondary position. By virtue of established
usage colonels and captains entertain their subordinates and thus
expend "much beyond their salaries."[5] This is one of the reasons why regiments are reserved for the sons of the best

[1] Mme. de Genlis, "Dict. des Etiquettes," I. 349.
[2] Barbier, "Journal," III. 211 (December, 1750).
[3] Aubertin, "L'Esprit public au dix-huitième siècle," 255.
[4] Mme. de Genlis, "Adèle et Théodore," III. 54.
[5] Duc de Lévis, 68. The same thing is found, previous to the late reform, in the English army. Cf. Voltaire, "Entretiens entre A, B, C," 15th entretien. "A regiment is not the reward for services but rather for the sum which the parents of a young man advance in order that he may go to the provinces for three months in the year and keep open house."

families, and companies in them for wealthy gentlemen. The vast royal tree, expanding so luxuriantly at Versailles, sends forth its offshoots to overrun France by thousands, and to bloom everywhere, as at Versailles, in bouquets of holiday sport and of drawing-room sociability.

VII.

Following this pattern, and as well through the effect of temperature, we see, even in remote provinces, all aristocratic branches tending to a worldly efflorescence. Lacking other employment, the nobles interchange visits, and the chief function of a prominent seignior is to do the honors of his house creditably. This applies as well to ecclesiastics as to laymen. The one hundred and thirty-one bishops and archbishops, the seven hundred abbés-commendatory, are all men of the world; they behave well, are rich, and are not austere, while their episcopal palace or abbey is for them a country-house, which they repair or embellish with a view to the time they pass in it, and to the company they welcome to it.[1] At Clairvaux, Dom Rocourt, very affable with men and still more gallant with the ladies, never drives out except with four horses, and with a mounted groom ahead; his monks do him the honors of a Monseigneur, and he maintains a veritable court. The chartreuse of Val Saint-Pierre is a sumptuous palace in the centre of an immense domain, and the father-procurator, Dom Effinger, passes his days in entertaining his guests.[2] At the convent of Origny, near Saint-Quentin,[3] "the abbess has her domestics and her carriage and horses, and receives men on visits, who dine in her apartments." The princess Christine, abbess of Remiremont, with her lady canonesses, are almost always travelling; and yet "they enjoy themselves in the abbey," entertaining there a good many people "in the private apartments of the princess, and in the strangers' rooms."[4] The twenty-five noble chapters of women, and the nineteen noble chapters of men, are as many permanent drawing-rooms and gathering places incessantly resorted to by the fine society which a slight ecclesiastical barrier scarcely divides from the great

[1] Beugnot, I. 79.
[2] Merlin de Thionville, "Vie et Correspondances." Account of his visit to the chartreuse of Val St. Pierre in Thierarche.
[3] Mme. de Genlis, "Mémoires," ch. vii.
[4] Mme. d'Oberkirk, I. 15.

world from which it is recruited. At the chapter of Alix, near
Lyons, the canonesses wear hoopskirts into the choir, "dressed
as in the world outside," except that their black silk robes and
their mantles are lined with ermine.[1] At the chapter of Ott-
marsheim in Alsace, "our week was passed in promenading, in
visiting the traces of Roman roads, in laughing a good deal, and
even in dancing, for there were many people visiting the abbey,
and especially talking over dresses." Near Sarrelouis, the canonesses of Loutre dine with the officers and are anything but pru-
dish.[2] Numbers of convents serve as agreeable and respectable
asylums for widowed ladies, for young women whose husbands
are in the army, and for young ladies of rank, while the superior,
generally some noble damsel, wields, with ease and dexterity, the
sceptre of this pretty feminine world. But nowhere is the pomp
of hospitality or the concourse greater, than in the episcopal palaces. I have described the situation of the bishops; with their
opulence, possessors of the like feudal rights, heirs and successors
to the ancient sovereigns of the territory, and besides all this, men
of the world and frequenters of Versailles, why should they not
keep a court? A Cicé, archbishop of Bordeaux, a Dillon, archbishop of Narbonne, a Brienne, archbishop of Toulouse, a Castellane, bishop of Mende and seignior-suzerain of the whole of
Gévaudan, an archbishop of Cambrai, duke of Cambray, seignior-suzerain of the whole of Cambrésis, and president by birth
of the provincial States-General, are nearly all princes;—why not
parade themselves like princes? Hence, they build, hunt and
have their clients and guests, a *lever*, an antechamber, ushers, officers, a free table, a complete household, equipages, and, oftener
still, debts, the finishing touch of a grand seignior. In the almost regal palace which the Rohans, hereditary bishops of Strasbourg and cardinals from uncle to nephew, erected for themselves
at Saverne,[3] there are 700 beds, 180 horses, 14 butlers, and 25
valets. "The whole province assembles there;" the cardinal
lodges as many as two hundred guests at a time, without counting the valets; at all times there are found under his roof "from
twenty to thirty ladies the most agreeable of the province, and

---

[1] Mme. de Genlis, I. ch. xxvi. Mme. d'Oberkirk, I. 62.
[2] De Lauzun, "Mémoires," 257.
[3] Marquis de Valfons, "Mémoires," 60. De Lévis, 156. Mme. d'Oberkirk, I. 127., II.
360.

this number is often increased by those of the court and from Paris. . . . The entire company sup together at nine o'clock in the evening, which always looks like a fête," and the cardinal himself is its chief ornament. Splendidly dressed, fine-looking, gallant, exquisitely polite, the slightest smile is a grace. "His face, always beaming, inspired confidence; he had the true physiognomy of a man expressly designed for pompous display."

Such likewise is the attitude and occupation of the principal lay seigniors, at home, in summer, when a love of the charms of fine weather brings them back to their estates. For example, Harcourt in Normandy and Brienne in Champagne are two chateaux the best frequented. " Persons of distinction resort to it from Paris, eminent men of letters, while the nobility of the canton pay there an assiduous court."[1] There is no residence where flocks of fashionable people do not light down permanently to dine, to dance, to hunt, to gossip, to unravel,[2] *(parfiler)* to play comedy. We can trace these birds from cage to cage; they remain a week, a month, three months, displaying their plumage and their prattle. From Paris to Ile-Adam, to Villers-Cotterets, to Frétoy, to Planchette, to Soissons, to Rheims, to Grisolles, to Sillery, to Braine, to Balincourt, to Vaudreuil, the Comte and Comtesse de Genlis thus bear about their leisure, their wit, their gaiety, at the domiciles of friends whom, in their turn, they entertain at Genlis. A glance at the exteriors of these mansions suffices to show that it was the chief duty in these days to be hospitable, as it was a prime necessity to be in society.[3] Their luxury, indeed, differs from ours. With the exception of a few princely establishments it is not great in the matter of country furniture ; a display of this description is left to the financiers. " But it is prodigious in all things which can minister to the enjoyment of others, in horses, carriages, and in an open table, in accommodations given even to people not belonging to the house, in boxes at the play which are lent to friends, and lastly, in servants, much more numerous than nowadays." Through this mutual and constant attention the most rustic nobles lose the rust still encrusting their brethren in Germany or in England. We find in France few Squire Westerns and Barons de Thunder-

---

[1] Beugnot, I. 71. Hippeau, " Le Gouvernement de Normandie," *passim.*
[2] An occupation explained farther on, page 145.—TR.
[3] Mme. de Genlis, " Mémoires," *passim.* " Dict. des Étiquettes," I. 348.

tentroenck ; an Alsatian lady, on seeing at Frankfort the grotesque country squires of Westphalia, is struck with the contrast.[1] Those of France, even in distant provinces, have frequented the drawing-rooms of the commandant and intendant, and have encountered on their visits some of the ladies from Versailles; hence "they always show some familiarity with superior manners and some knowledge of the changes of fashion and dress." The most barbarous will descend, with his hat in his hand, to the foot of his steps to escort his guests, thanking them for the honor they have done him. The greatest rustic, when in a woman's presence, dives down into the depths of his memory for some fragment of chivalric gallantry. The poorest and most secluded furbishes up his coat of royal blue and his cross of St. Louis that he may, when the occasion offers, tender his respects to his neighbor, the grand seignior, or to the prince who is passing by.

Thus is the feudal staff wholly transformed, from the lowest to the highest grades. Taking in at one glance its thirty or forty thousand palaces, mansions, manors and abbeys, what a brilliant and engaging scene France presents! She is one vast drawing-room, and I detect only drawing-room company. Everywhere the rude chieftains once possessing authority have become the masters of households administering favors. Their society is that in which, before fully admiring a great general, the question is asked, "is he amiable ? " Undoubtedly they still wear swords, and are brave through self-love and tradition, and they know how to die, especially in duels and according to form. But worldly traits have overspread the ancient military groundwork; at the end of the eighteenth century their genius is to be well-bred and their employment consists in entertaining or in being entertained.

---

[1] Mme. d'Oberkirk, I. 395. The Baron and Baroness de Sotenville in Molière are people well brought up although provincial and pedantic.

CHAPTER II.

SIMILAR circumstances have led other aristocracies in Europe
to nearly similar ways and habits. There also the monarchy
has given birth to the court and the court to a refined society.
But the development of this rare plant has been only partial.
The soil was unfavorable and the seed was not of the right sort.
In Spain, the king stands shrouded in etiquette like a mummy
in its wrappings, while a too rigid pride, incapable of yielding to
the amenities of the worldly order of things, ends in a sentiment
of morbidity and in insane display.[1] In Italy, under petty despotic sovereigns, and most of them strangers, the constant state
of danger and of hereditary distrust, after having tied all tongues,
turns all hearts towards the secret delights of love or towards
the mute gratifications of the fine arts. In Germany and in
England, a cold temperament, dull and rebellious to culture,

---

[1] De Loménie, "Beaumarchais et son temps," I. 403. Letter of Beaumarchais, Dec. 24,
1764. The travels of Mme. d'Aulnoy and the letters of Mme. de Villars. As to Italy see
Stendhal, "Rome, Naples et Florence." For Germany see the "Mémoires" of the Mar-
grave of Bareith, also of the Chevalier Lang. For England see my "Histoire de la littérature Anglaise," vols. III., IV.

keeps man, up to the close of the last century, within the Germanic habits of solitude, inebriety and brutality. In France, on the contrary, all things combine to make the social sentiment flourish; in this the national genius harmonizes with the political régime, the plant appearing to be selected for the soil beforehand.

The Frenchman loves company through instinct, and the reason is that he does well and easily whatever society calls upon him to do. He has not the false shame which renders his northern neighbors awkward, nor the powerful passions which absorb his neighbors of the south. Talking is no effort to him, having none of the natural timidity which begets constraint, and with no constant preoccupation to overcome. He accordingly converses at his ease, ever on the alert, and conversation affords him extreme pleasure. For the happiness which he requires is of a peculiar kind: delicate, light, rapid, incessantly renewed and varied, in which his intellect, his self-love, all his emotional and sympathetic faculties find nutriment; and this quality of happiness is provided for him only in society and in conversation. Sensitive as he is, personal attention, consideration, cordiality, delicate flattery, constitute his natal atmosphere, out of which he breathes with difficulty. He would suffer almost as much in being impolite as in encountering impoliteness in others. For his instincts of kindliness and vanity there is an exquisite charm in the habit of being amiable, and this is all the greater because it proves contagious. When we afford pleasure to others there is a desire to please us, and what we bestow in deference is returned in attentions. In company of this kind one can talk, for to talk is to amuse another in being oneself amused, a Frenchman finding no pleasure equal to it.[1] Lively and sinuous, conversation to him is like the flying of a bird; he wings his way from idea to idea, alert, excited by the inspiration of others, darting forward, wheeling round and unexpectedly returning, now up, now down, now skimming the ground, now aloft on the peaks, without sinking into quagmires, or getting entangled in the briers, and claiming nothing of the thousands of objects he slightly grazes but the diversity and the gaiety of their aspects.

---

[1] Volney, "Tableau du climat et du sol des Etats-Unis d'Amérique." The leading trait of the French colonist when compared with the colonists of other nations, is, according to this writer, the craving for neighbors and conversation.

Thus endowed, and thus disposed, he is made for a régime which, for ten hours a day, brings men together; natural feeling in accord with the social order of things renders the drawing-room perfect. The king, at the head of all, sets the example. Louis XIV. had every qualification for the master of a household: a taste for pomp and hospitality, condescension accompanied with dignity, the art of playing on the self-love of others and of maintaining his own position, chivalrous gallantry, tact, and even charms of intellectual expression. "His address was perfect; [1] whether it was necessary to jest, or he was in a playful humor, or deigned to tell a story, it was ever with infinite grace, and a noble refined air which I have found only in him." "Never was man so naturally polite, [2] nor of such circumspect politeness, so powerful by degrees, nor who better discriminated age, worth, and rank, both in his replies and in his deportment. . . . His salutations, more or less marked, but always slight, were of incomparable grace and majesty. . . . He was admirable in the different acknowledgments of salutes at the head of the army and at reviews. . . . But especially toward women there was nothing like it. . . . Never did he pass the most insignificant woman without taking off his hat to her; and I mean chambermaids whom he knew to be such. . . . Never did he chance to say anything disobliging to anybody. . . . Never before company anything mistimed or venturesome, but even to the smallest gesture, his walk, his bearing, his features, all were proper, respectful, noble, grand, majestic, and thoroughly natural."

Such is the model, and, nearly or remotely, it is imitated up to the end of the ancient régime. If it undergoes any change, it is only to become more sociable. In the eighteenth century, except on great ceremonial occasions, it is seen descending step by step from its pedestal. It no longer imposes "that stillness around it which lets one hear a fly walk." "Sire," said the Marshal de Richelieu, who had seen three reigns, addressing Louis XVI., "under Louis XIV. no one dared utter a word; under Louis XV. people whispered; under your Majesty they talk aloud." If authority is a loser, society is the gainer; etiquette, insensibly relaxed, allows the introduction of ease and cheerfulness. Henceforth the great, less concerned in overawing than in pleasing, cast

---

[1] Mme. de Caylus, "Souvenirs," p. 108.
[2] St. Simon, 461.

off stateliness like an uncomfortable and ridiculous garment, "seeking respect less than applause. It no longer suffices to be affable; one has to appear amiable at any cost with one's inferiors as with one's equals."[1] The French princes, says again a contemporary lady, "are dying with fear of being deficient in favors."[2] Even around the throne "the style is free and playful." The grave and disciplined court of Louis XIV. became at the end of the century, under the smiles of the youthful queen, the most seductive and gayest of drawing-rooms. Through this universal relaxation, a worldly existence gets to be perfect. "He who was not living before 1789," says Talleyrand at a later period, "knows nothing of the charm of living." It was too great; no other way of living was appreciated; it engrossed man wholly. When society becomes so attractive, people live for it alone.

II.

There is neither leisure nor taste for other matters, even for things which are of most concern to man, such as public affairs, the household, and the family. With respect to the first, I have already stated that people abstain from them, and are indifferent; the administration of things, whether local or general, is out of their hands and no longer interests them. They only allude to it in jest; events of the most serious consequence form the subject of witticisms. After the edict of the Abbé Terray, which half ruined the state creditors, a spectator, too much crowded in the theatre, cried out, "Ah, how unfortunate that our good Abbé Terray is not here to cut us down one-half!" Everybody laughs and applauds. All Paris the following day, is consoled for public ruin by repeating the phrase. Alliances, battles, taxation, treaties, ministries, *coups d'état*, the entire history of the country, is put

---

[1] Duc. le Lévis, p. 321.

[2] Mme. de Genlis, "Souvenirs de Félicie," p. 160. It is important, however, to call attention to the old-fashioned royal attitude under Louis XV. and even Louis XVI. "Although I was advised," says Alfieri, "that the king never addressed ordinary strangers, I could not digest the Olympian-Jupiter look with which Louis XV. measured the person presented to him, from head to foot, with such an impassible air; if a fly should be introduced to a giant, the giant, after looking at him, would smile, or perhaps remark.—'What a little mite!' In any event, if he said nothing, his face would express it for him." Alfieri, "Mémoires," I. 138, 1768. See in Mme. d'Oberkirk's "Mémoires," (II. 349), the lesson administered by Mme. Royale, aged seven and a half years, to a lady introduced to her.

into epigrams and songs. One day,[1] in an assembly of young people belonging to the court, one of them, as the current witticism was passing around, raised his hands in delight and exclaimed, "How can one help being pleased with great events, even with disturbances, when they give us such wit!" Thereupon the wit circulates, and every disaster in France is turned into nonsense. A song on the battle of Hochstaedt was pronounced poor, and some one in this connection said: "I am sorry that battle was lost—the song is so worthless."[2]

Even when eliminating from this trait all that belongs to the sway of impulse and the license of paradox, there remains the stamp of an age in which the State is almost nothing and society almost everything. We may on this principle divine what order of talent was required in the ministers. M. Necker, having given a magnificent supper with serious and comic opera, "finds that this festivity is worth more to him in credit, favor, and stability than all his financial schemes put together. . . . His last arrangement concerning the *vingtième* excited remark only for one day, while everybody is still talking about his fête; at Paris, as well as in Versailles, its attractions are dwelt on in detail, people emphatically declaring that Monsieur and Mme. Necker are a grace to society."[3] Good society devoted to pleasure imposes on those in office the obligation of providing pleasures for it. It might also say, in a half-serious, half-ironical tone, with Voltaire, "that the gods created kings only to give fêtes every day, provided they differ; that life is too short to make any other use of it; that lawsuits, intrigues, warfare, and the quarrels of priests, which consume human life, are absurd and horrible things; that man is born only to enjoy himself;" and that among the essential things we must put the "superfluous" in the first rank.

According to this, we can easily foresee that they will be as little concerned with their private affairs as with public affairs. Housekeeping, the management of property, domestic economy,

[1] Champfort, 26, 55; Bachaumont, I. 136 (Sept. 7, 1762). One month after the Parliament had passed a law against the Jesuits, little Jesuits in wax appeared, with a snail for a base. "By means of a thread the Jesuit was made to pop in and out from the shell. It is all the rage—there is no house without its Jesuit."
[2] On the other hand, the song on the battle of Rosbach is fine.
[3] "Correspondance secrète," by Métra, Imbert, etc., V. 277 (Nov. 17, 1777). Voltaire, "Princesse de Babylone."

are in their eyes vulgar, insipid in the highest degree, and only
suited to an intendant or a butler.   Of what use are such persons if we must have such cares ?   Life is no longer a festival if
one has to provide the ways and means.   Comforts, luxuries, the
agreeable must flow naturally and greet our lips of their own accord.   As a matter of course and without his intervention, a man
belonging to this world should find gold always in his pocket, a
handsome coat on his toilet table, powdered valets in his antechamber, a gilded coach at his door, a fine dinner on his table,
so that he may reserve all his attention to be expended in favors
on the guests in his drawing-room.   Such a mode of living
is not to be maintained without waste, and the domestics, left to
themselves, make the most of it.   What matter is it, so long as
they perform their duties ?   Moreover, everybody must live, and
it is pleasant to have contented and obsequious faces around one.
Hence the first houses in the kingdom are given up to pillage.
Louis XV., on a hunting expedition one day, accompanied by
the Duc de Choiseul,[1] inquired of him how much he thought
the carriage in which they were seated had cost.   M. de Choiseul replied that he should consider himself fortunate to get one
like it for 5,000 or 6,000 francs; but, " His Majesty paying for
it as a king, and not always paying cash, might have paid
8,000 francs for it. "   " You are wide of the mark, " rejoined the
king, "for this vehicle, as you see it, cost me 30,000 francs. . . .
The robberies in my household are enormous, but it is impossible to put a stop to them. "   In effect, the great help themselves
as well as the little, either in money, or in kind, or in services.
There are in the king's household fifty-four horses for the grand
equerry, thirty-eight of them being for Mme. de Brionne, the
administratrix of the office of the stables during her son's minority; there are two hundred and fifteen grooms on duty, and
about as many horses kept at the king's expense for various other
persons, entire strangers to the department.[2]   What a nest of
parasites on this one branch of the royal tree !   Elsewhere I find
Madame Elisabeth, so moderate, consuming fish amounting to
30,000 francs per annum ; meat and game to 70,000 francs; candles to 60,000 francs; Mesdames burn white and yellow candles to

---

[1] De Bezenval, "Mémoires," II. 206.   An anecdote related by the Duke.
[2] Archives nationales, a report by M. Texier (1780).   A report by M. Mesnard de Chousy
(O¹, 738).

the amount of 215,068 francs; the light for the queen comes to 157,109 francs. The street at Versailles is still shown, formerly lined with stalls, to which the king's valets resorted to nourish Versailles by the sale of his dessert. There is no article from which the domestic insects do not manage to scrape and glean something. The king is supposed to drink orgeat and lemonade to the value of 2,190 francs. "The grand broth, day and night," which Mme. Royale, aged six years, sometimes drinks, costs 5,201 francs per annum. Towards the end of the preceding reign [1] the *femmes-de-chambre* enumerate in the Dauphine's outlay "four pairs of shoes per week; three ells of ribbon per diem, to tie her dressing-gown; two ells of taffeta per diem, to cover the basket in which she keeps her gloves and fan." A few years earlier the king paid 200,000 francs for coffee, lemonade, chocolate, orgeat, and water-ices; several persons were inscribed on the list for ten or twelve cups a day, while it was estimated that the coffee, milk and bread each morning for each lady of the bed-chamber cost 2,000 francs per annum.[2] We can readily understand how, in households thus managed, the purveyors are willing to wait. They wait so well that often under Louis XV. they refuse to provide and "hide themselves." Even the delay is so regular that, at last, they are obliged to pay them five per cent. interest on their advances; at this rate, in 1778, after all Turgot's economic reforms, the king still owes nearly 800,000 livres to his wine merchant, and nearly three millions and a half to his purveyor.[3] The same disorder exists in the houses which surround the throne. "Mme. de Guéménée owes 60,000 livres to her shoe-maker, 16,000 livres to her paper-hanger, and the rest in proportion." Another lady, whom the Marquis de Mirabeau sees with hired horses, replies at his look of astonishment, "It is not because there are not seventy horses in our stables, but none of them are able to walk to-day."[4] Mme. de Montmorin, on ascertaining that her husband's debts are greater than his property, thinks she can save her dowry of 200,000 livres, but is informed that she had given security for a tailor's bill, which, "incredible

---

[1] "Marie Antoinette," by d'Arneth and Geffroy, I. 277 (February 29, 1772).
[2] De Luynes, XVII. 37 (August, 1758). D'Argenson, February 11, 1753.
[3] Archives nationales, O¹, 738. Various sums of interest are paid: 12,969 francs to the baker, 39,631 francs to the wine merchant, and 173,899 francs to the purveyor.
[4] Marquis de Mirabeau, "Traité de Population," 60. "Le Gouvernement de Normandie," by Hippeau, II. 204 (Sept. 30, 1780).

K

and ridiculous to say, amounts to the sum of 180,000 livres."[1]
"One of the decided manias of these days," says Mme. d'Oberkirk, "is to be ruined in everything and by everything." "The
two brothers Villemer build country cottages at from 500,000 to
600,000 livres; one of them keeps forty horses to ride occasionally in the Bois de Boulogne on horseback."[2]   In one night M.
de Chenonceaux, son of M. et Mme. Dupin, loses at play
700,000 livres. "M. de Chenonceaux and M. de Francueil ran
through seven or eight millions at this epoch."[3]   "The Duc de
Lauzun, at the age of twenty-six, after having run through the
capital of 100,000 crowns revenue, is prosecuted by his creditors for nearly two millions of indebtedness."[4]   "M. le Prince
de Conti lacks bread and wood, although with an income of
600,000 livres," for the reason that "he buys and builds wildly
on all sides."[5]   Where would be the pleasure if these people
were reasonable?   What kind of a seignior is he who studies the
price of things?   And how can the exquisite be reached if one
grudges money?   Money, accordingly, must flow and flow on
until it is exhausted, first by the innumerable secret or tolerated
bleedings through domestic abuses, and next in broad streams of
the master's own prodigality, through structures, furniture, toilets,
hospitality, gallantry, and pleasures.   The Comte d'Artois, that
he may give the queen a fête, demolishes, rebuilds, arranges, and
furnishes Bagatelle from top to bottom, employing nine hundred
workmen, day and night, and, as there is no time to go any distance for lime, plaster, and cut stone, he sends patrols of the
Swiss guards on the highways to seize, pay for, and immediately
bring in all carts thus loaded.[6]   The Marshal de Soubise, entertaining the king one day at dinner and over night, in his country
house, expends 200,000 livres.[7]   Mme. de Matignon makes a contract to be furnished every day with a new head-dress at 24,000
livres per annum.   Cardinal de Rohan has an alb bordered with

---

[1] Mme. de Larochejacquelein, "Mémoires," p. 30.   Mme. d'Oberkirk, II. 66.
[2] D'Argenson, January 26, 1753.
[3] George Sand, "Histoire de ma vie," I. 78.
[4] "Marie Antoinette," by d'Arneth and Geffroy, I. 61 (March 18, 1777).
[5] D'Argenson, January 26, 1753.
[6] "Marie Antoinette," III. 135, November 19, 1777.
[7] Barbier, IV., 155.   The Marshal de Soubise had a hunting lodge to which the king came
from time to time to eat an omelet of pheasants' eggs, costing 157 livres, 10 sous.   (Mercier,
XII. 192; also, according to the cook's statement who made it.)

point lace, which is valued at more than 100,000 livres, while his kitchen utensils are of massive silver.[1]

Nothing is more natural, considering their ideas of money; hoarded and piled up, instead of being a fertilizing stream, it is a useless marsh exhaling bad odors.   The queen, having presented the Dauphin with a carriage whose silver-gilt trappings are decked with rubies and sapphires, naïvely exclaims, " Has not the king added 200,000 livres to my treasury?   That is no reason for keeping them!"[2]   They would rather throw it out of the window,—which was actually done by the Marshal de Richelieu with a purse he had given to his grandson, and which the lad, not knowing how to use, brought back intact.   Money, on this occasion, was at least of service to the passing street-sweeper that picked it up.   But had there been no passer-by to pick it up, it would have been thrown into the river.   One day Mme. de B——, being with the Prince de Conti, hinted that she would like a miniature of her canary bird set in a ring.   The Prince offers to have it made. His offer is accepted, but on condition that the miniature be set plain and without jewels.   Accordingly the miniature is placed in a simple rim of gold.   But, to cover over the painting, a large diamond, made very thin, serves as a glass.   Mme. de B——, having returned the diamond, "M. le Prince de Conti had it ground to powder which he used to dry the ink of the note he wrote to Mme. de B—— on the subject."   This pinch of powder cost four or five thousand livres, but we may divine the turn and tone of the note.   The extreme of profusion must accompany the height of gallantry, the man of the world being so much the more important according to his contempt for money.

III.

In a drawing-room the wife who receives the least attention from a man is his own, and she returns the compliment.   Hence at a time like this, when people live for society and in society, there is no place for conjugal intimacy.   Moreover, when a married couple occupy an exalted position they are separated by cus-

---

[1] Mme. d'Oberkirk, I. 129, II. 257.

[2] Mme. de Genlis, "Souvenirs de Félicie," 80; and "Théâtre de l'Education," II. 367.   A virtuous young woman in ten months runs into debt to the amount of 70,000 francs: "Ten louis for a small table, 15 louis for another, 800 francs for a bureau, 200 francs for a small writing desk, 300 francs for a large one; hair rings, hair glass, hair chain, hair bracelets, hair clasps, hair necklace, hair box, 9,900 francs," etc.

tom and decorum.   Each party has his or her own household, or
at least their own apartments, servants, equipage, receptions and
distinct society, and, as self-parade entails ceremony, they stand
towards each other in deference to their rank on the footing of
polite strangers.   They are each announced in each other's apartment; they address each other " Madame, Monsieur," and not
alone in public, but in private; they shrug their shoulders when,
sixty leagues out from Paris, they encounter in some old chateau a
provincial wife ignorant enough to say " my dear " to her husband before company.[1]   Already separated at the fireside, the
two lives diverge beyond it at an ever increasing radius.   The
husband has a government of his own: his private command, his
private regiment, his post at court, which keeps him absent from
home; only in his declining years does his wife consent to follow
him into garrison or into the provinces.[2]   And rather is this the
case because she is herself occupied, and as seriously as himself;
often with a position near a princess, and always with an important
circle of company which she must maintain.   At this epoch woman
is as active as man,[3] following the same career, and with the same
resources, consisting of the flexible voice, the winning grace, the
insinuating manner, the tact, the quick perception of the right
moment, and the art of pleasing, demanding, and obtaining;
there is not a lady at court who does not bestow regiments and
benefices.   Through this right the wife has her personal retinue
of solicitors and protégés, also, like her husband, her friends, her
enemies, her own ambitions, disappointments, and rancorous feeling; nothing could be more effectual in the disruption of a
household than this similarity of occupation and this division of
interests.   The tie thus loosened ends by being sundered under

---

[1] Mme. de Genlis, " Adèle et Théodore," III. 14.

[2] Mme. d'Avray, sister of Mme. de Genlis, sets the example, for which she is at first much
criticized.

[3] "When I arrived in France M. de Choiseul's reign was just over.   The wife who could
please him, or even please his sister-in-law the Duchesse de Gramont, was sure of setting
crazy every colonel and lieutenant-general she was acquainted with.   Women were of consequence even in the eyes of the old and of the clergy; they were thoroughly familiar, to an
extraordinary degree, with the march of events; they knew by heart the characters and
habits of the king's friends and ministers.   One of these, on returning to his chateau from
Versailles, informed his wife about every thing with which he had been occupied; with us he
says one or two words to her about her water-color sketches, or remains silent and thoughtful,
pondering over what he has just heard in Parliament.   Our poor ladies are abandoned to the
society of those frivolous men who, for want of intellect, have no ambition, and of course no
employment (dandies)."   (Stendhal, "Rome, Naples, and Florence," 377.   A narrative by
Colonel Forsyth).

the ascendency of opinion. " It looks well not to live together," to grant each other every species of tolerance, and to devote oneself to society. Society, indeed, then fashions opinion, and through opinion it urges on the habits which it requires.

Toward the middle of the century the husband and wife lodge under the same roof, but that is all. " They are never at home in private ; they are never encountered in the same carriage ; they are never met in the same house ; nor, through the necessity of the case, are they ever together in public." Profound sentiment would have seemed odd and even " ridiculous ;" in any event unbecoming ; it would have been as unacceptable as an earnest " aside " in the general current of light conversation. Each has a duty to all, and for a couple to entertain each other is isolation ; in company there exists no right of the tête-à-tête.[1] It was hardly allowed for a few days to lovers.[2] And even then it was regarded unfavorably ; they were found too much occupied with each other. Their preoccupation diffused around them an atmosphere of " constraint and *ennui;* one had to be upon one's guard and to check oneself." They were " dreaded." The exigencies of society are those of an absolute king, and admit of no partition. " If morals lost by this, society was infinitely the gainer," says M. de Bezenval, a contemporary ; " having got rid of the annoyances and dulness caused by the husbands' presence, the freedom was extreme ; the coquetry both of men and women kept up social vivacity and daily provided piquant adventures." Nobody is jealous, not even when in love. " People are mutually pleased and become attached ; if one grows weary of the other, they part with as little concern as they came together. Should the sentiment revive they take to each other with as much vivacity as if it were the first time they had been engaged. They may again separate, but they never quarrel. As they have become enamored without love, they part without hate, deriving from the feeble desire they have inspired the advantage of being always ready to oblige."[3] Appearances, moreover, are respected. An uninformed stranger would detect

---

[1] De Bezenval, 49, 60. "Out of twenty seigniors at the court there are fifteen not living with their wives, and keeping mistresses. Nothing is so common at Paris among certain persons." (Barbier, IV. 496.)

[2] Ne soyez point epoux, ne soyez point amant.
Soyez l'homme du jour et vous serez charmant.

[3] Crébillon *fils,* "La nuit et le moment," IX. 14.

nothing to excite suspicion. An extreme curiosity, says Horace Walpole,[1] or a great familiarity with things, is necessary to detect the slightest intimacy between the two sexes. No familiarity is allowed except under the guise of friendship, while the vocabulary of love is as much prohibited as its rites apparently are. Even with Crébillon *fils*, even with Laclos, at the most exciting moments, the terms their characters employ are circumspect and irreproachable. Whatever indecency there may be, it is never expressed in words, the sense of propriety in language imposing itself not only on the outbursts of passion, but again on the grossness of instincts. Thus do the sentiments which are naturally the strongest lose their point and sharpness; their rich and polished remains are converted into playthings for the drawing-room, and, thus cast to and fro by the whitest hands, fall on the floor like a shuttlecock. We must, on this point, listen to the heroes of the epoch; their free and easy tone is inimitable, and it depicts both them and their actions. "I conducted myself," says the Duc de Lauzun, " very prudently, and even deferentially with Mme. de Lauzun; I knew Mme. de Cambis very openly, for whom I concerned myself very little; I kept the little Eugénie whom I loved a great deal; I played high, I paid my court to the king, and I hunted with him with great punctuality."[2] He had for others, withal, that indulgence of which he himself stood in need. "He was asked what he would say if his wife (whom he had not seen for ten years) should write to him that she had just discovered that she was *enceinte*. He reflected a moment and then replied, 'I would write, and tell her that I was delighted that heaven had blessed our union; be careful of your health; I will call and pay my respects this evening.'" There are countless replies of the same sort, and I venture to say that, without having read them, one could not imagine to what a degree social art had overcome natural instincts.

[1] Horace Walpole's letters (January 25, 1766). The Duke de Brissac, at Louveciennes, the lover of Mme. du Barry, and passionately fond of her, always in her society assumed the attitude of a polite stranger. (Mme. Vigée-Lebrun, "Souvenirs," I. 165.)

[2] De Lauzun, 51. Champfort, 39. "The Duc de ―― whose wife had just been the subject of scandal, complained to her mother-in-law; the latter replied with the greatest coolness, 'Eh, Monsieur, you make a good deal of talk about nothing. Your father was accustomed to better company.'" (Mme. d'Oberkirk, II. 135, 241). "A husband said to his wife, 'I allow you everybody excepting princes and lackeys.' He was true to the fact, these two extremes bringing dishonor on account of the scandal attached to them." (Sénac de Meilhan, "Considerations sur les Mœurs"). On a wife being discovered by a husband, he simply exclaims, "Madame, what imprudence! Suppose that I was any other man." ("La femme au dix-huitième siècle," 201.)

"Here at Paris," writes Mme. d'Oberkirk, "I am no longer my own mistress. I scarcely have time to talk with my husband and to answer my letters. I do not know what women do that are accustomed to lead this life; they certainly have no families to look after, nor children to educate." At all events they act as if they had none, and the men likewise. Married people not living together live but rarely with their children, and the causes which disintegrate wedlock also disintegrate the family. In the first place there is the aristocratic tradition, which interposes a barrier between parents and children with a view to maintain a respectful distance. Although enfeebled and about to disappear,[1] this tradition still subsists. The son says "Monsieur" to his father; the daughter comes "respectfully" to kiss her mother's hand at her toilet. A caress is rare and seems a favor; children generally, when with their parents, are silent, the sentiment that usually animates them being that of deferential timidity. At one time they were regarded as so many subjects, and up to a certain point they are so still; while the new exigencies of worldly life place them or keep them effectually aside. M. de Talleyrand stated that he had never slept under the same roof with his father and mother. And if they do sleep there, they are not the less neglected. "I was entrusted," says the Count de Tilly, "to valets, and to a kind of preceptor resembling these in more respects than one." During this time his father ran after women. "I have known him," adds the young man, "to have mistresses up to an advanced age; he was always adoring them and constantly abandoning them." The Duc de Lauzun finds it difficult to obtain a good tutor for his son; for this reason the latter writes, "he conferred the duty on one of my late mother's lackeys who could read and write tolerably well, and to whom the title of *valet-de-chambre* was given to insure greater consideration. They gave me the most fashionable teachers besides; but M. Roch (which was my mentor's name) was not qualified to arrange

[1] See in this relation the somewhat ancient types, especially in the provinces. "My mother, my sister, and myself, transformed into statues by my father's presence, only recover ourselves after he leaves the room." (Chateaubriand, "Mémoires," I. 17, 28, 130; "Mémoires de Mirabeau," I. 53.) The Marquis said of his father Antoine: "I never had the honor of kissing the cheek of that venerable man. . . . At the Academy, being two hundred leagues away from him, the mere thought of him made me dread every youthful amusement which could be followed by the least unfavorable results." Paternal authority seems almost as rigid among the middle and lower classes. ("Beaumarchais et son temps," by De Loménie, I. 23; "Vie de mon père," by Restif de la Bretonne, *passim*.)

their lessons, nor to qualify me to benefit by them. I was, more-over, like all the children of my age and of my station, dressed in the handsomest clothes to go out, and naked and dying with hunger in the house," [1] and not through unkindness, but through household oversight, dissipation, and disorder, attention being given to things elsewhere. One might easily count the fathers who, like the Marshal de Belle-Isle, brought up their sons under their own eyes, and themselves attended to their education me-thodically, strictly, and with tenderness. As to the girls, they were placed in convents; relieved from this care, their parents only enjoy the greater freedom. Even when they retain charge of them they are scarcely more of a burden to them. Little Fé-licité de Saint-Aubin [2] sees her parents "only on their waking up and at meal times." Their day is wholly taken up; the mother is making or receiving visits; the father is in his laboratory or en-gaged in hunting. Up to seven years of age the child passes her time with chambermaids who teach her only a little catechism, "with an infinite number of ghost stories." About this time she is taken care of, but in a way which well portrays the epoch. The Marquise, her mother, the author of mythological and pas-toral operas, has a theatre built in the chateau; a great crowd of company resorts to it from Bourbon-Lancy and Moulins; after rehearsing twelve weeks the little girl, with a quiver of arrows and blue wings, plays the part of Cupid, and the costume is so be-coming she is allowed to wear it in common during the entire day for nine months. To finish the business they send for a dancing-fencing master, and, still wearing the Cupid costume, she takes les-sons in fencing and in deportment. "The entire winter is devoted to playing comedy and tragedy." Sent out of the room after din-ner, she is brought in again only to play on the harpsichord or to declaim the monologue of Alzire before a numerous assembly. Undoubtedly such extravagances are not customary; but the spirit of education is everywhere the same; that is to say, in the eyes of parents there is but one intelligible and rational existence, that of society, even for children, and the attentions bestowed on these are solely with a view to introduce them into it or to prepare them for it.

---

[1] Sainte-Beuve, "Nouveaux Lundis," XII. 13; Comte de Tilly, "Mémoires," I. 12; Duc de Lauzun, 5; "Beaumarchais," by De Loménie, II. 298.
[2] Madame de Genlis, "Mémoires," ch. ii. and iii.

Even in the last years of the ancient régime[1] little boys have their hair powdered, "a pomatumed chignon *(bourse)*, ringlets, and curls"; they wear the sword, the chapeau under the arm, a frill, and a coat with gilded cuffs; they kiss young ladies' hands with the air of little dandies. A lass of six years is bound up in a whalebone waist; her large hoop-petticoat supports a skirt covered with wreaths; she wears on her head a skilful combination of false curls, puffs, and knots, fastened with pins, and crowned with plumes, and so high that frequently "the chin is half way down to her feet"; sometimes they put rouge on her face. She is a miniature lady, and she knows it; she is fully up in her part, without effort or inconvenience, by force of habit; the unique, the perpetual instruction she gets is that on her deportment; it may be said with truth that the fulcrum of education in this country is the dancing-master.[2] They could get along with him without any others; without him the others were of no use. For, without him, how could people go through easily, suitably, and gracefully the thousand and one actions of daily life, walking, sitting down, standing up, offering the arm, using the fan, listening and smiling, before eyes so experienced and before such a refined public? This is to be the great thing for them when they become men and women, and for this reason it is the thing of chief importance for them as children. Along with graces of attitude and of gesture, they already have those of the mind and of expression. Scarcely is their tongue loosened when they speak the polished language of their parents. The latter amuse themselves with them and use them as pretty dolls; the preaching of Rousseau, which, during the last third of the last century, brought children into fashion, produces no other effect. They are made to recite their lessons in public, to perform in proverbs, to take parts in pastorals. Their sallies are encouraged. They know how to turn a compliment, to invent a clever or affecting repartee, to be gallant, sensitive, and even *spirituelle*. The little Duc d'Angoulême, holding a book in his hand, receives Suffren, whom he addresses thus: "I was reading Plutarch and his illus-

---

[1] Mme. d'Oberkirk, II. 35. This fashion lasts until 1783. De Goncourt, "La femme au dix-huitième siècle," 415. "Les petits parrains," an engraving by Moreau. Berquin, "L'ami des enfants," *passim*. Mme. de Genlis, "Théâtre de l'Education," *passim*.

[2] Le Sage, "Gil Blas": the discourse of the dancing-master charged with the education of the son of Count d'Olivarès.

trious men. You could not have entered more *apropos.*"[1] The
children of M. de Sabran, a boy and a girl, one eight and the
other nine, having taken lessons from the comedians Sainval and
Larive, come to Versailles to play before the king and queen in
Voltaire's "Oreste," and on the little fellow being interrogated
about the classic authors, he replies to a lady, the mother of three
charming girls, "Madame, Anacreon is the only poet I can think
of here!" Another, of the same age, replies to a question of
Prince Henry of Prussia with an agreeable impromptu in verse.[2]
To cause witticisms, insipidities, and mediocre verse to germi-
nate in a brain eight years old, what a triumph for the culture of
the day! It is the last characteristic of the régime which, after
having stolen man away from public affairs, from his own affairs,
from marriage, from the family, hands him over, with all his sentiments and all his faculties, to social worldliness, him and all that
belong to him. Below him fine ways and forced politeness prevail, even with his servants and tradesmen. A Frontin has a gallant unconstrained air, and he turns a compliment.[3] An abigail
needs only to be a kept mistress to become a lady. A shoe-
maker is a "monsieur in black," who says to a mother on saluting
the daughter, "Madame, a charming young person, and I am
more sensible than ever of the value of your kindness," on which
the young girl, just out of a convent, takes him for a suitor and
blushes scarlet. Undoubtedly less unsophisticated eyes would
distinguish the difference between this pinchbeck louis d'or and a
genuine one; but their resemblance suffices to show the universal
action of the central mint—machinery which stamps both with
the same effigy, the base metal and the refined gold.

IV.

A society which obtains such ascendency must possess some
charm; in no country, indeed, and in no age has so perfect a

---

[1] "Correspondance," by Métra, XIV. 212; XVI. 100. Mme. d'Oberkirk, II, 302.
[2] De Ségur, I. 297.

> Ma naissance n'a rien de neuf,
> J'ai suivi la commune règle,
> Mais c'est vous qui sortez d'un œuf,
> Car vous êtes un aigle.

Mme. de Genlis, "Mémoires," ch. iv. Mme. de Genlis wrote verses of this kind at twelve
years of age.

[3] Already in the Précieuses of Molière, the Marquis de Mascarille and the Vicomte de Jode-
let. And the same in Marivaux, "L'épreuve, les jeux de l'amour et du hasard," etc. Le
Sage, "Crispin rival de son maître." Laclos, "Les liaisons dangéreuses," first letter.

social art rendered life so agreeable. Paris is the school-house of Europe, a school of urbanity to which the youth of Russia, Germany, and England resort to become civilized. Lord Chesterfield in his letters never tires of reminding his son of this, and of urging him into these drawing-rooms, which will remove "his Cambridge rust." Once familiar with them they are never abandoned, or if one is obliged to leave them, one always sighs for them. "Nothing is comparable," says Voltaire,[1] "to the genial life one leads there in the bosom of the arts and of a calm and refined voluptuousness; strangers and monarchs have preferred this repose, so agreeably occupied in it and so enchanting to their own countries and thrones. The heart there softens and melts away like aromatics slowly dissolving in moderate heat, evaporating in delightful perfumes." Gustavus III., beaten by the Russians, declares that he will pass his last days in Paris in a house on the boulevards; and this is not merely complimentary, for he sends for plans and an estimate.[2] A supper or an evening entertainment brings people two hundred leagues away. Some friends of the Prince de Ligne "leave Brussels after breakfast, reach the opera in Paris just in time to see the curtain rise, and, after the spectacle is over, return immediately to Brussels, travelling all night."—Of this delight, so eagerly sought, we have only imperfect copies, and we are obliged to revive it intellectually. It consists, in the first place, in the pleasure of living with perfectly polite people; there is no enjoyment more subtle, more lasting, more inexhaustible. The self-love of man being infinite, intelligent people are always able to produce some refinement of attention to gratify it. Worldly sensibility being infinite there is no imperceptible shade of it permitting indifference. After all, man is still the greatest source of happiness or of misery to man, and in those days the ever-flowing fountain brought to him sweetness instead of bitterness. Not only was it essential not to offend, but it was essential to please; one was expected to lose sight of oneself in others, to be always cordial and good-humored, to keep one's own vexations and grievances in one's own breast, to spare others melancholy ideas and to supply them with cheerful ideas. "Was any one old in those days? It is the Revolution which brought

---

[1] "Princesse de Babylone."
[2] "Gustave III.," by Geffroy, II. 37. Mme. Vigée-Lebrun, I. 81.

old age into the world. Your grandfather, my child,[1] was hand-some, elegant, neat, gracious, perfumed, playful, amiable, affec-tionate, and good-tempered to the day of his death. People then knew how to live and how to die; there was no such thing as troublesome infirmities. If any one had the gout, he walked along all the same and made no faces; people well brought up concealed their sufferings. There was none of that absorp-tion in business which spoils a man inwardly and dulls his brain. People knew how to ruin themselves without letting it appear, like good gamblers who lose their money without showing un-easiness or spite. A man would be carried half dead to a hunt. It was thought better to die at a ball or at the play than in one's bed, between four wax candles and horrid men in black. Peo-ple were philosophers; they did not assume to be austere, but often were so without making a display of it. If one was dis-creet, it was through inclination and without pedantry or prudish-ness. People enjoyed this life, and when the hour of departure came they did not try to disgust others with living. The last request of my old husband was that I would survive him as long as possible and live as happily as I could."

When, especially, women are concerned it is not sufficient to be polite; it is important to be gallant. Each lady invited by the Prince de Conti to Ile-Adam "finds a carriage and horses at her disposal; she is free to give dinners every day in her own rooms to her own friends."[2] Mme. de Civrac having to go to the springs, her friends undertake to divert her on the journey; they keep ahead of her a few posts, and, at every place where she rests for the night, they give her a little *fête champêtre*, disguised as villagers and in bourgeois attire, with bailiff and scrivener, and other masks all singing and reciting verses. A lady on the eve of Longchamp, knowing that the Vicomte de V—— possesses two calèches, makes a request for one of them; it is disposed of, but he is careful not to decline, and immediately has one of the greatest elegance purchased to lend it for three hours; he is only too happy that anybody should wish to borrow from him,

---

[1] George Sand, I. 58–60. A narration by her grandmother, who, at thirty years of age, married M. Dupin de Francueil, aged sixty-two.

[2] Mme. de Genlis, "Souvenirs de Félicie," 77. "Dict. des Etiquettes," I. 348. Mme. Campan, III. 74.

his prodigality appearing amiable but not astonishing.[1] The reason is that women then were queens in the drawing-room; it is their right; this is the reason why, in the eighteenth century, they prescribe the law and the fashion in all things.[2] Having formed the code of usages, it is quite natural that they should profit by it, and see that all its prescriptions are carried out. In this respect any circle " of the best company " is a superior tribunal, serving as a court of last appeal.[3] The Maréchale de Luxembourg is an authority; there is no point of manners which she does not justify with an ingenious argument. Any expression, any neglect of the standard, the slightest sign of pretension or of self-conceit incurs her disapprobation, from which there is no appeal, and the delinquent is for ever banished from refined society. Any subtle observation, any well-timed silence, an " oh " uttered in an appropriate place instead of an " ah," secures from her, as from M. Talleyrand, a diploma of good breeding which is the commencement of fame and the promise of a fortune. Under such an " instructress " it is evident that deportment, gesture, language, every act or omission in this mundane sphere, becomes, like a picture or poem, a veritable work of art; that is to say, infinite in refinement, at once studied and easy, and so harmonious in its details that its perfection conceals the difficulty of combining them.

A great lady " receives ten persons with one courtesy, bestowing on each, through the head or by a glance, all that he is entitled to;"[4] meaning by this the shade of regard due to each phase of position, consideration, and birth. " She has always to deal with easily irritated *amour-propres ;* consequently the slightest deficiency in proportion would be promptly detected."[5] But she is never mistaken, and never hesitates in these subtle distinctions; with incomparable tact, dexterity, and flexibility of tone, she regulates the degrees of her welcome. She has one " for women of condition, one for women of quality, one for women of the court, one for titled women, one for women of historic names, another

---

[1] See an anecdote concerning this species of royalty in " Adèle et Théodore, I. 69" by Mme. de Genlis. Mme. Vigée-Lebrun, I. 156. "Women ruled then ; the Revolution has dethroned them. . . . This gallantry I speak of has entirely disappeared."

[2] "Women in France to some extent dictate whatever is to be said and prescribe whatever is to be done in the fashionable world." ("A comparative view," by John Andrews, 1785.)

[3] Mme. d'Oberkirk, I. 299 ; Mme. de Genlis, " Mémoires," ch. xi.

[4] De Tilly, I. 24.

[5] Necker, " Œuvres Completes," XV. 259.

for women of high birth personally, but married to men beneath them; another for women who by marriage have changed a common into a distinguished name; another still for women of reputable names in the law; and, finally, another for those whose relief consists chiefly of expensive houses and good suppers." A stranger would be amazed on seeing with what certain and adroit steps she circulates among so many watchful vanities without ever giving or receiving a check. "She knows how to express all through the style of her salutations; a varied style, extending through imperceptible gradations, from the accessory of a single shrug of the shoulder, almost an impertinence, to that noble and deferential reverence which so few women, even of the court, know how to do well; that slow bending forward, with lowered eyes and straightened figure, gradually recovering and modestly glancing at the person while gracefully raising the body up, altogether much more refined and more delicate than words, but very expressive as the means of manifesting respect." This is but a single action, and very common; there are a hundred others, and of importance. Imagine, if it is possible, the degree of elegance and perfection to which they attained through good breeding. I select one at random—a duel between two princes of the blood, the Comte d'Artois and the Duc de Bourbon. [1] The latter being the offended party, the former, his superior, had to offer him a meeting. "As soon as the Comte d'Artois saw him he leaped to the ground, and walking directly up to him, said to him smiling: 'Monsieur, the public pretends that we are seeking each other.' The Duc de Bourbon, removing his hat, replied, 'Monsieur, I am here to receive your orders.' 'To execute your own,' returned the Comte d'Artois, 'but you must allow me to return to my carriage.' He comes back with a sword, and the duel begins. After a certain time they are separated, the seconds deciding that honor is satisfied. 'It is not for me to express an opinion,' says the Comte d'Artois. 'Monsieur le Duc de Bourbon is to express his wishes; I am here only to receive his orders.' 'Monsieur,' responds the Duc de Bourbon, addressing the Comte d'Artois, meanwhile lowering the point of his sword, 'I am overcome with gratitude for your kindness, and shall never be insensible to the honor you have done me.'" Could there be a

---

[1] Narrated by M. de Bezenval, a witness of the deed.

juster and more delicate sentiment of rank, position, and circumstance, and could a duel be surrounded with more graces?
There is no situation, however thorny, which is not saved by politeness. Through habit, and a suitable expression, even in the
face of the king, they conciliate resistance and respect. When
Louis XV., having exiled the Parliament, caused it to be proclaimed through Mme. Du Barry that his mind was made up and
that it would not be changed, "Ah, Madame," replied the Duc
de Nivernais, "when the king said that he was looking at yourself." "My dear Fontenelle," said one of his lady friends to
him, placing her hand on his heart, "the brain is there likewise."
Fontenelle smiled and made no reply. We see here, even with
an academician, how truths are forced down, a drop of acid in a
sugar-plum; the whole so thoroughly intermingled that the
piquancy of the flavor only enhances its sweetness. Night after
night, in each drawing-room, sugar-plums of this description are
served up, two or three along with the drop of acidity, all the
rest not less exquisite, but possessing only the sweetness and the
perfume. Such is the art of social worldliness, an ingenious and
delightful art, which, entering into all the details of speech and
of action, transforms them into graces; which imposes on man
not servility and falsehood, but civility and concern for others,
and which, in exchange, extracts for him out of human society all
the pleasure it can afford.

V.

One can very well understand this kind of pleasure in a summary way, but how is it to be made apparent? Taken by themselves the pastimes of society are not to be described; they are
too ephemeral; their charm arises from their accompaniments.
A narrative of them would be but tasteless dregs,—does the
libretto of an opera give any idea of the opera itself? If the
reader would revive for himself this vanished world let him seek
for it in those works that have preserved its externals or its accent, and first in the pictures and engravings of Watteau, Fragonard and the Saint-Aubins, and then in the novels and dramas of
Voltaire and Marivaux, and even in Collé and Crébillon *fils*;[1]

---

[1] See especially, Saint-Aubin, "Le bal paré," "Le Concert;" Moreau, "Les Elégants,"
"La Vie d'un Seigneur à la mode," the vignettes of "La nouvelle Héloise;" Beaudouin,
"La Toilette," "Le Coucher de la Mariée;" Lawrence, "Qu'en dit l'abbé?" Watteau, the
first in date and in talent, *transposes* these customs and depicts them the better by making

then do we see the breathing figures and hear their voices. What bright, winning, intelligent faces beaming with pleasure and with the desire to please! What ease in bearing and in gesture! What piquant grace in the toilet, in the smile, in vivaciousness of expression, in the control of the fluted voice, in the coquetry of hidden meanings! How involuntarily we stop to look and listen! Attractiveness is everywhere, in the small *spirituelle* heads, in the slender hands, in the rumpled attire, in the pretty features, in the demeanor. The slightest gesture, a pouting or mutinous turn of the head, a plump little wrist peering from its nest of lace, a yielding waist bent over an embroidery frame, the rapid rustling of an opening fan, is a feast for the eyes and the intellect. It is indeed all daintiness, a delicate caress for delicate senses, extending to the external decoration of life, to the sinuous outlines, the showy drapery, and the refinements of comfort in the furniture and architecture. Fill your imagination with these accessories and with these figures and you will take as much interest in their amusements as they did. In such a place and in such company it suffices to be together to be content. Their indolence is no burden to them for they sport with existence. At Chanteloup, the Duc de Choiseul, in disgrace, finds the fashionable world flocking to see him; nothing is done and yet no hours of the day are unoccupied.[1] " The Duchess has only two hours' time to herself, and these two hours are devoted to her toilet and her letters; the calculation is a simple one,—she gets up at eleven; breakfasts at noon, and this is followed by conversation, which lasts three or four hours; dinner comes at six, after which there is play and the reading of the memoirs of Mme. de Maintenon." Ordinarily " the company remains together until two o'clock in the morning." Intellectual freedom is complete. There is no confusion, no anxiety. They play whist and tric-trac in the afternoon and faro in the evening. " They do to-day what they did yesterday and what they will do to-morrow; the dinner-supper is to them the most important affair in life, and their only complaint in the world is of their diges-

---

them more poetic. Of the rest, read "Marianne," by Marivaux; "La Verité dans le vin," by Collé; "Le coin du feu," "La nuit et le moment," by Crébillon *fils ;* and two letters in the "Correspondance inédite" of Mme. du Deffant, one by the Abbé Barthélemy and the other by the Chevalier de Boufflers, (I. 258,341.).

[1] "Correspondance inédite de Mme. du Deffant," published by M. de Saint-Aulaire, I. 235, 258, 296, 302, 363.

tion. Time goes so fast I always fancy that I arrived only the evening before." Sometimes they get up a little race and the ladies are disposed to take part in it, "for they are all very agile and able to run around the drawing-room five or six times every day." But they prefer indoors to the open air; in these days true sunshine consists of candle-light and the finest sky is a painted ceiling,—is there any other less subject to inclemencies or better adapted to conversation and merriment? They accordingly chat and jest, in words with present friends, and by letters with absent friends. They lecture old Mme. du Deffant, who is too lively and whom they style the "little girl"; the young Duchesse, tender and sensible, is "her grandmama." As for "grandpapa," M. de Choiseul, "a slight cold keeping him in bed he has fairy stories read to him all day long, a species of reading to which we are all given; we find them as probable as modern history. Do not imagine that he is unoccupied. He has had a tapestry frame put up in the drawing-room at which he works, I cannot say with the greatest skill, but at least with the greatest assiduity. . . . Now, our delight is in flying a kite; grandpapa has never seen this sight and he is enraptured with it." The pastime, in itself, is nothing; it is resorted to according to opportunity or the taste of the hour, now taken up and now let alone, and the abbé soon writes: " I do not speak about our races because we race no more, nor of our readings because we do not read, nor of our promenades because we do not go out. What, then, do we do? Some play billiards, others dominoes, and others backgammon. We weave, we ravel and we unravel. Time pushes us on and we pay him back."

Other circles present the same spectacle. Every occupation being an amusement, a caprice or an impulse of fashion brings one into favor. At present, it is unravelling, every white hand at Paris, and in the chateaux, being busy in undoing trimmings, epaulettes and old stuffs, to pick out the gold and silver threads. They find in this employment the semblance of economy, an appearance of occupation, in any event something to keep them in countenance. On a circle of ladies being formed, a big unravelling bag in green taffeta is placed on the table, which belongs to the lady of the house; immediately all the ladies call for their bags and " *voilà les laquais en l'air.*" [1] It is all the rage. They

---

[1] Mme. de Genlis, "Dict. des Etiquettes," II. 38. "Adèle et Théodore," I. 212; II. 350. George Sand, "Histoire de ma vie," I. 228. De Goncourt, p. 111.

unravel every day and several hours in the day; some derive from
it a hundred louis d'or per annum. The gentlemen are expected
to provide the materials for the work; the Duc de Lauzun, accordingly, gives to Madame de V—— a harp of natural size
covered with gold thread; an enormous golden fleece, brought
as a present from the Comte de Lowenthal, and which cost two
or three thousand francs, brings, picked to pieces, five or six hundred francs. But they do not look into matters so closely. Some
employment is essential for idle hands, some manual outlet for
nervous activity; a humorous petulance breaks out in the middle
of the pretended work. One day, when about going out, Madame de R—— observes that the gold fringe on her dress would
be capital for unraveling, whereupon, with a dash, she cuts one of
the fringes off. Ten women suddenly surround a man wearing
fringes, pull off his coat and put his fringes and laces into their bags,
just as if a bold flock of tomtits, fluttering and chattering in the air,
should suddenly dart on a jay to pluck out its feathers; thenceforth a man who enters a circle of women stands in danger of
being stripped alive. All this pretty world has the same pastimes, the men as well as the women. Scarcely a man can
be found without some drawing-room accomplishment, some trifling way of keeping his mind and hands busy, and of filling up
the vacant hour; almost all make rhymes, or act in private theatricals; many of them are musicians and painters of still-life
subjects. M. de Choiseul, as we have just seen, works at tapestry; others embroider or make sword-knots. M. de Francueil
is a good violinist and makes violins himself, and besides this he
is " watchmaker, architect, turner, painter, locksmith, decorator,
cook, poet, music-composer and he embroiders remarkably well." [1]
In this general state of inactivity it is essential " to know how to
be pleasantly occupied in behalf of others as well as in one's own
behalf." Madame de Pompadour is a musician, an actress, a
painter and an engraver. Madame Adelaide learns watchmaking
and plays on all instruments from a horn to the jew's-harp ; not
very well, it is true, but as well as a queen can sing, whose fine
voice is ever only half in tune. But they make no pretensions.
The thing is to amuse oneself and nothing more; high spirits and
the amenities of the hour cover all. Rather read this capital fact

---

[1] George Sand, I. 59.

of Madame de Lauzun at Chanteloup: "Do you know," writes the abbé, "that nobody possesses in a higher degree one quality which you would never suspect of her, that of preparing scrambled eggs? This talent has been buried in the ground,—she cannot recall the time she acquired it; I believe that she had it at her birth. Accident made it known, and immediately it was put to the test. Yesterday morning, an hour for ever memorable in the history of eggs, the implements necessary for this great operation were all brought out, a heater, some gravy, some pepper, salt and eggs. Behold Madame de Lauzun, at first blushing and in a tremor, soon with intrepid courage, breaking the eggs, beating them up in the pan, turning them over, now to the right, now to the left, now up and now down, with unexampled precision and success! Never was a more excellent dish eaten." What laughter and gaiety in the group comprised in this little scene. And, not long after, what madrigals and allusions! Gaiety here resembles a dancing ray of sunlight; it flickers over all things and reflects its grace on every object.

VI.

"The Frenchman's characteristic," says an English traveller in 1785, "is to be always gay;"[1] and he remarks that he must be so because, in France, such is the tone of society and the only mode of pleasing the ladies, the sovereigns of society and the arbiters of good taste. Add to this the absence of the causes which produce modern dreariness, and which convert the sky above our heads into one of leaden gloom. There was no laborious, forced work in those days, no furious competition, no uncertain careers, no infinite perspectives. Ranks were clearly defined, ambitions limited, and there was less envy. Man was not habitually dissatisfied, soured and preoccupied as he is nowadays. Few free passes were allowed where there was no right to pass; we think of nothing but advancement; they thought only of amusing themselves. An officer, instead of raging and storming over the army list, busies himself in inventing some new disguise for a masked-ball; a magistrate, instead of counting the convictions he has secured, provides a magnificent supper. At Paris, every afternoon in the left avenue of the Palais-Royal, "fine company, very richly

---

[1] "A comparative view," etc., by John Andrews.

dressed, gather under the large trees ; " and in the evening "on leaving the opera at half-past eight, they go back there and remain until two o'clock in the morning." They have music in the open air by moonlight, Gavat singing, and the chevalier de Saint-George playing on the violin.[1] At Morfontaine, "the Comte de Vaudreuil, Lebrun the poet, the chevalier de Coigny, so amiable and so gay, Brongniart, Robert, compose charades every night and wake each other up to repeat them." At Maupertuis in M. de Montesquiou's house, at Saint-Ouen with the Marshal de Noailles, at Genevilliers with the Comte de Vaudreuil, at Rainay with the Duc d'Orléans, at Chantilly with the Prince de Condé, there is nothing but festivity. We read no biography of the day, no provincial document, no inventory, without hearing the tinkling of the universal carnival. At Monchoix,[2] the residence of the Comte de Bédée, Chateaubriand's uncle, "they had music, dancing and hunting, rollicking from morning to night, eating up both capital and income." At Aix and Marseilles, throughout the fashionable world, with the Comte de Valbelle, I find nothing but concerts, entertainments, balls, gallantries, and private theatricals with the Comtesse de Mirabeau for the leading performer. At Chateauroux, M. Dupin de Francueil entertains "a troop of musicians, lackeys, cooks, parasites, horses and dogs, bestowing everything lavishly, in amusements and in charity, wishing to be happy himself and everybody else around him," never casting up accounts, and going to ruin in the most delightful manner possible. Nothing arrests this gaiety, neither old age, exile, nor misfortune ; in 1793 it still subsists in the prisons of the Republic. A man in place is not then made uncomfortable by his official coat, puffed up by his situation, obliged to maintain a dignified and important air, constrained under that assumed gravity which democratic envy imposes on us as if a ransom. In 1753,[3] the parliamentarians, just exiled to Bourges, get up three companies of private theatricals and perform comedies, while one of them, M. Dupré de Saint-Maur, fights a rival with the sword. In 1787,[4] when the entire parliament is banished to Troyes the bishop, M. de Barral, returns from his chateau de

---

[1] Mme. Vigée-Lebrun, I. 15, 154.

[2] Chateaubriand, I. 34. "Mémoires de Mirabeau," *passim.* George Sand, I. 59, 76.

[3] Comptes rendus de la société de Berry (1863-1864).

[4] "Histoire de Troyes pendant la Révolution," by Albert Babeau, I. 46.

Saint-Lye expressly to receive it, presiding every evening at a dinner of forty persons. "There was no end to the fêtes and dinners in the town; the president kept open house," a triple quantity of food being consumed in the eating-houses and so much wood burned in the kitchens, that the town came near being put on short allowance. Feasting and jollity is but little less in ordinary times. A parliamentarian, like a seignior, must do credit to his fortune. See the letters of the President des Brosses concerning society in Dijon; it reminds us of the abbey of Thélème; then contrast this with the same town to-day.[1] In 1744, Monseigneur de Montigny, brother of the President de Bourbonne, *apropos* of the king's recovery, entertains the workmen, tradesmen and artisans in his employ to the number of eighty, another table being for his musicians and comedians, and a third for his clerks, secretaries, physicians, surgeons, attorneys and notaries; the crowd collects around a triumphal car covered with shepherdesses, shepherds and rustic divinities in theatrical costume; fountains flow with wine "as if it were water," and after supper the confectionery is thrown out of the windows. Each parliamentarian around him has his "little Versailles, a grand hotel between court and garden." This town, now so silent, then rang with the clatter of fine equipages. The profusion of the table is astonishing, "not only on gala days, but at the suppers of each week, and I could almost say, of each day." Amidst all these fête-givers, the most illustrious of all, the President des Brosses, so grave on the magisterial bench, so intrepid in his remonstrances, so laborious,[2] so learned, is an extraordinary stimulator of fun *(boute-entrain)*, a genuine Gaul, with a sparkling, inexhaustible fund of salacious humor: with his friends he throws off his perruque, his gown, and even something more. Nobody dreams of being offended by it; nobody conceives that dress is an extinguisher, which is true of every species of dress, and of the gown in particular. "When I entered society, in 1785," writes a parliamentarian, "I found myself introduced in a certain way, alike to the

---

[1] Foisset, "Le Président des Brosses," 65, 69, 70, 345. "Lettres du Président des Brosses," (ed. Coulomb), *passim.* Piron being uneasy concerning his "Ode à Priape," President Bouhier, a man of great and fine erudition, and the least starched of learned ones, sent for the young man and said to him, "You are a foolish fellow. If any one presses you to know the author of the offence tell him that I am." (Sainte-Beuve, "Nouveaux Lundis," VII. 414.)

[2] Foisset, *ibid.* 185. Six audiences a week and often two a day besides his labors as antiquarian, historian, linguist, geographer, editor and academician.

wives and the mistresses of the friends of my family, passing Monday evening with one, and Tuesday evening with the other. And I was only eighteen, and I belonged to a family of magistrates."[1] At Basville, at the residence of M. de Lamoignon, during the autumnal vacation and the Whitsuntide holidays, there are thirty persons at the table daily; there are three or four hunts a week, and the most prominent magistrates, M. de Lamoignon, M. Pasquier, M. de Rosambo, M. and Mme. d'Aguesseau, perform the "Barber of Seville" in the chateau theatre.

As for the cassock, it enjoys the same freedom as the robe. At Saverne, at Clairvaux, at Le Mans and at other places, the prelates wear it as freely as a court dress. The revolutionary upheaval was necessary to make it a fixture on their bodies, and, afterwards, the hostile supervision of an organized party and the fear of constant danger. Up to 1789 the sky is too serene and the atmosphere too balmy to lead them to button it up to the neck. "Freedom, facilities, Monsieur l'Abbé," said the Cardinal de Rohan to his secretary, "without these this life would be a desert."[2] This is what the good cardinal took care to avoid; on the contrary he had made Saverne an enchanting world according to Watteau, almost "a landing-place for Cythera." Six hundred peasants and keepers, ranged in a line a league long, form in the morning and beat up the surrounding country, while hunters, men and women, are posted at their stations. "For fear that the ladies might be frightened if left alone by themselves, the man whom they hated least was always left with them to tranquillize them," and as nobody was allowed to leave his post before the signal "it was impossible to be surprised." About an hour after noonday "the company gathered under a beautiful tent, on the bank of a stream or in some delightful place, where an exquisite dinner was served up, and, as every one had to be made happy, each peasant received a pound of meat, two of bread and half a bottle of wine, only asking to begin it all over again, as well as the ladies." The accommodating prelate might certainly have replied to scrupulous people along with Voltaire, that "nothing is wrong in good society." In fact, he so made answer, and in these very terms. One day, a lady accompanied

---

[1] "Souvenirs manuscripts," by M. X——. (As the author's name cannot be given I shall use this designation hereafter.)

[2] De Valfons, "Souvenirs," 60.

by a young officer, having come on a visit, and being obliged to keep them over night, his valet comes and whispers to him that there is no more room. "'Is the bath-room occupied?' 'No, Monseigneur!' 'Are there not two beds there?' 'Yes, Monseigneur, but they are both in the same chamber, and that officer—' 'Very well, didn't they come together? Shallow people like you always see something wrong. You will find that they will agree very well together,—there is not the slightest reason to object.'" And really nobody did object, either the officer or the lady. At Granselve, in the Gard, the Bernardines are still more hospitable.[1] People resort to the fête of St. Bernard which lasts a couple of weeks; during this time they dance, and hunt, and act comedies, "the tables being ready at all hours." The quarters of the ladies are provided with every requisite for the toilet; they lack nothing, and it is even said that it was not necessary for any of them to bring their officer. I might cite twenty prelates not less gallant,—the second Cardinal de Rohan, the hero of the necklace, M. de Jarente, bishop of Orleans, who keeps the record of benefices, the young M. de Grimaldi, bishop of Le Mans, M. de Breteuil, bishop of Montauban, M. de Cicé, archbishop of Bordeaux, the Cardinal de Montmorency, grand-almoner, M. de Talleyrand, bishop of Autun, M. de Conzié, bishop of Arras,[2] and, in the first rank, the Abbé de Saint-Germain des Près, Comte de Clermont, prince of the blood, who, with an income of three hundred and seventy thousand francs succeeds in ruining himself twice, who performs in comedies in his town and country residences, who writes to Collé in a pompous style and, who, in his abbatial mansion at Berny, installs Mademoiselle Leduc, a dancer, to do the honors of his table. There is no hypocrisy. In the house of M. Trudaine, four bishops attend the performance of a piece by Collé entitled " Les accidents ou les Abbés," the substance of which, says Collé himself, is so free that he did not dare print it along with his other pieces. A little later, Beaumarchais, on reading his "Marriage of Figaro " at the Maréchal de Riche-

---

[1] Montgaillard (an eye-witness), "Histoire de France," II. 246.
[2] M. de Conzié is surprised at four o'clock in the morning by a rival, an officer in the guards. "Make no noise," said he to him, "my coat which is like yours will be brought to me and I will make a *queue* so that we shall be on the same footing." A valet brings him his weapons. He descends into the garden of the mansion, fights with the officer and disarms him. ("Correspondance," by Métra, XIV. May 20, 1783.) "Le Comte de Clermont," by Jules Cousin, *passim.* "Journal de Collé," III. 232 (July, 1769).

lieu's domicile, not expurgated, much more crude and coarse than it is to-day, has bishops and archbishops for his auditors, and these, he says, "after being infinitely amused by it, did me the honor to assure me that they would state that there was not a single word in it offensive to good morals : "[1] thus was the piece accepted against reasons of State, against the king's will, and through the connivance of all those most interested in suppressing it. "There is something more irrational than my piece, and that is its success," said its author. The attraction was too strong. People devoted to pleasure could not dispense with the liveliest comedy of the age. They came to applaud a satire on themselves; and better still, they themselves acted in it. A prevalent taste ends, like a powerful passion, in extremes which become follies; it must enjoy what is offered to it at any cost; any momentary gratification of it is as with a child tempted by fruit; nothing arrests it, neither the danger to which it is insensible, nor the sense of propriety it establishes for itself.

VII.

To divert oneself is to turn aside from oneself, to get away from oneself, and to forget oneself; and to forget oneself fully one must be transported into another, put himself in the place of another, take his mask and play his part. Hence the liveliest of diversions is the comedy in which one is an actor. It is that of children who, as authors, actors and audience, improvise and represent petty scenes the livelong day. It is that of a people whose political régime excludes manly solicitudes, and who sport with life after the fashion of children. At Venice, in the eighteenth century, the carnival lasts six months; in France, under another form, it lasts the entire year. Less familiar and less picturesque, more refined and more elegant, it abandons the public square where it lacks sunshine, to shut itself up in drawing-rooms where chandeliers are the most suitable for it. It has retained of the vast popular masquerade only a fragment, the opera ball, very splendid and frequented by princes, princesses and the queen; but this fragment, brilliant as it is, does not suffice; consequently, in every chateau, in every mansion, at Paris and in the provinces, it sets up travesties on society and domestic com-

---

[1] De Loménie, "Beaumarchais et son temps," II. 304.

edies. On welcoming a great personage, on celebrating the birth-
day of the master or mistress of the house, its guests or invited
persons perform in an improvised operetta, in an ingenious,
laudatory pastoral, sometimes dressed as gods, as Virtues, as
mythological abstractions, as operatic Turks, Laplanders and
Poles, similar to the figures then gracing the frontispieces of
books, sometimes in the dress of peasants, pedagogues, pedlars,
milkmaids and flower-girls like the fanciful villagers with which the
current taste then fills the stage. They sing, they dance, and
come forward in turn to recite petty verses composed for the occasion consisting of so many well-turned compliments.[1] At Chantilly
"the young and charming Duchesse de Bourbon, attired as a
voluptuous Naiad, guides the Comte du Nord, in a gilded gon-
dola, across the grand canal to the island of Love;" the Prince
de Conti, in his part, serves as pilot to the Grand Duchesse;
other seigniors and ladies "each in allegorical guise," form the
escort,[2] and on these limpid waters, in this new garden of Alci-
nous, the smiling and gallant retinue seems a fairy scene in Tasso.
At Vaudreuil, the ladies, advised that they are to be carried off to
scraglios, attire themselves as vestals, while the high-priest welcomes them with pretty couplets into his temple in the park;
meanwhile over three hundred Turks arrive who force the enclosure to the sound of music, and bear away the ladies in palanquins
along the illuminated gardens. At the little Trianon, the park is
arranged as a fair, and the ladies of the court are the saleswomen,
"the queen keeping a café," while, here and there, are processions
and theatricals; this festival costs, it is said, one hundred thousand livres, and a repetition of it is designed at Choisy attended
with a larger outlay.

Alongside of these masquerades which stop at costume and
require only an hour, there is a more important diversion, the
private theatrical performance, which completely transforms the
man, and which for six weeks, and even for three months, absorbs
him entirely at rehearsals. Towards 1770[3] "the rage for it is

---

[1] De Luynes, XVI. 161 (September, 1757). The village festival given to King Stanislas
by Mme. de Mauconseil at Bagatelle. Bachaumont, III. 247 (September 7, 1767). Festival
given by the Prince de Condé.

[2] "Correspondance," by Métra, XIII. 97 (June 15, 1782), and V. 232 (June 24 and 25,
1777). Mme. de Genlis "Mémoires," chap. xiv.

[3] Bachaumont, November 17, 1770. "Journal de Collé," III. 136 (April 29, 1767). De
Montlosier, "Mémoires," I. 43. "At the residence of the Commandant (at Clermont) they
would have been glad to enlist me in private theatricals."

incredible; there is not an attorney in his cottage who does not wish to have a stage and his company of actors." A Bernardine living in Bresse, in the middle of a wood, writes to Collé that he and his brethren are about to perform "La Partie de Chasse de Henri IV.," and that they are having a small theatre constructed "without the knowledge of bigots and small minds." Reformers and moralists introduce theatrical art into the education of children; Mme. de Genlis composes comedies for them, considering these excellent for the securing of a good pronunciation, proper self-confidence and the graces of deportment. The theatre, indeed, then prepares man for society as society prepares him for the theatre; in either case he is on representation, composing his attitude and tone of voice, and playing a part; the stage and the drawing-room are on an equal footing. Towards the end of the century everybody becomes an actor, everybody having been one before.[1] "We hear of nothing but little theatres set up in the country around Paris." For a long time those of highest rank set the example. Under Louis XV. the Ducs d'Orléans, de Nivernais, d'Ayen, de Coigny, the Marquises de Courtenvaux, and d'Entraigues, the Comte de Maillebois, the Duchesse de Brancas, the Comtesse d'Estrades form, with Madame de Pompadour, the company of the "small cabinets;" the Duc de la Vallière is the director of them; when the piece contains a ballet the Marquis de Courtenvaux, the Duc de Beuvron, the Comtes de Melfort and de Langeron are the titulary dancers.[2] "Those who are accustomed to such spectacles," writes the sedate and pious Duc de Luynes, "agree in the opinion that it would be difficult for professional comedians to play better and more intelligently." The passion reaches at last still higher, even to the royal family. At Trianon, the queen, at first before forty persons and then before a more numerous audience, performs Colette in "Le Devin de Village," Gotte, in "La Gageure imprévue," Rosine in "Le Barbier de Seville," Pierette in "Le Chasseur et la Laitière,"[3] while the other comedians consist of the principal men of the court, the Comte d'Artois, the Comtes d'Adhémar and de

---

[1] "Correspondance," by Métra, II. 245 (Nov. 18, 1775).

[2] Julien, "Histoire du Théâtre de Madame de Pompadour." These representations last seven years and cost during the winter alone of 1749, 300,000 livres. De Luynes, X. 45. Mme. du Hausset, 230.

[3] Mme. Campan, I. 130. Cf. with caution the very suspicious Memoirs, much made up, of Fleury. De Goncourt, 114.

Vaudreuil, the Comtesse de Guiche, and the Canoness de Polignac. A theatre is formed in Monsieur's domicile; there are two in the Comte d'Artois's house, two in that of the Duc d'Orléans, two in the Comte de Clermont's, and one in the Prince de Condé's. The Comte de Clermont performs serious characters; the Duc d'Orléans represents, with completeness and naturalness, peasants and financiers; M. de Miromesnil, keeper of the seals, is the smartest and most finished of Scapins; M. de Vaudreuil seems to rival Molé; the Comte de Pons plays the "Misanthrope" with rare perfection.[1] "More than ten of our ladies of high rank," writes the Prince de Ligne, "play and sing better than the best of those I have seen in our theatres." By their talent judge of their study, assiduity and zeal. It is evident that for many of them it is the principal occupation. In a certain chateau, that of Saint-Aubin, the lady of the house, to secure a large enough troupe, enrolls her four chambermaids in it, making her little daughter, ten years old, play the part of Zaire, and for over twenty months she has no vacation. After her bankruptcy, and in her exile, the first thing done by the Princess de Guéménée was to send for upholsterers to arrange a theatre. In short, as nobody went out in Venice without a mask so here nobody comprehended life without the masqueradings, metamorphoses, representations and triumphs of the player.

The last trait I have to mention, yet more significant, is the after-piece. Really, in this fashionable circle, life is a carnival as free and almost as rakish as that of Venice. The play commonly terminates with a parade borrowed from La Fontaine's tales or from the farces of the Italian drama, which are not only pointed but more than free, and sometimes so broad "that they can be played only before princes and courtesans;"[2] a morbid palate, indeed, having no taste for orgeat, and demanding a dram. The Duc d'Orléans sings on the stage the most spicy songs, playing Bartholin in "Nicaise," and Blaise in "Joconde." "Le Marriage sans Curé," "Leandre grosse," "L'amant poussif," "Leandre Etalon," are the showy titles of the

---

[1] Jules Cousin, "Le Comte de Clermont," p. 21. Mme. de Genlis, "Mémoires," chap. iii. and xi. De Goncourt, 14.

[2] Bachaumont, III. 343 (February 23, 1768) and IV. 174, III. 232. "Journal de Collé," *passim.* Collé, Laujon and Poisinet are the principal purveyors for these displays; the only one of merit is "La Verité dans la Vin." In this piece instead of "Mylord," there is the "bishop of Avranches," and the piece was thus performed at Villers-Cotterets in the house of the Duc d'Orléans.

pieces composed by Collé "for the amusement of His Highness and the Court." For one which contains salt there are ten stuffed with strong pepper. At Brunoy, at the residence of Monsieur, so gross are they[1] the king regrets having attended; "nobody had any idea of such license; two women in the auditorium had to go out, and, what is most extraordinary, they had dared to invite the queen." Gaiety is a sort of intoxication which draws the cask down to the dregs, and when the wine is gone it draws on the lees. Not only at their little suppers, and with courtesans, but in the best society and with ladies, they commit the follies of a bagnio. Let us use the right word, they are blackguards, and the word is no more offensive to them than the action. "For five or six months," writes a lady in 1782,[2] "the suppers are followed by a blindman's-buff or by a draw-dance, and they end in *general mischievousness, (une polissonnerie générale).*" Guests are invited a fortnight in advance. "On this occasion they upset the tables and the furniture; they scattered twenty caraffes of water about the room; I finally got away at half-past one, wearied out, pelted with handkerchiefs, and leaving Madame de Clarence hoarse, with her dress torn to shreds, a scratch on her arm, and a bruise on her forehead, but delighted that she had given such a gay supper and flattered with the idea of its being the talk the next day." This is the result of a craving for amusement. Under its pressure, as under the sculptor's thumb, the face of the century becomes transformed and insensibly loses its seriousness; the formal expression of the courtier at first becomes the sprightly physiognomy of the worldling, and then, on these smiling lips, their contours changed, we see the bold, unbridled grin of the scamp.[3]

---

[1] Mme. d'Oberkirk, II. 82. On the tone of the best society see "Correspondance" by Métra, I. 20, III. 68, and Bezenval (Ed. Barrière) 387 and 349.

[2] Mme. de Genlis, "Adèle et Théodore," II. 362.

[3] George Sand, I. 85. "At my grandmother's I have found boxes full of couplets, madrigals and biting satires. I burned some of them so obscene that I would not dare read them through, and these written by abbés I had known in my infancy and by a marquis of the best blood." Among other examples, toned down, the songs on the Bird and the Shepherdess may be read in "Correspondance," by Métra.

CHAPTER III.

I.

MERE pleasure, in the long run, ceases to gratify, and however agreeable this drawing-room life may be, it ends in a certain hollowness. Something is lacking without any one being able to say precisely what that something is; the soul becomes restless, and slowly, aided by authors and artists, it sets about investigating the cause of its uneasiness and the object of its secret longings. Barrenness and artificiality are the two traits of this society, the more marked because it is more complete, and, in this one, pushed to extreme, because it has attained to supreme refinement. In the first place naturalness is excluded from it; everything is arranged and adjusted,—decoration, dress, attitude, tone of voice, words, ideas and even sentiments. "A genuine sentiment is so rare," said M. de V——, "that, when I leave Versailles, I sometimes stand still in the street to see a dog gnaw a bone."[1] Man, in abandoning himself wholly to society, had withheld no portion of his personality for himself, while decorum, clinging to him like so much ivy, had abstracted from him the substance of his being and subverted every principle of activity. "There was then," says one who was educated in this style,[2] "a certain way of walking, of sitting down, of saluting, of picking up a glove, of holding a fork, of tendering any article, in fine, a com-

---

[1] Champfort, 110.
[2] George Sand, V. 59. "I was rebuked for everything; I never made a movement which was not criticized."

plete mimicry, which children had to be taught at a very early
age in order that habit might become a second nature, and this
conventionality formed so important an item in the life of men
and women in aristocratic circles that the actors of the present
day, with all their study, are scarcely able to give us an idea
of it." Not only was the outward factitious but, again, the inward; there was a certain prescribed mode of feeling and of
thinking, of living and of dying. It was impossible to address a
man without placing oneself at his orders, or a woman without
casting oneself at her feet. Fashion, *le bon ton*, regulated every
important or petty proceeding, the manner of making a declaration to a woman and of breaking an engagement, of entering
upon and managing a duel, of treating an equal, an inferior and
a superior. If any one failed in the slightest degree to conform
to this code of universal custom, he is called "a specimen." A
man of heart or of talent, D'Argenson, for example, bore a
surname of "simpleton," because his originality transcended the
conventional standard. "That has no name, there is nothing like
it!" embodies the strongest censure. In conduct as in literature,
whatever departs from a certain type is rejected. The quantity
of authorized actions is as great as the number of authorized
words. The same super-refined taste impoverishes the initiatory
act as well as the initiatory expression, people acting as they
write, according to acquired formulas and within a circumscribed
circle. Under no consideration can the eccentric, the unforeseen,
the spontaneous, vivid inspiration be accepted. Among twenty
instances I select the least striking since it merely relates to a
simple gesture, and is a measure of other things. Mademoiselle
de —— obtains, through family influence, a pension for Marcel,
a famous dancing-master, and runs off, delighted, to his domicile
to convey him the patent. Marcel receives it and at once flings
it on the floor: "Mademoiselle, did I teach you to offer an object
in that manner? Pick up that paper and hand it to me as you
ought to." She picks up the patent and presents it to him with
all suitable grace. "That's very well, Mademoiselle, I accept it, although your elbow was not quite sufficiently rounded,
and I thank you."[1] So many graces end in becoming weari-

---

[1] "Paris, Versailles et les provinces," I. 162. "The king of Sweden is here; he wears
rosettes on his breeches; all is over; he is ridiculous, and a provincial king." ("Le Gouvernement de Normandie," by Hippeau, IV. 237, July 4, 1784.)

some; after having eaten rich food for years, a little milk and dry bread becomes welcome.

Among all these social flavourings one is especially abused; one which, unremittingly employed, communicates to all dishes its frigid and piquant relish, I mean insincerity *(badinage)*. Society does not tolerate passion, and in this it exercises its right. One does not enter company to be either vehement or sombre; a strained air or one of concentration would appear incongruous. The mistress of a house is always right in reminding a man that his emotional constraint brings on silence. " Monsieur Such-a-one, you are not amiable to-day." To be always amiable is, accordingly, an obligation, and, through this training, a sensibility that is diffused through innumerable little channels never produces a broad current. " One has a hundred friends, and out of these hundred friends two or three may have some chagrin every day; but one could not award them sympathy for any length of time as, in that event, one would be wanting in consideration for the remaining ninety-seven; "[1] one might sigh for an instant with some one of the ninety-seven, and that would be all. Madame du Deffant, having lost her oldest friend, the President Hénault, that very day goes to sup in a large assemblage: " Alas," she exclaimed, "he died at six o'clock this evening; otherwise you would not see me here." Under this constant régime of distractions and diversions there are no longer any profound sentiments; we have nothing but an epidermic exterior; love itself is reduced to "the exchange of two phantasies." And, as one always falls on the side to which one inclines, levity becomes deliberate and a matter of elegance.[2] Indifference of the heart is in fashion; one would be ashamed to show any genuine emotion. One takes pride in playing with love, in treating woman as a mechanical puppet, in touching one inward spring, and then another, to force out, at will, her anger or her pity. Whatever she may do, there is no deviation from the most insulting politeness; the very exaggeration of false respect which is lavished on her is a mockery by which indifference for her is fully

---

[1] Stendhal, " Rome, Naples and Florence," 379. Stated by an English lord.

[2] Marivaux, " Le Petit-Maître corrigé." Gresset, "Le Méchant." Crébillon *fils*, " La Nuit et le Moment," (especially the scene between Clitandre and Lucinde). Collé, " La Verité dans le Vin," (the part of the abbé with the *présidente*). De Bezenval, 79. (The Comte de Frise and Mme. de Blot). " Vie privée du Maréchal de Richelieu," (scenes with Mme. Michelin). De Goncourt, 167 to 174.

manifested. But they go still further, and in souls naturally un-feeling, gallantry turns into wickedness. Through *ennui* and the demand for excitement, through vanity, and as a proof of dexterity, delight is found in tormenting, in exciting tears, in dishonoring and in killing women by slow torture. At last, as self-love is a bottom-less pit, there is no species of blackness of which these polished exe-cutioners are not capable; the personages of Laclos are derived from these originals.[1] Monsters of this kind are, undoubtedly, rare; but there is no need of reverting to them to ascertain how much egotism is harbored in the gallantry of society. The women who erected it into an obligation are the first to realize its deceptive-ness, and, amidst so much homage without heat, to pine for the communicative warmth of a powerful sentiment. The character of the century obtains its last trait when "the man of feeling" comes on the stage.

II.

It is not that the groundwork of habits becomes different, for these remain equally worldly and dissipated up to the last. But fashion authorizes a new affectation, consisting of effusions, rev-eries, and sensibilities as yet unknown. The point is to return to nature, to admire the country, to delight in the simplicity of rustic manners, to be interested in village people, to be humane, to have a heart, to find pleasure in the sweetness and tenderness of natural affections, to be a husband and a father, and still more, to possess a soul, virtues, and religious emotions, to believe in Prov-idence and immortality, to be capable of enthusiasm. One wants to be all this, or at least show an inclination that way. In any event, if the desire does exist it is on the implied condition, that one shall not be too much disturbed in his ordinary pursuits, and that the sensations belonging to the new order of life shall in no respect interfere with the enjoyments of the old one. Ac-cordingly the exaltation which arises is little more than cerebral fer-mentation, and the idyl is to be almost entirely performed in the drawing-room. Behold, then, literature, the drama, painting and all the arts pursuing the same sentimental road to supply heated imaginations with factitious nourishment.[2] Rousseau, in labored

---

[1] Laclos, "Les Liaisons Dangereuses." Mme. de Merteuil was copied after a Marquise de Grenoble. Remark the difference between Lovelace and Valmont, one being stimulated by pride and the other by vanity.

[2] The growth of sensibility is indicated by the following dates: Rousseau, "Sur l'influence

periods, preaches the charms of an uncivilized existence, while other masters, between two madrigals, fancy the delight of sleeping naked in the primeval forest. The lovers in "La Nouvelle Héloise" interchange passages of fine style through four volumes, whereupon a person "not merely methodical but prudent," the Comtesse de Blot, exclaims, at a social gathering at the Duchesse de Chartres's, "a woman truly sensitive, unless of extraordinary virtue, could refuse nothing to the passion of Rousseau."[1] People collect in a dense crowd in the Exhibition around "L'Accordée de Village," "La Cruche Cassée," and the "Retour de nourrice," with other rural and domestic idyls by Greuze; the voluptuous element, the tempting undercurrent of sensuality made perceptible in the fragile simplicity of his artless maidens, is a dainty bit for the libertine tastes which are kept alive beneath moral aspirations.[2]   After these, Ducis, Thomas, Parny, Colardeau, Boucher, Delille, Bernardin de St. Pierre, Marmontel, Florian, the mass of orators, authors and politicians, the misanthrope Champfort, the logician La Harpe, the minister Necker, the versifiers and the imitators of Gessner and Young, the Berquins, tho Bitaubés, nicely combed and bedizened, holding embroidered handkerchiefs to wipe away tears, are to marshal forth the universal eclogue down to the acme of the Revolution.   Marmontel's "Moral Tales" appear in the columns of the "Mercure" for 1791 and 1792,[3] while the number following the massacres of September opens with verses "to the manes of my canary-bird."

Consequently, in all the details of private life, sensibility displays its magniloquence.   A small temple to Friendship is erected in a park.   A little altar to Benevolence is set up in a private closet.   Dresses *à la Jean-Jacques-Rousseau* are worn "analogous to the principles of that author."   Head-dresses are selected with "puffs *au sentiment*" in which one may place the portrait of one's daughter, mother, canary or dog, the whole "garnished with the

---

des lettres et des arts," 1749; "Sur l'inégalité," 1753; "Nouvelle Héloise," 1759. Greuze, "Le Père de Famille lisant la Bible," 1755; "L'Accordée de Village," 1761. Diderot, "Le fils naturel," 1757; "Le Père de Famille," 1758.

[1] Mme. de Genlis, "Mémoires," chap. xvii.   George Sand, I. 72.   The young Mme. de Francueil, on seeing Rousseau for the first time, burst into tears.

[2] This point has been brought out with as much skill as accuracy by Messieurs de Goncourt in "L'Art au dix-huitième siècle," I. 433-438.

[3] The number for August, 1792, contains "Les Rivaux d'eux-mêmes." About the same time other pieces are inserted in the "Mercure," such as "The federal union of Hymen and Cupid," "Le Jaloux," "A Pastoral Romance," "Ode Anacréontique à Mlle. S. D. . . . ." etc.

M

hair of one's father or intimate friend."[1] People keep intimate friends for whom "they experience something so warm and so tender that it nearly amounts to a passion" and whom they cannot go three hours a day without seeing. "Every time female companions interchange tender ideas the voice suddenly changes into a pure and languishing tone, each fondly regarding the other with approaching heads and frequently embracing," and suppressing a yawn a quarter of an hour after, with a nap in concert, because they have no more to say. Enthusiasm becomes an obligation. On the revival of "Le père de famille" there are as many handkerchiefs counted as spectators, and ladies faint away. "It is customary, especially for young women, to be excited, to turn pale, to melt into tears and, generally, to be seriously affected on encountering M. de Voltaire; they rush into his arms, stammer and weep, their agitation resembling that of the most passionate love."[2] When a society-author reads his work in a drawing-room, fashion requires that the company should utter exclamations and sob, and that some pretty fainting subject should be unlaced. Mme. de Genlis, who laughs at these affectations, is no less affected than the rest. Suddenly some one in the company is heard to say to the young orphan whom she is exhibiting: "Pamela, show us Héloise," whereupon Pamela, loosening her hair, falls on her knees and turns her eyes up to heaven with an air of inspiration, to the great applause of the assembly.[3] Sensibility becomes an institution. The same Madame de Genlis founds an order of Perseverance which soon includes "as many as ninety chevaliers in the very best society." To become a member it is necessary to solve some riddle, to answer a moral question and pronounce a discourse on virtue. Every lady or chevalier who discovers and publishes "three well-verified virtuous actions" obtains a gold medal. Each chevalier has his "brother in arms," each lady has her bosom friend and each member has a device, and each device, framed in a little pict-

---

[1] Mme. de Genlis, "Adèle et Théodore," I. 312. De Goncourt, "La Femme au dix-huitième siècle," 318. Mme. d'Oberkirk, I. 56. Description of the puff *au sentiment* of the Duchesse de Chartres (de Goncourt, 311): "In the background is a woman seated in a chair and holding an infant, which represents the Duc de Valois and his nurse. On the right is a paroquet pecking at a cherry, and on the left a little negro, the duchess's two pets : the whole is intermingled with locks of hair of all the relations of Mme. de Chartres, the hair of her husband, father and grandfather."

[2] Mme. de Genlis, "Les Dangers du Monde." I. scene vii. ; II. scene iv. ; "Adèle et Théodore," I. 312; "Souvenirs de Félicie," 199; Bachaumont, IV., 320.

[3] Mme. de Larochejacquelein, "Mémoires."

ure, figures in the " Temple of Honor," a sort of tent gallantly decorated, and which M. de Lauzun causes to be erected in the middle of a garden.[1] The sentimental parade is complete, a drawing-room masquerade being visible even in this chivalric revival.

The froth of enthusiasm and of fine words nevertheless leaves in the heart a residuum of active benevolence, trustfulness, and even happiness, or, at least, expansiveness and freedom. Wives, for the first time, are seen accompanying their husbands into garrison; mothers desire to nurse their infants, and fathers begin to interest themselves in the education of their children. Simplicity again forms an element of manners. Hair-powder is no longer put on little boys' heads; many of the seigniors abandon laces, embroideries, red heels and the sword, except when in full dress. People appear in the streets "dressed à la Franklin, in coarse cloth, with a knotty cane and thick shoes."[2] The taste no longer runs on cascades, statues and stiff and pompous decorations; the preference is for the English garden. The queen arranges a village for herself at the Trianon, where, "dressed in a frock of white cambric muslin and a gauze neck-handkerchief, and with a straw hat," she fishes in the lake and sees her cows milked. Etiquette falls away like the paint scaling off from the skin, disclosing the bright hue of natural emotions. Madame Adelaide takes up a violin and replaces an absent musician to let the peasant girls dance.[3] The Duchesse de Bourbon goes out early in the morning incognito to bestow alms, and "to see the poor in their garrets." The Dauphine jumps out of her carriage to assist a wounded postilion, a peasant knocked down by a stag. The king and the Comte d'Artois help a carter to extract his cart from the mud. People no longer think about self-constraint, and self-adjustment, and of keeping up their dignity under all circumstances, and of subjecting the weaknesses of human nature to the exigencies of rank. On the demise of the first Dauphin,[4] whilst the people in the room place themselves before

[1] Mme. de Genlis, "Mémoires," chap. xx. De Lauzun, 270.
[2] Mme. d'Oberkirk, II. 35 (1783–1784). Mme. Campan, III. 371. Mercier, "Tableau de Paris," *passim.*
[3] "Correspondance" by Métra (XVII. 55, 1784). Mme. d'Oberkirk, II. 234. "Marie Antoinette," by d'Arneth and Geffroy, II. 63, 29.
[4] "Le Gouvernement de Normandie," by Hippeau, IV. 387 (Letters of June 4, 1789, by an eye-witness).

the king to prevent him from entering it, the queen falls at his
knees, and he says to her, weeping, "Ah, my wife, our dear child
is dead, since they do not wish me to see him." And the narrator adds with admiration; "I always seem to see a good husbandman and his excellent partner a prey to the deepest despair
at the loss of their beloved child." Tears are no longer concealed, as it is a point of honor to be a man. One becomes human and familiar with one's inferiors. A prince, on a review,
says to the soldiers on presenting the princess to them, "My
boys, here is my wife." There is a disposition to make people
happy, and to take great delight in their gratitude. To be kind,
to be loved is the object of the head of a government, of a man
in place. This goes so far that God is prefigured according to
this model. The "harmonies of nature" are construed into the
delicate attentions of Providence; on instituting filial affection the
Creator "deigned to choose for our best virtue our sweetest pleasure."[1] The idyl which is imagined to take place in heaven cor-
responds with the idyl practised on earth. From the public up
to the princes, and from the princes down to the public, in prose,
in verse, in compliments at festivities, in official replies, in the style
of royal edicts down to the songs of the market-women, there is
a constant interchange of graces and of sympathies. Applause
bursts out in the theatre at any verse containing an allusion to
princes, and, a moment after, at the speech which exalts the
merits of the people, the princes return the compliment by applauding in their turn.[2] On all sides, just as this society is van-
ishing, a mutual deference, a spirit of kindliness arises, like a soft
and balmy autumnal breeze, to dissipate whatever harshness remains of its aridity and to mingle with the radiance of its last
hours the perfume of dying roses. We now encounter acts and

---

[1] Florian, "Ruth."

[2] Hippeau, IV. 86 (June 23, 1773), on the representation of "Le Siege de Calais," at the
Comédie Française, at the moment when Mlle. Vestris uttered these words:

> Le Français dans son prince aime à trouver un frère
> Qui, né fils de l'Etat, en devienne le père.

"Long and universal plaudits greeted the actress who had turned in the direction of the
Dauphin." In another place these verses occur:

> Quelle leçon pour vous, superbes potentats!
> Veillez sur vos sujets dans le rang le plus bas,
> Tel, loin de vos regards, dans le misère expire,
> Qui quelque jour peut-être, eut sauvé votre empire.

"The Dauphin and the Dauphine in turn applauded the tirade. This demonstration of their
sensibility was welcomed with new transports of affection and gratitude."

words of infinite grace, unique of their kind, like a lovely, ex-quisite little figure on old Sèvres porcelain. One day, on the Comtesse Amélie de Boufflers speaking somewhat flippantly of her husband, her mother-in-law interposes, "You forget that you are speaking of my son." "True, mamma, I thought I was only speaking of your son-in-law." It is she again who, on playing "the boat," and obliged to decide between this beloved mother-in-law and her own mother, whom she scarcely knew, replies, "I would save my mother and drown with my mother-in-law."[1] The Duchesse de Choiseul, the Duchesse de Lauzun, and others be-sides, are equally charming miniatures. When the affections and the intellect combine their refinements they produce masterpieces, and these, like the art, the refinements and the society which surrounds them, possess a charm unsurpassed by anything except their own fragility.

III.

The reason is that, the better adapted men are to a certain sit-uation the less prepared are they for the opposite situation. The habits and faculties which serve them in the previous condition become prejudicial to them in the new one. In acquiring talents adapted to tranquil times they lose those suited to times of agita-tion, reaching the extreme of feebleness at the same time with the extreme of urbanity. The more polished an aristocracy be-comes the weaker it becomes, and when no longer possessing the power to please it no longer possesses the strength to struggle. And yet, in this world, we must struggle if we would live. In humanity, as in nature, empire belongs to force. Every creature that loses the art and energy of self-defence becomes so much more certainly a prey according as its brilliancy, imprudence and even gentleness, deliver it over in advance to the gross appetites roaming around it. Where find resistance in characters formed by the habits we have just described? To defend ourselves we must, first of all, look carefully around us, see and foresee, and provide for danger. How could they do this living as they did? Their circle is too narrow and too carefully enclosed. Confined to their castles and mansions they see only those of their own sphere, they hear only the echo of their own ideas, they imagine that there is nothing beyond; the public seems to consist of two hundred persons. Moreover, disagreeable truths are not ad-

---

[1] Madame de Genlis, "Souvenirs de Félicie," 76, 161.

mitted into a drawing-room, especially when of personal import, an idle fancy there becoming a dogma because it becomes conventional. Here, accordingly, we find those who, already deceived by the limitations of their accustomed horizon, fortify their delusion still more by delusions about their fellow-men. They comprehend nothing of the vast world which envelopes their little world ; they are incapable of entering into the sentiments of a bourgeois, of a villager ; they have no conception of the peasant as he is but as they would like him to be. The idyl is in fashion, and no one dares dispute it ; any other supposition would be false because it would be disagreeable, and as the drawing-rooms have decided that all will go well, all must go well. Never was a delusion more complete and more voluntary. The Duc d'Orléans offers to wager a hundred louis that the States-General will dissolve without accomplishing anything, not even abolishing the *lettre-de-cachet.* After the demolition has begun, and yet again after it is finished, they will form opinions no more accurate. They have no idea of social architecture ; they know nothing about either its materials, its proportions, or its harmonious balance ; they have had no hand in it, they have never worked at it. They are entirely ignorant of the old building[1] in which they occupy the first story. They are not qualified to calculate either its pressure or its resistance.[2] They conclude, finally, that it is better to let the thing tumble in, and that the restoration of the edifice in their behalf will follow its own course, and that they will return to their drawing-room, expressly rebuilt for them, and freshly gilded, to begin over again the pleasant conversation which an accident, some tumult in the street, had interrupted.[3] Clear-sighted in society, they are obtuse in politics. They examine everything by the artificial light of candles ; they are disturbed and bewildered in the powerful light of open day. The eyelid has grown stiff through age. The organ so long bent on the petty details of one refined life no longer takes in the popular life of the masses, and, in the new sphere into which it is sud-

---

[1] M. de Montlosier, in the Constituent Assembly, is about the only person familiar with feudal laws.

[2] "A competent and impartial man who would estimate the chances of the success of the Revolution would find that there are more against it than against the five winning numbers in a lottery ; but this is possible, and unfortunately, this time, they all came out." (Duc de Lévis, "Souvenirs," 328.)

[3] "Corinne," by Madame de Staël, the character of the Comte d'Erfeuil. Malonet, "Mémoires," II. 297 (a memorable instance of political stupidity).

denly plunged, its refinement becomes the source of its blindness. Nevertheless action is necessary, for danger is seizing them by the throat. But the danger is of an ignoble species, while their education has provided them with no arms suitable for warding it off. They have learned how to fence, but not how to box. They are still the sons of those at Fontenoy, who, instead of being the first to fire, courteously raised their hats and addressed their English antagonists, " No, gentlemen, fire yourselves." Being the slaves of good-breeding they are not free in their movements. Numerous acts, and those the most important, those of a sudden, vigorous and rude stamp, are opposed to the respect a well-bred man entertains for others, or at least to the respect which he owes to himself. They do not consider these allowable among themselves ; they do not dream of their being allowed, and, the higher their position the more their rank fetters them. When the royal family sets out for Varennes the accumulated delays by which they are lost are the result of etiquette. Madame de Touzel insists on her place in the carriage to which she is entitled as governess of the Children of France. The king, on arriving, is desirous of conferring the marshal's baton on M. de Bouillé, and after running to and fro to obtain a baton he is obliged to borrow that of the Duc de Choiseul. The queen cannot dispense with a travelling dressing-case and one has to be made large enough to contain every imaginable implement from a warming-pan to a silver porridge-dish, with other dishes besides ; and, as if there were no shifts to be had in Brussels, there had to be a complete outfit in this line for herself and her children.[1] A narrow fidelity, humanity in its own despite *(quand même)*, the frivolity of the small literary spirit, graceful urbanity, profound igno rance,[2] the nullity or rigidity of the understanding and of the will are still greater with the princes than with the nobles. All are impotent against the wild and roaring outbreak. They have not the physical superiority that can master it, the vulgar charlatanism which can charm it away, the tricks of a Scapin to throw it off the scent, the bull's neck, the mountebank's gestures, the stentor's lungs, in short, the resources of the energetic temperament and of animal cunning, alone capable of diverting the rage of the unchained

---

[1] Mme. Campan, II. 140, 313.   Duc de Choiseul, "Mémoires."
[2] Journal of Dumont d'Urville, commander of the vessel which transported Charles X. into exile in 1830. See note 4 at the end of the volume.

brute.   To secure wrestlers of this stamp they seek for three
or four men of a different race and education, men having suffered and roamed about, a brutal plebeian like the abbé Maury,
a colossal and dirty satyr like Mirabeau, a bold and prompt
adventurer like that Dumouriez who, at Cherbourg, when,
through the feebleness of the Duc de Beuvron, the stores of grain
were given up and the riot began, hooted at and nearly cut to
pieces, suddenly sees the keys of the storehouse in the hands of
a Dutch sailor, and, yelling to the mob that it was betrayed through
a foreigner having got hold of the keys, himself jumps down
from the railing, seizes the keys and hands them to the officer
of the guard, saying to the people, "I am your father,—I
am the man to be responsible for the storehouse!"[1]   To entrust
oneself with porters and brawlers, to be collared by a political club,
to improvise on the highways, to bark louder than the barkers,
to fight with the fists or a cudgel, as with the gay youths of a
later day, against brutes and lunatics incapable of employing
other arguments, and who must be answered in the same vein, to
mount guard over the Assembly, to act as volunteer constable,
to spare neither one's own hide nor that of others, to be one of
the people to face the people, are simple and effectual proceedings, but so vulgar as to appear to them disgusting.   The idea
of resorting to such means never enters their head; they neither
know how, nor do they care to make use of their hands in such
business.[2]   They are skilled only in the duel and, almost immediately, the brutality of opinion, by means of assaults, stops the way
to polite combats.   Their arms, the shafts of the drawing-room,
epigrams, witticisms, songs, parodies, and other needle thrusts are
impotent against the popular bull.[3]   This character lacks both
roots and resources; through super-refinement it has become
etiolated; nature, impoverished by culture, is incapable of the
transformations by which we are renewed and survive.   An all-

---

[1] Dumouriez, "Mémoires," III. chap. iii. (July 21, 1789).

[2] "All these fine ladies and gentlemen who knew so well how to bow and courtesy and walk over a carpet, could not take three steps on God's earth without getting dreadfully fatigued. They could not even open or shut a door; they had not even strength enough to lift a log to put it on the fire; they had to call a servant to draw up a chair for them; they could not come in or go out by themselves.   What could they have done with their graces, without their valets to supply the place of hands and feet?" (George Sand, V. 61.)

[3] When Madame de F—— had expressed a clever thing she felt quite proud of it.   M—— remarked that on uttering something clever about an emetic she was quite surprised that she was not purged   Champfort, 107.

powerful education has repressed, mollified, enfeebled instinct itself. About to die, they experience none of the reactions of blood and rage, the universal and sudden restoration of the forces, the murderous spasm, the blind irresistible need of striking those who strike them. If a gentleman is arrested in his own house by a Jacobin we never find him splitting his head open.[1] They allow themselves to be taken, going quietly to prison; to make an uproar would be bad taste; it is necessary, above all things, to remain what they are, well-bred people of society. In prison both men and women dress themselves with great care, pay each other visits and keep up a drawing-room; it may be at the end of a corridor, by the light of three or four candles; but here they circulate jests, compose madrigals, sing songs and pride them selves on being as gallant, as gay and as gracious as ever: need people be morose and ill-behaved because accident has con- signed them to a poor inn? They preserve their dignity and their smile before their judges and on the cart; the women, es- pecially, mount the scaffold with the ease and serenity characteris- tic of an evening entertainment. It is the supreme characteristic of good-breeding, erected into an unique duty, and become to this aristocracy a second nature, which is found in its virtues as well as in its vices, in its faculties as well as in its impotencies, in its prosperity as at its fall, and which adorns it even in the death to which it conducts.

---

[1] The following is an example of what armed resistance can accomplish for a man in his own house. "A gentleman of Marseilles, proscribed and living in his country domicile, has provided himself with gun, pistols and sabre, and never goes out without this armament, de- claring that he will not be taken alive. Nobody has dared to execute the order of arrest." (Anne Plumptre, "A Residence of three years in France," 1802–1805, II. 115.

BOOK THIRD.

𝔗𝔥𝔢 𝔖𝔭𝔦𝔯𝔦𝔱 𝔞𝔫𝔡 𝔱𝔥𝔢 𝔇𝔬𝔠𝔱𝔯𝔦𝔫𝔢.

CHAPTER I.

THE COMPOSITION OF THE REVOLUTIONARY SPIRIT.—Scientific acquisitions its first element.—I. The accumulation and progress of discoveries in science and in nature.—They serve as a starting-point for the new philosophers.—II. Change of the point of view in the science of man.—It is detached from theology and is united with the natural sciences.—III. The transformations of history.—Voltaire.—Criticism and conceptions of unity.—Montesquieu.—An outline of social laws.—IV. The transformation of psychology.—Condillac.—The theory of sensation and of signs.—V. The analytical method.—Its principle.—The conditions requisite to make it productive.—These conditions wanting or inadequate in the 18th century.—The truth and survival of the principle.

ON seeing a man with a somewhat feeble constitution, but healthy in appearance and of steady habits, greedily swallow some new kind of cordial and then suddenly fall to the ground, foam at the mouth, act deliriously and writhe in convulsions, we at once surmise that this agreeable beverage contained some dangerous substance; but a delicate analysis is necessary to detect and decompose the poison. The philosophy of the eighteenth century contained poison, and of a kind as potent as it was peculiar; for, not only is it a long historic elaboration, the final and condensed essence of the tendency of the thought of the century, but again, its two principal ingredients have this peculiarity, that, separate, they are salutary, and in combination they form a venomous compound.

I.

The first is scientific discovery, admirable on all sides, and beneficent in its nature; it is made up of masses of facts slowly

accumulated and then summarily presented,or in rapid succession.
For the first time in history the sciences expand and affirm
each other to the extent of providing, not, as formerly, under
Galileo and Descartes, constructive fragments, or a provisional
scaffolding, but a definite and demonstrated system of the universe, that of Newton.[1] Around this capital fact, almost all the
discoveries of the century, either as complementary or as pro-
longations, range themselves. In pure mathematics we have the
Infinitesimal Calculus discovered simultaneously by Leibnitz and
Newton, mechanics reduced by d'Alembert to a single theorem,
and that superb collection of theories which, elaborated by the
Bernouillis, Euler, Clairaut, d'Alembert, Taylor and Maclaurin, is
finally completed at the end of the century by Monge, Lagrange,
and Laplace.[2] In astronomy, the series of calculations and
observations which, from Newton to Laplace, transforms science
into a problem of mechanics, explains and predicts the movements
of the planets and of their satellites, indicating the origin and
formation of our solar system, and, extending beyond this, through
the discoveries of Herschel, affording an insight into the distribution of the stellar archipelagos, and of the grand outlines of
celestial architecture. In physics, the decomposition of light and
the principles of optics discovered by Newton, the velocity of
sound, the form of its undulations, and from Sauveur to Chladni,
from Newton to Bernouilli and Lagrange, the experimental laws
and leading theorems of Acoustics, the primary laws of the radiation of heat by Newton, Kraft and Lambert, the theory of
latent heat by Black, the proportions of caloric by Lavoisier 'and
Laplace, the first true conceptions of the source of fire and heat,
the experiments, laws, and means by which Dufay, Nollet,
Franklin, and especially Coulomb explain, manipulate and, for
the first time, utilize electricity. In Chemistry, all the foundations
of the science : isolated oxygen, nitrogen and hydrogen, the composition of water, the theory of combustion, chemical nomenclature, quantitative analysis, the indestructibility of matter, in short,
the discoveries of Scheele, Priestley, Cavendish and Stahl,

---

[1] " Philosophiæ naturalis principia," 1687 ; " Optics," 1704.
[2] See concerning this development Comte's " Philosophie Positive," vol. I. At the
beginning of the eighteenth century, mathematical instruments are carried to such perfection as to warrant the belief that all physical phenomena may be analysed, light, electricity,
sound, crystallization, heat, elasticity, cohesion and other effects of molecular forces. See
" Whewell's History of the Inductive Sciences," II., III.

crowned with the clear and concise theory of Lavoisier. In Mineralogy, the goniometer, the constancy of angles and the primary laws of derivation by Romé de Lisle, and next the discovery of types and the mathematical deduction of secondary forms by Haüy. In Geology, the verification and results of Newton's theory, the exact form of the earth, the depression of the poles, the expansion of the equator,[1] the cause and the law of the tides, the primitive fluidity of the planet, the constancy of its internal heat, and then, with Buffon, Desmarets, Hutton and Werner, the aqueous or igneous origin of rocks, the stratifications of the earth, the structure of beds of fossils, the prolonged and repeated submersion of continents, the slow growth of animal and vegetable deposits, the vast antiquity of life, the denudations, fractures and gradual transformation of the terrestrial surface,[2] and, finally, the grand picture in which Buffon describes in approximative manner the entire history of our globe, from the moment it formed a mass of glowing lava down to the time when our species, after so many lost or surviving species, was able to inhabit it.

Upon this science of inorganic matter we see arising at the same time the science of organic matter. Grew, and then Vaillant had just demonstrated the sexual system and described the fecundation of plants; Linnæus invents botanic nomenclature and the first complete classifications; the Jussieus discover the subordination of characteristics and natural classification. Digestion is explained by Réaumur and Spallanzani, respiration by Lavoisier; Prochaska verifies the mechanism of reflex actions; Haller and Spallanzani experiment on and describe the conditions and phases of generation. Scientists penetrate to the lowest stages of animal life. Réaumur publishes his admirable observations on insects and Lyonnet devotes twenty years to portraying the willow-caterpillar; Spallanzani resuscitates his rotifers, Tremblay dissects his fresh-water polyps, and Needham reveals his infusoria. The experimental conception of life is deduced from these various researches. Buffon already, and especially Lamarck, in their great and incomplete sketches, outline with penetrating divination the leading features of modern physiology and zool-

---

[1] The travels of La Condamine in Peru and of Maupertuis in Lapland.
[2] Buffon, "Théorie de la Terre," 1749; "Epoques de la Nature," 1788. "Carte géologique de l'Auvergne," by Desmarets, 1766.

ogy. Organic molecules everywhere diffused or everywhere growing, species of globules constantly in course of decay and restoration, which, through blind and spontaneous development, transform themselves, multiply and combine, and which, without either foreign direction or any preconceived end, solely through the effect of their structure and surroundings, unite together to form those masterly organisms which we call plants and animals : in the beginning, the simplest forms, and next a slow, gradual, complex and perfected organization; the organ created through habits, necessities and surrounding medium; heredity transmitting acquired modifications,[1] all denoting in advance, in a state of conjecture and approximation, the cellular theory of later physiologists[2] and the conclusions of Darwin. In the picture which the human mind draws of nature, the general outline is marked by the science of the eighteenth century, the arrangement of its plan and of the principal masses being so correctly marked, that to-day the leading lines remain intact. With the exception of a few partial corrections we have nothing to efface.

This vast supply of positive or probable facts, either demonstrated or anticipated, furnishes food, substance and impulse to the intellect of the century. Consider the leaders of public opinion, the promoters of the new philosophy : they are all, in various degrees, versed in the physical and natural sciences. Not only are they familiar with theories and authorities, but again they have personal knowledge of facts and objects. Voltaire[3] is among the first to explain the optical and astronomical theories of Newton, and again to make calculations, observations and experiments of his own. He writes memoirs for the Academy of Sciences "On the Measure of Motive Forces," and "On the Nature and Diffusion of Heat." He handles Réaumur's thermometer, Newton's prism, and Muschenbrock's pyrometer. In his laboratory at Cirey he has all the known apparatus for physics and

---

[1] See a lecture by M. Lacaze-Duthier on Lamarck, "Revue Scientifique," III. 276–311.

[2] Buffon, "Histoire Naturelle," II. 340: "All living beings contain a vast quantity of living and active molecules. Vegetal and animal life seem to be only the *results of the actions of all the small lives peculiar* to each of the active molecules whose life is primary." Cf. Diderot, "Revue de d'Alembert."

[3] "Philosophie de Newton," 1738, and "Physique," by Voltaire. Cf. du Bois-Raymond, "Voltaire physicien," (Revue des Cours Scientifique, V. 539), and Saigey, "la Physique de Voltaire." "Voltaire," writes Lord Brougham, "had he continued to devote himself to experimental physics would undoubtedly have inscribed his name among those of the greatest discoverers of his age."

chemistry. He experiments with his own hand on the reflection of light in space, on the increase of weight in calcined metals, on the renewal of amputated parts of animals, and in the spirit of a true savant, persistently, with constant repetitions, even to the beheading of forty snails and slugs, to verify an assertion made by Spallanzani. The same curiosity and the same preparation prevails with all imbued with the same spirit. In the other camp, among the Cartesians, about to disappear, Fontenelle is an excellent mathematician, the competent biographer of all eminent men of science, the official secretary and true representative of the Academy of Sciences. In other places, in the Academy of Bordeaux, Montesquieu reads discourses on the mechanism of the echo, and on the use of the renal glands; he dissects frogs, tests the effect of heat and cold on animated tissues, and publishes observations on plants and insects. Rousseau, the least instructed of all, attends the lectures of the chemist Rouelle, botanizing and appropriating to himself all the elements of human knowledge with which to write his "Emile." Diderot taught mathematics and devoured every science and art even to the technical processes of all industries. D'Alembert stands in the first rank of mathematicians. Buffon translated Newton's theory of fluxions, and the Vegetable Statics of Hales; he is in turn a metallurgist, optician, geographer, geologist and, last of all, an anatomist. Condillac, to explain the use of signs and the filiation of ideas, writes abridgments of arithmetic, algebra, mechanics and astronomy.[1] Maupertuis, Condorcet and Lalande are mathematicians, physicists and astronomers; d'Holbach, Lamettrie and Cabanis are chemists, naturalists, physiologists and physicians. Prophets of a superior or inferior kind, masters or pupils, specialists or simple amateurs, all draw directly or indirectly from the living source that has just burst forth. From this they all start to teach man what he is, from whence he came, where he is going, what he may become and what he should be. A new point of departure leads to new points of view, and hence the idea which was then entertained of man is to effect a complete transformation.

---

[1] See his "Logique des Calculs" and his "Art de Raisonner."

II.

Suppose a mind thoroughly imbued with these new truths; place the spectator on the orbit of Saturn, and let him observe.[1] Amidst this vast and overwhelming space and in these boundless solar archipelagoes, how small is our own sphere, and the earth, what a grain of sand! What multitudes of worlds beyond our own, and, if life exists in them, what combinations are possible other than those of which we are the result! What is life, what is organic substance in this monstrous universe but an indifferent mass, a passing accident, the corruption of a few epidermic particles? And if this be life, what is that humanity which is so small a fragment of it? Such is man in nature, an atom, an ephemeral particle; let this not be lost sight of in our theories concerning his origin, his importance, and his destiny. "A mite that would consider itself as the centre of all things would be grotesque, and therefore it is essential that an insect almost infinitely small should not show conceit almost infinitely great."[2] How slow has been the evolution of the globe itself! What myriads of ages between the first cooling of its mass and the beginnings of life![3] Of what consequence is the turmoil of our ant-hill alongside of the geological tragedy in which we have borne no part, the strife between fire and water, the thickening of the earth's crust, the formation of the universal sea, the construction and separation of continents! Previous to our historical record what a long history of vegetable and animal existences! What a succession of flora and fauna! What generations of marine organisms in forming the strata of sediment! What generations of plants in forming the deposits of coal! What transformations of climate to drive the pachydermata away from the pole! And now comes man, the latest of all, shooting up as the terminal

---

[1] For a popular exposition of these ideas see Voltaire, *passim*, and particularly the "Micromégas" and "Les Oreilles du Comte de Chesterfield."

[2] Cf. Buffon, *ibid.* I. 31: "Those who imagine a reply with final causes do not reflect that they take the effect for the cause. The relationship which things bear to us having no influence whatever on their origin, moral fitness can never become a physical explanation." Voltaire, "Candide": "When His High Mightiness sends a vessel to Egypt is he in any respect embarrassed about the comfort of the mice that happen to be aboard of it?"

[3] Buffon, *ibid.* "Supplement," II. 513; IV. ("Epoques de la Nature"), 65, 167. According to his experiments with the cooling of a cannon ball he based the following periods: From the glowing fluid mass of the planet to the fall of rain 35,000 years. From the beginning of life to its actual condition 40,000 years. From its actual condition to the entire congealing of it and the extinction of life 93,000 years. He gives these figures simply as the minima. We now know that they are much too limited.

bud of the top of a lofty ancient tree, growing there a few seasons, but destined to perish, like the tree, after a few seasons,
when the increasing and foretold congelation allowing the tree
to live shall force the tree to die. He is not alone on the
branch: beneath him, around him, on a level with him, other
buds shoot forth, born of the same sap; but he must not forget,
if he would comprehend his own being, that, along with himself,
other lives exist in his vicinity, graduated up to him and issuing
from the same trunk. If he is unique he is not isolated, being
an animal among other animals;[1] in him and with them, substance, organization and birth, the formation and renewal of
the functions, senses and appetites, are similar, while his superior intelligence, like their rudimentary intelligence, has for
an indispensable organ a nervous matter whose structure is the
same with him and with them. Thus surrounded, brought forth
and borne along by nature, is it to be supposed that in nature he is
an empire within an empire ? He is there as the part of a whole,
by virtue of being a physical body, a chemical composition, an
animated organism, a sociable animal, among other bodies, other
compositions, other social animals, all analogous to him; and, by
virtue of these classifications, he is, like them, subject to laws.
For, if the first cause is unknown to us, and we dispute among
ourselves to know what it is, whether innate or external, we affirm
with certainty the mode of its action, and that it operates only
according to fixed and general laws. Every circumstance, whatever it may be, is conditioned, and, its conditions being given, it
never fails to conform to them. Of two links forming a chain,
the first always draws on the second. There are laws for numbers, forms, and motions, for the revolutions of the planets and
the fall of bodies, for the diffusion of light and the radiation of
heat, for the attractions and repulsions of electricity, for chemical
combinations, and for the growth, equilibrium and dissolution of
organized matter. They exist for the growth, support, and development of human societies, for the formation, conflict, and
direction of the ideas, the passions and the wills of human individuals.[2] In all this, man continues nature; hence, if we would

---

[1] Buffon, *ibid.* I. 12: "The first truth derived from this patient investigation of nature is,
perhaps, a humiliating truth for man, that of taking his place in the order of animals."

[2] Voltaire, "Philosophie, Du principe d'action : " "All beings, without exception, are subject to invariable laws."

comprehend him, we must observe him in her, after her, and like her, with the same independence, the same precautions, and in the same spirit. Through this remark alone the method of the moral sciences is fixed. In history, in psychology, in morals, in politics, the thinkers of the preceding century, Pascal, Bossuet, Descartes, Fenelon, Malebranche, and La Bruyère, still start from dogma; it is plain to every one qualified to read them that their position is already determined. Religion provided them with a complete theory of the moral order of things; according to this theory, latent or exposed, they described man and accommodated their observations to the preconceived type. The writers of the eighteenth century overthrow this method: they dwell on man, on the observable man, and on his surroundings; in their eyes, conclusions about the soul, its origin, and its destiny, must come afterwards and depend wholly, not on that which revelation, but on that which observation, furnishes. The moral sciences are divorced from theology and attach themselves, as if a prolongation of them, to the physical sciences.

III.

Through this substitution and this combination they become sciences. In history, every foundation is laid on which we of the present day build. Compare Bossuet's "Discours sur l'histoire universelle," and Voltaire's "Essai sur les mœurs," and we at once see how new and deep these foundations were. Criticism at once obtains its fundamental principle: considering that the laws of nature are universal and immutable it concludes from this that, in the moral world, as in the physical world, there can be no infringement of them, and that no arbitrary or foreign force intervenes to disturb the regular course of things, which affords a sure means of discerning myth from truth.[1] Biblical exegesis is born out of this maxim, and not alone that of Voltaire, but the exegetical methods of the future. Meanwhile it sceptically examines the annals of all people, carelessly cutting away and suppressing; too hastily, extravagantly, especially where the ancients are concerned, because its historical expedition is simply

---

1 "Essai sur les Mœurs," chap. cxlvii., the summary: "The intelligent reader readily sees that he must believe only in great events possessing some probability, and view with pity the fables with which fanaticism, romantic taste and credulity have at all times filled the world"

a reconnoitring journey; but everywhere bestowing such accurate glances that we now preserve almost all the outlines
of its summary chart. The primitive man was not a superior
being, enlightened from above, but a coarse savage, naked and
miserable, slow of growth, sluggish in progress, the most destitute
and most needy of all animals, and, on this account, sociable,
endowed like the bee and the beaver with an instinct for living
in groups, and moreover, an imitator like the monkey, but more
intelligent, capable of passing by degrees from the language
of gesticulation to that of articulation, beginning with a mono-
syllabic idiom which gradually increases in richness, precision
and subtlety.[1]   How many centuries are requisite to attain to
this primitive language!   How many centuries more to the
discovery of the most necessary arts, the use of fire, the fabrica-
tion of "hatchets of silex and jade," the melting and refining
of metals, the domestication of animals, the production and
modification of edible plants, the formation of early civilized and
durable communities, the discovery of writing, figures and astronomical periods.[2]   Only after a dawn of vast and infinite
length do we see in Chaldea and in China the commencement
of an accurate chronological history.   There are five or six
of these great independent centres of spontaneous civilization,
China, Babylon, ancient Persia, India, Egypt, Phœnicia, and the
two American empires.   On collecting these fragments together,
on reading such of their books as have been preserved, and
which travellers bring to us, the five Kings of the Chinese, the
Vedas of the Hindoos, the Zendavesta of the ancient Persians,
we find that all contain religions, moral theories, philosophies
and institutions, as worthy of study as our own.   Three of
these codes, those of India, China and the Mussulmans, still at
the present time govern countries as vast as our Europe, and
nations of equal importance.   We must not, like Bossuet, "overlook the universe in a universal history," and subordinate humanity to a small population confined to a desolate region

---

1 "Traité de Metaphysique," chap. i.   "Having fallen on this little heap of mud, and
with no more idea of man than man has of the inhabitants of Mars or Jupiter, I set foot on
the shore of the ocean of the country of Caffraria and at once began to search for a man.   I
encounter monkeys, elephants and negroes, with gleams of imperfect intelligence, etc."
The new method is here clearly apparent.

2 "Introduction à l'Essai sur les Mœurs: Des Sauvages."   Buffon, in "Epoques de la
nature," the seventh epoch, precedes Darwin in his ideas on the modifications of the useful
species of animals.

around the Dead Sea.[1] Human history is a thing of natural
growth like the rest; its direction is due to its own elements;
no external force guides it, but the inward forces that create it;
it is not tending to any prescribed end but developing a result.
And the chief result is the progress of the human mind.
"Amidst so many ravages and so much destruction, we see
a love of order secretly animating the human species, and fore-
stalling its utter ruin.   It is one of the springs of nature ever
recovering its energy; it is the source of the formation of the
codes of nations; it causes the law and the ministers of the
law to be respected in Tonquin and in the islands of Formosa
as well as in Rome."   Man thus possesses "a principle of reason," namely, a "mechanical instinct" suggesting to him useful
implements;[2] also an instinct of right suggesting to him his
moral conceptions.   These two instincts form a part of his
organization; he has them from his birth, "as the birds have
their feathers, and bears their hair."   Hence he is perfectible
through nature, and merely conforms to nature in improving his
mind and in bettering his condition.   The savage, "the Brazilian,
is an animal that has not yet attained to the completeness of its
species; a worm enclosed in its chrysalis envelope, and not
to become a butterfly until after the lapse of centuries."   Extend
the idea farther along with Turgot and Condorcet,[3] and, with all
its exaggerations, we see arising, before the end of the century,
our modern theory of progress, that which founds all our aspirations on the boundless advance of the sciences, on the increase
of comforts which their applied discoveries constantly bring
to the human condition, and on the increase of good sense
which their discoveries, popularized, slowly deposit in the human
brain.

A second principle has to be established to complete the foundations of history.   Discovered by Montesquieu it still to-day
serves as a constructive support, and, if we resume the work, as if
on the substructure of the master's edifice, it is simply owing to accumulated erudition placing at our disposal more substantial and
more abundant materials.   In human society all parts are inter-

---

[1] "Remarques de l'Essai sur les Mœurs." "We may speak of this people in connection
with theology but they are not entitled to a prominent place in history." "Entretien entre
A, B, C," the seventh.

[2] Franklin defined man as a maker of tools.

[3] Condorcet, "Esquisse d'un tableau historique des progrès de l'esprit humain."

dependent; no modification of one can take place without effect-
ing proportionate changes in the others.   Institutions, laws and
customs are not mingled together, as in a heap, through chance or
caprice, but connected one with the other through convenience
or necessity, as in a harmony.[1]   According as authority is in all,
in several or in one hand, according as the sovereign admits or
rejects laws superior to himself, with intermediary powers below
him, everything differs or tends to differ in an understood sense
and in a constant quantity,—public intelligence, education, the
form of judgments, the nature and order of penalties, the condition of women, military organization and the nature and extent
of taxation.   A multitude of subordinate wheels depend on the
great central wheel.   For, if the clock goes, it is owing to the harmony of its various parts, from which it follows that, on this
harmony ceasing, the clock gets out of order.   But, besides the
principal spring, there are others which, acting on or in combination with it, give to each clock a special character and a peculiar movement.   Such, in the first place, is climate, that is to say,
the degree of heat or cold, humidity or dryness, with its infinite
effects on man's physical and moral attributes, followed by its influence on political, civil and domestic servitude or freedom.
Likewise the soil, according to its fertility, its position and its extent.   Likewise the physical régime, according as a people is
composed of hunters, shepherds or agriculturists.   Likewise the
fecundity of the race, and the consequent slow or rapid increase
of population, and also the excess in number, now of males and
now of females.   And finally, likewise, are national character and
religion.   All these causes, each added to the other, or each limited by the other, contribute together to form a total result, namely
society.   Simple or complex, stable or unstable, barbarous or
civilized, this society contains within itself its explanations of its
being.   Strange as its structure may be, it can be explained;
also its institutions, however contradictory.   Neither prosperity,
nor decline, nor despotism, nor freedom, is a cast of the die
brought on by the vicissitudes of chance, nor so many passages
of theatrical display improvised by individual wills.   They are

---

[1] "Esprit des Lois," preface. "I, at first, examined men, thinking that, in this infinite
diversity of laws and customs, they were not wholly governed by their fancies. I brought
principles to bear and I found special cases yielding to them as if naturally, the histories of
all nations being simply the result of these, each special law being connected with another
law or depending on some general law."

conditions from which we cannot abstract ourselves. In any event it is serviceable to know these conditions, either to better ourselves or take all things patiently, now to carry out opportune reforms, now to renounce impracticable reforms, now to acquire the skill which enables us to succeed, and now to acquire the prudence which leads us to abstain.

IV.

The centre of the moral sciences is herein reached; the question now is concerning man in general. The natural history of the soul has to be set forth, and this must be done as we have done the others, by discarding all prejudice and adhering to facts, taking analogy for our guide, beginning with origins and following, step by step, the development by which the infant, the savage, the uncultivated primitive man, is converted into the rational and cultivated man. Let us consider life at the outset, the animal at the lowest degree on the scale, man as soon as he is born. The first thing we find is sensation, of this or that species, agreeable or painful, and next a want, tendency or desire, and next after these, through physiological mechanism, voluntary or involuntary movements, more or less exactly and more or less quickly appropriated and co-ordinated. And this elementary fact is not merely primitive; it is, again, constant and universal, since we encounter it at each moment of each life, and in the most complicated as well as in the simplest. Let us accordingly ascertain whether it is not the thread with which all our mental cloth is woven, and whether its spontaneous unfolding, and the knotting of mesh after mesh, is not finally to produce the entire network of our thought and passion. Condillac, with a mind of incomparable precision and lucidity, provides replies to nearly all the important questions arising from this idea, and which a revival of theological prejudice and the importation of German metaphysics into France was to bring into discredit at the beginning of the nineteenth century, but which fresh observation, the establishment of mental pathology, and multiplied vivisections now come to reanimate, to justify and to complete.[1]   Locke had already stated that our ideas all

---

[1] Pinel (1791), Esquirol (1838), on mental diseases. Prochaska, Legallois (1812), and then Flourens for vivisection. Hartley and James Mill at the end of the eighteenth century follow Condillac on the same psychological road; all contemporary psychologists have entered upon it. (Wundt, Helmholtz, Fechner, in Germany, Bain, Stuart Mill, Herbert Spencer and Carpenter, in England).

originate in outward or inward experience. Condillac shows additionally that the *actual elements* of perception, memory, idea, imagination, judgment, reasoning, knowledge are sensations, properly so called, or revived sensations; our loftiest ideas are derived from no other materials, for they can be reduced to signs which are themselves sensations of a certain kind. Sensations accordingly form the substance of human or of animal intelligence; but the former infinitely surpasses the latter in this, that, through the creation of signs, it succeeds in isolating, abstracting and noting fragments of sensations, that is to say, in forming, combining and employing general conceptions. This being granted, we are able to verify all our ideas, for, through reflection, we can revive and reconstruct the ideas we had formed without any reflection. No abstract definitions exist at the outset; abstraction is ulterior and derivative; at the head of each science must be placed examples, experiences, evident facts; from these we derive our general idea. In like manner we derive from several general ideas of the same degree another general idea, and so on successively, step by step, always proceeding according to the natural order of things, by constant analysis, using expressive signs, as with mathematicians in passing from calculation by the fingers to calculation by numerals, and from this to calculation by letters, and who, calling upon the eyes to aid reason, depict the inward analogy of quantities by the outward analogy of symbols. In this way science becomes complete by means of a properly organized language.[1] Through this reversal of the usual method we summarily dispose of disputes about words, escaping the illusions of human speech, simplifying study, remodelling education, insuring discoveries, subjecting every assertion to control, and bringing all truths within reach of all understandings.

V.

Such is the course to be pursued with all the sciences, and especially with the moral and political sciences. To consider in turn each distinct province of human activity, to decompose the leading notions out of which we form our conceptions, those of religion, society and government, those of utility, wealth and ex-

---

[1] Condillac, *passim.*, and especially in his last two works the "Logique," and the "Langue des Calculs."

change, those of justice, right and duty; to revert to palpable facts, to first experiences, to the simple circumstances harboring the elements of our ideas; to derive from these the precious ore without loss or alloy; to recompose our ideas with this, to fix its meaning and determine its value; to substitute for the vague and vulgar notion with which we started the precise scientific definition we arrive at, for the base metal we receive the refined metal we obtain, constituted the prevalent method taught by the philosophers under the name of analysis, and which sums up the whole progress of the century. Up to this point, and no farther, they are right; truth, every truth, is found in observable objects, and only from thence can it be derived; there is no other pathway leading to discovery. The operation, undoubtedly, is productive only when the vein is rich, and we possess the means of extracting the ore. To obtain a just notion of government, of religion, of right, of wealth, a man must be a historian beforehand, a jurisconsult and economist, and have gathered up myriads of facts; and, besides all this, he must possess a vast erudition and practised and special acuteness. If these conditions are only partially complied with, the operation again doubtless affords but incomplete results or a dubious alloy, a few rough drafts of the sciences, the rudiments of pedagogy along with Rousseau, of political economy with Quesnay, Smith, and Turgot, of linguistics with Des Brosses, and of arithmetical morals and criminal legislation with Bentham. Finally, if none of these conditions are complied with, the same operation in the hands of closet speculators, drawing-room amateurs, and oratorical charlatans in public places, will undoubtedly end only in mischievous compounds and in destructive explosions. Nevertheless a good law remains good even when the ignorant and the impetuous make a bad use of it; and if we of to-day resume the abortive effort of the eighteenth century, it is within the lines it transmitted to us.

CHAPTER II.

THIS grand and magnificent edifice of new truths resembles a tower of which the first story, quickly finished, at once becomes accessible to the public. The public ascends the structure and is requested by its constructors to look about, not at the sky and at surrounding space, but right before it and on the ground, so as to know the country on which it dwells. The point of view is certainly favorable, and the recommendation is judicious. To conclude, however, that the public will see accurately would not be warranted, for the state of its eyes must be examined, to ascertain whether it is near or far-sighted, or if the retina naturally, or through habit, is sensitive to certain colors. In like manner the French of the eighteenth century must be considered, the structure of their inward vision, that is to say, the fixed form of understanding they bear with them, unconsciously or undesignedly, into the tower.

I.

I. This fixed form consists of the classic spirit, which, applied to the scientific acquisitions of the period, produces the philosophy of the century and the doctrines of the Revolution. Various signs denote its presence, and notably its oratorical, regular and correct style, wholly consisting of generalized expressions and of related ideas. It lasts two centuries, from Malherbe and

Balzac to Delille and de Fontanes, and during this long period, no man of intellect, save two or three, and then only in private memoirs, as in the case of St. Simon, also in familiar letters like those of the Marquis and bailly de Mirabeau, either dares or can withdraw himself from its empire. Far from disappearing with the ancient régime it forms the matrix out of which every discourse and document issues, even the phrases and vocabulary of the Revolution. Now, what is more efficacious than a mould prepared beforehand, either imposed or accepted, in which by virtue of natural tendency, of tradition and of education, every mind can shut itself up to think? This one, accordingly, is a historic force, and of the highest order. Fully to comprehend it, let us study its formation.

Its establishment is coeval with that of the regular monarchy and polished intercourse, and it accompanies these, not accidentally, but in the natural order of things. For it is the work of the new public which the new régime and new habits then formed, consisting of an aristocracy rendered listless by the encroaching monarchy, of people well born and well educated who, withdrawn from activity, fall back on conversation and devote their leisure to enjoying the calm or refined pleasures of the intellect.[1] Finally, they find no other occupation or interest : to talk, to listen, to entertain themselves agreeably and with ease, on all subjects, grave or gay, of any interest to the men, and especially to the women, of society is their great affair. In the seventeenth century they are styled " honest folk ; " and thenceforth a writer, even the most abstract, addresses himself to them. " The honest man," says Descartes, " need not have read all books nor have studiously acquired all that is taught in the schools , " and he entitles his last treatise, " A search for Truth according to natural light, which alone, without the aid of Religion or Philosophy, determines the truths an *honest man* should possess on all matters forming the subjects of his thoughts." [2] In short, from one end

---

[1] Voltaire, "Dict. Phil.," see the article on Language. "Of all the languages in Europe the French is most generally used because it is the best adapted to conversation. Its character is derived from that of the people who speak it. For more than a hundred and fifty years past, the French have been the most familiar with society and the first to discard all discomfort in it. . . . It is a better currency than any other, even if it should lack weight."

[2] Descartes, ed. Cousin, XI. 333, I. 121. Descartes depreciates " simple knowledge acquired without the aid of reflection, such as languages, history, geography, and, generally, whatever is not based on experience. . . . It is no more the duty of an honest man to know Greek or Latin than to know the Swiss or Breton languages, nor the history of the Romano-Germanic empire any more than of the smallest country in Europe."

of his philosophy to the other, the only qualification he demands of his readers is "natural good sense," added to the common stock of experience acquired by contact with the world.   As these form the auditory they are likewise the judges.   "One must study the taste of the court," says Molière,[1] "for in no place are verdicts more just. . . . With simple common sense and intercourse with people of refinement, a habit of mind is there obtained which, without comparison, forms a more accurate judgment of things than the rusty attainments of the pedants." From this time forth, it may be said that the arbiter of truth and of taste is not, as before, an erudite Scaliger, but a man of the world, a Larochefoucauld, or a Tréville.[2]   The pedant and, after him, the savant, the specialist, is set aside.   "True honest people," says Nicole after Pascal, "require no sign.   They need not be divined ; they join in the conversation going on as they enter the room.   They are not styled either poets or geometers, but they are the judges of all these." [3]   In the eighteenth century they constitute the sovereign authority.   In the great crowd of "imbeciles," mingled with vulgar pedants, there is, says Voltaire, "a small group apart called *good society*, which group, rich, well brought up, well informed and polished, forms, so to say, the flower of humanity ; for it the greatest men have labored ; it is that which creates fame." [4]   Admiration, favor, importance, belong not to those who are worthy of it but to those who address themselves to this group.   "In 1789," said the Abbé Maury, "the French Academy alone enjoyed any consideration in France, and it really gave a position.   That of the Sciences signified nothing in public opinion, any more than that of Inscriptions. . . . Languages form the science of simpletons.   D'Alembert was ashamed of belonging to the Academy of Sciences.   Only a handful of people listen to a mathematician, a chemist, etc. ; the man of letters,

---

[1] Molière, "Les Femmes Savantes," and "La Critique de l'école des femmes." The parts of Dorante with Lycidas and of Clitandre with Trissotin.

[2] The learned Huet, (1630–1721), true to the taste of the sixteenth century, describes this change very well from his point of view. " When I entered the world of letters these were still flourishing; great reputations maintained their supremacy. I have seen letters decline and finally reach an almost entire decay. For I scarcely know a person of the present time that one can truly call a savant." The few Benedictines like Ducange and Mabillon, and later, the academician Fréret, the president Bouhier of Dijon, in short, the veritable erudites exercise no influence.

[3] Nicole, "Œuvres morales," in the second essay on Charity and Self-love, 142 .

[4] Voltaire, "Dialogues," "L'intendant des menus et l'abbé Grizel," 129.

the orator, addresses the universe." [1] Under a strong pressure of this kind the mind necessarily accommodates itself to the exigencies, the proprieties, the tastes, and the degree of attention and of instruction of its public. Hence the classic mould,—formed out of the habit of speaking, writing and thinking for a drawing-room audience.

This is evidently the case, and at the first glance, in relation to style and language. Between Amyot, Rabelais and Montaigne on the one hand, and Chateaubriand, Victor Hugo and Honoré de Balzac on the other, classic French comes into being and dies. Its title is ensured at the start; it is the language of honest people; it is fashioned not merely for them, but by them, and Vaugelas,[2] their secretary, devotes himself for thirty years to the registry of decisions according to the usages only of good society. Hence, in all its parts, both in its vocabulary and in its grammar, language is refashioned over and over again, according to the cast of their intellects, which is the prevailing intellect. In the first place the vocabulary is diminished. Most of the words specially employed on erudite and technical subjects, expressions that are too Greek and too Latin, terms peculiar to the schools, to science, to occupations, to the household, are excluded from discourse; those too closely denoting a particular occupation or profession are not considered proper in general conversation. A vast number of picturesque and expressive words are dropped, all that are crude, *gaulois* or *naïfs*, all that are local and provincial, or personal and made-up, all familiar and proverbial locutions,[3] many brusque, familiar and frank turns of thought, every haphazard, telling metaphor, almost every description of impulsive and dexterous utterance throwing a flash of light into the imagination and bringing into view the precise, colored and complete form, but of which a too vivid impression would run counter to the proprieties of polite conversation. " One improper word," said

---

[1] Mably adds with his accustomed coarseness, "We, in the French Academy, looked upon the members of the Academy of Sciences as our valets." These valets at that time consisted of Lavoisier, Fourcroy, Lagrange, Laplace, etc. (A narrative by Joseph de Maistre, quoted by Sainte-Beuve, "Causeries du lundi," IV. 283.)

[2] Vaugelas, "Remarques sur la langue française:" "It is the mode of speech of the most sensible portion of the court, as well as the mode of writing of the most sensible authors of the day. It is better to consult women and those who have not studied than those who are very learned in Greek and in Latin."

[3] One of the causes of the fall and discredit of the Marquis d'Argenson in the eighteenth century, was his habit of using these.

Vaugelas, " is all that is necessary to bring a person in society into contempt," and, on the eve of the Revolution, an objectionable term denounced by Madame de Luxembourg still consigns a man to the rank of " *espèces,*" because correct expression is ever an element of good manners. Language, through this constant screening, becomes attenuated and colorless : Vaugelas estimates that one-half of the phrases and terms employed by Amyot are set aside.[1] With the exception of La Fontaine, an isolated and spontaneous genius, who reopens the old sources, and La Bruyère, a bold seeker, who opens a fresh source, and Voltaire, an incarnate demon who, in his anonymous and pseudonymous writings, gives the rein to the violent, crude expressions of his inspiration,[2] the terms which are most appropriate fall into desuetude. One day, Gresset, in a discourse at the Academy, dares utter four or five of these,[3] relating, I believe, to carriages and head-dresses, whereupon murmurs at once burst forth. During his long retreat he had become provincial and lost the tone. By degrees, discourses are composed of " general expressions " only. These are even employed, in accordance with Buffon's precept, to designate particular objects. They are more in conformity with the urbane disposition which effaces, smooths away and avoids brusque and familiar accents, to which a crowd of ideas seems gross or trivial when not enveloped in a semi-transparency. They are better suited to a languid attention ; general terms in conversation alone suddenly arouse current and common ideas ; they are intelligible to every man from the single fact that he belongs to the drawing-room ; special terms, on the contrary, demand an effort of the memory or of the imagination. Suppose that, in relation to Franks or to savages, I should mention " a battle-axe," which would be at once understood ; should I mention a " tomahawk," or a "*francisque,*"[4] many would imagine that I was speaking Teuton or Iroquois.[5] In this respect the more elevated the genus,

---

[1] Vaugelas, *ibid.* "Although we may have eliminated one-half of his phrases and terms we nevertheless obtain in the other half all the riches of which we boast and of which we make a display." Compare together a lexicon of two or three writers of the sixteenth century and one of two or three writers of the seventeenth. A brief statement of the results of the comparison is here given. Let any one, with pen in hand, note the differences on a hundred pages of any of these texts, and he will be surprised at it. Take, for example, two writers of the same category, and of secondary grade, Charron and Nicole.

[2] For instance, in the article "Ignorance," in the "Dict. Philosophique."

[3] La Harpe, "Cours de Littérature," ed. Didot. II. 142.

[4] A battle-axe used by the Franks.—TR.

[5] I cite an example haphazard from the "Optimiste" (1788), by Colin d'Harleville. In

the more powerful the scruple; every appropriate word is ban-ished from poetry; if one happens to enter the mind it must be evaded or replaced by a paraphrase.   An eighteenth century poet avails himself of but little more than one-third of the dictionary, and poetic language at last becomes so restricted as to compel a man with anything to utter not to utter it in verse.

On the other hand the more pruning language undergoes the clearer it becomes.   Reduced to a select vocabulary the French-man says fewer things, but he says them more agreeably and more accurately.   "Urbanity, exactitude," these two words, born at the same time with the French Academy, are an abridgment of the reform of which it is the organ, and which the drawing-room, by it, and alongside of it, imposes on the public.   Grand seigniors in retirement, and unoccupied fine ladies, obtain amusement in an examination of the subtleties of words for the purpose of com-posing maxims, definitions and characters.   With admirable scrupulousness and infinitely delicate tact, writers and people of society apply themselves to weighing each word and each phrase in order to fix its sense, to measure its force and bearing, to determine its affinities, use and connections; and this work of precision is carried on from the earliest academicians, Vaugelas, Chapelain and Conrart, to the end of the classic epoch, in the "Synonymes" of Bauzée and Girard, in the "Remarques" by Duclos, in the "Commentaire" by Voltaire, in Corneille, in the "Lycée" of La Harpe,[1] in the efforts, the example, the practice and the authority of the great and the inferior writers of which all are correct.   Never did architects, obliged to use the common stones of a highway in building, better understand each piece, its dimensions, its shape, its resistance, its possible connections and suitable position.   All this understood, the question arises how to construct with the least trouble and with the utmost so-lidity, while the grammar undergoes reformation in the same sense as the dictionary.   Words following each other according to the variable order of impressions and emotions are no longer allow-able; they must be regularly and rigorously assigned accord-

---

a certain description, "The scene represents a bosquet filled with odoriferous trees."   The classic spirit rebels against stating the species of tree, whether lilacs, lindens or hawthorns. In the landscapes of this era we have the same thing, the trees being generalized,—of no known species.

[1] See in the "Lycée," by La Harpe, after the analysis of each piece, his remarks on detail in style.

ing to the unchangeable order of ideas. The author loses the right of placing first, or as a vidette, the object or trait which first and most vividly impresses him; the plan is arranged and positions are assigned beforehand. Each portion of the discourse has its own plan; no omission or transposition is permitted, as was done in the sixteenth century;[1] all are necessary to it, and in definite positions, at first the subject of the sentence with its appendices, then the verb, then the object direct, and, finally, the indirect connections. In this way the sentence forms a graduated scaffolding, the substance coming foremost, then the quality, then the modes and varieties of the quality, just as a good architect in the first place poses his foundation, then the building, then the accessories, economically and prudently, with a view to adapt each section of the edifice to the support of the section following after it. No sentence demands any less attention than another, nor is there any in which one may not at every step verify the connection or incoherence of the parts.[2] The method governing the arrangement of the simple sentence also governs that of the period, the paragraph and the series of paragraphs; it forms the style as it forms the syntax. Each small edifice occupies a distinct position, and but one, in the great total edifice. As the discourse advances, each section must in turn file in, never before, never after, no parasitic member being allowed to intrude, and no regular member being allowed to encroach on its neighbor, while all these members bound together by their very positions must move onward, combining all their forces on one single point. Finally, we have for the first time in a writing, natural and distinct groups, complete and compact harmonies, none of which infringe on the others or allow others to infringe on them. It is no longer allowable to write haphazard, according to the caprice of one's inspiration, to discharge one's ideas in bulk, to let oneself be interrupted by parentheses, to string along interminable rows of citations and enumerations. An end is proposed; some truth is to be demonstrated, some definition to be ascertained, some conviction to be brought about; to do this we must march, and ever directly onward. Order, sequence, progress,

---

[1] The omission of the pronouns, *I, he, we, you, they*, the article *the*, and of the verb, especially the verb *to be*. Any page of Rabelais, Amyot or Montaigne, suffices to show how numerous and various were the transpositions.

[2] Vaugelas, *ibid.* "No language is more inimical to ambiguities and every species of obscurity."

proper transitions, constant development constitute the characteristics of this style.   To such an extent is this pushed, that from the very first, familiar letters, romances, humorous pieces, and all ironical and gallant effusions, consist of morsels of systematic eloquence.[1] At the Hôtel Rambouillet, the explanatory period is displayed with as much fulness and as rigorously as with Descartes himself. One of the words most frequently occurring with Mme. de Scudéry is the conjunction *for*. Passion is worked out through close-knit arguments. Drawing-room compliments stretch along in sentences as finished as those of an academical oration. Scarcely completed, the instrument already discloses its aptitudes ; we are aware of its being made to explain, to demonstrate, to persuade and to popularize ; Condillac, a century later, is justified in saying that it is in itself a systematic means of decomposition and of recomposition, a scientific method analogous to arithmetic and algebra. At the very least it possesses the incontestable advantage of starting with a few ordinary terms, and of leading the reader along with facility and promptness, by a series of simple combinations, up to the loftiest.[2] By virtue of this, in 1789, the French tongue ranks above every other. The Berlin Academy establishes a prize to secure an explanation of its pre-eminence. It is spoken throughout Europe. No other language is used in diplomacy. As formerly with Latin, it is international, and henceforth seems to be the chosen organ of reasoning.

It is the organ only of a certain species of reasoning, *la raison raisonnante*, that requiring the least preparation for thought, giving itself as little trouble as possible, content with its acquisitions, taking no pains to increase or renew them, incapable of, or unwilling to embrace the plenitude and complexity of actualities. In its purism, in its disdain of terms suited to the occasion, in its avoidance of lively sallies, in the extreme regularity of its developments, the classic style is powerless to fully portray or to record the infinite and varied details of experience. It declines

---

[1] See the principal romances of the seventeenth century, the " Roman Bourgeois," by Furetière, the " Princesse de Clèves," by Madame de Lafayette, the " Clélie," by Mme. de Scudéry, and even Scarron's " Roman Comique." See Balzac's letters, and those of Voiture and their correspondents, the " Récit des grands jours d'Auvergne," by Fléchier, etc. On the oratorical peculiarities of this style cf. Sainte-Beuve, " Port-Royal," 2d ed. I. 515.

[2] Voltaire, ' Essai sur le poème épique' : " Our nation, regarded by strangers as superficial, is, with the pen in its hand, the wisest of all. Method is the dominant quality of all our writers.

to render the outward guise of things, the immediate sensations
of the spectator, the heights and depths of passion, the physiognomy, at once so composite and absolutely personal, of the
breathing individual, in short, that unique harmony of countless
traits, blended together and animated, which compose not human
character in general but one particular character, and which
a Saint-Simon, a Balzac, or a Shakespeare himself could not
render if the copious language they used, and which was en-
riched by their temerities, did not contribute its subtleties to the
multiplied details of their observation.[1] Neither the Bible, nor
Homer, nor Dante, nor Shakespeare[2] could be translated with
this style. Read Hamlet's monologue in Voltaire and see what
remains of it, an abstract piece of declamation, with about as
much of the original in it as there is of Othello in his Orosmane.
Look at Homer and then at Fenelon in the island of Calypso;
the wild, rocky island, where "gulls and other sea-birds with
long wings," build their nests, becomes in pure French prose an
orderly park arranged "for the pleasure of the eye." In the
eighteenth century, contemporary novelists, themselves belonging
to the classic epoch, Fielding, Swift, Defoe, Sterne and Richardson, are admitted into France only after excisions and much
weakening; their expressions are too free and their scenes are too
impressive; their freedom, their coarseness, their quaintness, would
form blemishes; the translator abbreviates, softens, and sometimes, in his preface, apologizes for what he retains. Room is
found, in this language, only for a portion of the truth, a scanty
portion, and which constant refining daily renders still more
scanty. Considered in itself, the classic style is always in danger
of accepting slight, unsubstantial *commonplaces* for its materials.
It spins them out, mingles and weaves them together; only
a fragile filagree, however, issues from its logical apparatus; we
may admire the elegant workmanship; but in practice, the work
is of little, none, or dangerous service.

1 "Shakespeare, who displayed a greater variety of expression than probably any writer in
any language, produced all his plays with about 15,000 words. Milton's works are built up
with 8,000; and the Old Testament says all it has to say with 5,642 words." (Max Müller,
"Lectures on the Science of Language," I. 309.) It would be interesting to place alongside
of this Racine's restricted vocabulary. That of Mme. de Scudery is extremely limited. In
the best romance of the XVIIth century, the "Princesse de Clèves," the number of words
is reduced to the minimum. The Dictionary of the old French Academy contains 29,712
words; the Greek Thesaurus, by H. Estienne, contains about 150,000.

2 Compare together the translations of the Bible made by de Sacy and Luther; those of
Homer by Dacier, Bitaubé and Lecomte de Lisle; those of Herodotus, by Larcher and
Courrier, the popular tales of Perrault and those by Grimm, etc.

From these characteristics of style we divine those of the mind for which it serves as the organ. Two principal operations constitute the activity of the human understanding. Placed before objects, it receives a more or less complete, profound and exact impression of these ; and after this, turning away from them, it analyses its impression, and classifies, distributes, and more or less skilfully expresses the ideas derived from them. In the second of these operations the classicist is superior. Obliged to adapt himself to his audience, that is to say, to people of society who are not specialists and yet critical, he necessarily carries to perfection the art of exciting attention and of making himself heard ; that is to say, the art of composition and of writing. With patient industry, and multiplied precautions, he carries the reader along with him by a series of easy rectilinear conceptions, step by step, omitting none, beginning with the lowest and thus ascending to the highest, always progressing with steady and measured pace, securely and agreeably as on a promenade. No interruption or diversion is possible : on either side, along the road, balustrades keep him within bounds, each idea extending into the following one by such an insensible transition, that he involuntarily advances, without stopping or turning aside, until brought to the final truth where he is to be seated. Classic literature throughout bears the imprint of this talent ; there is no branch of it into which the qualities of a good discourse do not enter and form a part. It is paramount in those branches which, in themselves, are only half-literary, but which, by its means, become fully so, transforming writings into fine works of art which their matter would seem to class with scientific works, with the instrumentalities of action, with historical documents, with philosophical treatises, with doctrinal expositions, with sermons, polemics, dissertations and demonstrations, even with dictionaries, from Descartes to Condillac, from Bossuet to Buffon and Voltaire, from Pascal to Rousseau and Beaumarchais, in short, prose almost entirely, even official despatches and diplomatic correspondence, and private correspondence, from Madame de Sévigné to Madame du Deffant; including so many perfect letters escaping from the pens of women who never thought of it. It is paramount in those kinds which, in themselves, are literary, but which derive from it an oratorical turn. Not only does it impose a rigid plan,

o

a regular distribution of parts [1] in dramatic works, accurate proportions, suppressions and connections, a sequence and progress, as in a passage of eloquence, but again it tolerates only the most perfect discourses. There is no character that is not an accomplished orator; with Corneille and Racine, with Molière himself, the confidant, the barbarian king, the young cavalier, the drawing-room coquette, the valet, show themselves adepts in the use of language. Never have we encountered such adroit exordiums, such well-arranged evidence, such just reflections, such delicate transitions, such conclusive perorations. Never have dialogues borne such a strong resemblance to oratorical tilts. Each narration, each piece of portraiture, each detail of action, might be detached and serve as a good example for schoolboys, along with the masterpieces of the ancient tribune. So strong is this tendency that, on the approach of the final moment, in the agony of death, alone and without witnesses, a character contrives to plead his own frenzy and to die eloquently.

II.

This excess marks a defect. In the two operations which the human mind performs, the classicist is more successful in the second than in the first. The second, indeed, stands in the way of the first, the obligation of saying things perfectly always impeding the utterance of what should be said. With him the form is more admirable than the substance is rich, the general impression which serves as the animating source losing, in the regular channels to which it is confined, its force, depth and impetuosity. Poetry, properly so called, the outflow of meditation and of insight, is an impossibilty. Lyric poetry proves abortive, and likewise the epic poem.[2] Nothing springs up on these remote and sublime confines where speech is in accordance with music and painting. Never do we hear the involuntary outburst of vivid impressions, the lonely

---

[1] See the "Discours académique," by Racine, on the reception of Thomas Corneille: "In this chaos of dramatic poetry your illustrious brother brought *reason* on the stage, but reason associated with all the pomp and the ornamentation our language is capable of."

[2] Voltaire, "Essai sur le poème épique," 290. "It must be admitted that a Frenchman has more difficulty in writing an epic poem than anybody else. . . . Dare I confess it? Our own is the least poetic of all polished nations. The works in verse the most highly esteemed in France are those of the drama, which must be written in a familiar style approaching conversation."

confession of an overcharged soul,[1] which gives itself voice only for relief and expansion. When a creation of characters is imperative, as in dramatic poetry, the classic mould fashions but one species, those which through education, birth, or imitatively, always speak correctly, in other words, so many people of society. No others are visible on the stage or elsewhere, from Corneille and Racine to Marivaux and Beaumarchais. So strong is the yoke as even to impose itself on La Fontaine's animals, on the servants and valets of Molière, on Montesquieu's Persians, and on the Babylonians, the Indians and the Micromégas of Voltaire. It must be stated, furthermore, that these personages are only partially real. In each living being two kinds of characteristics are found, the first not numerous or common to all individuals of its class, and which any reader or observer may readily distinguish, and the second in large number, appertaining to it alone, and not to be detected without some effort. Classic art concerns itself only with the former; it purposely effaces, neglects or subordinates the latter. Its creations are not veritable individuals, but generalized characters, a king, a queen, a young prince, a confidant, a high-priest, a captain of the guards, possessing some general passion, habit or inclination, such as love, ambition, fidelity or perfidy, a despotic or a yielding temper, some species of wickedness or of native goodness. As to the circumstances of time and place, which exercise the most powerful influence in fashioning and diversifying man, it scarcely indicates them, making an abstraction of them. In tragedy the scene is really everywhere and of all centuries, the opposite affirmation being equally true, that it is nowhere and of no century. It consists of any palace or of any temple,[2] in which, to get rid of all historic or personal impressions, habits and costumes are introduced conventionally, being neither French nor foreign, nor ancient, nor modern. In this abstract world the address is always "you,"[3] "Seigneur" and "Mad-

---

[1] Except in the "Pensées," by Pascal, a few notes dotted down by a morbidly exalted Christian, and which certainly, in the perfected work, would not have been allowed to remain as they are.

[2] See in the Cabinet of Engravings the theatrical costumes of the middle of the XVIIIth century. Nothing could be more opposed to the spirit of the classic drama than the parts of Esther and Brittannicus, as they are played nowadays, in the accurate costumes and with scenery derived from late discoveries at Pompeii or Nineveh.

[3] The formality which this indicates will be understood by those familiar with the use of the pronoun *thou* in France, denoting intimacy and freedom from restraint in contrast with ceremonious and formal intercourse.—TR.

ame," the noble style always clothing the most opposite characters with the same drapery. When Corneille and Racine, through the stateliness and elegance of their verse, afford us a glimpse of contemporary figures they do it unconsciously, imagining that they are portraying man in himself; and, if we of the present time recognize in their pieces either the cavaliers, the duellists, the bullies, the politicians or the heroines of the Fronde, or the courtiers, princes and bishops, the ladies and gentlemen in waiting of the regular monarchy, it is owing to their brush having been involuntarily dipped in their own experience and some of its color having fallen accidentally on the bare ideal outline which they wished to trace. We have simply a contour, a general sketch, filled up with the harmonious gray tone of correct diction. Even in comedy, necessarily portraying surrounding habits, even with Molière, so frank and so bold, the model shows its incompleteness, all individual peculiarities being suppressed, the face becoming for a moment a theatrical mask, and the personage, especially when talking in verse, sometimes losing its animation in becoming the speaking-trumpet of a tirade or of a dissertation.[1] The stamp of rank, condition or fortune, whether gentleman or bourgeois, provincial or Parisian, is frequently overlooked.[2] We are rarely made to appreciate physical externals, as in Shakespeare—the temperament, the state of the nervous system, the bluff or drawling tone, the impulsive or restrained action, the emaciation or obesity of a character.[3] Frequently no trouble is taken to find a suitable name, this being either Chrysale, Orgon, Damis, Dorante, or Valère. The name designates only a simple quality, that of a father, a youth, a valet, a grumbler, a gallant, and, like an ordinary cloak, fitting indifferently all forms alike, as it passes from the wardrobe of Molière to that of Regnard, Destouche, Le Sage or Marivaux.[4]

---

[1] See the parts of the moralizers and reasoners like Cléante in "Tartuffe," Ariste in "Les Femmes Savantes," Chrysale in "L'Ecole des femmes," etc. See the discussion between the two brothers in "Le Festin de Pierre," III. 5; the discourse of Ergaste in "L'Ecole des Maris"; that of Eliante, imitated from Lucretius in the "Misanthrope," II. 5; the portraiture, by Dorine in "Tartuffe," I. 1; the portrait of the hypocrite, by Don Juan in "Le Festin de Pierre," V. 2.

[2] For instance the parts of Harpagon and Arnolphe.

[3] We see this in Tartuffe, but only through an expression of Dorine, and not directly. Cf. in Shakespeare, the parts of Coriolanus, Hotspur, Falstaff, Othello, Cleopatra, etc.

[4] Balzac passed entire days in reading the "Almanach des cent mille adresses," also in a cab in the streets during the afternoons, examining signs for the purpose of finding suitable names for his characters. This little circumstance shows the difference between two diverse conceptions of mankind.

The character lacks the personal badge, the unique, authentic appellation serving as the primary stamp of an individual. All these details and circumstances, all these aids and accompaniments of a man, remain outside of the classic theory. To secure the admission of some of them required the genius of Molière, the fulness of his conception, the wealth of his observation, the extreme freedom of his pen. It is equally true again that he often omits them, and that, in other cases, he introduces only a small number of them, because he avoids giving to these general characters a richness and complexity that would embarrass the action. The simpler the theme the clearer its development, the first duty of the author throughout this literature being to clearly develop the restricted theme of which he makes a selection.

There is, accordingly, a radical defect in the classic spirit, the defect of its qualities, and which, at first kept within proper bounds, contributes towards the production of its purest masterpieces, but which, in accordance with the universal law, goes on increasing and turns into a vice through the natural effect of age, use, and success. Contracted at the start, it is to become yet more so. In the eighteenth century the portrayal of living realities, an actual individual, just as he is in nature and in history, that is to say, an undefined unit, a rich plexus, a complete organism of peculiarities and traits, superposed, commingled and co-ordinated, is improper. The capacity to receive and contain all these is wanting. Whatever can be discarded is cast aside, and to such an extent that nothing is left at last but a condensed extract, an evaporated residuum, an almost empty name, in short, what is called a hollow abstraction. The only characters in the eighteenth century exhibiting any life are the off-hand sketches, made in passing and as if contraband, by Voltaire,—Baron de Thundertentronk and Milord Watthen,—the lesser figures in his stories, and five or six portraits of secondary rank,—Turcaret, Gil Blas, Marianne, Manon Lescaut, Rameau, and Figaro,—two or three of the rough sketches of Crébillon the younger and of Collé, all so many works in which sap flows through a familiar knowledge of things, comparable with those of the minor masters in painting,—Watteau, Fragonard, Saint-Aubin, Moreau, Lancret, Pater, and Beaudouin,—and which, accepted with difficulty, or as a surprise, by the official drawing-room are still to subsist after the grander and soberer canvases shall have become mouldy through their wearisome exhalations. Every-where else the sap dries up, and, instead of blooming plants, we encounter only flowers of painted paper. What are all the serious poems, from the "Henriade" of Voltaire to the "Mois" by Roucher or the "Imagination" by Delille, but so many pieces of rhetoric garnished with rhymes? Examine the innumerable tragedies and comedies of which Grimm and Collé give us mort-uary extracts, even the meritorious works of Voltaire and Cré-billon, and later, those of authors of repute, Du Belloy, La Harpe, Ducis, and Marie Chénier? Eloquence, art, situations, correct verse, all exist in these except human nature; the per-sonages are simply well-taught puppets, and generally mere mouthpieces by which the author makes his declamation public; Greeks, Romans, mediæval knights, Turks, Arabs, Peruvians, Giaours, or Byzantines, all form the same declamatory mechanism. The public, meanwhile, betrays no surprise. It does not possess the historic sentiment. It accepts humanity as everywhere the same. It establishes the success alike of the "Incas" by Mar-montel, and of "Gonsalve" and the "Nouvelles" by Florian; also of the peasants, mechanics, negroes, Brazilians, Parsees, and Malabarites that appear before it uttering their amplifications. Man is simply regarded as a reasoning being, alike in all ages and alike in all places; Bernardin de Saint-Pierre endows his pariah with this habit, like Diderot, in his Otaheitians. The one recognized principle is that every human being must think and talk like a book.

Accordingly how inadequate are historical productions! With the exception of Charles XII., a contemporary on whom Voltaire bestows fresh life, through the accounts of him by eye-witnesses, also his spirited sketches of Englishmen, Frenchmen, Spaniards, Italians and Germans, scattered through his stories, where are men found? With Hume, Gibbon and Robertson, belonging to the French school, and who are at once adopted in France, in the researches into our middle ages of Dubos and of Mably, in the "Louis XI." of Duclos, in the "Anacharsis" of Barthélemy, even in the "Essai sur les Mœurs," and in the "Siècle de Louis XIV." of Voltaire, even in the "Grandeur des Romains" and in the "Esprit des Lois" of Montesquieu, what remarkable incompleteness! Erudition, criticism, common sense, an almost exact exposition of dogmas and of institutions, philosophic views of the relation of events and on the general course of things, nothing is wanting but souls! On reading these it seems as if the climates, institutions and civilizations transforming the human mind from one given whole to another, are simply so many externals, so many accidental coverings, which, far from reaching down to its depths scarcely penetrate beneath its surface. The vast differences separating the men of two centuries, or of two races, escape them entirely.[1] The ancient Greek, the early christian, the conquering Teuton, the feudal man, the Arab of Mahomet, the German, the Renaissance Englishman, the puritan, appear in their books about the same as in engravings and frontispieces, with some difference in costume, but the same in form, feature and expression, attenuated, faded and respectable, and adapted to the conventionalities of good-breeding. That sympathetic imagination by which the writer enters into the mind of another, and reproduces in himself a system of habits and feelings opposed to his own, is the talent the most wanting in the eighteenth century. With the exception of Diderot, who uses it badly and capriciously, it almost entirely disappears in the last half of the century. Consider in turn, during the same period, in France and in England, where it is most extensively used, the romance, a sort of mirror everywhere transportable, the best adapted to reflect all phases of nature and of life. After reading the series of English novelists, Defoe, Richardson, Fielding, Smollett, Sterne, and Goldsmith down to Miss Burney and Miss Austen, I am familiar with England in the eighteenth century; I have encountered clergymen, country gentlemen, farmers, innkeepers, sailors, people of every condition in life, high and low; I know the details of fortunes and of careers, how much is earned, how much is expended, how journeys are made and how people eat and drink: I have accumulated for myself a file of precise biographical events, a complete picture in a thousand scenes of an entire community, the amplest stock of information to guide me should I wish to frame a history of this vanished world. On reading a corresponding list of French novelists, the younger Crébillon, Rous-

---

[1] "At the present day, whatever may be said, there is no such thing as Frenchmen, Germans, Spaniards, and Englishmen, for all are Europeans. All have the same tastes, the same passions, the same habits, none having obtained a national form through any specific institution." Rousseau, "Sur le gouvernement de Pologne," 170.

seau, Marmontel, Laclos, Restif de la Breton, Louvet, Madame de Staël, Madame de Genlis and the rest, including Mercier and even Mme. Cottin, I scarcely take any notes; all precise and instructive little facts are left out; I find civilities, polite acts, gallantries, mischief-making, social dissertations and nothing else. They carefully abstain from mentioning money, from giving me figures, from describing a wedding, a trial, the administration of a piece of property; I am ignorant of the situation of a curate, of a rustic noble, of a resident prior, of a steward, of an intendant. Whatever relates to a province or to the rural districts, to the bourgeoisie or to the shop,[1] to the army or to a soldier, to the clergy or to convents, to justice or to the police, to business or to housekeeping remains vaguely in my mind or is falsified; to clear up any point I am obliged to recur to that marvellous Voltaire who, on laying aside the great classic coat, finds plenty of elbow room and tells all. On the organs of society of vital importance, on the practices and regulations that provoke revolutions, on feudal rights and seigniorial justice, on the mode of recruiting and governing monastic bodies, on the revenue measures of the provinces, of corporations and of trade-unions, on the tithes and the *corvées*,[2] literature provides me with scarcely any information. Drawing-rooms and men of letters are apparently its sole material. The rest is null and void. Under the good society that is able to converse France appears perfectly empty. On the approach of the Revolution the elimination increases. Glance over the harangues of the clubs and of the tribune, over reports, legislative bills and pamphlets, and through the mass of writings prompted by passing and exciting events; in none of them do we see any sign of the human creature as we see him in the fields and in the street; he is always regarded as a simple automaton, a well-known mechanism. Among writers he was but lately regarded as a mechanical warbler; with politicians he is now a mechanical voter; touch him in the proper place and he responds in the desired manner. Facts are never apparent; only abstractions, long arrays of sentences on nature, reason, and the

---

[1] Previous to 1750 we find something about these in "Gil-Blas," and in "Marianne," (Mme. Dufour the sempstress and her shop). Unfortunately the Spanish travesty prevents the novels of Le Sage from being as instructive as they might be.

[2] Interesting details are found in the little stories by Diderot as, for instance, "Les deux amis de Bourbonne." But elsewhere he is a partisan, especially in the "Religieuse," and conveys a false impression of things.

people, on tyrants and liberty, like inflated balloons, uselessly conflicting with each other in space. Were we not aware that all this would terminate in terrible practical effects we should regard it as so much logical sportiveness, as school exercises, or academic parades, or ideological compositions. Ideology, the last emanation of the century, is in effect about to give of the classic spirit the final formula and the last word.

III.

To pursue in every research, with the utmost confidence, without either reserve or precaution, the mathematical method; to derive, limit and isolate a few of the simplest generalized notions; and then, setting experience aside, comparing them, combining them, and, from the artificial compound thus obtained, deducing all the consequences they involve by pure reasoning, is the natural process of the classic spirit. It is so deeply implanted as to be equally encountered in both centuries, as well with Descartes, Malebranche [1] and the partisans of innate ideas as with the partisans of sensation, of physical needs and of primary instinct, Condillac, Rousseau, Helvétius, and, later, Condorcet, Volney, Sieyès, Cabanis and Destutt de Tracy. In vain do the latter assert that they are the followers of Bacon and reject innate ideas; with another starting point than the Cartesians they pursue the same path, and, as with the Cartesians, after borrowing a little, they leave experience behind them. In this vast moral and social world, they only remove the superficial bark from the human tree with its innumerable roots and branches; they are unable to penetrate to or grasp at anything beyond it; their hands cannot contain more. They have no suspicion of anything outside of it; the classic spirit, with limited comprehension, is not far-reaching. To them the bark is the entire tree, and, the operation once completed, they retire, bearing along with them the dry, dead epidermis, never returning to the trunk itself. Through intellectual incapacity and literary

---

[1] "To attain to the truth we have only to fix our attention on the ideas which each one finds within his own mind." (Malebranche, "Recherche de la Vérité," book I. ch. i.) "Those long chains of reasoning, all simple and easy, which geometers use to arrive at their most difficult demonstrations, suggested to me that all things which come within human knowledge must follow each other in a similar chain." Lewes, (Descartes, "Discours de la Methode," I. 142). In the eighteenth century *à priori* ideas were employed, in the eighteenth century sensations, but always following the same mathematical method fully displayed in the "Ethics" of Spinoza.

pride they omit the characteristic detail, the animating fact, the specific circumstance, the significant, convincing and complete example. Scarcely one of these is found in the "Logique" and in the "Traité des Sensations" by Condillac, in the "Idéologie" by Destutt de Tracy, or in the "Rapports du Physique et du Morale" by Cabanis.[1] Never, with them, are we on the solid and visible ground of personal observation and narration, but always in the air, in the empty space of pure generalities. Condillac declares that the arithmetical method is adapted to psychology and that the elements of our ideas can be defined by a process analogous "to the rule of three." Sieyès holds history in profound contempt, and believes that he had "perfected the science of politics"[2] at one stroke, through an effort of the brain, in the style of Descartes, who thus discovers analytic geometry. Destutt de Tracy, in undertaking to comment on Montesquieu, finds that the great historian has too servilely confined himself to history, and attempts to do the work over again by organizing society as it should be, instead of studying society as it is. Never were such systematic and superficial institutions built up with such a moderate extract of human nature. Condillac, employing sensation, animates a statue, and then, by a process of pure reasoning, following up its effects, as he supposes, on smell, taste, hearing, sight and touch, fashions a complete human soul. Rousseau, by means of a contract, founds political association, and, with this given idea, pulls down the constitution, government and laws of every balanced social system. In a book which serves as the philosophical testament of the century,[3] Condorcet declares that this method is "the final step of philosophy, that which places a sort of eternal barrier between humanity and its ancient infantile errors." "In its application to morals, politics and political economy" we succeed in obtaining a foothold in the moral sciences "as certain as in the natural sciences; through it we have been able to discover the rights of man." A single fundamental proposition is deduced, as in

---

[1] See especially his memoir: "De l'influence du climat sur les habitudes morales," vague, and wholly barren of illustrations excepting one citation from Hippocrates.

[2] These are his own words. He adds elsewhere, "There is no more reality in assumed historical truths than in assumed religious truths." ("Papiers de Sieyès," the year 1772, according to Sainte-Beuve, "Causeries du lundi," V. 194). Descartes and Malebranche already expressed this contempt for history.

[3] Condorcet, "Esquisse d'un tableau historique de l'esprit humain," ninth epoch.

mathematics, which proposition, similar to a first principle in mathematics, becomes a fact of daily experience, verified by everybody and therefore self-evident. This school is to subsist throughout the Revolution, the Empire and even into the Restoration,[1] along with the tragedy of which it is the sister, with the classic spirit their common parent, a primordial, sovereign power as hurtful as it is useful, as destructive as it is creative, as capable of propagating error as truth, as astonishing in the rigidity of its code, in the limitations of its authority and in the uniformity of its works as in the duration of its reign and the universality of its ascendency.

---

[1] See the "Tableau historique," presented to the Institute by Chénier in 1808, showing by its statements that the classic spirit still prevails in all branches of literature. Cabanis died in 1818, Volney in 1820, de Tracy and Sieyès in 1836, Daunon in 1848. In May, 1845, Saphary and Valette are still professors of Condillac's philosophy in the two lycées in Paris.

CHAPTER III.

I.

OUT of the scientific acquisitions thus set forth, elaborated by the spirit we have just described, is born a doctrine, seemingly a revelation, and which, under this title, assumes to regulate the government of human affairs. On the approach of 1789 it is generally admitted that man is living in " a century of light," in " the age of reason; " that, previously, the human species was in its infancy and that now it has attained to its " majority." Truth, finally, is made manifest and, for the first time, its reign on earth is apparent. The right is supreme because it is truth itself. It must direct all things because through its nature it is universal. The philosophy of the eighteenth century, in these two articles of faith, resembles a religion, the puritanism of the seventeenth century, and Mahometanism in the seventh century. We see the same outburst of faith, hope and enthusiasm, the same spirit of propagandism and of dominion, the same rigidity and intolerance, the same ambition to recast man and to remodel human life according to a preconceived type. The new doctrine is also to have its doctors, its dogmas, its popular catechism, its fanatics, its inquisitors and its martyrs. It is to speak as loudly as those preceding it, as a legitimate authority to which dictatorship belongs by right of birth, and against which rebellion is criminal or insane. It differs, however, from the preceding religions in this respect, that instead of imposing itself in the name of God, it imposes itself in the name of Reason.

The authority, indeed, was a new one. Up to this time, in the control of human actions and opinions, reason had played but a small and subordinate part. Both the motive and its direction were obtained elsewhere; faith and obedience were an inheritance ; a man was a Christian and a subject because he was born Christian and subject. Surrounding this budding philosophy and the reason which enters upon its great investigation, is a system of recognized laws, an established power, a reigning religion ; all the stones of this structure hold together and each story is supported by a preceding story. But what does the common cement consist of, and what is its first foundation ? Who authorizes all these civil regulations which control marriages, testaments, inheritances, contracts, property and persons, these fanciful and often contradictory regulations ? In the first place immemorial custom, varying according to the province, according to the title to the soil, according to the quality and condition of the person; and next, the will of the king who caused the custom to be inscribed and who sanctioned it. Who authorizes this will, this sovereignty of the prince, this first of public obligations ? In the first place, eight centuries of possession, a hereditary right similar to that by which each one enjoys his own field and domain, a property established in a family and transmitted from one eldest son to another, from the first founder of the State to his last living successor; and, in addition to this, a religion directing men to submit to the constituted powers. And who, finally, authorizes this religion ? At first, eighteen centuries of tradition, the immense series of anterior and concordant proofs, the steady belief of sixty preceding generations; and after this, at the beginning of it, the presence and teachings of Christ, then, farther back, the creation of the world, the command and the voice of God. Thus, throughout the moral and social order of things the past justifies the present; antiquity provides its title, and if, beneath all these supports which age has consolidated, the deep primitive rock is sought for in subterranean depths, we find it in the divine will. During the whole of the seventeenth century this theory still absorbs all souls in the shape of a fixed habit and of inward respect; it is not open to question. It is regarded in the same light as the heart of the living body; whoever would lay his hand upon it would instantly draw back, moved by a vague sentiment of its ceasing to beat in case it were touched. The most independent, with Descartes at the head, "would be grieved" at being confounded with those chimerical speculators who, instead of pursuing the beaten track of custom, dart blindly forward "across mountains and over precipices." In subjecting their belief to systematic investigation not only do they except and set aside "the truths of faith,"[1] but again the dogma they suppose to have been discarded remains in their mind latent and effective, to lead them on without their knowledge and to convert their philosophy into a preparation for, or a confirmation of, Christianity.[2] Summing it all up, faith, the performance of religious duties, with religious and political institutions, provide the mother ideas of the seventeenth century. Reason, whether she admits it or is ignorant of it, is only a subaltern, an oratorical agency, a setter-in-motion, forced by religion and the monarchy to labor in their behalf. With the exception of La Fontaine, whom I regard as unique in this as in other matters, the greatest and most independent, Pascal, Descartes, Bossuet, La Bruyère, derive from the established system their first conception of nature, of man, of society, of right and of government.[3] So long as reason is limited to this function its work is that of a councillor of State, an extra preacher which its superiors despatch on a missionary tour in the departments of philosophy and of literature. Far from proving destructive it consolidates; in fine, even down to the Regency, its chief employment is to produce good Christians and loyal subjects.

---

[1] "Discours de la Methode."

[2] This is evident with Descartes in the second step he takes. (The theory of pure spirit, the idea of God, the proof of his existence, the veracity of our intelligence demonstrated by the veracity of God, etc.)

[3] See Pascal, "Pensées" (on the origin of property and rank). The "Provinciales" (on homicide and the right to kill). Nicole, "Deuxième traité de la charité, et de l'amour-propre" (on the natural man and the object of society). Bossuet, "Politique tirée de l'Ecriture sainte." La Bruyère, "Des Esprits forts."

But here the parts become inverted; tradition descends from the upper to the lower ranks, while reason ascends from the latter to the former.   On the one hand religion and the monarchy, through their excesses and misdeeds under Louis XIV., and their laxity and incompetency under Louis XV., demolish piece by piece the basis of hereditary reverence and filial obedience so long serving them as a foundation, and which maintained them aloft above all dispute and free of investigation; hence the authority of tradition insensibly declines and disappears.   On the other hand science, through its imposing and multiplied discoveries, erects piece by piece a basis of universal trust and deference, raising itself up from an interesting subject of curiosity to the rank of a public power; hence the authority of reason augments and occupies its place.   A time comes when, the latter authority having dispossessed the former, the mother ideas tradition had reserved to itself fall into the grasp of reason.   Investigation penetrates into the forbidden sanctuary.   Instead of deference there is verification, and religion, the state, the law, custom, all the organs, in short, of moral and practical life, become subject to analysis, to be preserved, restored or replaced, according to the prescriptions of the new doctrine.

II.

Nothing could be better had the doctrine been complete, and had reason, instructed by history and rendered critical, been qualified to comprehend the rival she replaced.   For then, instead of regarding her as an usurper to be repelled she would have recognized in her an elder sister whose part must be left to her. Hereditary prejudice is a sort of reason operating unconsciously. It has claims as well as reason, but it is unable to present these; instead of advancing those that are authentic it puts forth the doubtful ones.   Its archives are buried; to exhume these it is necessary to make researches of which it is incapable; nevertheless they exist, and history at the present day is bringing them to light.   Careful investigation shows that, like science, it issues from a long accumulation of experiences : men, after a multitude of gropings and efforts, have satisfied themselves that a certain way of living and thinking is the only one adapted to their situation, the most practical and the most salutary, the system or dogma now seeming arbitrary to us being at first a confirmed expedient of public safety. Frequently it is so still; in any event, in its leading features, it is indispensable; it may be stated with certainty that, if the leading prejudices of the community should suddenly disappear, man, deprived of the precious legacy transmitted to him by the wisdom of ages, would at once fall back into a savage condition and again become what he was at first, namely, a restless, famished, wandering, hunted brute. There was a time when this heritage was lacking; there are populations to-day with which it is still utterly lacking.[1] To abstain from eating human flesh, from killing useless or burdensome aged people, from exposing, selling or killing children one does not know what to do with, to be the one husband of but one woman, to hold in horror incest and unnatural practices, to be the sole and recognized owner of a distinct field, to be mindful of the superior injunctions of modesty, humanity, honor and conscience, all these observances, formerly unknown and slowly established, compose the civilization of human beings. Because we accept them in full security they are not the less sacred, and they become only the more sacred when, submitted to investigation and traced through history, they are disclosed to us as the secret force which has converted a herd of brutes into a society of men. In general, the older and more universal a custom, the more it is based on profound motives, on physiological motives on those of hygiene, and on those instituted for social protection. At one time, as in the separation of castes, a heroic or thoughtful race must be preserved by preventing the mixtures by which inferior blood introduces mental debility and low instincts.[2] At another, as in the prohibition of spirituous liquors, and of animal food, it is necessary to conform to the climate prescribing a vegetable diet, or to the race-temperament for which strong drink is pernicious.[3] At another, as in the institution of the right of primogeniture, it was important to prepare and designate beforehand the military commander whom the tribe would obey, or the civil chieftain that would preserve the domain, super-

---

[1] Cf. Sir John Lubbock, " Early Civilization." Gerand-Teulon, "Les Origines de la famille."

[2] The principle of caste in India; we see this in the contrast between the Aryans and the aborigines, the Soudras and the pariahs.

[3] In accordance with this principle the inhabitants of the Sandwich Islands passed a law forbidding the sale of liquor to the natives and allowing it to Europeans. (De Varigny, " Quatorze ans aux iles Sandwich.")

intend its cultivation, and support the family.[1] If there are valid reasons for legitimising custom there are reasons of higher import for the consecration of religion. Consider this point, not in general and according to a vague notion, but at the outset, at its birth, in the texts, taking for an example one of the faiths which now rule in society, Christianity, brahminism, the law of Mahomet or of Buddha. At certain critical moments in history, a few men, emerging from their narrow and daily routine of life, form some generalized conception of the infinite universe; the august face of nature is suddenly unveiled to them; in their sublime emotion they seem to have detected its first cause; they have at least detected some of its elements. Through a fortunate conjunction of circumstances these elements are just those which their century, their race, a group of races, a fragment of humanity, is in a state to comprehend. Their point of view is the only one at which the graduated multitudes below them are able to place themselves. For millions of men, for hundreds of generations, only through them is any access to divine things to be obtained. Theirs is the unique utterance, heroic or affecting, enthusiastic or tranquillizing; the only one which the hearts and minds around them and after them will heed; the only one adapted to profound cravings, to accumulated aspirations, to hereditary faculties, to a complete intellectual and moral organism; yonder that of Hindostan or of the Mongolian; here that of the Semite or of the European; in our Europe that of the German, the Latin or the Sclave; in such a way that its contradictions, instead of condemning it, justify it, its diversity producing its adaptation and its adaptation producing its benefits.

This is no barren formula. A sentiment of such grandeur, of such comprehensive and penetrating insight, an idea by which man, compassing the vastness and depth of things, so greatly oversteps the ordinary limits of his mortal condition, resembles an illumination; it is easily transformed into a vision; it is never remote from ecstasy; it can express itself only through symbols; it evokes divine figures.[2] Religion in its nature is a metaphysical poem accompanied by faith. Under this title it is popular and efficacious; for, apart from an invisible select few, a pure abstract

[1] Cf. Leplay, "De l'Organization de la famille," the history of a domain in the Pyrenees.
[2] See, especially, in Brahminic literature the great metaphysical poems and the Puranas.

P

idea is only an empty term, and truth, to be apparent, must be clothed with a body. It requires a form of worship, a legend, and ceremonies in order to address the people, women, children, the credulous, every one absorbed by daily cares, any understanding in which ideas involuntarily translate themselves through imagery. Owing to this palpable form it is able to give its weighty support to the conscience, to counterbalance natural egoism, to curb the mad onset of brutal passions, to lead the will to abnegation and devotion, to tear man away from himself and place him wholly in the service of truth, or of his kind, to form ascetics, martyrs, sisters of charity and missionaries. Thus, throughout society, religion becomes at once a natural and precious instrumentality. On the one hand men require it for the contemplation of infinity and to live properly; if it were suddenly to be taken away from them their souls would be a mournful void, and they would do greater injury to their neighbors. Besides, it would be vain to attempt to take it away from them; the hand raised against it would encounter only its envelope; it would be repelled after a sanguinary struggle, its germ lying too deep to be extirpated.

And when, at length, after religion and habit, we regard the State, that is to say, the armed power possessing both physical force and moral authority, we find for it an almost equally noble origin. In Europe at least, from Russia to Portugal, and from Norway to the two Sicilies it is, in its origin and essence, a military foundation in which heroism constitutes itself the champion of right. Here and there, in the chaos of mixed races and of crumbling societies, some man has arisen who, through his ascendency, rallies around him a loyal band, driving out intruders, overcoming brigands, re-establishing order, reviving agriculture, founding a patrimony, and transmitting as property to his descendants his office of hereditary justiciary and born general. Through this permanent delegation a great public office is removed from competitors, fixed in one family, sequestered in safe hands; thenceforth the nation possesses a vital centre and each right obtains a visible protector. If the sovereign confines himself to his attributions, is restrained in despotic tendencies, and avoids falling into egotism, he provides the country with the best government of which the world has any knowledge, not alone the most stable, the most capable of continuance, the most suitable for maintaining together a body of twenty or thirty thousand men, but again one of the best because self-sacrifice dignifies both command and obedience and, through the prolongation of military tradition, fidelity and honor, from grade to grade, attaches the chieftain to his duty and the soldier to his chieftain.

Such are the strikingly valid claims of hereditary prejudice. Like instinct, it appears to us as a blind form of reason. That which makes it fully legitimate is reason herself being obliged to borrow its form to obtain any efficacy. A doctrine becomes inspiring only through a blind medium. To become of practical use, to take upon itself the government of souls, to be transformed into a spring of action, it must be deposited in minds given up to systematic belief, of fixed habits, of established tendencies, of domestic traditions, and, from the stormy heights of the intellect, descend into and become amalgamated with the passive forces of the will; then only does it form a part of the character and become a social force. At the same time, however, it ceases to be critical and clairvoyant; it no longer tolerates doubt and contradiction, nor admits further restrictions or nice distinctions; it is either no longer cognizant of, or badly appreciates, its own evidences. We of the present day believe in infinite progress about the same as people once believed in original sin; we still receive ready-made opinions from above, the Academy of Sciences occupying in many respects the place of the ancient councils. Except with a few special savants, belief and obedience will always be unreflecting, while reason would wrongfully resent the leadership of prejudice in human affairs, since, to lead, it must itself become prejudice.

III.

Unfortunately, in the eighteenth century, reason was classic; not only the aptitude but the documents which enable it to comprehend tradition were absent. In the first place, there was no knowledge of history; there was a repugnance to erudition, because of its dulness and tediousness; learned compilations, vast collections of extracts and the slow work of criticism were held in disdain. Voltaire rallied the Benedictines. Montesquieu, to ensure the acceptance of his "Esprit des lois," indulged in wit about laws. Raynal, to give an impetus to his history of commerce in the Indies, welded to it the declamation of Diderot.

The Abbé Barthélemy covered over the realities of Greek manners and customs with his literary varnish. Science was expected to be either epigrammatic or oratorical; crude or technical details would have been objectionable to a public composed of people of society; correctness of style drove out or falsified the little significant facts which give a peculiar sense and their original relief to antiquated characters. Even if writers had dared to note them, their sense and bearing would not have been understood. The sympathetic imagination did not exist; people were incapable of going out of themselves, of betaking themselves to distant points of view, of conjecturing the peculiar and violent states of the human brain, the decisive and fruitful moments during which it gives birth to a vigorous creation, a religion destined to rule, a state that is sure to endure. The imagination of man is limited to personal experiences, and where, in their experience, could individuals in this society find the materials with which to imagine the pains of the parturition? How could minds, as polished and as amiable as these, fully adopt the sentiments of an apostle, of a monk, of a barbaric or feudal founder; see these in the *milieu* which explains and justifies them; picture to themselves the surrounding crowd, at first souls in despair and haunted by mystic dreams, and next the rude and violent intellects given up to instinct and imagery, thinking with half-visions, their wills consisting of irresistible impulses? A reason of this stamp forms no conception of figures like these. To bring them within its rectilinear limits they require to be reduced and made over; the Macbeth of Shakespeare becomes that of Ducis, and the Mahomet of the Koran that of Voltaire. Consequently, as they failed to see souls, they misconceived institutions. The suspicion that truth could have been conveyed only through the medium of legends, that justice could have been established only by force, that religion was obliged to assume the sacerdotal form, that the State necessarily took a military form, and that the Gothic edifice possessed, as well as other structures, its own architecture, proportions, balance of parts, solidity, utility, and even beauty, never entered their heads. Consequently again, unable to comprehend the past, they were unable to comprehend the present. They had no accurate conception of the present, of the mechanic, of the provincial bourgeois, or even of the inferior rural noble; these were

visible only at a distance, half-effaced, and wholly transformed
through philosophic theories and sentimental mistiness. "Two or
three thousand" [1] polished and cultivated individuals formed the
circle of honest folks, and they never went outside of this. If
they obtained glimpses of the people from their chateaux and
on their journeys, it was in passing, the same as of their post-
horses, or of the cattle on their farms, showing compassion undoubtedly, but never divining their anxious thoughts and their
obscure instincts. The structure of the still primitive mind of
the people was never imagined, the paucity and tenacity of their
ideas, the narrowness of their mechanical, routine existence, devoted to manual labor, absorbed with anxieties for daily bread,
confined to the bounds of a visible horizon; their attachment to
the local saint, to rites, to the priest, their deep-seated rancor,
their inveterate distrust, their credulity growing out of the imagination, their lack of capacity for conceiving abstract right and
of comprehending public events, the silent operation by which
political novelties became transformed in their brain into nursery
fables or into ghost stories, their contagious infatuations like
those of sheep, their blind fury like that of bulls, and all those
traits of character the Revolution was about to bring to light.
Twenty millions of men and more had scarcely passed out of the
mental condition of the middle ages; hence, in its grand lines,
the social edifice in which they could dwell was necessarily mediæval. It had to be made healthy and cleaned, windows put
in and walls pulled down, but without disturbing the foundations,
or the main building and its general arrangement; otherwise,
after demolishing it and living encamped for ten years in the open
air like savages, its inmates would have been obliged to rebuild
it on the same plan. In uneducated minds, those having not yet
attained to reflection, faith attaches itself only to the corporeal
symbol, obedience being brought about only through physical
restraint; there is no religion outside of the curate, and no state
outside of the soldier. But one writer, Montesquieu, the best
instructed, the most sagacious, and the best balanced of all the
spirits of the age, made these truths apparent, because he was at
once an erudite, an observer, a historian and a jurisconsult. He,
however, spoke as an oracle, in sentences and enigmatically; he

---

[1] Voltaire, "Dict. Phil." the article on Punishments.

ran off as if upon live coals, every time that he touched matters belonging to his country and epoch. Hence, he remained
respected, but isolated, his fame exercising no influence. The
classic reason declined[1] to go so far as to laboriously study the
ancient man and the actual man. It found the way shorter and
more convenient to follow its original bent, to shut its eyes on
man as he is, to fall back on its stores of current notions, to
derive from these an idea of man in general, and build in empty
space. Through this natural and determined state of blindness, it no longer heeds the old and living roots of contemporary
institutions ; no longer seeing them it denies that they exist.
Hereditary prejudice to it becomes pure prejudice ; the titles of
tradition are lost, and royalty is an usurpation. Thenceforward
behold reason armed and at war with its predecessor to wrest
away the government of souls and to substitute the reign of truth
for the reign of error.

IV.

In this great undertaking there are two halting-places.
Through good sense or through timidity many stop half-way.
Through passion or through logic others go to the end.
A first campaign results in carrying the enemy's out-works and
his frontier fortresses, the philosophical army being led by Voltaire. To combat hereditary prejudice, other prejudices are
opposed to it whose empire is as extensive and whose authority
is not less recognized. Montesquieu looks at France through
the eyes of a Persian, and Voltaire, on his return from England,
describes the English, an unknown species. Confronting dogma
and the prevailing system of worship, accounts are given, either
with open or with covert irony, of the various christian sects,
the anglicans, the quakers, the presbyterians, the socinians, those
of ancient or of remote people, the Greeks, Romans, Egyptians,
Mahometans and Guebers, of the worshippers of Brahma, of
the Chinese and of pure idolaters. In relation to established laws
and customs, expositions are made, with evident intentions,
of other constitutions and other social habits, of despotism,
of limited monarchy, of a republic, here the church subject
to the state, there the church free of the state, in this country
castes, in another polygamy, and, from country to country, from
century to century, the diversity, contradiction and antagonism

---

1 "Resumé des cahiers," by Prud'homme, preface, 1789.

of fundamental customs which, each on its own ground, are all equally consecrated by tradition, all legitimately forming the system of public rights. From this time forth the charm is broken. Ancient institutions lose their divine prestige; they are simply human works, the fruits of the place and of the moment, and born out of convenience and a covenant. Scepticism enters through all the breaches. With regard to Christianity it at once enters into open hostility, into a bitter and prolonged polemical warfare; for, under the title of a state religion this occupies the ground, censuring free thought, burning writings, exiling, imprisoning or disturbing authors, and everywhere acting as a natural and official adversary. Moreover, by virtue of being an ascetic religion, it condemns not only the free and cheerful ways tolerated by the new philosophy but again the natural tendencies it sanctions, and the promises of terrestrial felicity with which it everywhere dazzles the eyes. Thus the heart and the head both agree in their opposition. Voltaire, with texts in hand, pursues it from one end to the other of its history, from the first biblical narration to the latest papal bulls, with unflagging animosity and energy, as critic, as historian, as geographer, as logician, as moralist, questioning its sources, opposing evidences, driving ridicule like a pick-axe into every weak spot where an outraged instinct beats against its mystic walls, and into all doubtful places where ulterior patchwork disfigures the primitive structure. He respects, however, the first foundation, and, in this particular, the greatest writers of the day follow the same course. Under positive religions that are false there is a natural religion that is true. This is the simple and authentic text of which the others are altered and amplified translations. Discard ulterior and divergent accretions and the original remains; this common extract, through which all copies harmonize, is deism.—The same operation ensues with civil and political laws. In France, where so many institutions survive their utility, where privileges are no longer sanctioned by services, where rights are changed into abuses, how incoherent is the architecture of the old Gothic building! How poorly adapted to a modern nation! Of what use, in an unique and compact state, are those feudal compartments separating orders, corporations and provinces? What a living paradox is the archbishop of a semi-province, a chapter owning twelve thousand serfs, a drawing-room abbé well supported by a monastery he never saw, a seignior liberally pensioned to figure in antechambers, a magistrate purchasing the right to administer justice, a colonel leaving college to take the command of his inherited regiment, a Parisian trader who, renting a house for one year in Franche-Comté, alienates the ownership of his property and of his person. Throughout Europe there are others of the same character. The best that can be said of "a polished nation" is that its laws, customs and practices are composed "one-half of abuses and one-half of tolerable usages." But, underneath these positive laws, which contradict each other, and of which each contradicts itself, a natural law exists, implied in the codes, applied socially, and written in all hearts. "Show me a country where it is honest to steal the fruits of my labor, to violate engagements, to lie for injurious purposes, to calumniate, to assassinate, to imprison, to be ungrateful to one's benefactor, to strike one's father and mother on offering you food." "Justice and injustice is the same throughout the universe," and, as in the worst community force always, in some respects, is at the service of right, so, in the worst religion, the extravagant dogma always in some fashion proclaims a supreme architect. Religions and communities, accordingly, disintegrated under the investigating process, disclose at the bottom of the crucible, some a residuum of truth, others a residuum of justice, a small but precious balance, a sort of gold ingot preserved by tradition, purified by reason, and which little by little, freed from its alloys, elaborated and devoted to all usages, must solely provide the substance of religion and all the threads of the social warp.

V.

Here begins the second philosophic expedition. It consists of two armies, the first composed of the encyclopedists, some of them sceptics like d'Alembert, others pantheists like Diderot and Lamarck, others open atheists and materialists like d'Holbach, Lamettrie and Helvétius, and later, Condorcet, Lalande and Volney, all differing and independent of each other, but all unanimous in regarding tradition as the common enemy. Such is the effect of prolonged hostilities: the duration of warfare begets exasperation; the desire to be master of everything, to push the adversary to the wall, to drive him out of all his positions. They refuse to admit that reason and tradition can occupy and defend the same citadel together; as soon as one enters the other must depart; henceforth one prejudice is established against another prejudice. In fact, Voltaire, "the patriarch, does not desire to abandon his redeeming and avenging God;"[1] let us tolerate in him this remnant of superstition on account of his great services; but let us examine this phantom in man which he regards with infantile vision. We admit it into our minds through faith, and faith is always suspicious. It is forged by ignorance, fear, and imagination, which are all deceptive powers. At first it was simply the fetish of savages; in vain have we striven to purify and aggrandize it; its origin is always apparent; its history is that of a hereditary dream which, arising in a rude and doting brain, prolongs itself from generation to generation, and still lasts in the healthy and cultivated brain. Voltaire would have this dream true because, otherwise, he could not explain the admirable order of the world, and that a watch suggests a watchmaker; prove, first, that the world is a watch and, then, let us see if the arrangement, such as it is, incomplete, which we have observed, cannot be better explained by a simpler supposition and more conformable to experience, that of eternal matter in which motion is eternal. Mobile and active particles, of which the different kinds are in different states of equilibrium, afford minerals, inorganic substances, marble, lime, air, water and coal.[2] I form humus out of this, " I sow peas, beans and cabbages;" plants find their nourishment in the humus, and " I find my nourishment in the plants." At every meal, within me, and through me, inanimate matter becomes animate; "I convert it into flesh. I animalize it. I render it sensitive." It harbors latent, imperfect sensibility rendered perfect and made manifest. Organization is the cause, and life and sensation are the effects; I need no spiritual monad to account for effects since I am in possession of the cause. "Look at this egg, with which all schools of theology and all the temples of the earth can be overthrown. What is this egg? A sensationless mass previous to the introduction of

---

[1] Voltaire, "Dict. Phil.," the article on Religion.   "If there is a hamlet to be governed it must have a religion."
[2] "Le rêve de d'Alembert," by Diderot, *passim.*

the germ. And what is it after the introduction of the germ? An insensible mass, an inert fluid." Add heat to it, keep it in an oven, and let the operation continue of itself, and we have a chicken, that is to say, "sensibility, life, memory, conscience, passions and thought." That which you call soul is the nervous centre in which all sensitive chords concentrate. Their vibrations produce sensations; a quickened or reviving sensation is memory; our ideas are the result of sensations, memory and signs. Matter, accordingly, is not the work of an intelligence; but matter, through its own arrangement, produces intelligence. Let us fix intelligence where it is, in the organized body; we must not detach it from its support to perch it in the sky on an imaginary throne. This disproportionate conception, once introduced into our minds, ends in perverting the natural play of our sentiments, and, like a monstrous parasite, abstracts for itself all our substance.[1] The first duty of a sound man is to get rid of it, to discard every superstition, every "fear of invisible powers."[2] Then only can he establish a moral order of things and distinguish "the natural law." The sky consisting of empty space, we have no need to seek commands from on high. Let us look down to the ground; let us consider man in himself, as he appears in the eyes of the naturalist, namely, an organized body, a sensitive animal possessing wants, appetites and instincts. Not only are these indestructible but they are legitimate. Let us throw open the prison in which prejudice confines them; let us give them free air and space; let them be displayed in all their strength and all will go well. According to Diderot,[3] a lasting marriage is an abuse, being "the tyranny of a man who has converted the possession of a woman into property." Purity is an invention and conventional, like a dress;[4] happiness and morals go together only in countries where instinct is sanctioned; as in Otaheite, for instance, where

---

[1] "If a misanthrope had proposed to himself to injure humanity what could he have invented better than faith in an incomprehensible being, about which men never could come to any agreement, and to which they would attach more importance than to their own existence?" Diderot, "Entretien d'un philosophe avec la Maréchale ——."

[2] Cf. "Catéchisme Universel," by Saint-Lambert, and the "Loi naturelle ou Catéchisme du citoyen français," by Volney.

[3] "Supplément au voyage de Bougainville."

[4] Cf. "Mémoires de Mme. d'Epinay," a conversation with Duclos and Saint-Lambert at the house of Mlle. Quinault. Rousseau's "Confessions," part i. book V. These are the same principles taught by M. de la Tavel to Mme. de Warens.

marriage lasts but a month, often only a day, and sometimes a quarter of an hour, where, in the evening and with hospitable intent, a host offers his daughters and wife to his guest, where the son espouses his mother out of politeness, where the union of the sexes is a religious festivity celebrated in public. And, pushing things to extremes, the logician ends with five or six pages calculated "to make one's hair stand on end,"[1] himself avowing that his doctrine is "not suited to children or the great." With Diderot, to say the least, these paradoxes have their correctives. In his pictures of modern ways and habits, he is the moralist. He not only is familiar with all the chords of the human keyboard, but he classifies each according to its rank. He loves fine and pure tones, and is full of enthusiasm for noble harmonies; his heart is equal to his genius.[2] And better still, on the question of primitive impulsions arising, he assigns, side by side with self-love, an independent and superior position to pity, sympathy, benevolence and well-doing; to every generous affection of the heart displaying sacrifice and devotion without calculation or personal benefit. But associated with him are others, cold and narrow, who form moral systems according to the mathematical methods of the ideologists, after the style of Hobbes.[3] One motive alone satisfies these, the simplest and most palpable, utterly gross, almost mechanical, completely physiological, the natural animal tendency of avoiding pain and seeking pleasure. "Pain and pleasure," says Helvétius, "form the only springs of the moral universe, while the sentiment of self-love is the only basis on which we can lay the foundations of moral usefulness. What motive but that of self-interest could lead a man to perform a generous action? He can as little love good for the sake of good as evil for the sake of evil."[4] "The principles of natural law, say the disciples, are reduced to one unique and fundamental principle, self-preservation."[5] "To preserve oneself, to be happy," is instinct, right and duty. "Oh,

---

[1] "Suite du rêve de d'Alembert." "Entretien entre Mlles. de Lespinasse et Bordeu." "Mémoires de Diderot," a letter to Mlle. Volant, III. 66.

[2] Cf. his admirable tales, "Entretiens d'un père avec ses enfants," and "Le neveu de Rameau."

[3] Volney, *ibid.* "The natural law consists wholly of facts of which the demonstration is unceasingly renewed to the senses and which compose a science as precise and accurate as geometry and mathematics."

[4] Helvétius, "De l'Esprit," *passim.*

[5] Volney, *ibid.* chap. iii.   Saint-Lambert, *ibid.* the first dialogue.

ye,"[1] says nature, "who, through the impulsion I bestow on you,
tending towards happiness at every moment of your being, resist
not my sovereign law, strive for your own felicity, enjoy fearlessly
and be happy!" But, to be happy, contribute to the happiness
of others; if you wish them to be useful to you, be useful to
them; your interest, properly understood, commands you to
serve them. "Every man, from birth to death, has need of mankind." "Live then for them, that they may live for you." "Be
good, because goodness links hearts together; be gentle, because
gentleness wins affection; be modest, because pride repels beings
full of their self-importance. . . . Be citizens, because the country is necessary to ensure your safety and well-being. Defend
your country, because it renders you happy and contains your
possessions." Virtue thus is simply egotism furnished with a
spy-glass; man has no other reason for doing good but the fear
of doing himself harm, while self-devotion consists of self-interest.
One goes fast and far on this road. When the sole law for each
person is to be happy, each wishes to be so immediately and in
his own way; the herd of appetites is let loose, rushing ahead and
breaking down all barriers. And the more readily because it
has been demonstrated to them that every barrier is an evil, invented by cunning and malicious shepherds, the better to milk and
shear them. "The state of society is a state of warfare of the
sovereign against all, and of each member against the rest.[2] . . .
We see on the face of the globe only incapable, unjust sovereigns,
enervated by luxury, corrupted by flattery, depraved through un-
punished license, and without talent, morals, or good qualities.
. . . Man is wicked not because he is wicked, but because he
has been made so." "Would you know the story, in brief, of
almost all our wretchedness?[3] Here it is. There existed the
natural man, and into this man was introduced an artificial man,
whereupon a civil war arose within him, lasting through life.
. . . If you propose to become a tyrant over him, . . . do your
best to poison him with a theory of morals against nature; impose
every kind of fetter on him; embarrass his movements with a
thousand obstacles; place phantoms around him to frighten him.
. . . Would you see him happy and free? Do not meddle with

---

i D'Holbach, "Système de la Nature," II. 408–493.   ² *Ibid.* I. 347.
³ Diderot, "Supplément au voyage de Bougainville."

his affairs. . . . Remain convinced of this, that these wise legislators have formed and shaped you as they have done, not for your benefit, but for their own. I appeal to every civil, religious, and political institution; examine these closely, and, if I am not mistaken, you will find the human species, century after century, subject to a yoke which a mere handful of knaves chose to impose on it. . . . Be wary of him who seeks to establish order; to order is to obtain the mastery of others by giving them trouble." All this must come to an end; the passions are honest, and if the herd would eat freely, its first care must be to trample under its *sabots* the mitred and crowned animals who keep it in the fold for their own advantage.[1]

VI.

A return to nature, meaning by this the abolition of society, is the war-cry of the whole encyclopedic battalion. The same shout is heard in another quarter, coming from the Rousseau battalion, and that of the socialists who, in their turn, march up to the assault of the established régime. The mining and sapping of the walls practised by the latter seems less extensive, but only the more efficacious, while the distinctive machinery it employs consists likewise of a new conception of human nature. Rousseau derived this conception wholly from the spectacle he contemplated in his own breast:[2] a strange, original and superior man, who, from his infancy, harbored within him a germ of insanity, and who finally became wholly insane; a wonderful, ill-balanced mind in which sensations, emotions and images are too powerful: at once blind and perspicacious, a veritable poet

---

[1] Diderot, "Les Eleuthéromanes."
     Et mes mains, ourdissant les entrailles du prêtre,
     En feraient un cordon pour le dernier des rois.
Brissot: "Wants being the sole title to property the result is that when a want is satisfied man is no longer a property owner. . . . Two prime necessities are due to the animal constitution, food and waste. . . . May men nourish themselves on their fallen creatures?' (Yes, for) all beings may justly nourish themselves on any material calculated to supply their wants. . . . Man of nature, fulfil your desire, give heed to your cravings, your sole masters and your only guide. Do you feel your veins throbbing with inward fires at the sight of a charming creature? She is yours, your caresses are innocent and your kisses pure. Love alone entitles to enjoyment as hunger is the warrant for property." (An essay published in 1780, and reprinted in 1782 in the "Bibliothèque du Législateur," quoted by Roux and Buchez "Histoire parlementaire," XIII. 431.
[2] The words of Rousseau himself ("Rousseau juge de Jean-Jacques," third dialogue, p. 193): "From whence may the painter and apologist of nature, now so disfigured and so calumniated. derive his model if not from his own heart?"

and a morbid poet, who, instead of objects beheld reveries, living in a romance and dying in a nightmare of his own creation; incapable of self-mastery and of self-management, regarding resolutions as acts, a slight impulse for a resolution, and the part he assumed for the character he thought he possessed ; wholly disproportionate to the ordinary ways of the world, striking against, wounding himself and sullying himself at every barrier by the wayside ; committing absurdities, meannesses and crimes, and yet preserving up to the end delicate and profound sensibility, humanity, pity, the gift of tears, the faculty of loving, the passion for justice, the sentiment of religion and of enthusiasm, like so many vigorous roots in which generous sap is always fermenting, whilst the stem and the branches prove abortive and become deformed or wither under the inclemencies of the atmosphere. How explain such a contrast ? How did Rousseau himself account for it ? A critic, a psychologist would merely regard him as a singular case, the effect of an extraordinarily discordant mental formation, analogous to that of Hamlet, Chatterton, René or Werther, adapted to poetic spheres, but unsuitable for real life. Rousseau generalizes ; occupied with himself, even to infatuation, and regarding no one in the world but himself, he imagines man accordingly, and " describes him as he feels him within." Self-esteem, moreover, finds its account in this ; one is gratified at considering himself the type of humanity ; the statue one erects of himself becomes more important ; one rises in his own estimation when, in confessing to himself, he thinks he is confessing the human species. Rousseau convokes the assembly of generations with the trumpet of the day of judgment, and boldly stands up in the eyes of all men and of the Supreme Judge, exclaiming, " Let one of you dare to say I am better than thou ! "[1] His contaminations all come to him from without ; his vices and his baseness must be attributed to circumstances : " If I had fallen into the hands of a better

---

[1] " Confessions," Book I. p. 1, and at the end of the fifth book. See his letter to Malesherbes : " I know my great faults, and am profoundly sensible of my vices. With all that I shall die under the persuasion that of all the men I have encountered no one was better than myself." To Madame B——, March 16, 1770, he writes : " You have awarded me esteem for my writings ; your esteem would be yet greater for my life if it were open to your inspection, and still greater for my heart if it were exposed to your view. Never was there a better one, a heart more tender or more just. . . . My misfortunes are all due to my virtues." To Madame de la Tour, " Whoever is not enthusiastic in my behalf is unworthy of me."

master. . . . I should have been a good Christian, a good father, a good friend, a good workman, a good man in all things." The wrong is thus all on the side of society. In like manner nature, with man in general, is good. "His first impulses are always right. . . . The fundamental principle of all moral questions, on which I have argued in all my writings, is that *man is naturally good, and loving justice and order.* 'Emile,' especially, is a treatise on the natural goodness of man, intended to show how vice and error, foreign to his constitution, gradually find their way into it from without and insensibly change him. . . . Nature made man to be happy and good, while society has made him depraved and miserable."[1] Divest him, in thought, of his factitious habits, of his superadded necessities, of his false prejudices; put aside systems, study your own heart, listen to the inward dictates of feeling, let yourself be guided by the light of instinct and of conscience, and you will again find the first Adam, like an incorruptible marble statue that has fallen into a marsh, a long time lost under a crust of slime and mud, but which, released from its foul covering, may be replaced on its pedestal in the completeness of its form and in the perfect purity of its whiteness.

Around this central idea a reform occurs in the spiritualistic doctrine. A being so noble cannot possibly consist of a simple collection of organs; he is something more than mere matter; the impressions he derives from his senses do not constitute his full being. "I am not merely a sensitive and passive being, but an active and intelligent being, and, whatever philosophy may say, I dare claim the honor of thinking." And better still, this thinking principle, in man, at least, is of a superior kind. "Show me another animal on the globe capable of producing fire and of admiring the sun. What! I who am able to observe, to comprehend beings and their associations; who can appreciate order, beauty and virtue; who can contemplate the universe and exalt myself to the hand which controls it; who can love the good and do good, I compare myself to brutes!" Man is free, capable of deciding between two actions, and therefore the creator of his actions; he is accordingly a first and original cause, "an immaterial substance," distinct from the body, a soul hampered by the body and which may survive the body. This immortal soul imprisoned within the flesh has conscience for its organ.

[1] The letter to M. de Beaumont, p. 24. "Rousseau juge de Jean-Jacques," third dialogue, 193.

" O Conscience, divine instinct, immortal and celestial voice, un-
failing guide of an ignorant and finite but free and intelligent being, infallible judge between good and evil, and rendering
man similar to God, thou formest the superiority of his nature ! "
Alongside of self-love, by which we subordinate everything to ourselves, there is a love of order by which we subordinate ourselves
to the whole.   Alongside of egotism, by which man seeks happiness even at the expense of others, is sympathy, by which he
seeks the happiness of others even at the expense of his own.
Personal enjoyment does not suffice him; he still needs tranquillity of conscience and the effusions of the heart.   Such is man
as God designed and created him; in his organization there is
no defect.   Inferior elements are as serviceable as the superior
elements; all are essential, proportionate, in proper place, not
only the heart, the conscience, the intellect, and the faculties by
which we surpass brutes, but again the inclinations in common
with animals, the instinct of self-preservation and of self-defence,
the need of physical activity, sexual appetite, and other primitive
impulses as we observe them in the child, the savage and the
uncultivated man.[1]   None of these in themselves are either
vicious or injurious.   None are too strong, even the love of self.
None come into play out of season.   If we would not interfere
with them, if we would impose no constraint on them, if we
would permit these sparkling fountains to flow according to their
bent, if we would not confine them to our artificial and foul
channels, we should never see them boiling over and becoming
turbid.   We look with wonder on their ravages and on their
contaminations; we forget that, in the beginning, they were pure
and undefiled.   The fault is with us, in our social arrangements, in
our incrusted and formal channels whereby we cause deviations
and windings, and make them heave and bound.   "Your very
governments are the cause of the evils which they pretend to
remedy.   Ye scepters of iron! ye absurd laws, ye we reproach
for our inability to fulfil our duties on earth ! "   Away with
these dykes, the work of tyranny and routine !   An emancipated nature will at once resume a direct and healthy course and
man, without effort, will find himself not alone happy but virtuous.[2]

---

[1] "Emile," book I. and the letter to M. de Beaumont, *passim.*
[2] Article I.   " All Frenchmen shall be virtuous."   Article II.   " All Frenchmen shall be
happy."   (Draft of a constitution found among the papers of Sismondi, at that time in
school.)

On this principle the attack begins : there is none that is pushed further, nor conducted with more bitter hostility. Thus far existing institutions are exhibited simply as oppressive and unreasonable; they are now charged with being unjust and corrupting. Reason and the appetites were the only insubordinates; conscience and pride are now in rebellion. With Voltaire and Montesquieu fewer evils might be anticipated. With Diderot and d'Holbach the horizon discloses only a glowing Eldorado or a comfortable Cythera. With Rousseau I behold within reach an Eden where I shall immediately recover the nobleness inseparable from felicity. It is my right; nature and Providence summon me to it; it is my heritage. One arbitrary institution alone keeps me away from it, the creator of my vices as of my misery. With what rage and fury will I overthrow this ancient barrier! We detect this in the vehement tone, in the embittered style, and in the sombre eloquence of the new doctrine. Humor and scurrility are no longer an object; a serious tone is maintained; people become exasperated, while the powerful voice now heard penetrates beyond the drawing-room, to the rude and suffering crowd to which no word has yet been spoken, whose mute resentment for the first time finds an interpreter, and whose destructive instincts are soon to be set in motion at the summons of its herald. Rousseau is one of the people, and not a man of society. He feels awkward in a drawing-room.[1] He is not capable of conversing and of appearing amiable; his wit is late, coming to him on the steps as he leaves the house; he keeps silent with a sulky air or utters stupidities, redeeming his awkwardness with the sallies of a clown or with the phrases of a vulgar pedant. Elegance annoys him, luxuriousness makes him uncomfortable, politeness is a lie, conversation mere prattle, ease of manner a grimace, gaiety a conventionalism, wit a parade, science so much charlatanry, philosophy an affectation and morals utter corruption. All is factitious, false and unwholesome,[2]

---

[1] "Confessions," part 2, book IX. 368. "I cannot comprehend how any one can converse in a circle. . . . I stammer out a few words, with no meaning in them, as quickly as I can, very glad if they convey no sense. . . . I should be as fond of society as anybody if I were not certain of appearing not merely to disadvantage but wholly different from what I really am." Cf. in the "Nouvelle Héloise," 2d part, the letter of Saint-Preux on Paris. Also in "Emile," the end of book IV.

[2] "Confessions," part 2, IX. 361. "I was so weary of drawing-rooms, of jets of water, of bowers, of flower-beds and of those that showed them to me; I was so overwhelmed with pamphlets, harpsichords, games, knots, stupid witticisms, simpering looks, petty story-

from the paint, toilet and beauty of women to the atmosphere of
the apartments and the ragouts on the dinner-table, in sentiment
as in amusement, in literature as in music, in government as in
religion.   This civilization, which boasts of its splendour, is simply
the restlessness of over-excited, servile monkeys each imitating the
other, and each corrupting the other to attain to super-refinement,
discomfort and ennui.   Human culture, accordingly, is in itself
bad, while the fruit it produces is merely excrescence and poison.
Of what service are the sciences?   Uncertain and useless, they
afford merely a pasture-ground for idlers and wranglers.[1]   " Who
could pass a lifetime in sterile observation, did each person, consulting human duties and nature's demands, bestow his time on
his country, on the unfortunate and on his friends?"   Of what
use are the fine arts?   They serve only as public flattery of dominant passions.   "The more pleasing and the more perfect the
drama, the more baneful its influence;" the theatre, even with
Molière, is a school of bad morals, "inasmuch as it excites per-
fidious souls to inflict punishment, under the guise of stupidity, on
the candor of the innocent."   Tragedy, said to be moralizing,
wastes in counterfeit effusions the little virtue that still remains.
" After a man has seen and admired admirable conduct in fables
what more is expected of him?   After paying homage to virtue
is he not discharged from all that he owes to it?   What more
would they have him do?   Must he practise it himself?   He
has no part to play, he is not a comedian."   The sciences, the
fine arts, the arts of luxury, philosophy, literature, all is adapted
to enervating and dissipating the soul; all is contrived for the
small crowd of brilliant and noisy insects buzzing around elevated places in society and sucking away the public substance.
As for the sciences, but one is important, that of our duties,
and, without so many subtleties and so much study, innate sentiment suffices for our teaching.   As regards the arts, only those

---

tellers and heavy suppers, that when I spied out a corner in a hedge, a bush, a barn, a
meadow, or when, on passing through a hamlet, I caught the smell of a good parsely omelet
. . I sent to the devil all the rouge, furbelows and perfumery, and, regretting a plain
dinner and common wine, I would gladly have pommelled both the head cook and the
master of the house who forced me to dine when I generally sup, and to sup when I
generally go to bed, but, especially the lackeys that envied me every morsel I ate and who,
at the risk of my dying with thirst, sold me the drugged wine of their master at ten times
the price I would have to pay for better wine at a tavern."

   [1] " Discours sur l'influence des sciences et des arts "   The letter to d'Alembert on
theatrical performances.

should be tolerated which, ministering to our prime necessities, provide us with bread for our support, a roof to shelter us, clothing to cover our bodies and arms with which to defend ourselves. In the way of existence that only is healthy which enables us to live in the fields, requiring no preparation, without display, in family union, devoted to cultivation, living on the products of the soil and among neighbors that are equals and with servants that one trusts as friends.   As for the classes, but one is respectable, that of laboring men, especially that of men working with their own hands, artisans and mechanics, only these being really of service, the only ones who, through their situation, are in close proximity to the natural state, and who preserve, under a rough exterior, the warmth, the goodness and the integrity of primitive instincts. Accordingly, call by its true name this elegance, this luxury, this urbanity, this literary delicacy, this philosophical eccentricity, admired by the prejudiced as the flower of the life of humanity, but which is only its mould and moss.   In like manner esteem at its just value the swarm that live upon it, namely, the indolent aristocracy, the fashionable world, the privileged who direct and make a display, the idlers of the drawing-room who talk, divert themselves and regard themselves as the elect of humanity, but who are simply so many parasites. Whether parasitic or excretory, one attracts the other, and the tree can only again become healthy by getting rid of one or the other.

If civilization is bad, society is worse.[1]   For this could not have been established except by destroying primitive equality, while its two principal institutions, property and government, are usurpations.   "He who first enclosed a plot of ground, and who took it into his head to say *this belongs to me,* and who found people simple enough to believe him,[2] was the true founder of civil society. What crimes, what wars, what murders, what misery and what horrors would have been spared the human race if he who, pulling up the landmark and filling up the ditch, had cried out to his fellows: Be wary of that impostor; you are lost if you forget that no one has a right to the ground and that its fruits are the property of

---

[1] "Society is as natural to the human species as decrepitude to the individual. The people require arts, laws, and governments, as old men require crutches." See the letter to M. Philopolis, p. 248.

[2] See the discourse on the "Origine de l'Inégalité," *passim.*

all!" The first property right was a robbery by which an individual abstracted from the community a portion of the public domain. Nothing could justify the outrage, nothing added by him to the soil, neither his industry, nor his trouble, nor his valor. " In vain may he assert that he built this wall, and acquired this land by his labor. Who marked it out for him, one might ask, and how do you come to be paid for labor which was never imposed on you? Are you not aware that a multitude of your brethren are suffering and perishing with want because you have too much, and that the express and unanimous consent of the whole human species is requisite before appropriating to yourself more than your share of the common subsistence?" Underneath this theory we recognize the personal animus, the rancor of the poor embittered plebeian, who, on entering society, finds the places all taken, and who is incapable of creating one for himself; who, in his confessions, marks the day when he ceased to feel hungry; who, for lack of something better, lives in concubinage with a serving-woman and places his five children in a hospital; who is in turn valet, clerk, vagabond, teacher and copyist, always on the watch and making shift to maintain his independence, disgusted with the contrast between what he is outwardly and what he feels himself inwardly, avoiding envy only by disparagement, and preserving in the folds of his heart an old grudge "against the rich and the fortunate in this world as if they were so at his expense, as if their assumed happiness had been an infringement on his happiness."[1] Not only is there injustice in the origin of property but again there is injustice in the power it secures to itself, the wrong increasing like a canker under the partiality of law. "Are not all the advantages of society for the rich and for the powerful? Do they not absorb to themselves all lucrative positions? Is not the public authority wholly in their interest? If a man of position robs his creditors or commits other offences is he not certain of impunity? Are not the cudgellings he bestows, his violent assaults, the murders and the assassinations he is guilty of, matters that are hushed up and forgotten in a few months? Let this same man be robbed and the entire police set to work, and woe to the poor innocents they suspect! Has he to pass a dangerous place, escorts overrun the country. If the axle

---

[1] "Emile," book IV. Rousseau's narrative. p. 14.

of his coach breaks down everybody runs to help him. Is a noise made at his gate, a word from him and all is silent. Does the crowd annoy him, he makes a sign and order reigns. Does a carter chance to cross his path, his attendants are ready to knock him down, while fifty honest pedestrians might be crushed rather than a puppy be stopped on his headlong career. All this deference to him costs him not a penny. What a difference in the pict ure of the poor! The more humanity owes to it the more soci ety refuses it. All doors are closed to it even when it has the right to have them opened, and if it sometimes obtains justice it experiences more trouble than another in obtaining favors. If there are *corvées* to work out, a militia to raise, the poor are the most eligible. It always bears burdens from which its wealthier neighbor with influence secures exemption. At the least accident to a poor man everybody abandons him. Let his cart upset and I regard him as fortunate if he escapes the insults of the smart companions of a young duke passing by. In a word all gratuitous assistance is withheld from him in time of need, precisely because he cannot pay for it. I regard him as a lost man if he is so unfortunate as to be honest and have a pretty daughter and a powerful neighbor. Let us sum up in few words the social pact of the two estates: *You need me because I am rich and you are poor : let us then make an agreement together. I will allow you the honor of serving me on condition that you give me the little that remains to you for the trouble I have in governing you."*

This shows the spirit, the object and the effect of political society. At the start, according to Rousseau, it consisted of an iniquitous bargain, made by an adroit rich man with a poor dupe, "providing new fetters for the weak and fresh power for the rich," and, under the title of legitimate property, hallowing the usurpation of the soil. To-day the contract is still more iniquitous "as a child may govern an old man, a fool lead the wise, and a handful of people burst with superfluities whilst a famished multitude lack the necessaries of life." It is the nature of inequality to grow; hence the authority of some increases along with the dependence of the rest, so that the two conditions, having at last reached their extremes, the hereditary and perpetual subjection of the people seems to be a divine right equally with the hereditary and perpetual despotism of the king.

This is the present condition of things, and if a change occurs it is for the worse. "For,[1] the occupation of all kings, or of those charged with their functions, consists wholly of two objects, to extend their sway abroad and to render it more absolute at home." If any other aim is alleged it is a pretext. "The terms *public welfare, happiness of subjects*, the glory of the nation, so pretentiously employed in public edicts, never denote other than disastrous commands, and the people shudder beforehand when its masters allude to their paternal solicitude." However, this fatal point once reached, "the contract with the government is dissolved; the despot is master only while remaining the most powerful, and, as soon as he can be expelled, he has no reclamation against violence." Right exists only through consent, and no consent nor right can exist between master and slave. "Whether between one man and another man, or between one man and a people, the following is an absurd address: '*I make an agreement with you wholly at your expense and to my advantage which I shall respect as long as I please and which you shall respect as long as it pleases me.*'" Madmen may sign such a treaty, but, as madmen, they are not in a condition to negotiate and their signature is not binding. Those who are stricken to the ground, with swords pointed at their throats, may accept such conditions but, being under constraint, their promise is null and void. Madmen and the conquered may for a thousand years have bound over all subsequent generations, but a contract for a minor is not a contract for an adult, and on the child arriving at the age of reason he belongs to himself. We at last have become adults, and we have only to examine into the authority calling itself legitimate to bring its pretensions to their just value. It has power on its side and nothing more. But "A pistol, in a brigand's hand is power," and will you say that I am conscientiously obliged to hand him my purse? I obey through force and I will have my purse back if I can take his pistol away from him.

VII.

We stop here. It is not worth while to follow the forlorn hope of the party, Naigeon and Sylvain Maréchal, Mably and Morelly, the fanatics that erected atheism into an obligatory dogma and

---

[1] "Discours sur l'Origine de l'Inégalité," 178. "Contrat Social," I. ch. iv.

into a superior duty; the socialists who, to suppress egoism, propose a community of goods, and who found a republic in which any man that proposes to re-establish "detestable owner-ship" shall be declared an enemy of humanity, treated as a "raging maniac" and shut up in a dungeon for life. It is sufficient to have studied the operations of large armies and of great campaigns. With different resources and contrary tactics, the various attacks are all directed to the same end. Every in-stitution is undermined at its foundations. The dominant philosophy withdraws all authority from custom, from religion, from the State. Not only is it admitted that tradition in itself is false, but again that it is baneful through its works, that it builds up injustice on error, and that by rendering man blind it leads him to oppress. Henceforth it is proscribed. Let this "infamous thing" with its upholders be crushed out. It is the great wrong of the human species, and, when suppressed, only the right will remain. "The time will then come[1] when the sun will shine only on free men recognizing no other master than reason; when tyrants and slaves, and priests with their senseless or hypocritical instruments will exist only in history and on the the stage; when attention will no longer be bestowed on them except to pity their victims and their dupes, keeping oneself vigilant and useful through horror of their excesses, and able to recognize and extinguish by the force of reason the first germs of superstition and of tyranny, should they ever venture to reappear." The millenium is approaching and reason must be its own organizer. We are thus to owe everything to its salutary authority, the foundation of the new order of things as well as the destruction of the old one.

- Condorcet, "Tableau des progrès de l'esprit humain," the tenth epoch.

CHAPTER IV.

I.

CONSIDER future society as it appears at this moment to our legislators of the closet, and bear in mind that it will soon appear under the same aspect to the legislators of the Assembly. In their eyes the decisive moment has come. Henceforth two histories are to exist; [1] one, that of the past, the other, that of the future, formerly a history of man still deprived of his reason, and at present the history of the rational man. At length the rule of right is to begin. Of all that the past has founded and transmitted nothing is legitimate. Overlaying the natural man it has created an artificial man, either ecclesiastic or laic, noble or plebeian, sovereign or subject, proprietor or proletary, ignorant or cultivated, peasant or citizen, slave or master, all being factitious qualities which we are not to heed, as their origin is tainted with violence and robbery. Strip off these superadded

---

[1] Barrère, "Point du jour," No. 1, (June 15, 1789). "You are summoned to give history a fresh start."

garments; let us take man in himself, the same under all conditions, in all situations, in all countries, in all ages, and strive to
ascertain what sort of association is the best adapted to him.
The problem thus stated, the rest follows.

Conformably to the ways of the classic spirit, and to the pre-
cepts of the prevailing ideology, a political system is constructed
after a mathematical model.[1] A simple proposition is selected,
and set apart, very general, familiar, readily apparent, and easily
understood by the most ignorant and inattentive schoolboy.
Reject every difference which separates one man from other
men; retain of him only the portion common to him and to
others. This remainder constitutes man in general, or in other
words, "a sensitive and rational being who, thus endowed, avoids
pain and seeks pleasure," and therefore aspiring to "happiness,
namely, a stable condition in which one enjoys greater pleasure
than pain,"[2] or, again, "a sensitive being capable of forming
rational opinions and of acquiring moral ideas."[3] The first
comer is cognizant of this notion in his own experience, and can
verify it at the first glance. Such is the social unit; let several
of these be combined, a thousand, a hundred thousand, a million,
twenty-six millions, and you have the French people. Men
born at twenty-one years of age, without relations, without a
past, without traditions, without a country, are supposed to be
assembled for the first time and, for the first time, to treat with
each other. In this position, at the moment of contracting
together, all are equal: for, as the definition states, the extrinsic
and spurious qualities through which alone all differ have been
rejected. All are free; for, according to the definition, the unjust
thraldom imposed on all by brute force and by hereditary preju
dice has been suppressed. But, if all men are equal, no reason exists why, in this contract, any special advantage should be
conceded to one more than to another. Accordingly all shall
be equal before the law; no person, or family, or class, shall be
allowed any privilege; no one shall claim a right of which

---

[1] Condorcet, *ibid.* "The methods of the mathematical sciences, applied to new objects,
have opened new roads to the moral and political sciences." Cf. Rousseau, in the "Contrat
Social," the mathematical calculation of the fraction of sovereignty to which each individual
is entitled.

[2] Saint-Lambert, "Catéchisme universel," the first dialogue, p. 17.

[3] Condorcet, *il id.*, ninth epoch. "From this single truth the publicists have been able to
derive the rights of man."

another might be deprived ; no one shall be subject to any duty from which another is exempt. On the other hand, all being free, each enters with a free will along with the group of wills constituting the new community ; it is necessary that in the common resolutions he should fully concur. Only on these conditions does he bind himself; he is bound to respect laws only because he has assisted in making them, and to obey magistrates only because he has aided in electing them. Underneath all legitimate authority his consent or his vote must be apparent, while, in the humblest citizen, the most exalted of public powers must recognize a member of their own sovereignty. No one may alienate or lose this portion of his sovereignty; it is inseparable from his person, and, on delegating it to another, he reserves to himself full possession of it. The liberty, equality and sovereignty of the people constitute the first articles of the social contract. These are rigorously deduced from a primary definition ; other rights of the citizen are to be no less rigorously deduced from it, the main features of the constitution, the most important civil and political laws, in short, the order, the form and the spirit of the new state.

II.

Hence, two consequences. In the first place, a society thus organized is the only just one ; for, the reverse of all others, it is not the result of a blind subjection to traditions, but of a contract concluded among equals, examined in open daylight, and assented to in full freedom.[1] The social contract, composed of demonstrated theorems, has the authority of geometry ; hence an equal value at all times, in every place, and for every people ; it is accordingly rightfully established. Whatever interposes any obstacle thereto is inimical to the human race ; whether a government, an aristocracy or a clergy, it must be overthrown. Revolt

---

[1] Rousseau still entertained admiration for Montesquieu but, at the same time, with some reservation; afterwards, however, the theory developed itself, every historical right being rejected. "Then," says Condorcet, (*ibid.*, ninth epoch), "they found themselves obliged to abandon a false and crafty policy which, forgetful of men deriving equal rights through their nature, attempted at one time to estimate those allowed to them according to extent of territory, the temperature of the climate, the national character, the wealth of the population, the degree of perfection of their commerce and industries, and again to apportion the same rights unequally among diverse classes of men, bestowing them on birth, riches and professions, and thus creating opposite interests and opposite powers, for the purpose of subsequently establishing an equilibrium alone rendered necessary by these institutions themselves and which the danger of their tendencies by no means corrects."

is simply just defence ; in withdrawing ourselves from its hands
we only recover what it wrongfully withholds and which
legitimately belongs to us.   In the second place, this social code,
as just set forth, once promulgated, is applicable without misconception or resistance ; for it is a species of moral geometry,
simpler than any other, reduced to first principles, founded on
the clearest and most popular notions, and, in four steps, leading
to capital truths.   The comprehension and application of these
truths demand no preparatory study or profound reflection ; good
sense suffices, and even common sense.   Prejudice and selfishness alone impair the testimony ; but never will testimony be
wanting in a sound brain and in an upright heart.   Explain the
rights of man to a laborer or to a peasant and at once he becomes an able politician ; teach children the citizen's catechism
and, on leaving school, they comprehend duties and rights as well
as the four fundamental principles.—Thereupon hope spreads
her wings to the fullest extent ; all obstacles seem removed.
It is admitted that, of itself, and through its own force, the theory
engenders its own application, and that it suffices for men to
decree or accept the social compact to acquire suddenly by this
act the capacity for comprehending it and the disposition to
carry it out.

Such trust, marvellous, and, at the first glance, inexplicable,
suggests an idea then entertained by man which we no longer
possess.   Man, indeed, was regarded as essentially good and reasonable.—Reasonable, that is to say, capable of assenting to a
plain obvious principle, of following an ulterior chain of argument, of understanding and accepting the final conclusion, of extracting for himself, on the occasion calling for it, the varied consequences to which it leads : such is the ordinary man in the eyes
of the writers of the day ; they judge him by themselves.   To
them the human intellect is their own, the classic intellect.   For
a hundred and fifty years it rules in literature, in philosophy, in
science, in education, in conversation, by virtue of tradition, of
usage and of good taste.   No other is tolerated and no other is
imagined ; and if, within this closed circle, a stranger succeeds in
introducing himself, it is on condition of adopting the oratorical
idiom which the *raison raisonnante* imposes on all its guests, on
Greeks, Englishmen, barbarians, peasants and savages, however different from each other and however different they may be

amongst themselves.   In Buffon, the first man, on narrating the
first hours of his being, analyses his sensations, emotions and impulses, with as much subtlety as Condillac himself.   With
Diderot, Otou the Otaheitian, with Bernardin de St. Pierre, a
semi-savage Hindoo and an old colonist of the Ile-de-France,
with Rousseau a country vicar, a gardener and a juggler, are accomplished conversationists and moralists.   In Marmontel and
in Florian, in all the literature of inferior rank preceding or accompanying the Revolution, also in the tragic or comic drama,
the chief talent of the personage, whoever he may be, whether
an uncultivated rustic, tattooed barbarian or naked savage, consists in explaining himself, in arguing and in following an
abstract discourse with intelligence and attention, in tracing for
himself, or in the footsteps of a guide, the rectilinear pathway of
general ideas.   Thus, to spectators of the eighteenth century,
reason is everywhere and she stands alone in the world.   A
form of intellect so universal necessarily strikes them as natural,
they resemble people who, speaking but one language, and one
they have always spoken with facility, cannot imagine any other
language being spoken, or that they may be surrounded by the
deaf and the dumb.   And so much the more inasmuch as their
theory authorizes this prejudice.   According to the new ideology
all minds are within reach of all truths.   If the mind does not
attain to them the fault is ours in not being properly prepared; it
will attain to them if we take the trouble to guide it properly.
For it has senses the same as our own; and sensations, revived,
combined and noted by signs, suffice to form "not only all our
conceptions but again all our faculties."[1]   An exact and constant
filiation of ideas attaches our simplest perceptions to the most
complex sciences, and, from the lowest to the highest degree, a
scale is practicable; if the scholar stops on the way it is owing
to our having left too great an interval between two degrees of
the scale; let no intermediary degrees be omitted and he will
mount to the top of it.   To this exalted idea of the faculties of
man is added a no less exalted idea of his heart.   Rousseau having declared this to be naturally good, the refined class plunge into
the belief with all the exaggerations of fashion and all the sentimentality of the drawing-room.   The conviction is widespread that

---

[1] Condillac, " Logique."

man, and especially the man of the people, is sensitive and affectionate by nature; that he is immediately impressed by benefactions and disposed to be grateful for them, that he softens at the slightest sign of interest in him, and that he is capable of every refinement. A series of engravings represents two children in a dilapidated cottage,[1] one five and the other three years of age, by the side of an infirm grandmother, one supporting her head and the other giving her drink; the father and mother enter and, on seeing this touching incident, "these good people find themselves so happy in possessing such children they forget they are poor." "Oh, my father," cries a shepherd youth of the Pyrenees,[2] "accept this faithful dog, so true to me for seven years; in future let him follow and defend you, for never will he have served me so usefully." It would require too much space to follow in the literature of the end of the century, from Marmontel to Bernardin de Saint-Pierre, and from Florian to Berquin and Bitaubé, the interminable repetition of these sweet insipidities. The illusion even reaches statesmen. "Sire," says Turgot, on presenting the king with a plan of political education,[3] "I venture to assert that in ten years your nation will no longer be recognizable, and through enlightenment and good morals, in intelligent zeal for your service and for the country, it will rise above all other nations. Children who are now ten years of age will then be men prepared for the state, loving their country, submissive to authority, not through fear but through reason, aiding their fellow-citizens, and accustomed to recognizing and respecting justice." In the month of January, 1789,[4] Necker, to whom M. de Bouillé pointed out the imminent danger arising from the unswerving efforts of the Third-Estate, "coldly replied, turning his eyes upward, 'reliance must be placed on the moral virtues of man.'" In the main, on the imagination forming any conception of human society, this consists of a vague, semi-bucolic, semi-theatric scene, somewhat

---

[1] "Histoire de France par Estamps," 1789.

[2] Mme. de Genlis, "Souvenirs de Félicie," 371-391.

[3] De Tocqueville, "L'Ancien régime," 237. Cf. "L'an 2440," by Mercier, III. vols. One of these imaginings in all its details may be found here. The work was first published in 1770. "The Revolution," says one of the characters, "was brought about *without an effort*, through the heroism of a great man, a royal philosopher worthy of power, because he despised it," etc. (Tome II. 109.)

[4] "Mémoires de M. de Bouillé," p. 70. Cf. Barante, "Tableau de la litt. française au dix-huitième siècle," p. 318. "Civilization and enlightenment were supposed to have allayed all passions and softened all characters. It seemed as if morality had become easy of practice and that the balance of social order was so well adjusted that nothing could disturb it."

resembling those displayed on the frontispieces of illustrated works on morals and politics. Half-naked men with others clothed in skins, assemble together under a large oak tree; in the centre of the group a venerable old man arises and makes an address, using "the language of nature and reason," proposing that all should be united, and explaining how men are bound together by mutual obligations; he shows them the harmony of private and of public interests, and ends by making them sensible of the beauties of virtue.[1] All utter shouts of joy, embrace each other, gather round the speaker and elect him chief magistrate; dancing is going on under the branches in the background, and henceforth happiness on earth is fully established. This is no exaggeration. The National Assembly addresses the nation in harangues of this style. For many years the government speaks to the people as it would to one of Gessner's shepherds. The peasants are entreated not to burn castles because it is painful for their good king to see such sights. They are exhorted "to surprise him with their virtues in order that he may be the sooner rewarded for his own."[2] At the height of the Jacquerie tumults the sages of the day seem to think they are living in a state of pastoral simplicity, and that with an air on the flute they may restore to its fold the howling pack of bestial animosities and unchained appetites.

III.

It is a sad thing to fall asleep in a sheepcot and, on awakening, to find the sheep transformed into wolves. And yet, in case of a revolution this is what we may expect. What we call reason in man is not an innate endowment, primitive and enduring, but a tardy acquisition and a fragile composition. The slightest physiological knowledge suffices to show that it is a state of unstable equilibrium, dependent on the no less greater instability of the brain, nerves, circulation and digestion. Take women that are hungry and men that have been drinking; place a thousand of these together, and let them excite each other with their exclamations, their anxieties, and the contagious reaction of their

---

1 See in Rousseau, in the "Lettre à M. de Beaumont," a scene of this description, the establishment of deism and toleration, associated with a similar discourse.

2 Roux et Buchez, "Histoire parlementaire," IV. 322, the address made on the 11th Feb., 1790. "What an affecting and sublime address," says a deputy. It was greeted by the Assembly with "unparalleled applause." The whole address should be quoted entire.

ever-deepening emotions; it will not be long before you find them
a crowd of dangerous maniacs. This is evident in 1789 ; and
more besides. Now, interrogate psychology. The simplest mental operation, a sensuous perception, an act of memory, the appliance of a name, an ordinary act of judgment is the play of
complicated mechanism, the joint and final result of several millions of wheels which, like those of a clock,[1] turn and propel
blindly, each for itself, each through its own force, and each kept
in place and in functional activity by a system of balance and
compensation. If the hands mark the hour with any degree of
accuracy it is due to a wonderful if not miraculous conjunction,
while hallucination, delirium and monomania, ever at the door,
are always ready to enter it. Properly speaking man is imbecile,
as the body is morbid, by nature; the health of our mind, like
the health of our organs, is simply a repeated achievement and a
happy accident. If such happens to be the case with the coarse
woof and canvas, with the large and approximatively strong
threads of our intellect, what risks are imminent for the ulterior
and superadded embroidery, the subtle and complicated netting
forming reason properly so called, and which is composed of
general ideas ? Formed by a slow and delicate process of weaving, through a long system of signs, amidst the agitations of
pride, of enthusiasm and of dogmatic obstinacy, how many
chances there are, even in the most perfect brain, of these ideas
inadequately corresponding with outward things! All that we
require in this connection is to witness the operation of the idyl in
vogue with the philosophers and politicians. These being the
superior minds, what can be said of the masses of the people, of
the uncultivated or semi-cultivated brains ? According as reason
is crippled in man so is it rare in humanity. General ideas
and accurate reasoning are found only in a select few. The
comprehension of abstract terms and the habit of making accurate deductions requires previous and special preparation, a prolonged mental exercise and steady practice, and besides this,
where political matters are concerned, a degree of composure
which, affording every facility for reflection, enables a man to detach himself for a moment from himself for the consideration of
his interests as a disinterested observer. If one of these con-

---

[1] The number of cerebral cells is estimated (the cortical layer) at twelve hundred
millions, and the fibres binding them together at four thousand millions.

ditions is wanting, reason, especially in relation to politics, is absent.—In a peasant or a villager, in any man brought up from infancy to manual labor, not only is the network of superior conceptions defective, but again the internal machinery by which
they are woven is not perfected. Accustomed to the open air, to
the exercise of his limbs, his attention flags if he stands inactive
for a quarter of an hour; generalized expressions find their way
into his mind only as sound; the mental combination they ought
to excite cannot be produced., He becomes drowsy unless a
powerful vibrating voice contagiously arouses in him the instincts
of flesh and blood, the personal cravings, the secret enmities which,
restrained by outward discipline, are always ready to be set free.
In the half-cultivated mind, even with the man who thinks himself
cultivated and who reads the newspapers, principles are generally
disproportionate guests; they are above his comprehension; he
does not measure their bearings, he does not appreciate their
limitations, he is insensible to their restrictions and he fal-
sifies their application. They are like those preparations of
the laboratory which, harmless in the chemist's hands, become
destructive in the street under the feet of passing people. Too
soon will this be apparent when, in the name of popular
sovereignty, each commune, each mob, shall regard itself as the
nation and act accordingly; when reason, in the hands of its new
interpreters, shall inaugurate riots in the streets and peasant insurrections in the fields.

This is owing to the philosophers of the age having been
mistaken in two ways. Not only is reason not natural to man
nor universal in humanity, but again, in the conduct of man and
of humanity, its influence is small. Except with a few cool and
clear intellects, a Fontenelle, a Hume, a Gibbon, with whom it
may prevail because it encounters no rivals, it is very far from
playing the leading part; it belongs to other forces born within us,
and which, by virtue of being the first comers, remain in possession of the field. The place obtained by reason is always restricted;
the office it fulfils is generally secondary. Openly or secretly,
it is only a convenient subaltern, a domestic advocate unceasingly
suborned, employed by the proprietors to plead in their behalf; if they yield it precedence in public it is only through
decorum. Vainly do they proclaim it the recognized sovereign;
they grant it only a' passing authority, and, under its nominal

control, they remain the inward masters. These masters of man consist of physical temperament, bodily needs, animal instinct, hereditary prejudice, imagination, generally the dominant passion, and more particularly personal or family interest, also that of caste or party. We should labor under serious error were we to suppose ourselves naturally good, generous, sympathetic, or, even at the least, gentle, pliable, and ready to sacrifice ourselves to social interests or to those of others. There are several of them and those of the most powerful kind, which, if left to themselves, would make only havoc. In the first place, if there is no certainty of man being a remote blood cousin of the monkey, it is at least certain that, in his structure, he is an animal closely related to the monkey, provided with canine teeth, carnivorous, formerly cannibal and, therefore, a hunter and bellicose. Hence there is in him a steady substratum of brutality and ferocity, and of violent and destructive instincts, to which must be added, if he is French, gaiety, laughter, and a strange propensity to gambol and act insanely in the havoc he makes;—we shall see him at work. In the second place, at the outset, his condition casts him naked and destitute on an ungrateful soil, on which subsistence is difficult, where, at the risk of death, he is obliged to save and to economize. Hence a constant preoccupation and the rooted idea of acquiring, accumulating, and possessing, rapacity and avarice, more particularly in the class which, tied to the glebe, fasts for sixty generations in order to support other classes, and whose crooked fingers are always outstretched to clutch the soil whose fruits they cause to grow;—we shall see this class at work. Finally, his more delicate mental organization makes of him from the earliest days an imaginative being in which swarming fancies develop themselves into monstrous chimeras to expand his hopes, fears and desires beyond all bounds. Hence an excess of sensibility, sudden outbursts of emotion, contagious transports, irresistible currents of passion, epidemics of credulity and suspicion, in short, enthusiasm and panic, especially if he is French, that is to say, excitable and communicative, easily thrown off his balance and prompt to accept foreign impulsion, deprived of the natural ballast which a phlegmatic temperament and the concentration of lonely meditations secure to his German or Latin neighbors;—and all this we shall see at work. These constitute some of the brute forces that control human life. In ordinary

R

times we pay no attention to them; being subordinated they do
not seem to us formidable.   We take it for granted that they are
allayed and pacified; we flatter ourselves that the discipline
imposed on them has made them natural, and that by dint of
flowing between dykes they are settled down into their accustomed beds.   The truth is that, like all brute forces, like a stream
or a torrent, they only remain in these under constraint; it is the
dyke which, through its resistance, produces this moderation.
Another force equal to their force had to be installed against their
outbreaks and devastations, graduated according to their scale, all
the firmer as they are more menacing, despotic if need be against
their despotism, in any event constraining and repressive, at the
outset a tribal chief, later an army general, all modes consisting
in an elective or hereditary gendarme, possessing vigilant eyes and
vigorous arms, and who, with blows, excites fear and, through
fear, maintains order.   In the regulation and limitation of his
blows divers instrumentalities are employed, a pre-established
constitution, a division of powers, a code of laws, tribunals, and
legal formalities.   At the bottom of all these wheels ever appears
the principal lever, the efficacious instrument, namely, the
gendarme armed against the savage, brigand and madman each
of us harbors, in repose or manacled, but always living, in the recesses of his own breast.

On the contrary, in the new theory, every principle promulgated, every precaution taken, every suspicion awakened is aimed
at the gendarme.   In the name of the sovereignty of the people
all authority is withdrawn from the government, every prerogative, every initiative, its continuance and its force.   The people
being sovereign the government is simply its clerk, and less than
its clerk, merely its domestic.   Between them "no contract"
indefinite or at least enduring, "and which may be cancelled
only by mutual consent or the unfaithfulness of one of the two
parties."   "It is against the nature of a political body for the
sovereign to impose a law on himself which he cannot set aside."
There is no sacred and inviolable charter "binding a people
to the forms of an established constitution."   "The right to
change these is the first guarantee of all rights."   "There is not,
and never can be, any fundamental, obligatory law for the entire
body of a people, not even the social contract."   It is through
usurpation and deception that a prince. an assembly, and a body

of magistrates declare themselves representatives of the people. "Sovereignty is not to be represented for the same reason that it is not to be alienated. . . . The moment a people gives itself representatives it is no longer free, it exists no more. . . . The English people think themselves free but they deceive themselves; they are free only during an election of members of parliament; on the election of these they become slaves and are null. . . . The deputies of the people are not, nor can they be, its representatives; they are simply its commissioners and can establish no final compact. Every law not ratified by the people themselves is null and is no law." "A body of laws sanctioned by an assembly of the people through a fixed constitution of the State does not suffice; other fixed and periodical assemblies are necessary which cannot be abolished or prorogued, so arranged that on a given day the people may be legitimately convoked by the law, no other formal convocation being requisite. . . . The moment the people are thus assembled the jurisdiction of the government is to cease, and the executive power is to be suspended," society commencing anew, while citizens, restored to their primitive independence, may reconstitute at will, for any period they determine, the provisional contract to which they have assented only for a determined time. "The opening of these assemblies, whose sole object is to maintain the social compact, should always take place with two propositions, never suppressed, and which are to be voted on separately ; the first one, *whether the sovereign is willing to maintain the actual form of the government ;* and the second, *whether the people are willing to leave its administration in the hands of those actually performing its duties."* Thus, "the act by which a people is subject to its chiefs is absolutely only a commission, a service in which, as simple officers of their sovereign, they exercise in his name the power of which he has made them depositaries, and which he may modify, limit and resume at pleasure."[1] Not only does it always reserve to itself "the legislative power which belongs to it and which can belong only to it," but again, it delegates and withdraws the executive power according to its fancy. Those who exercise it are its employés. "It may establish and depose them when it pleases." In relation to it they have no

---

[1] Rousseau, "Contrat social," I, ch. 7; III. ch. 13, 14, 15, 18; IV. ch. 1, 18; IV. 3. Cf. Condorcet, ninth epoch.

rights. "It is not a matter of contract with them but one of obedience;" they have "no conditions" to prescribe; they cannot demand of it the fulfilment of any engagement. It is useless to raise the objection that, according to this, every man of spirit or of culture will decline our offices, and that our chiefs will bear the character of lackeys. We will not leave them the freedom of accepting or declining office; we impose it on them authoritatively. "In every true democracy the magistrature is not an advantage but an onerous burden, not. to be assigned to one more than to another." We can lay hands on our magistrates, take them by the collar and seat them on their benches in their own despite. By fair means or foul they are the working subjects *(corvéables)* of the State, in a lower condition than a valet or a mechanic, since the mechanic does his work according to acceptable conditions, and the discharged valet can claim his eight days' notice to quit. When government throws off this humble attitude it usurps, while constitutions are to proclaim that, in such an event, insurrection is not only the most sacred right but the most imperative duty.

Practice, accordingly, accompanies the theory, and the dogma of the sovereignty of the people, interpreted by the mass, is to produce a perfect anarchy, up to the moment when, interpreted by its chiefs, it produces a perfect despotism.

IV.

For there are two sides to this theory; whilst one side leads to the perpetual demolition of government, the other terminates in the illimitable dictation of the State. The new contract is not a historic fact, like the English Declaration of Rights in 1688, or the Dutch federation in 1579, entered into by actual and living individuals, admitting acquired situations, groups already formed, established positions, and drawn up to recognize, define, guarantee and complete an anterior right. Antecedent to the social contract no veritable right exists; for veritable rights are born solely out of the social contract, the only valid one, since it is the only one agreed upon between beings perfectly equal and perfectly free, so many abstract creatures, so many species of mathematical units, all of the same value, all playing the same part and whose inequality or constraint never disturbs the common understanding. Hence, at the moment of its completion, all other facts are nullified. Property, family, church, no ancient institution may invoke any right against the new State. The area on which it is built up must be considered vacant; if old structures are partly allowed to remain it is only in its name and for its benefit, to be enclosed within its barriers and appropriated to its use; the entire soil of humanity is its property. On the other hand it is not, according to the American doctrine, an association for mutual protection, a society like other societies, circumscribed in its purpose, restricted to its office, limited in its powers, and by which individuals reserving to themselves the better portion of their property and persons, assess each other for the maintenance of an army, a police, tribunals, highways, schools, in short, the major instrumentalities of public safety and utility, at the same time withholding the remainder of local, general, spiritual and material services in favor of private initiative and of spontaneous associations that may arise as occasion or necessity calls for them. Our State is not to be a simple utilitarian machine, a convenient, handy implement, of which the workman avails himself without abandoning the free use of his hand, or the simultaneous use of other implements. Being elder born, the only son and sole representative of reason, it must, to ensure its sway, leave nothing beyond its grasp. In this respect the old régime paves the way for the new one, while the established system inclines minds beforehand to the budding theory. Through administrative centralization the State already, for a long time, has its hands everywhere.[1] " You must know," says Law to the Marquis d'Argenson, " that the kingdom of France is governed by thirty intendants. You have neither parliaments, assemblies or governors, simply thirty masters of requests, provincial clerks, on whom depends the happiness or misery, the fruitfulness or sterility of these provinces." The king, in fact, sovereign, father, and universal guardian, manages local affairs through his delegates, and intervenes in private affairs through his favors or *lettres-de-cachet.* Such an example and such a course followed for fifty years excites the imagination. No other instrumentality is better calculated to effect reforms on a large scale and at one stroke. Hence, far from restricting the central power the economists are desirous of extending its action.

---

[1] De Tocqueville, " L'Ancien régime," book II. entire, and book III. ch. 3.

Instead of setting up new dykes against it they interest themselves only in destroying what is left of the old dykes still in-
terfering with it. " The system of counter-forces in a government," say Quesnay and his disciples, " is a fatal idea. . . . The
speculations on which the system of counter-balance is founded
are chimerical. . . . Let the government have a full comprehension of its duties and be left free. . . . The State must govern
according to the essential laws of order, and in this case unlimited
power is requisite." On the approach of the Revolution the
same doctrine reappears, except in the substitution of one term
for another term. In the place of the sovereignty of the king
the " *Contrat social*" substitutes the sovereignty of the people.
The latter, however, is much more absolute than the former, and,
in the democratic convent which Rousseau constructs, on the
Spartan and Roman model, the individual is nothing and the
State everything.

In effect, "the clauses of the social contract reduce themselves
to one, namely, the total transfer of each associate with all his
rights to the community." [1] Every one surrenders himself entirely, "just as he stands, he and all his forces, of which his
property forms a portion." There is no exception nor reservation; whatever he may have been previously and whatever may
have belonged to him is no longer his own. Henceforth whatever he becomes or whatever he may possess devolves on him
only through the delegation of the social body, the universal
proprietor and absolute master. All rights must be vested in the
State and none in the individual; otherwise there would be litigation between them, and, "as there is no common superior to
decide between them " their litigation would never end. On the
contrary, through the complete donation which each one makes
of himself, "the unity is as perfect as possible; " having renounced all and renounced himself " he has no further claim to
make."

This being admitted, let us trace the consequences. In the
first place, I enjoy my property only through tolerance and at
second-hand; for, according to the social contract, I have surren-
dered it; [2] "it now forms a portion of the national estate;" if I

---

[1] Rousseau, "Contrat social." I. 6.

[2] *Ibid.* I. 9. "The State in relation to its members is master of all their possessions according to the social compact; possessors are considered as depositaries of the public wealth."

retain the use of it for the time being it is through a concession of the State which makes me a "depositary" of it. And this favor must not be considered as a restitution. "Far from accepting the property of individuals society despoils them of it, simply converting the usurpation into a veritable right, the enjoyment of it into proprietorship." Previous to the social contract I was possessor not by right but in fact, and even unjustly if I had large possessions; for, "every man has naturally a right to whatever he needs," and I have robbed other men of all that I possessed beyond my subsistence. Hence, so far from the State being under obligation to me, I am under obligation to it, the property which it returns to me not being mine but that with which the State favors me. It follows, accordingly, that the State may impose conditions on its gift, limit the use I may make of it according to its fancy, restrict and regulate my disposition of it, my right to bequeath it. "According to nature,[1] the right of property does not extend beyond the life of its owner; the moment he dies his possessions are no longer his own. Thus, to prescribe the conditions on which he may dispose of it is really less to change his right in appearance than to extend it in effect." In any event as my title is an effect of the social contract it is precarious like the contract itself; a new stipulation suffices to limit it or to destroy it. "The sovereign[2] may legitimately appropriate to himself all property, as was done in Sparta in the time of Lycurgus." In our lay convent whatever each monk possesses is only a revocable gift by the convent.

In the second place, this convent is a seminary. I have no right to bring up my children in my own house and in my own way. "As the reason of each man[3] must not be the sole arbiter of his rights, so much less should the education of children, which is of more consequence to the State than to fathers, be left to the intelligence and prejudices of their fathers." "If public authority, taking the place of fathers in assuming this important function, acquires their rights in fulfilling their duties, they have so much the less reason to complain inasmuch as they merely undergo a change of name, and, under the title of citizens, exercise in common the same authority over their children that they have

[1] Rousseau, "Discours sur l'Economie politique," 308.
[2] *Ibid.* "Emile," book V. 175.
[3] *Ibid.* "Discours sur l'Economie politique," 302.

separately exercised under the title of fathers." In other words you cease to be a father, but, in exchange, become a school inspector; one is as good as the other, and what complaint have you to make? Such was the case in that perpetual army called Sparta; there, the children, genuine regimental children, equally obeyed all properly-formed men. Thus, "public education, within laws prescribed by the government and under magistrates appointed by sovereign will, is one of the fundamental maxims of popular or legitimate government." Through this the citizen is formed in advance. "It gives the national form to souls.[1] Nations, in the long run, are what the government makes them—soldiers, citizens, men when so disposed, a populace, *canaille* if it pleases," being fashioned by their education. "Would you obtain an idea of public education? Read Plato's 'Republic.'[2] . . . The best social institutions are those the best qualified to change man's nature, to destroy his absolute being, to give him a relative being, and to convert *self* into the common unity, so that each individual may not regard himself as one by himself, but a part of the unity, and no longer sensitive but through the whole. An infant, on opening its eyes, must behold the common patrimony and, to the day of its death, behold that only. . . . He should be disciplined so as never to contemplate the individual except in his relations with the body of the State." Such was the practice of Sparta, and the sole aim of the " great Lycurgus." "All being equal through the law, they must be brought up together and in the same manner." "The law must regulate the subjects, the order and the form of their studies." They must, at the very least, take part in public exercises, in horse-races, in the games of strength and of agility instituted "to accustom them to law, equality, fraternity, and competition ; " to teach them how "to live under the eyes of their fellow-citizens and to crave public applause." Through these games they become democrats from their early youth, since, the prizes being awarded, not through the arbitrament of masters, but through the cheers of spectators, they accustom themselves to recognizing as sovereign the legitimate sovereignty, consisting of the verdict of the assembled people. The important interest of the State is, always, to form the wills of those by which it lasts, to prepare the votes that are

---

[1] Rousseau, on the "Gouvernement de Pologne," 277, 283, 287.
[2] *Ibid.* "Emile," book I.

to maintain it, to uproot passions in the soul that might be opposed to it, to implant passions that will prove favorable to it, to fix firmly within the breasts of its future citizens the sentiments and prejudices it will at some time need.[1]   If it does not secure the children it will not possess the adults.   Novices in a convent must be educated as monks, otherwise, when they grow up, the convent will no longer exist.

Finally, our lay convent has its own religion, a lay religion. If I possess any other it is through its condescension and under restrictions.   It is, by nature, hostile to other associations than its own ; they are rivals, they annoy it, they absorb the will and pervert the votes of its members.   "To ensure a full declaration of the general will it is an important matter not to allow any special society in the State, and that each citizen should pronounce according to it alone."[2]   "Whatever breaks up social unity is worthless," and it would be better for the State if there were no Church.   Not only is every church suspicious but, if I am a Christian, my belief is regarded unfavorably.   According to this new legislator "nothing is more opposed to the social spirit than Christianity. . . . A society of true Christians would no longer form a society of men."   For, "the Christian patrimony is not of this world."   It cannot zealously serve the State, being bound by its conscience to support tyrants.   Its law "preaches only servitude and dependence . . . it is made for a slave," and never will a citizen be made out of a slave.   "*Christian Republic,* each of these two words excludes the other."   Therefore, if the future Republic assents to my profession of Christianity, it is on the understood condition that my doctrine shall be shut up in my mind, without even affecting my heart.   If I am a Catholic, (and twenty-five out of twenty-six million Frenchmen are like me), my condition is worse.   For the social pact does not tolerate an intolerant religion ; any sect that condemns other sects is a public enemy ; "whoever presumes to say that *there is no salvation out of the church,* must be driven out of the State."   Should I be, finally, a free-thinker, a positivist or sceptic, my situation is little better.   "There is a civil religion," a catechism, "a profession of faith, of which the sovereign has the right to dictate the

---

[1] Morelly, "Code de la nature."   "At the age of five all children should be removed from their families and brought up in common, at the charge of the State, in a uniform manner." A similar project, perfectly Spartan, was found among the papers of St. Just.
[2] Rousseau, "Contrat social," II. 3 ; IV. 8.

articles, not exactly as religious dogmas but as sentiments of social import without which we cannot be a good citizen or a loyal
subject." These articles embrace "the existence of a powerful,
intelligent, beneficent, foreseeing and provident divinity, the future life, the happiness of the good, the punishment of the
wicked, the sacredness of the social contract and of the laws.[1]
Without forcing any one to believe in this creed, whoever does
not believe in it must be expelled from the State; it is necessary
to banish such persons not on account of impiety, but as un-
sociable beings, incapable of sincerely loving law and justice and,
if need be, of giving up life for duty." Take heed that this profession of faith be not a vain one, for a new inquisition is to test
its sincerity. "Should any person, after having publicly assented
to these dogmas, act as an unbeliever, let him be punished with
death. He has committed the greatest of crimes: he has lied before the law." Truly, as I said above, we are in a convent.

V.

These articles are all necessary sequels of the social contract.
The moment I enter the corporation I abandon my own personality; I abandon, by this step, my possessions, my children, my
church, and my opinions. I cease to be proprietor, father, Christian and philosopher. The State is my substitute in all these
functions. In place of my will, there is henceforth the public
will, that is to say, in theory, the mutable absolutism of a majority
counted by heads, while in fact, it is the rigid absolutism of
the assembly, the faction, the individual who is custodian of
the public authority. On this principle an outburst of boundless
infatuation takes place. The very first year Grégoire states in the
tribune of the Constituent Assembly," we might change religion if
we pleased, but we have no such desire." A little later the desire
comes, and it is to be carried out; that of Holbach is proposed, then
that of Rousseau, and they dare go much farther. In the name
of Reason, of which the State alone is the representative and interpreter, they undertake to unmake and make over, conformably to
reason and to reason alone, all customs, festivals, ceremonies, and
costumes, the era, the calendar, weights and measures, the names

---

[1] Cf. Mercier, "L'an 2240," I. ch. 17 and 18. From 1770 on, he traces the programme of
a system of worship similar to that of the Theo-philanthropists, the chapter being entitled
" Pas si éloigné qu'on le pense."

of the seasons, months, weeks and days, of places and monuments, family and baptismal names, complimentary titles, the tone of discourse, the mode of salutation, of greeting, of speaking and of writing, in such a fashion, that the Frenchman, as formerly with the puritan or the quaker, remodelled even in his inward substance, exposes, through the minutest details of his conduct and exterior, the dominance of the all-powerful principle which refashions his being and the inflexible logic which controls his thoughts.   This constitutes the final result and complete triumph of the classic spirit.   Installed in narrow brains, incapable of entertaining two related ideas, it is to become a cold or furious monomania, maddened in the destruction of a past it curses, and in the establishment of the millennium it pursues, and all in the name of an imaginary contract, at once anarchical and despotic, which unfetters insurrection and justifies dictation ; all to end in a social antagonism, resembling now a bacchanalian orgy of demons, and now a Spartan conventual group ; all with a view to substitute for the existing man, enduring and slowly formed by history, an improvised automaton that is to fall away through its own debility when the external and mechanical force that keeps it up will no longer sustain it.

BOOK FOURTH.

𝕮𝔥𝔢 𝔓𝔯𝔬𝔭𝔞𝔤𝔞𝔱𝔦𝔬𝔫 𝔬𝔣 𝔱𝔥𝔢 𝔇𝔬𝔠𝔱𝔯𝔦𝔫𝔢.

CHAPTER I.

SUCCESS OF THIS PHILOSOPHY IN FRANCE.—Failure of the same philosophy in England.—I. Causes of this difference.—The art of writing in
France.—Its superiority at this epoch.—It serves as the vehicle of new
ideas.—Books are written for people of the world.—The philosophers are
people of the world and consequently writers.—This accounts for philosophy
descending to the drawing-room.—II. Owing to this method it becomes
popular.—III. Owing to style it becomes pleasing.—Two stimulants peculiar
to the 18th century, coarse humor and irony.—IV. The art and processes
of the masters.—Montesquieu.—Voltaire.—Diderot.—Rousseau.—"The
Marriage of Figaro."

ANALOGOUS theories have many times traversed the imaginations of men, and analogous theories will yet traverse them more
than once again. In all ages and in all countries, any considerable change effected in the conception of human nature
suffices to disclose, by way of counterstroke, utopias and discoveries springing up on the territories of politics and religion.
But this does not suffice for the propagation of the new doctrine
nor, above all, for speculation to become application. Although
born in England, the philosophy of the eighteenth century could
not develop itself in England; the fever for demolition and
reconstruction remained superficial there and momentary. Deism, atheism, materialism, scepticism, ideology, the theory of the
return to nature, the proclamation of the rights of man, all the
temerities of Bolingbroke, Collins, Toland, Tindal and Mande-
ville, the bold ideas of Hume, Hartley, James Mill and Bentham,
all the revolutionary doctrines, were so many conservatory plants

produced, here and there, in the isolated studies of a few thinkers : in the open air they proved abortive, after blooming for a little time under the too vigorous competition with the old vegetation to which the soil belonged.[1] On the contrary, in France, the seed imported from England takes root and spreads with extraordinary vigor. After the Regency it is in full bloom.[2] Like any species favored by soil and climate, it invades all soils, appropriating light and atmosphere to itself, scarcely allowing in its shadow a few abortions of an inimical species, the survival of an antique flora like Rollin, or a specimen of an eccentric flora like Saint-Martin. Large trees and dense thickets, masses of brushwood and low plants,—Voltaire, Montesquieu, Rousseau, Diderot, d'Alembert and Buffon,—Duclos, Mably, Condillac, Turgot, Beaumarchais, Bernardin de Saint-Pierre, Barthélemy and Thomas, the crowd of journalists, compilers and conversationists, the *élite* of the philosophical, scientific and literary multitude,—absorb the Academy, the stage, the drawing-room and conversation. Every lofty form of the century is one of its offshoots, and among these are some of the loftiest produced by the human species. This is owing to the seed having fallen on suitable ground, that is to say, on the patrimony of the classic spirit. In this land of the *raison raisonnante* it no longer encounters the rivals that impeded its growth on the other side of the Channel, and it not only immediately acquires vigor of sap but, again, the propagating organ which it required.

I.

This organ is the "art of expression, eloquence applied to the gravest subjects, the talent for making things clear."[3] "The great writers of this nation," says their great adversary, "express themselves better than those of any other nation. Their books give but little information to true savants," but "through the art of expression they influence men" and "the mass of men, constantly repelled from the sanctuary of the sciences by the dry style and

---

[1] "Who, born within the last forty years, ever reads a word of Collins, and Toland, and Tindal, or of that whole race who called themselves freethinkers?" (Burke, "Reflexions on the French Revolution," 1790).

[2] The "Œdipe," by Voltaire, belongs to the year 1718, and his "Lettres sur les Anglais," to the year 1728. The "Lettres Persanes," by Montesquieu, published in 1721, contain the germs of all the leading ideas of the century.

[3] Joseph de Maistre, "Œuvres inédites," pp. 8, 11.

bad taste of (other) scientific writers, cannot resist the seductions of the French style and method." Thus the classic spirit that furnishes the ideas likewise furnishes the means of conveying them, the theories of the eighteenth century being like those seeds provided with wings which float and distribute themselves on all soils. There is no book of that day not written for people of the world, and even for women of the world. In Fontenelle's dialogues on the Plurality of Worlds the principal personage is a marchioness. Voltaire composes his "Métaphysique" and his "Essai sur les Mœurs" for Madame du Chatelet, and Rousseau his "Emile" for Madame d'Epinay. Condillac wrote the "Traité des Sensations" from suggestions of Mademoiselle Ferrand, and he sets forth instructions to young ladies how to read his "Logique." Baudeau dedicates and explains to a lady his "Tableau Economique." Diderot's most profound work is a conversation between Mademoiselle de l'Espinasse and d'Alembert and Bordeu.[1] Montesquieu had placed an invocation to the muses in the middle of the "Esprit des Lois." Almost every work is a product of the drawing-room, and of one obtaining the first fruits of the work before being presented to the public. In this respect the habit is so strong as to last up to the end of 1789; the harangues about to be made in the National Assembly are passages of *bravura* previously rehearsed before ladies at an evening entertainment. The American Ambassador, a practical man, explains to Washington with sober irony the fine academic and literary parade preceding the political tournament in public.[2] "The speeches are made beforehand in a small society of young men and women, and generally the fair friend of the speaker is one, or else the fair whom he means to make his friend, and the society very politely give their approbation, unless the lady who gives the tone to that circle chances to reprehend something, which is of course altered, if not amended." It is not surprising, with customs of this kind, that professional philosophers should become men of society. At no time nor in any place have they been so to the same extent, nor so habitually. The great delight of a man of genius or of learning here, says an English traveller, is to reign over a brilliant assembly of people of fashion.[3]

---

[1] His letters on the Blind and on the Deaf and Dumb are addressed in whole or in part to women.

[2] Works of Governor Morris, II. 89. (Letter of January 24, 1790).

[3] John Andrews in "A comparative view," etc. (1785). Arthur Young, I. 123. "I should pity the man who expected, without other advantages of a very different nature, to be well

Whilst in England they bury themselves morosely in their books, living amongst themselves and appearing in society only on condition of "doing some political drudgery," that of journalist or pamphleteer in the service of a party, in France they dine out every evening, and constitute the ornaments and amusement of the drawing-rooms to which they resort to converse.[1] There is not a house in which dinners are given that has not its titular philosopher, and, later on, its economist and man of science. In the various memoirs, and in the collections of correspondence, we track them from one drawing-room to another, from one chateau to another, Voltaire to Cirey at Madame du Chatelet's, and then home, at Ferney where he has a theatre and entertains all Europe; Rousseau to Madame d'Epinay's, and M. de Luxembourg's; the Abbé Barthélemy to the Duchesse de Choiseul's; Thomas, Marmontel and Gibbon to Madame Necker's; the encyclopedists to d'Holbach's ample dinners, to the plain and discreet table of Madame Geoffrin, and to the little drawing-room of Mademoiselle de L'Espinasse, all belonging to the great central state drawing-room, that is to say, to the French Academy, where each newly-elected member appears to parade his style and obtain from a polished body his commission of master in the art of discourse. Such a public imposes on an author the obligation of being more a writer than a philosopher. The thinker is expected to concern himself with his sentences as much as with his ideas. He is not allowed to be a mere scholar in his closet, a simple erudite, diving into folios in German fashion, a metaphysician absorbed with his own meditations, having an audience of pupils who take notes, and, as readers, men devoted to study and willing to give themselves trouble, a Kant, who forms for himself a special language, who waits for a public to comprehend him and who leaves the room in which he labors only for the lecture-room in which he delivers his lectures. Here, on the contrary, in the matter of expression, all

received in a brilliant circle in London, because he was a fellow of the Royal Society. But this would not be the case with a member of the Academy of Sciences at Paris, he is sure of a good reception everywhere."

[1] " I met in Paris the d'Alemberts, the Marmontels, the Baillys at the houses of duchesses, which was an immense advantage to all concerned. . . . When a man with us devotes himself to writing books he is considered as renouncing the society equally of those who govern as of those who laugh. . . . Taking literary vanity into account the lives of your d'Alemberts and Baillys are as pleasant as those of your seigniors." (Stendhal, "Rome, Naples et Florence," 377, in a narrative by Col. Forsyth).

are experts and even professional. The mathematician d'Alembert publishes a small treatise on elocution; Buffon, the naturalist, pronounces a discourse on Style; the legist Montesquieu composes an essay on Taste; the psychologist Condillac writes a volume on the art of writing. In this consists their greatest glory; philosophy owes its entry into society to them. They withdrew it from the closet, the clique and the school, to introduce it into company and into conversation.

II.

"Madame la Maréchale," says one of Diderot's personages,[1] "I must consider things from a somewhat higher point of view."—"As high as you please so long as I understand you."— "If you do not understand me it will be my fault."—"You are very polite, but you must know that I have studied nothing but my prayer-book." That makes no difference; the pretty woman, ably led on, begins to philosophize without knowing it, arriving without effort at the distinction between good and evil, comprehending and deciding on the highest doctrines of morality and religion. Such is the art of the eighteenth century, and the art of writing. People are addressed who are perfectly familiar with life, but who are commonly ignorant of orthography, who are curious in all directions, but ill prepared for any; the object is to bring truth down to their level. Scientific or too abstract terms are inadmissible; they tolerate only those used in ordinary conversation. And this is no obstacle; it is easier to talk philosophy in this language than to use it in discussing precedences and mantua-making. For, in every abstract question there is some leading and simple conception on which the rest depends, those of unity, proportion, mass and motion in mathematics; those of organ, function and being in physiology; those of sensation, pain, pleasure and desire in psychology; those of utility, contract and law in politics and morality; those of capital, production, value, exchange in political economy, and the same in the other sciences, all of these being conceptions derived from passing experience; from which it follows that, in appealing to common experience by means of a few familiar circumstances, such as short stories, anecdotes, agreeable tales, and the like,

---

[1] " Entretien d'un philosophe avec la Maréchale ——."

these conceptions are fashioned anew and rendered precise. This being accomplished, almost everything is accomplished; for nothing then remains but to lead the listener along step by step, flight by flight, to the remotest consequences. "Will Madame la Maréchale have the kindness to recall my definition?"—"I remember it well—do you call that a definition?"—"Yes."—"That, then, is philosophy!"—"Admirable!"—"And I have been philosophical?"—"As you read prose, without being aware of it." The rest is simply a matter of reasoning, that is to say, of leading on, of putting questions in the right order, and of analysis. With the conception thus renewed and rectified the truth nearest at hand is brought out, then out of this, a second truth related to the first one, and so on to the end, no other obligation being involved in this method but that of carefully advancing step by step, and of omitting no intermediary step.

With this method one is able to explain all, to make everything understood, even by women, and even by women of society. In the eighteenth century it forms the substance of all talents, the warp of all masterpieces, the lucidity, popularity and authority of philosophy. The "Eloges" of Fontenelle, the "Philosophe ignorant et le principe d'action" by Voltaire, the "Lettre à M. de Beaumont," and the "Vicaire Savoyard" by Rousseau, the "Traité de l'homme" and the "Epoques de la Nature" by Buffon, the "Dialogues sur les blés" by Galiani, the "Considérations" by d'Alembert, on mathematics, the "Langue des Calculs" and the "Logique" by Condillac, and, a little later, the "Exposition du système du Monde" by Laplace, and the "Discours généraux" by Bichat and Cuvier; all are based on this method.[1] Finally, this is the method which Condillac erects into a theory under the name of ideology, soon acquiring the ascendency of a dogma, and which then seems to sum up all methods. At the very least it sums up the process by which the philosophers of the century obtained their audience, propagated their doctrine and achieved their success.

III.

Thanks to this method one can be understood; but, to be read, something more is necessary. I compare the eighteenth century

---

[1] The same process is observable in our day in the "Sophismes économiques" of Bastiat, the "Eloges historiques" of Flourens, and in "Le Progrès," by Edmond About.

to a company of people around a table; it is not sufficient that
the food before them be well prepared, well served, within reach
and easy to digest, but it is important that it should be some
choice dish or, better still, some dainty. The intellect is epicurean; let us supply it with savory, delicate viands adapted to its
taste; it will eat so much the more owing to its appetite being
sharpened by sensuality. Two special condiments enter into the
cuisine of this century, and, according to the hand that makes
use of them, they furnish all literary dishes with a coarse or
delicate seasoning. In an epicurean society, to which a return
to nature and the rights of instinct are preached, voluptuous
images and ideas present themselves involuntarily; this is the
appetizing, exciting spice-box. Each guest at the table uses or
abuses it; many empty its entire contents on their plate. And I
do not allude merely to the literature read in secret, to the
extraordinary books Madame d'Audlan, governess to the French
royal children, peruses, and which stray off into the hands of the
daughters of Louis XV.,[1] nor to other books, still more extraordinary,[2] in which philosophical arguments appear as an interlude
between filth and the illustrations, and which are kept by the
ladies of the court on their toilet-tables, under the title of
" Heures de Paris." I refer here to the great men, to the masters
of the public intellect. With the exception of Buffon, all put
pimento into their sauces, that is to say, loose talk or coarseness
of expression. We find this even in the " Esprit des Lois ;" there
is an enormous amount of it, open and covered up, in the " Lettres
Persanes." Diderot, in his two great novels, puts it in by handfuls, as if during an orgy. The teeth crunch on it like so many
grains of pepper, on every page of Voltaire. We find it, not
only piquant, but strong and of burning intensity, in the
' Nouvelle Héloise," scores of times in " Emile," and, in the
" Confessions," from one end to the other. It was the taste of
the day. M. de Malesherbes, so upright and so grave, committed
" La Pucelle" to memory and recited it. We have from the pen
of Saint-Just, the gloomiest of the " Mountain," a poem as
lascivious as that of Voltaire, while Madame Roland, the noblest
of the Girondins, has left us confessions as venturesome and
specific as those of Rousseau.[3]

---

[1] The "Portier de Chartres."
[2] "Thérese Philosophe." There is a complete literature of this species.
[3] See the edition of M. Dauban in which the suppressed passages are restored.

On the other hand there is a second box, that containing the old Gallic salt, that is to say, humor and raillery. Its mouth is wide open in the hands of a philosophy proclaiming the sovereignty of reason. Whatever is contrary to reason is to it absurd and therefore open to ridicule. The moment the solemn hereditary mask covering up an abuse is brusquely and adroitly torn aside, we feel a curious spasm, the corners of our mouth stretching apart and our breast heaving violently, as at a kind of sudden relief, an unexpected deliverance, experiencing a sense of our recovered superiority, of our revenge being gratified and of an act of justice having been performed. But it depends on the mode in which the mask is struck off whether the laugh shall be in turn light or loud, suppressed or unbridled, now amiable and cheerful, or now bitter and sardonic. Humor *(la plaisanterie)* comports with all aspects, from buffoonery to indignation ; no literary seasoning affords such a variety, or so many mixtures, nor one that so well enters into combination with that above-mentioned. The two together, from the middle ages down, form the principal ingredients employed by the French *cuisine* in the composition of its most agreeable dainties,—fables, tales, witticisms, jovial songs and waggeries, the eternal heritage of a good-humored, mocking race, preserved by La Fontaine athwart the pomp and sobriety of the seventeenth century, and, in the eighteenth, reappearing everywhere at the philosophic banquet. Its charm is great to the brilliant company at this table, so amply provided, whose principal occupation is pleasure and amusement. It is all the greater because, on this occasion, the passing disposition is in harmony with hereditary instinct, and because the taste of the epoch is fortified by the national taste. Add to all this the exquisite art of the cooks, their talent in commingling, in apportioning and in concealing the condiments, in varying and arranging the dishes, the certainty of their hand, the finesse of their palate, their experience in processes, in the traditions and practices which, already for a hundred years, form of French prose the most delicate aliment of the intellect. It is not strange to find them skilled in regulating human speech, in extracting from it its quintessence and in distilling its full delight.

IV.

In this respect four among them are superior, Montesquieu, Voltaire, Diderot and Rousseau. It seems sufficient to mention their names.   Modern Europe has no greater writers.   And yet their talent must be closely examined to properly comprehend their power.

In tone and style Montesquieu is the first.   No writer is more master of himself, more outwardly calm, more sure of his meaning.   His voice is never boisterous; he expresses the most powerful thoughts with moderation.   There is no gesticulation; exclamations, the abandonment of impulse, all that is irreconcilable with decorum is repugnant to his tact, his reserve, his dignity. He seems to be always addressing a select circle of people with acute minds, and in such a way as to render them at every moment conscious of their acuteness.   No flattery could be more delicate; we feel grateful to him for making us satisfied with our intelligence.   We must possess some intelligence to be able to read him, for he deliberately curtails developments and omits transitions; we are required to supply these and to comprehend his hidden meanings.   He is rigorously systematic but the system is concealed, his concise completed sentences succeeding each other separately, like so many precious coffers or caskets, now simple and plain in aspect, now superbly chased and decorated, but always full.   Open them and each contains a treasure; here is placed in narrow compass a rich store of reflections, of emotions, of discoveries, our enjoyment being the more intense because we can easily retain all this for a moment in the palm of our hand.   "That which usually forms a grand conception," he himself says, "is a thought so expressed as to reveal a number of other thoughts, and suddenly disclosing what we could not anticipate without patient study."   This, indeed, is his manner; he thinks with summaries; he concentrates the essence of despotism in a chapter of three lines.   The summary itself often bears the air of an enigma, of which the charm is twofold; we have the pleasure of comprehension accompanying the satisfaction of divining.   In all subjects he maintains this supreme discretion, this art of indicating without enforcing, these reticences, the smile that never becomes a laugh.   "In my defence of the 'Esprit des Lois,'" he says, "that which gratifies me is not to see venerable theologians crushed to the ground but to see them glide down gently."   He excels in tranquil irony, in polished disdain,[i] in disguised sarcasm.   His Persians judge France

---

[1] "Esprit des Lois," ch. xv. book V. (Reasons in favor of slavery).   The "Defence of the Esprit des Lois," I. Reply to the second objection. II. Reply to the fourth objection.

as Persians, and we smile at their errors; unfortunately the laugh is not against them but against ourselves, for their error is found to be a verity.[1] This or that letter, in a sober vein, seems a comedy at their expense without reflecting upon us, full of Mahometan prejudices and of oriental infatuation;[2] reflect a moment, and our infatuation, in this relation, appears no less. Blows of extraordinary force and reach are given in passing, as if thoughtlessly, against existing institutions, against the transformed Catholicism which "in the present state of Europe, cannot last five hundred years," against the degenerate monarchy which causes useful citizens to starve to fatten parasite courtiers.[3] The entire new philosophy blooms out in his hands with an air of innocence, in a pastoral romance, in a simple prayer, in an artless letter.[4]   None of the gifts which serve to arrest and fix the attention are wanting in this style, neither grandeur of imagination nor profound sentiment, vivid characterization, delicate gradations, vigorous precision, a sportive grace, unlooked for burlesque, nor variety of representation.   But, amidst so many ingenious devices, apologues, tales, portraits and dialogues, in earnest as well as when masquerading, his deportment throughout is irreproachable and his tone is perfect.   If, as an author, he develops a paradox it is with almost English gravity.   If he fully exposes indecency it is with decent terms.   In the full tide of buffoonery, as well as in the full blast of license, he is ever the well-bred man, born and brought up in the aristocratic circle in which full liberty is allowed but where good-breeding is supreme, where every idea is permitted but where words are weighed, where one has the privilege of saying what he pleases, but on condition that he never forgets himself.

A circle of this kind is a small one, comprising only a select few; to be understood by the multitude requires another tone of voice. Philosophy demands a writer whose principal occupation is a diffusion of it, who is unable to keep it to himself, who pours it out like a gushing fountain, who offers it to everybody, daily and in every form, in broad streams and in small drops,

---

[1] Letter 24 (on Louis XIV.)

[2] Letter 18 (on the purity and impurity of things). Letter 39 (proofs of the mission of Mahomet).

[3] Letters 75 and 118.

[4] Letters 98 (on the modern sciences), 46 (on a true system of worship), 11 and 14 (on the nature of justice).

without exhaustion or weariness, through every crevice and by
every channel, in prose, in verse, in imposing and in trifling
poems, in the drama, in history, in novels, in pamphlets, in
pleadings, in treatises, in essays, in dictionaries, in correspondence,
openly and in secret, in order that it may penetrate to all depths
and in every soil ; such was Voltaire. " I have accomplished
more in my day," he says somewhere, "than either Luther or Cal-
vin," in which he is mistaken. The truth is, however, he has
something of their spirit. Like them he is desirous of changing
the prevailing religion, he takes the attitude of the founder of a
sect, he recruits and binds together proselytes, he writes letters
of exhortation, of direction and of predication, he puts watch-
words in circulation, he furnishes "the brethren" with a device ;
his passion resembles the zeal of an apostle or of a prophet.
Such a spirit is incapable of reserve ; it is militant and fiery by
nature ; it apostrophizes, reviles and improvises ; it writes under
the dictation of impressions ; it allows itself every species of utterance and, if need be, the coarsest. It thinks by explosions ; its
emotions are sudden starts, and its images so many sparks ; it lets
the rein go entirely ; it gives itself up to the reader and hence it
takes possession of him. Resistance is impossible ; the contagion
is too overpowering. A creature of air and flame, the most excitable that ever lived, composed of more ethereal and more
throbbing atoms than those of other men ; none is there whose
mental machinery is more delicate, nor whose equilibrium is at
the same time more shifting and more exact. He may be compared to those accurate scales that are affected by a breath, but
alongside of which every other measuring apparatus is incorrect
and clumsy. But, in this delicate balance only the lightest
weights, the finest specimen must be placed ; on this condition
only it rigorously weighs all substances ; such is Voltaire, involuntarily, through the demands of his intellect, and in his own behalf as much as in that of his readers. An entire philosophy,
ten volumes of theology, an abstract science, a special library, an
important branch of erudition, of human experience and invention, is thus reduced in his hands to a phrase or to a stanza.
From the enormous mass of riven or compact scoriæ he extracts
whatever is essential, a grain of gold or of copper as a specimen
of the rest, presenting this to us in its most convenient and most
manageable form, in a simile, in a metaphor, in an epigram that

becomes a proverb. In this no ancient or modern writer approaches him; in simplification and in popularization he has not his equal in the world. Without departing from the usual conversational tone, and as if in sport, he puts into little portable phrases the greatest discoveries and hypotheses of the human mind, the theories of Descartes, Malebranche, Leibnitz, Locke and Newton, the diverse religions of antiquity and of modern times, every known system of physics, physiology, geology, morality, natural law, and political economy,[1] in short, all the generalized conceptions in every order of knowledge to which humanity had attained in the eighteenth century. His tendency in this direction is so strong as to carry him too far; he belittles great things by rendering them accessible. Religion, legend, ancient popular poesy, the spontaneous creations of instinct, the vague visions of primitive times are not thus to be converted into small current coin; they are not subjects of amusing and lively conversation. A piquant witticism is not an expression of all this, but simply a travesty. But how charming to Frenchmen, and to people of the world! And what reader can abstain from a book containing all human knowledge summed up in piquant witticisms? For it is really a summary of human knowledge, no important idea, as far as I can see, being wanting to a man whose breviary consisted of the "Dialogues," the "Dictionary," and the "Novels." Read them over and over five or six times, and we then form some idea of their vast contents. Not only do views of the world and of man abound in them, but again they swarm with positive and even technical details, thousands of little facts scattered throughout, multiplied and precise details on astronomy, physics, geography, physiology, statistics, and on the history of all nations, the innumerable and personal experiences of a man who has himself read the texts, handled the instruments, visited the countries, taken part in the industries, and associated with the persons, and who, in the precision of his marvellous memory, in the liveliness of his ever-blazing imagination, revives or sees, as with the eye itself, everything that he states and as he states it. It is a unique talent, the rarest in a classic era, the most precious of all, since it consists in the display of actual be-

---

[1] Cf. "Micromégas," "L'homme aux quarantes écus," "Dialogues entre A, B, C," "Dict. Philosophique," *passim.* In verse, "Les systèmes," "La loi naturelle," "Le pour et le contre," "Discours sur l'homme," etc.

ings, not through the gray veil of abstractions, but in themselves, as they are in nature and in history, with their visible color and forms, with their accessories and surroundings in time and space, a peasant at his cart, a quaker in his meeting-house, a German baron in his castle, Dutchmen, Englishmen, Spaniards, Italians, Frenchmen, in their homes,[1] a great lady, a designing woman, provincials, soldiers, courtesans,[2] and the rest of the human medley, on every step of the social ladder, each an abridgment of his kind and in the passing light of a sudden flash.

For, the most striking feature of this style is the prodigious rapidity, the dazzling and bewildering stream of novelties, ideas, images, events, landscapes, narratives, dialogues, brief little pictures, following each other rapidly as if in a magic-lantern, withdrawn almost as soon as presented by the impatient magician who, in the twinkling of an eye, girdles the world and, constantly accumulating one on top of the other, history, fable, truth and fancy, the present time and times past, frames his work now with a parade as absurd as that of a country fair, and now with a fairy scene more magnificent than all those of the opera. To amuse and be amused, "to diffuse his spirit in every imaginable mode, like a glowing furnace into which all substances are thrown by turns to evolve every species of flame, coruscation and odor," is his first instinct. "Life," he says again, "is an infant to be rocked until it goes to sleep." Never was mortal more excited and more exciting, more incapable of silence and more hostile to ennui,[3] better endowed for conversation, more evi dently.destined to become the king of a sociable century in which, with six pretty stories, thirty witticisms and some confidence in himself, a man could obtain a social passport and the certainty of being everywhere welcome. Never was there a writer possessing to so high a degree and in such abundance every qualification of the conversationist, the art of animating and of enlivening

---

1 "Traité de métaphysique," chap. i. p. 1. (on the peasantry). "Lettres sur les Anglais," *passim.* "Candide," *passim.* "La Princesse de Babylone," ch. vii viii. ix. x. and xi.

2 "Dict. Phil." articles "Maladie," (Replies to the princess). "Candide," at Madame de Parolignac. The sailor in the wreck. Narrative of Paquette. The "Ingénu," the first chapters.

3 "Candide," the last chapter. When there was no dispute going on, it was so wearisome that the old woman one day boldly said to nim: "I should like to know which is worse, to be ravished a hundred times by negro pirates, to have one's rump gashed, or be switched by the Bulgarians, to be scourged or hung in an auto-da-fé, to be cut to pieces, to row in the galleys, to suffer any misery through which we have passed, or sit still and do nothing?" "That is a great question," said Candide.

discourse, the talent for giving pleasure to people of society. Perfectly refined when he chose to be, confining himself without inconvenience to strict decorum, of finished politeness, of exquisite gallantry, deferential without being servile, fond without being mawkish,[1] and always at his ease, it suffices that he should be before the public, to fall naturally into the proper tone, the discreet ways, the winning half-smile of the well-bred man who, introducing his readers into his mind, does them the honors of the place. Are you on familiar terms with him, and of the small private circle in which he freely unbends himself, with closed doors ? You never tire of laughing. With a sure hand and without seeming to touch it, he abruptly tears aside the veil hiding a wrong, a prejudice, a folly, in short, any human idolatry. The real figure, whether deformed, odious or spiritless, suddenly appears in this instantaneous flash; we shrug our shoulders. This is the risibility of an agile, triumphant reason. We have another in that of the gay temperament, of the droll improvisator, of the man keeping youthful, a child, a boy even to the day of his death, and who " gambols on his own tombstone." He is fond of caricature, exaggerating the features of faces, bringing grotesques on the stage,[2] walking them about in all lights like marionettes, never weary of taking them up and of making them dance in new costumes; in the very midst of his philosophy, of his propagandism and polemics, he sets up his portable theatre in full blast, exhibiting oddities, the scholar, the monk, the inquisitor, Maupertuis, Pompignan, Nonotte, Fréron, King David, and countless others who appear before us, capering and gesticulating in their harlequin attire. When a farcical talent is thus added to the requirements of truth humor becomes all powerful; for it gratifies the profound and universal instincts of human nature, a mischievous curiosity, the spirit of disparagement, the aversion to constraint, that groundwork of ill-nature which is established within us by conventionality, etiquette and the social obligation of wearing the burdensome cloak of respect and of decency; moments occur in life when the wisest is not sorry to throw this

---

[1] For example, in the lines addressed to the Princess Ulrique in the preface to "Alzire," dedicated to Madame du Chatelet.
"Souvent un peu de verité," etc.
[2] The scholar in the dialogue of " Les Mais," (Jenny). The canonization of Saint Cucufin Advice to brother Pediculoso. The diatribe of Doctor Akakia. Conversation of the emperor of China with brother Rigolo, etc.

half aside and even cast it off entirely. On each page, now with the bold stroke of a hardy naturalist, now with the quick turn of a mischievous monkey, Voltaire lets the solemn or serious drapery fall, disclosing man, the poor biped, and in such attitudes![1] Swift alone dared to present similar pictures. What physiological crudities relating to the origin and end of our most exalted sentiments! What disproportion between such feeble reason and such powerful instincts! What recesses in the wardrobes of politics and religion concealing their foul linen! We laugh at all this so as not to weep, and yet behind this laughter there are tears; he ends sneeringly, subsiding into a tone of profound sadness, of mournful pity. In this degree, and with such subjects, it is only an effect of habit, or as an expedient, a mania of inspiration, a fixed condition of the nervous machinery rushing headlong over everything, without a break and in full speed. Gaiety, let it not be forgotten, is still a mainspring of action, the last that keeps man erect in France, the best in maintaining the tone of his spirit, his strength and his powers of resistance, the most intact in an age when men, and women too, believed it incumbent on them to die people of good society, with a smile and a jest on their lips.[2]

When the talent of a writer thus accords with public inclinations it is a matter of little import whether he deviates or fails since he is following the universal tendency. He may wander off or besmirch himself in vain, for his audience is only the more pleased, his defects serving him as advantageously as his good qualities. After the first generation of healthy minds the second one comes on, the intellectual balance here being equally inexact. " Diderot," says Voltaire, " is too hot an oven, everything that is baked in it getting burnt." Or rather, he is an eruptive volcano which, for forty years, discharges ideas of every order and species, boiling and fused together, precious metals, coarse scoriæ and fetid mud; the steady stream overflows at will according to the roughness of the ground, but always displaying the ruddy light and acrid fumes of glowing lava. He is not master of his ideas, but his ideas master him; he is under submission to them; he has not that firm foundation of common practical sense

---

1 "Dict. Philosophique," the article "Ignorance." "Les Oreilles du Comte de Chesterfield," "L'homme au quarante écus," chap. vii. and xi.

2 Bachaumont, III. 194. (The death of the Comte de Maugiron).

which controls their impetuosity and ravages, that inner dyke of social caution which, with Montesquieu and Voltaire, bars the way to outbursts.   Everything with him rushes out of the surcharged crater, never picking its way, through the first fissure or crevice it finds, according to his haphazard reading, a letter, a conversation, an improvisation, and not in frequent small jets as with Voltaire, but in broad currents tumbling blindly down the most precipitous declivities of the century.   Not only does he descend thus to the very depths of anti-religious and anti-social doctrines, with logical and paradoxical rigidity, more impetuously and more obstreperously than d'Holbach himself; but again he falls into and sports himself in the slime of the age, consisting of obscenity, and into the beaten track of declamation.   In his leading novels he dwells a long time on salacious equivocation, or on a scene of lewdness.   Crudity with him is not extenuated by malice or glossed over by elegance.   He is neither refined nor pungent; he is quite incapable, like the younger Crébillon, of depicting the scapegrace of ability.   He is a new-comer, a parvenu in standard society; you see in him a plebeian, a powerful reasoner, an indefatigable workman and great artist, introduced, through the customs of the day, at a supper of fashionable livers.   He engrosses the conversation, directs the orgy, and in the contagion, or on a wager, says more filthy things, more " *gueulées*," than all the guests put together.[1]   In like manner, in his dramas, in his " Essays on Claudius and Nero," in his " Commentary on Seneca," in his additions to the " Philosophical History " of Raynal, he forces the tone of things.   This tone, which then prevails by virtue of the classic spirit and of the new fashion, is that of sentimental rhetoric.   Diderot carries it to extremes in the exaggeration of tears or of rage, in exclamations, in apostrophes, in tenderness of feeling, in violences, in indignations, in enthusiasms, in full-orchestra tirades, in which the fire of his brain finds employment and an outlet.

On the other hand, among so many superior writers, he is the

---

[1] "The novels of the younger Crébillon were in fashion.   My father conversed with Madame de Puisieux on the ease with which licentious works were composed; he contended that it was only necessary to find an amusing idea as a peg to hang others on in which intellectual libertinism should be a substitute for taste.   She challenged him to produce one of this kind.   At the end of a fortnight he brought her 'Les bijoux indiscrets' and fifty louis." (Mémoires of Diderot, by his daughter).   "La Religieuse," has a similar origin, its object being to mystify M. de Croismart.

only genuine artist, the creator of souls, the mind in which objects, events and personages are born and become organized of
themselves, through their own forces, by virtue of natural affinities,
involuntarily, without foreign intervention, in such a way as to
live for and in themselves, safe from the author's intentions, and
outside of his combinations. The composer of the "Salons," the
"Petits Romans," the "Entretien," the "Paradoxe du Comédien,"
and especially the "Rêve de d'Alembert" and the " Neveu de
Rameau " is a man of an unique species in his time. However alert
and brilliant Voltaire's personages may be, they are always puppets; their action is derivative; always behind them you catch a
glimpse of the author pulling the strings. With Diderot, the
strings are severed; he is not speaking through the lips of his
characters; they are not his comical speaking-trumpets or danc-
ing-jacks, but independent and detached creations, with an action
of their own, a personal accent, with their own temperament,
passions, ·ideas, philosophy, style and spirit, and occasionally, as
in the "Neveu de Rameau," a spirit so original, complex and complete, so alive and so deformed that, in the natural history of
man, it becomes an incomparable monster and an immortal
document. He has expressed everything concerning nature,[1] art
morality and life[2] in two small treatises of which twenty successive readings exhaust neither the charm nor the sense. Find
elsewhere, if you can, a similar stroke of power and a greater
masterpiece, "anything more absurd and more profound!"[3]

Such is the advantage of men of genius possessing no control over themselves. They lack discernment but they have inspiration. Among twenty works, either shapeless, unwholesome
or foul, they produce one that is a creation, and still better, an
animated thing, able to live by itself, before which others, fabri-
cated by merely intellectual people, resemble simply well-dressed
puppets. Hence it is that Diderot is so great a narrator, a master of dialogue, the equal in this respect of Voltaire, and, through
a quite opposite talent, believing all he says at the moment of
saying it; forgetful of his very self, carried away by his own re-
cital, listening to inward voices, surprised with the responses
which come to him unexpectedly, borne along, as if on an un-

---

[1] "Le Rêve de d'Alembert."
[2] "Le neveu de Rameau."
[3] The words of Diderot himself in relation to the "Rêve de d'Alembert."

known river, by the current of action, by the sinuosities of the conversation inwardly and unconsciously developed, aroused by the flow of ideas and the leap of the moment to the most unlooked-for imagery, extreme in burlesque or extreme in magnificence, now lyrical even to providing Musset with an entire strophe,[1] now comic and droll with outbursts unheard of since the days of Rabelais, always in good faith, always at the mercy of his subject, of his inventions, of his emotions, the most natural of writers in an age of artificial literature, resembling a foreign tree which, transplanted to a parterre of the epoch, swells out and decays on one side of its stem, but of which five or six branches, thrust out into full light, surpass the neighboring underwood in the freshness of their sap and in the vigor of their growth.

Rousseau also is an artisan, a man of the people, ill-adapted to elegant and refined society, out of his element in a drawing-room and, moreover, of low birth, badly brought up, sullied by a vile and precocious experience, highly and offensively sensual, morbid in mind and in body, fretted by superior and discordant faculties, possessing no tact, and carrying the contamination of his imagination, temperament and past life into his austere morality and into his purest idyls:[2] besides this he has no fervor, and in this he is the opposite of Diderot, avowing himself " that his ideas arrange themselves in his head with the utmost difficulty, that certain sentences are turned over and over again in his brain for five or six nights before putting them on paper, and that a letter on the most trifling subject costs him hours of fatigue," that he cannot fall into an easy and agreeable tone, nor succeed otherwise than "in works which demand application."[3]   As an offset to this, style, in this ardent brain, under the influence of intense, pro-

---

[1] One of the finest strophes in "Souvenir" is almost literally transcribed (involuntarily, I suppose), from the dialogue on Otaheite.

[2] "Nouvelle Héloïse," *passim.*, and notably Julie's extraordinary letter, second part, number 15. "Emile," the preceptor's discourse to Emile and Sophie the morning after their marriage. Letter of the Comtesse de Boufflers to Gustavus III., published by Geffroy, ("Gustave III. et la cour de France"). "I entrust to Baron de Lederheim, though with reluctance, a book for you which has just been published, the infamous memoirs of Rousseau entitled 'Confessions.' They seem to me those of a common scullion and even lower than that, being dull throughout, whimsical and vicious in the most offensive manner. I do not recur to my worship of him (for such it was); I shall never console myself for its having caused the death of that eminent man David Hume, who, to gratify me, undertook to entertain that filthy animal in England."

[3] "Confessions," part 1, book III.

longed meditation, incessantly hammered and re-hammered, becomes more concise and of higher temper than is elsewhere found. Since La Bruyère we have seen no more ample, virile phrases, in which anger, admiration, indignation, studied and concentrated passion, appear with more rigorous precision and more powerful relief. He is almost the equal of La Bruyère in the arrangement of skilful effects, in the aptness and ingenuity of developments, in the terseness of impressive summaries, in the overpowering directness of unexpected arguments, in the multiplicity of literary achievements, in the execution of those passages of bravura, portraits, descriptions, comparisons, creations, wherein, as in a musical crescendo, the same idea, varied by a series of yet more animated expressions, attains to or surpasses, at the last note, all that is possible of energy and of brilliancy. Finally, he has that which is wanting in La Bruyère; his passages are linked together; he is not a writer of pages but of books; no logician is more condensed. His demonstration is knitted together, mesh by mesh, for one, two and three volumes like a great net without an opening in which, willingly or not, we remain caught. He is a systematizer who, absorbed with himself, and with his eyes stubbornly fixed on his own reverie or his own principle, buries himself deeper in it every day, weaving its consequences off one by one, and always holding fast to the various ends. Do not go near him. Like a solitary, enraged spider he weaves this out of his own substance, out of the most cherished convictions of his brain and the deepest emotions of his heart. He trembles at the slightest touch; ever on the defensive, he is terrible,[1] beside himself,[2] even venomous through suppressed exasperation and wounded sensibility, furious against an adversary, whom he stifles with the multiplied and tenacious threads of his web, but still more redoubtable to himself than to his enemies, soon caught in his own meshes,[3] believing that France and the universe conspire against him, deducing with wonderful subtlety the proofs of this chimerical conspiracy, made desperate, at last, by his over-plausible romance, and strangling in the cunning toils which, by dint of his own logic and imagination, he has fashioned for himself.

---

[1] Letter to M. de Beaumont.

[2] "Emile," letter IV. 193. "People of the world must necessarily put on disguise; let them show themselves as they are and they would horrify us," etc.

[3] See, especially, his book entitled "Rousseau juge de Jean-Jacques," his connection with Hume and the last books of the "Confessions."

One runs a risk of killing himself with arms of this description, but there is power in it. Rousseau was powerful, equally so with Voltaire; it may be said that the last half of the eighteenth century belongs to him. A foreigner, a protestant, original in temperament, in education, in heart, in mind and in habits, at once misanthropic and philanthropic, living in an ideal world constructed by himself, entirely opposed to the world as it is, he finds himself standing in a new position. No one is so sensitive to the evils and vices of actual society. No one is so affected by the virtues and happiness of the society of the future. This accounts for his having two holds on the public mind, one through satire and the other through the idyl. These two holds are undoubtedly slighter at the present day; the substance of their grasp has disappeared; we are not the auditors to which it appealed. The famous discourse on the influence of literature and on the origin of inequality seems to us a collegiate oration; an effort of the will is required to read the " Nouvelle Héloise." The author is repulsive in the persistency of his spitefulness or in the exaggeration of his enthusiasm. He is always in extremes, now moody and with knit brows, and now streaming with tears and with arms outstretched to Heaven. Hyperbole, prosopopæia, and other literary machinery are too often andtoo deliberately used by him. We are tempted to regard him now as a sophist making the best use of his arts, now as a rhetorician cudgelling his brains for a purpose, now as a preacher becoming excited, that is to say, an actor ever maintaining a thesis, striking an attitude and aiming at effects. Finally, with the exception of the " Confessions " his style soon wearies us; it is too studied, and too constantly overstrained. The author is always the author, and he communicates the defect to his personages. His Julie argues and descants for twenty successive pages on duelling, on love, on duty, with a logical completeness, a talent and phrases that would do honor to an academical moralist. Commonplace exists everywhere, general themes, a raking fire of abstractions and arguments, that is to say, truths more or less empty and paradoxes more or less hollow. The smallest detail of fact, an anecdote, a trait of habit, would suit us much better, and hence we of to-day prefer the precise eloquence of objects to the lax eloquence of words. In the eighteenth century it was otherwise; to every writer this oratorical style was the prescribed ceremonial costume, the dress-coat he had to put on for admission into the company of select people. That which seems to us affectation was then only proper; in a classic epoch the perfect period and the sustained development constitute decorum, and are therefore to be observed. It must be noted, moreover, that this literary drapery which, with us of the present day, conceals truth did not conceal it to his contemporaries; they saw under it the exact feature, the perceptible detail no longer detected by us. Every abuse, every vice, every excess of refinement and of culture, all that social and moral disease which Rousseau scourged with an author's emphasis, existed before them under their own eyes, in their own breasts, visible and daily manifested in thousands of domestic incidents. In applying satire they had only to observe or to remember. Their experience completed the book, and, through the co-operation of his readers, the author possessed power which he is now deprived of. If we were to put ourselves in their place we should recover their impressions. His denunciations and sarcasms, the harsh things of all sorts he says of the great, of fashionable people and of women, his rude and cutting tone, provoke and irritate, but are not displeasing. On the contrary, after so many compliments, insipidities and petty versification all this quickens the blunted taste; it is the sensation of strong common wine after long indulgence in orgeat and preserved citron. Accordingly, his first discourse against art and literature "lifts one at once above the clouds." But his idyllic writings touch the heart more powerfully than his satires. If men listen to the moralist that scolds them they throng in the footsteps of the magician that charms them; especially do women and the young adhere to one who shows them the promised land. All accumulated dissatisfactions, weariness of the world, *ennui*, vague disgust, a multitude of suppressed desires gush forth, like subterranean waters, under the sounding line that for the first time brings them to light. Rousseau with his soundings struck deep and true through his own trials and through genius. In a wholly artificial society where people are drawing-room puppets, and where life consists in a graceful parade according to a recognized model, he preaches a return to nature, independence, earnestness, passion, and effusion, a manly, active, ardent and happy existence in the open air and in sunshine. What an outlet for restrained faculties, for the broad and luxurious fountain ever bubbling in man's breast, and for which no issue is provided into this beautiful world! A woman of the court is familiar with love as then practised, simply a preference, often only a pastime, mere gallantry of which the exquisite polish poorly conceals the shallowness, coldness and, occasionally, wickedness; in short, adventures, amusements and personages as described by Crébillon the younger. One evening, about to go out to the opera ball, she finds the "Nouvelle Héloise" on her toilet-table; it is not surprising that she keeps her horses and footmen waiting from hour to hour, and that at four o'clock in the morning she orders the horses to be unharnessed, and then passes the rest of the night in reading, and that she is stifled with her tears; for the first time in her life she finds a man that loves.[1] In like manner if you would comprehend the success of "Emile," call to mind the children we have described, the embroidered, gilded, dressed-up, powdered little gentlemen, decked with sword and sash, carrying the chapeau under the arm, bowing, presenting the hand, rehearsing fine attitudes before a mirror, repeating prepared compliments, pretty little puppets in which everything is the work of the tailor, the hairdresser, the preceptor and the dancing-master; alongside of these, little ladies of six years, still more artificial, bound up in whalebone, harnessed in a heavy skirt composed of hair and a girdle of iron, supporting a head-dress two feet in height, so many veritable dolls to which rouge is applied, and with which a mother amuses herself each morning for an hour and then consigns them to her maids for the rest of the day.[2] This mother reads "Emile." It is not surprising that she immediately strips the poor little thing, and determines to nurse her next child herself.

It is through these contrasts that Rousseau is strong. He revealed the dawn to people who never got up until noon, the landscape to eyes that had thus far rested only on palaces and drawing-rooms, a natural garden to men who had never prome-

---

[1] "Confessions," part 2. book XI. "The women were intoxicated with the book and with the author to such an extent that there were few of them, even of high rank, whose conquest I could not have made if I had undertaken it. I possess evidence of this which I do not care to publish, and which, without having been obliged to prove it by experience, warrants my statement." Cf. G. Sand, "Histoire de ma vie," I. 73.

[2] See an engraving by Moreau called "Les Petits Parrains." Berquin, *passim.*, and among others "L'épée." Remark the ready-made phrases, the style of an author common to children, in Berquin and Madame de Genlis.

naded outside of clipped shrubs and rectilinear borders, the country, the family, the people, simple and endearing pleasures, to townsmen made weary by social avidity, by the excesses and complications of luxury, by the uniform comedy which, in the glare of hundreds of lighted candles, they played night after night in their own and in the homes of others.[1] An audience thus disposed makes no clear distinction between pomp and sincerity, between sentiment and sentimentality. They follow their author as one who makes a revelation, as a prophet, even to the end of his ideal world, much more through his exaggerations than through his discoveries, as far on the road to error as on the pathway of truth.

These are the great literary powers of the century. With inferior successes, and through various combinations, the elements which contributed to the formation of the leading talents also form the secondary talents, like those below Rousseau,—Bernardin de St. Pierre, Raynal, Thomas, Marmontel, Mably, Florian, Dupaty, Mercier, Madame de Staël; below Voltaire,— the lively and piquant intellects of Duclos, Piron, Galiani, President Des Brosses, Rivarol, Champfort, and to speak with precision, all other talents. Whenever a vein of talent, however meagre, peers forth above the ground it is for the propagation and carrying forward of the new doctrine; scarcely can we find two or three little streams that run in a contrary direction, like the journal of Fréron, a comedy by Palissot, or a satire by Gilbert. Philosophy winds through and overflows all channels public and private, through manuals of impiety, like the "Théologies portatives," and in the lascivious novels circulated secretly, through epigrams and songs, through daily novelties, through the amusements of fairs,[2] and the harangues of the Academy, through tragedy and the opera, from the beginning to the end of the century, from the " Œdipe " of Voltaire, to the " Tarare " of Beaumarchais. It seems as if there was nothing else in the world. At least it is found everywhere and it floods all literary efforts; nobody cares whether it deforms them, content in making them serve as a

---

[1] See the description of sunrise in "Emile," of the Elysée (a natural garden), in "Héloise." And especially in "Emile," at the end of the fourth book, the pleasures which Rousseau would enjoy if he were rich.

[2] See in Marivaux, ("La double inconstance,") a satire on the court, courtiers and the corruptions of high life, opposed to the inferior class who have maintained primitive simplicity, the village swains and lasses.

conduit.   In 1763, in the tragedy of Manco-Capac[1] the "principal part," writes a contemporary, "is that of a savage who utters in verse all that we have read, scattered through ' Emile ' and the ' Contrat Social,' concerning kings, liberty, the rights of man and the inequality of conditions." This virtuous savage saves a king's son over whom a high-priest raises a poniard, and then, designating the high-priest and himself by turns, he cries, " Behold the civilized man,—here is the savage man!" At this line the applause breaks forth, and the success of the piece is such that it is demanded at Versailles and played before the court.

The same ideas have to be expressed with skill, brilliancy, gaiety, energy and scandal, and this is accomplished in " The Marriage of Figaro." Never were the ideals of the age displayed under a more transparent disguise, nor in an attire that rendered them more attractive. Its title is the " Folle journée," and indeed it is an evening of folly, an after-supper like those occurring in the fashionable world, a masquerade of Frenchmen in Spanish costumes, with a parade of dresses, changing scenes, couplets, a ballet, a singing and dancing village, a medley of odd characters, gentlemen, servants, duennas, judges, notaries, lawyers, music-masters, gardeners, *pastoureaux;* in short, a spectacle for the eyes and the ears, for all the senses, the very opposite of the prevailing drama in which three pasteboard characters, seated on classic chairs, exchange didactic arguments in an abstract saloon. And still better, it is an imbroglio displaying a superabundance of action, amidst intrigues that cross, interrupt and renew each other, through a *pêle-mêle* of travesties, exposures, surprises, mistakes, leaps from windows, quarrels and slaps, and all in sparkling style, each phrase flashing on all sides, where responses seem to be cut out by a lapidary, where the eyes would forget themselves in contemplating the multiplied brilliants of the dialogue if the mind were not carried along by its rapidity and the excitement of the action. But here is another charm, the most welcome of all in a society passionately fond of Parny; according to an expression of the Comte d'Artois, which I dare not quote, this appeals to the senses, the arousing of which constitutes the spiciness and savor of the piece. The fruit that hangs ripening

---

[1] Bachaumont, I. 254.

and savory on the branch never falls but always seems on the
point of falling; all hands are extended to catch it, its voluptuousness somewhat veiled but so much the more provoking,
declaring itself from scene to scene, in the Count's gallantry, in
the Countess's agitation, in the simplicity of Fanchette, in the
jestings of Figaro, in the liberties of Susanne, and reaching its
climax in the precocity of Cherubino.   Add to this a continual
double sense, the author hidden behind his characters, truth put
into the mouth of a clown, malice enveloped in simple utterances,
the master duped but saved from being ridiculous by his deportment, the valet rebellious but preserved from acrimony by his
gaiety, and you can comprehend how Beaumarchais could have
the ancient régime played before its head, put political and social
satire on the stage, publicly attach an expression to each wrong
so as to become a by-word, and ever making a loud report,[1]
gather up into a few traits the entire polemics of the philosophers
against the prisons of the State, against the censorship of literature, against the venality of office, against the privileges of birth,
against the arbitrary power of ministers, against the incapacity of
people in office, and still better, to sum up in one character
every public demand, give the leading part to a plebeian, bastard, bohemian and valet, who, by dint of dexterity, courage
and good-humor, keeps himself up, swims with the tide, and
shoots ahead in his little skiff, avoiding contact with larger craft
and even supplanting his master, accompanying each pull on
the oar with a shower of wit cast broadside at all his rivals.

   After all, in France at least, the chief power is intellect.   Literature in the service of philosophy is all-sufficient.   The public
opposes but a feeble resistance to their complicity, the mistress
finding no trouble in convincing those who have already been
won over by the servant.

---

   [1] "A calculator was required for the place but a dancer got it."   "The sale of offices is a
great abuse."   "Yes, it would be better to give them for nothing."   "Only small men fear
small literature."   "Chance makes the interval, the mind only can alter that!"   "A courtier?—they say it is a very difficult profession."   "To receive, to take, and to ask, is the secret in three words," etc.   Also the entire monologue by Figaro, and all the scenes with
Bridoisin.

CHAPTER II.

I.

THIS public has yet to be made willing to be convinced and to be won over; belief occurs only when there is a disposition to believe, and, in the success of books, its share is often greater than that of their authors.   On addressing men about politics or religion their opinions are, in general, already formed; their prejudices, their interests, their situation have confirmed them beforehand; they listen to you only after you have uttered aloud what they inwardly think.   Propose to them to demolish the great social edifice and to rebuild it anew on quite an opposite plan: ordinarily your auditors will consist only of those who are poorly lodged or shelterless, who live in garrets or cellars, or who sleep under the stars, on the bare ground in the vicinity of houses. The common run of people, whose lodgings are small but tolerable, dread moving and adhere to their accustomed ways.   The difficulty becomes much greater on appealing to the upper classes who occupy superior habitations; their acceptance of your proposal depends either on their great delusions or on their great disinterestedness. In England they quickly foresee the danger. In vain is philosophy there indigenous and precocious; it does not become acclimatised. In 1729, Montesquieu writes in his memorandum-book: " No religion in England; four or five members of the House of Commons attend mass or preaching in the House. . . . When religion is mentioned everybody begins to laugh. A man having said: I believe that as an *article of faith*, everybody laughed. A committee is appointed to consider the state of religion, but it is regarded as absurd." Fifty years later the public mind undergoes a reaction; all with a good roof over their heads and a good coat on their backs[1] see the bearing of the new doctrines. In any event they feel that closet speculations are not to become street preaching. Impiety seems to them an indiscretion; they consider religion as the cement of public order. This is owing to the fact that they are themselves public men, engaged in active life, taking a part in the government, and instructed through their daily and personal experience. Practical life fortifies them against the chimeras of theorists; they have proved to themselves how difficult it is to lead and to control men. Having had their hand on the machine they know how it works, its value, its cost, and they are not tempted to cast it aside as rubbish to try another, said to be superior, but which, as yet, exists only on paper. The baronet, or squire, a justice on his own domain, has no trouble in discerning in the clergyman of his parish an indispensable co-worker and a natural ally. The duke or marquis, sitting in the upper house by the side of bishops, requires their votes to pass bills, and their assistance to rally to his party the fifteen hundred curates who influence the rural conscience. Thus all have a hand on some social wheel, large or small, principal or accessory, and this endows them with earnestness, foresight and good sense. On coming in contact with realities there is no temptation to soar away into the imaginary world; the fact of one being at work on solid ground of itself makes one dislike aerial excursions in empty space. The more occupied one is the less one dreams, and, to men of business, the

---

[1] Macaulay.

geometry of the " *Contrat Social*" is merely intellectual gymnastics.

II.

It is quite the reverse in France.   " I arrived there in 1774,"[1] says an English gentleman, " having just left the house of my father, who never came home from Parliament until three o'clock in the morning, and who was busy the whole morning correcting the proofs of his speech for the newspapers, and who, after hastily kissing us, with an absorbed air, went out to a political dinner. . . . In France I found men of the highest rank enjoying perfect leisure.   They had interviews with the ministers but only to interchange compliments ; in other respects they knew as little about the public affairs of France as they did about those of Japan ; and less of local affairs than of general affairs, having no knowledge of their peasantry other than that derived from the accounts of their stewards.   If one of them, bearing the title of governor, visited a province, it was, as we have seen, for outward parade ; whilst the intendant carried on the administration, he exhibited himself with grace and magnificence by giving receptions and dinners.   To receive, to give dinners, to entertain guests agreeably is the sole occupation of a grand seignior ; hence it is that religion and government only serve him as subjects of conversation.   The conversation, moreover, occurs between him and his equals, and a man may say what he pleases in good company.   Moreover the social system turns on its own axis, like the sun, from time immemorial, through its own energy, and shall it be deranged by what is said in the drawing-room ?   In any event he does not control its motion and he is not responsible. Accordingly there is no uneasy undercurrent, no morose preoccupation in his mind.   Carelessly and boldly he follows in the track of his philosophers ; detached from affairs he can give himself up to ideas, just as a young man of family, on leaving college, lays hold of some principle, deduces its consequences, and forms a system for himself without concerning himself about its application.[2]

---

[1] Stendhal, " Rome, Naples et Florence," 371.

[2] Morellet, " Mémoires," I. 139 (on the writings and conversations of Diderot, d'Holbach and the atheists).   " At that time, in this philosophy, all seemed innocent enough, it being confined to the limits of speculation, and never seeking, even in its boldest flights, anything beyond a calm intellectual exercise."

Nothing is more enjoyable than this speculative inspiration. The mind soars among the summits as if it had wings; it embraces vast horizons in a glance, taking in all of human life, the economy of the world, the origin of the universe, of religions and of societies. Where, accordingly, would conversation be if people abstained from philosophy? What circle is that in which serious political problems and profound criticism are not admitted? And what motive brings intellectual people together if not the desire to debate questions of the highest importance? For two centuries in France all this forms the pabulum of conversation, and hence its great charm. Strangers find it irresistible; nothing like it is found at home; Lord Chesterfield sets it forth as an example. It always turns, he says, on some point in history, on criticism or even philosophy which is much better suited to rational beings than our English discussions about the weather and whist. Rousseau, so querulous, admits "that a moral subject could not be better discussed in a society of philosophers than in that of a pretty woman in Paris." Undoubtedly there is a good deal of idle talk, but with all the chattering "let a man of any authority make a serious remark or start a grave subject and the attention is immediately fixed on this point; men and women, the old and the young, all give themselves up to its consideration on all its sides, and it is surprising what an amount of reason and good sense issues, as if in emulation, from these frolicsome brains." The truth is that, in this constant holiday which this brilliant society gives itself, philosophy is the principal amusement. Without philosophy the ordinary ironical chit-chat would be vapid. It is a sort of superior opera in which every grand conception that can interest a reflecting mind passes before it, now in comic and now in sober attire, and each in conflict with the other. The tragedy of the day scarcely differs from it except in this respect, that it always bears a solemn aspect and is performed only in the theatres; the other assumes all sorts of physiognomies and is found everywhere because conversation is everywhere carried on. Not a dinner nor a supper is given at which it does not find place. One sits at a table amidst refined luxuriousness, among agreeable and well-dressed women and pleasant and well-informed men, a select company, in which comprehension is prompt and intercourse safe. After the second course the inspiration breaks out in the liveliest sallies, all minds flashing and scintillating.   When the dessert comes on what is to prevent the gravest of subjects from being put into witticisms ?   On the appearance of the coffee questions on the immortality of the soul and on the existence of God come up.

To form any idea of this attractive and bold conversation we must consult the correspondence of the day, the short treatises and dialogues of Diderot and Voltaire, whatever is most animated, most delicate, most piquant and most profound in the literature of the century; and yet this is only a residuum, a lifeless fragment.   The whole of this written philosophy was uttered in words, with the accent, the impetuosity, the inimitable naturalness of improvisation, with the versatility of malice and of enthusiasm.   Even to-day, chilled and on paper, it still transports and seduces us.   What must it have been issuing breathing and vibrating from the lips of Voltaire and Diderot ?   Daily, in Paris, suppers took place like those described by Voltaire,[1] at which "two philosophers, three clever intellectual ladies, M. Pinto the famous Jew, the chaplain of the Batavian ambassador of the reformed church, the secretary of the Prince de Galitzin of the Greek church, and a Swiss calvinist captain," seated around the same table, for four hours interchanged their anecdotes, their flashes of wit, their remarks and their decisions "on all subjects of interest relating to science and taste."   The most learned and distinguished foreigners daily visited, in turn, the house of the Baron d'Holbach,—Hume, Wilkes, Sterne, Beccaria, Veri, the Abbé Galiani, Garrick, Franklin, Priestley, Lord Shelburne, the Comte de Creutz, the Prince of Brunswick and the future Elector of Mayence.   With respect to society in general the Baron entertained Diderot, Rousseau, Helvétius, Duclos, Saurin, Raynal, Suard, Marmontel, Boulanger, the Chevalier de Chastellux, the traveller La Condamine, the physician Barthèz, and Rouelle, the chemist.   Twice a week, on Sundays and Thursdays, "without prejudice to other days," they dine at his house, according to custom, at two o'clock; a significant custom which thus leaves to conversation and gaiety a man's best powers and the best hours of the day.   Conversation, in those days, was not relegated to night and late hours; a man was not forced, as at the present

---

[1] "L'Homme aux quarante écus."   Cf. Voltaire, "Mémoires," the suppers given by Frederick II.   "Never in any place in the world was there greater freedom of conversation concerning the superstitions of mankind."

day, to subordinate it to the exigencies of work and money, of the Assembly and the Exchange. Talking is the main business. "Entering at two o'clock," says Morellet,[1] "we almost all remained until seven or eight o'clock in the evening. . . . Here could be heard the most liberal, the most animated, the most instructive conversation that ever took place. . . . There was no political or religious temerity which was not brought forward and discussed pro and con. . . . Frequently some one of the company would begin to speak and state his theory in full, without interruption. At other times it would be a combat of one against one, of which the rest remained silent spectators. Here I heard Roux and Darcet expose their theory of the earth, Marmontel the admirable principles he collected together in his ' Eléments de la Littérature,' Raynal, telling us in *livres*, *sous* and *deniers*, the commerce of the Spaniards with Vera-Cruz and of the English with their colonies." Diderot improvises on the arts and on moral and metaphysical subjects, with that incomparable fervor and wealth of expression, that flood of logic and of illustration, those happy hits of style and that mimetic power which belonged to him alone, and of which but two or three of his works preserve even the feeblest image. In their midst Galiani, secretary of the Neapolitan Embassy, a clever dwarf, a genius, "a sort of Plato or Machiavelli with the spirit and action of a harlequin," inexhaustible in stories, an admirable buffoon, and an accomplished sceptic, "having no faith in anything, on anything or about anything,"[2] not even in the new philosophy, braves the atheists of the drawing-room, beats down their dithyrambs with puns, and, with his perruque in his hand, sitting cross-legged on the chair on which he is perched, proves to them in a comic apologue that they *raisonnent* (reason) or *résonnent* (resound or echo) if not as *cruches* (blockheads) at least as *cloches* (bells);" in any event almost as poorly as theologians. One of those present says, "It was the most diverting thing possible and worth the best of plays."

How can the nobles, who pass their lives in talking, refrain from the society of people who talk so well? They might as well expect their wives, who frequent the theatre every night, and who perform at home, not to attract famous actors and singers to

---

[1] Morellet, "Mémoires," I. 133.

[2] Galiani, "Correspondance," *passim.*

their receptions, Jelyotte, Sainval, Préville, and young Molé who, quite ill and needing restoratives, "receives in one day more than two thousand bottles of wine of different sorts from the ladies of the court," Mlle. Clairon, who, consigned to prison in Fort l'Eveque, attracts to it "an immense crowd of carriages," presiding over the most select company in the best apartment of the prison.[1]   With life thus regarded, a philosopher with his ideas is as necessary in a drawing-room as a chandelier with its lights. He forms a part of the new system of luxuriousness.   He is an article of export.   Sovereigns, amidst their splendor, and at the height of their success, invite them to their courts to enjoy for once in their life the pleasure of perfect and free discourse.   When Voltaire arrives in Prussia Frederic II. is willing to kiss his hand, fawning on him as on a mistress, and, at a later period, after such mutual fondling, he cannot dispense with carrying on conversations with him by letter.   Catherine II. sends for Diderot, and, for two or three hours every day, she plays with him the great game of the intellect.   Gustavus III., in France, is intimate with Marmontel, and considers a visit from Rousseau as the highest honor.[2]   It is said with truth of Voltaire that "he holds the four kings in his hand," those of Prussia, Sweden, Denmark and Russia, without mentioning lower cards, the princes, princesses, grand dukes and margraves.   The principal *rôle* in this society evidently belongs to authors; their ways and doings form the subject of gossip; people never weary of paying them homage.   Here, writes Hume to Robertson,[3] " I feed on ambrosia, drink nothing but nectar, breathe incense only and walk on flowers.   Every man I meet, and especially every woman, would consider themselves as failing in the most indispensable duty if they did not favor me with a lengthy and ingenious discourse on my celebrity."   Presented at court, the future Louis XVI., aged ten years, the future Louis XVIII., aged eight years, and the future Charles X., aged four years, each recites a compliment to him on his works.   I need not narrate the return of Voltaire, his triumphant entry,[4] the Academy in a body coming to welcome him, his carriage stopped by the crowd, the

---

[1] Bachaumont, III. 93 (1766), II. 202 (1765).
[2] Geffroy, "Gustave III.," I. 114.
[3] Villemain, "Tableau de la Littérature au dix-huitième siècle," IV. 409.
[4] Grimm, "Corresp. littéraire," IV. 176.   De Ségur, "Mémoires," I. 113.

thronged streets, the windows, steps and balconies filled with admirers, an intoxicated audience in the theatre incessantly applauding, outside an entire population carrying him off with huzzas, in the drawing-rooms a continual concourse equal to that of the king, grand seigniors pressed against the door with outstretched ears to catch a word, and great ladies standing on tiptoe to observe the slightest gesture. " To form any conception of what I experienced," says one of those present, " one should breathe the atmosphere of enthusiasm I lived in. I spoke with him." This expression at that time converted any new-comer into an important character. He had, in fact, seen the wonderful orchestra-leader who, for more than fifty years, conducted the tumultuous concert of serious or *court-vêtues* ideas, and who, always on the stage, always chief, the recognized leader of universal conversation, supplied the motives, gave the pitch, marked the measure, stamped the inspiration, and drew the first note on the violin.

III.

Listen to the shouts that greet him : Hurrah for the author of the *Henriade !* the defender of Calas, the author of *la Pucelle !* Nobody of the present day would utter the first, nor especially the last hurrah. This indicates the tendency of the century ; not only were writers called upon for ideas, but again for antagonistic ideas. To render an aristocracy inactive is to render it fault-finding ; man willingly accepts a law only when he assists in applying it. Would you rally him to the support of the government ? Then let him take part in it. If not he stands by as a looker-on and sees nothing but the mistakes it commits, feeling only its irritations, and disposed only to criticize and to hoot at it. In fact, in this case, he is as if in the theatre, where he goes to be amused, and, especially, not to be put to any inconvenience. What inconveniencies in the established order of things, and indeed in any established order ! In the first place, as regards religion. To the amiable "idlers " whom Voltaire describes,[1] to " the hundred thousand persons with nothing to do but to play and to amuse themselves," she is the most disagreeable of pedagogues, always scolding, hostile to sensible amusement and free

---

[1] "Princesse de Babylone." Cf. "le Mondain."

discussion, burning books which one wants to read, and imposing dogmas that are no longer comprehensible. In plain terms she is an eyesore, and whoever wishes to throw stones at her is welcome. There is another bond, the moral law of the sexes. It seems onerous to men of pleasure, to the companions of Richelieu, Lauzun and Tilly, to the heroes of Crébillon the younger, and all others belonging to that libertine and gallant society for whom license has become the rule. Our fine gentlemen are quite ready to adopt a theory which justifies their practices. They are very glad to be told that marriage is conventional and a thing of prejudice. Saint-Lambert obtains their applause at supper when, raising a glass of champagne, he proposes as a toast a return to nature and the customs of Otaheite.[1] The last fetter of all is the government, the most galling, for it enforces the rest and keeps man down with its weight, along with the added weight of the others. It is absolute, it is centralized, it works through favorites, it is backward, it makes mistakes, it has reverses,—how many causes of discontent embraced in a few words! It is opposed by the vague and suppressed resentment of the former powers which it has dispossessed, the provincial assemblies, the parliaments, the grandees of the provinces, the old stock of nobles, who, like the Mirabeaus, retain the old feudal spirit, and like Chateaubriand's father, call the Abbé Raynal a " master-man." Against it is the spite of all those who imagine themselves frustrated in the distribution of offices and of favors, not only the provincial nobility who remain outside[2] while the court nobility are feasting at the royal banquet, but again the majority of the courtiers who are obliged to be content with crumbs, while the little circle of intimate favorites swallow down the large morsels. It has against it the ill-humor of those under its direction who, seeing it play the part of Providence and providing for all, accuses it of everything, the dearness of bread as well as of the decay of a highway. It has against it the new humanity which, in the most elegant drawing-rooms, lays to its charge the maintenance of the antiquated remains of a barbarous epoch, ill-imposed, ill-

---

[1] Mme. d'Epinay, ed. Boiteau, I. 216: at a supper given by Mlle. Quinault, the comedian, at which are present Saint-Lambert, the Prince de ——, Duclos and Mme. d'Epinay.

[2] For example, the father of Marmont, a military gentleman, who, having won the cross of St. Louis at twenty-eight, abandons the service because he finds that promotion is only for people of the court. In retirement on his estates he is a liberal, teaching his son to read the reports made by Necker. (Marshal Marmont, " Mémoires," I. 9).

apportioned and ill-collected taxes, sanguinary laws, blind prosecutions, atrocious punishments, the persecution of the protestants, *lettres-de-cachet*, and prisons of State. And I do not include its excesses, its scandals, its disasters and its disgraces,—Rosbach, the treaty of Paris, Madame du Barry, and bankruptcy. Disgust intervenes, for everything is decidedly bad. The spectators of the play say to each other that not only is the piece itself poor, but the theatre is badly built, uncomfortable, stifling and contracted, to such a degree that, to be at one's ease, the whole thing must be torn down and rebuilt from cellar to garret.

Just at this moment the new architects appear, with their specious arguments and their ready-made plans, proving that every great public structure, religious and moral, and all communities, cannot be otherwise than barbarous and insalubrious, since, thus far, they are built up out of bits and pieces, by degrees, and generally by fools and savages, in any event by common masons, who built haphazard, feeling their way and devoid of principles. They are genuine architects, and they have principles, that is to say, reason, nature, and the rights of man, all being simple and fruitful principles which everybody can understand, the consequences derived from them sufficing to substitute for the ill-shapen tenements of the past the admirable edifice of the future. To irreverent, epicurean and philanthropic malcontents the temptation is a great one. They readily adopt maxims which seem in conformity with their secret wishes ; at least they adopt them in theory and in words. The imposing terms of liberty, justice, public good, man's dignity, are so admirable, and besides so vague! What heart can refuse to cherish them, and what intelligence can foretell their innumerable applications ? And all the more because, up to the last, the theory does not descend from the heights, being confined to abstractions, resembling an academic oration, always treating of man in himself, of the social contract, and of the imaginary and perfect civic body. Is there a courtier at Versailles who would refuse to proclaim equality in the city of the Salentini! Communication between the two stories of the human intellect, the upper where abstract reasoning spins its arguments, and the lower where an active faith reposes, is neither complete nor immediate. A certain set of principles never leave the upper stories ; they remain there in the position of curiosities, so many delicate, ingenious subtleties of which a parade is willingly made, but which scarcely ever enter into actual service.   If the proprietor sometimes transfers them to the lower story he makes but a partial use of them ; established customs, anterior and more powerful interests and instincts restrict their employment.   In this respect he is not acting in bad faith, but as a man ; each of us professing truths which he does not put in practice.   One evening Target, a dull lawyer, having taken a pinch from the snuff-box of the Maréchale de Beauvau, the latter, whose drawing-room is a small democratic club, is amazed at such monstrous familiarity.   Later, Mirabeau, on returning home just after having voted for the abolition of nobility titles, takes his servant by the ear and bawls out to him in his stentorian voice, "Look here, *drôle*, I trust that to you I shall always be Monsieur le Comte !"   This shows to what extent new theories are admitted into an aristocratic brain. They occupy the whole of the upper story, and there, with a pleasing murmur, they weave the web of interminable conversation ; their buzzing lasts throughout the century ; never have the drawing-rooms seen such an outpouring of fine sentences and of fine words.   Something of all this drops from the upper to the lower story, if only as dust, that is to say, hope, faith in the future, belief in reason, a love of truth, the generosity of youthful feeling, the enthusiasm that quickly passes but which is often exalted into self-abnegation and devotion.

IV.

Let us follow the progress of philosophy in the upper class. Religion is the first to receive the severest attacks.   The small group of sceptics, which is hardly perceptible under Louis XIV , has obtained its recruits in the dark ; in 1698 the Palatine, the mother of the Regent, writes that "we scarcely meet a young man now who is not ambitious of being an atheist."[1]   Under the Regency, unbelief comes out into open daylight.   "I doubt," says this lady again, in 1722, "if, in all Paris, a hundred individuals can be found, either ecclesiastics or laymen, who have any true faith, or even believe in our Lord.   It makes one tremble. . . ."   The position of an ecclesiastic in society is already difficult.   He is looked upon, apparently, as either a puppet or a

---

[1] Aubertin, "L'Esprit-public," in the 18th century, p. 7.

butt.[1] "The moment we appear," says one of them, "we are forced into discussion; we are called upon to prove, for example, the utility of prayer to an unbeliever in God, and the necessity of fasting to a man who has all his life denied the immortality of the soul; the effort is very irksome, while those who laugh are not on our side." It is not long before the continued scandal of confession tickets and the stubbornness of the bishops in not allowing ecclesiastical property to be taxed, excites opinion against the clergy, and, as a matter of course, against religion itself. "There is danger," says Barbier in 1751, "that this may end seriously; we may some day see a revolution in this country in favor of protestantism." [2] " The hatred against the priests," writes d'Argenson in 1753, "is carried to extremes. They scarcely show themselves in the streets without being hooted at. . . . As our nation and our century are quite otherwise enlightened (than in the time of Luther), it will be carried far enough; they will expel the priests, abolish the priesthood and get rid of all revelation and all mystery. . . . One dare not speak in behalf of the clergy in social circles; one is scoffed at and regarded as a familiar of the inquisition. The priests remark that, this year, there is a diminution of more than one-third in the number of communicants. The College of the Jesuits is being deserted ; one hundred and twenty boarders have been withdrawn from these so greatly defamed monks. It has been observed also that, during the carnival in Paris, the number of masks counterfeiting ecclesiastical dress,—bishops, abbés, monks and nuns,—was never so great." So deep is this antipathy, the most mediocre books become the rage so long as they are antichristian and condemned as such. In 1748 a work by Toussaint called "Les Mœurs," in favor of natural religion, suddenly becomes so famous "that there is no one among a certain class of people," says Barbier, "man or woman, pretending to be intellectual, who is not eager to see it." People accost each other on their promenades, Have you read "Les Mœurs ? " Ten years later they are beyond deism. "Materialism," again says Barbier, "is the great grievance." "Almost all people of acquirements and of wit," writes d'Argenson, "inveigh against our holy re-

---

[1] Montesquieu, "Lettres Persanes," (Letter 61). Cf. Voltaire, ("Diner du Comte de Boulainvilliers").
[2] Aubertin, pp. 281, 282, 285, 280.

ligion. . . . It is attacked on all sides, and what animates unbe-
lievers still more is the efforts made by the devout to compel
belief. They publish books which are but little read; disputes
no longer take place, everything being laughed at, while people
persist in materialism." Horace Walpole, who returns to France
in 1765,[1] and whose good sense anticipates the danger, is astonished at such imprudence: "I dined to-day with a dozen
savans, and although all the servants were waiting, the conversation was much more unrestrained, even on the Old Testament,
than I would suffer at my own table in England even if a single
footman was present." People dogmatize everywhere. "Laughing is as much out of fashion as pantins or bilboquets. Good
folks, they have no time to laugh! There is God and the king
to be pulled down first; and men and women, one and all, are
devoutly employed in the demolition. They think me quite
profane for having any belief left. . . . Do you know who *the
philosophers* are, or what the term means here? In the first
place it comprehends almost everybody; and in the next, means
men, who, avowing war against popery, aim, many of them, at
a subversion of all religion. . . . These *savans*—I beg their par-
dons, the *philosophers*—are insupportable, superficial, overbear-
ing and fanatic: they preach incessantly, and their avowed doctrine is atheism; you would not believe how openly. Voltaire
himself does not satisfy them. One of their lady devotees said
of him, ' He is a bigot, a deist!' "

This is very strong, and yet we have not come to the end of
it; for, thus far, impiety is less a conviction than the fashion.
Walpole, a careful observer, is not deluded by it. "By what I
have said of their religious or rather irreligious opinions, you must
not conclude their people of quality atheists—at least not the
men. Happily for them, poor souls! they are not capable of going so far into thinking. They assent to a great deal because it
is the fashion, and because they don't know how to contradict."
Now "that dandies are antiquated" and everybody is "a philosopher" "they are philosophers." It is essential to be like all the
rest of the world. But that which they best appreciate in the
new materialism is the pungency of paradox and the freedom
given to pleasure. They are like the boys of good families, fond

---

[1] Horace Walpole, "Letters and Correspondence," Sept. 27th, October 19th and 28th,
November 19, 1765, January 25, 1766.

of playing tricks on their ecclesiastical preceptor. They take out of learned theories just what is wanted to make a dunce-cap, and derive the more amusement from the fun if it is seasoned with impiety. A seignior of the court having seen Doyen's picture of "St. Genevieve and the plague-stricken," sends to a painter the following day to come to him at his mistress's domicile: "I would like," he says to him, "to have Madame painted in a swing put in motion by a bishop; you may place me in such a way that I may see the ankles of that handsome woman, and even more, if you want to enliven your picture."[1] The licentious song "Marotte" "spreads like wildfire;" "a fortnight after its publication," says Collé, "I met no one without a copy; and it is the vaudeville, or rather, the clerical assembly, which gives it its popularity." The more irreligious a licentious book is the more it is prized; when it cannot be printed it is copied in manuscript. Collé counts "perhaps two thousand manuscript copies of ' La Pucelle ' by Voltaire, scattered about Paris in one month." The magistrates themselves burn it only for form's sake. " It must not be supposed that the hangman is allowed to burn the books whose titles figure in the decree of the Court. Messieurs would be loath to deprive their libraries of the copy of those works which fall to them by right, and make the registrar supply its place with a few poor records of chicanery of which there is no scanty provision."[2]

But, as the century advances, infidelity becomes less obstreperous and more resolute. It invigorates itself at the fountain-head ; the women themselves begin to be infatuated with the sciences. In 1782,[3] one of Mme. de Genlis's characters writes, " Five years ago I left them thinking only of their attire and the preparation of their suppers ; I now find them all scientific and witty." We find in the study of a fashionable woman, alongside of a small altar dedicated to Benevolence or Friendship, a dictionary of natural history and treatises on physics and chemistry. A woman no longer has herself painted as a goddess on a cloud, but in a laboratory, seated amidst squares and telescopes.[4] The

---

[1] "Journal et Mémoires de Collé," published by H. Bonhomme, II. 24 (October, 1755), and III. 165 (October 1767).

[2] "Corresp. littéraire," by Grimm (September, October, 1770).

[3] Mme. de Genlis, "Adèle et Théodore," I. 312.

[4] De Goncourt, "La femme au dix-huitième siècle," 371–373. Bachaumont, I. 224 (April 13, 1763).

Marquise de Nesle, the Comtesse de Brancas, the Comtesse de Pons, the Marquise de Polignac, are with Rouelle when he undertakes to melt and volatilize the diamond.   Associations of twenty or twenty-five persons are formed in the drawing-rooms to attend lectures either on physics, applied chemistry, mineralogy or on botany.   Fashionable women at the public meetings of the Academy of Inscriptions applaud dissertations on the bull Apis, and reports on the Egyptian, Phœnician and Greek languages. Finally, in 1786, they succeed in opening the doors of the College de France.   Nothing deters them.   Many of them use the lancet and even the scalpel; the Marquise de Voyer attends at dissections, and the young Comtesse de Coigny dissects with her own hands.   The current infidelity finds fresh support on this foundation, which is that of the prevailing philosophy.   Towards the end of the century[1] "we see young persons who have been in society six or seven years openly pluming themselves on their irreligion, thinking that impiety makes up for wit, and that to be an atheist is to be a philosopher."   There are, undoubtedly, a good many deists, especially after Rousseau appeared, but I question whether, out of a hundred persons, there were in Paris at this time ten Christian men or women.   "The fashionable world for ten years past," says Mercier[2] in 1783, "has not attended mass.   People go only on Sundays so as not to scandalize their lackeys, while the lackeys well know that it is on their account." The Duc de Coigny,[3] on his estate near Amiens, refuses to be prayed for and threatens his curate if he takes that liberty to have him cast out of his pulpit; his son becomes ill and he prohibits the administering of the sacraments; the son dies and he opposes the usual obsequies, burying the body in his garden; becoming ill himself he closes his door against the bishop of Amiens, who comes to see him twelve times, and dies as he had lived.   A scandal of this kind is doubtless notorious and, therefore, rare. Almost everybody, male and female, "ally with freedom of ideas a proper observance of forms."[4]   When a maid appears and says to her mistress, "Madame la Duchesse, the Host (*le bon Dieu*) is outside, will you allow him to enter?   He desires to have the

---

[1] Mme. de Genlis, "Adèle et Théodore," II. 326.
[2] "Tableau de Paris," III. 44.
[3] Métra, "Correspondance secrète," XVII. 387 (March 7, 1785).
[4] De Goncourt, *ibid.* 456. Vicomtesse de Noailles, "Vie de la Princesse de Foix," formerly de Beauvau.

honor of administering to you," appearances are kept up. The
troublesome individual is admitted and he is politely received.
If they slip away from him it is under a decent pretext ; but if
he is humored it is only out of a sense of decorum. " At Sura
when a man dies, he holds a cow's tail in his hand." Society
was never more detached from Christianity. In its eyes a positive religion is only a popular superstition, good enough for
children and innocents but not for " sensible people" and the
great. It is your duty to raise your hat to the Host as i' passes,
but your duty is only to raise your hat.

The last and gravest sign of all ! If the curates who work and
who are of the people hold the people's ideas, the prelates who
talk, and who are of society hold the opinions of society. And
I do not allude merely to the abbés of the drawing-room, the
domestic courtiers, bearers of news, and writers of light verse,
those who fawn in boudoirs, and who, when in company, answer
like an echo, and who, between one drawing-room and another,
serve as speaking-tubes ; an echo, a speaking-tube only repeats
the phrase, whether sceptical or not, with which it is charged. I
refer to the dignitaries, and, on this point, the witnesses all concur.
In the month of August, 1767, the Abbé Bassinet, grand vicar of
Cahors, on pronouncing the panegyric of St. Louis in the Louvre
chapel,[1] "suppressed the sign of the cross, making no quotation
from Scripture and never uttering a word about Christ and the
Saints. He considered Louis IX. merely on the side of his political, moral and military virtues. He animadverted on the Crusades, setting forth their absurdity, cruelty and even injustice.
He struck openly and without caution at the see of Rome."
Others "avoid the name of Christ in the pulpit and merely allude
to him as a Christian legislator."[2] In the code which the prevailing opinions and social decency impose on the clergy a delicate observer [3] thus specifies distinctions in rank with their proper
shades of behavior : " A plain priest, a curate, must have a little
faith, otherwise he would be found a hypocrite ; at the same time,

---

[1] The Abbé de Latteignaut, canon of Rheims, the author of some light poetry and con-
vivial songs, "has just composed for Nicolet's theatre a parade in which the intrigue is supported by a good many broad jests, very much in the fashion at this time. The courtiers who
give the tone to this theatre think the canon of Rheims superb." (Bachaumont, IV. 174,
November, 1768).

[2] Bachaumont, III. 253. Chateaubriand, "Mémoires," I. 246.

[3] Champfort, 279.

he must not be too well satisfied, for he would be found intolerant.   On the contrary, the grand vicar may smile at an expression against religion, the bishop may laugh outright, and the cardinal may add something of his own to it."   "A little while ago,"
a chronicle narrates, "some one put this question to one of the
most respectable curates in Paris: Do you think that the bishops
who insist so strenuously on religion have much of it themselves?
The worthy pastor replied, after a moment's hesitation: There
may be four or five among them who still believe."   To one who
is familiar with their birth, their social relations, their habits and
their tastes, this does not appear at all improbable.   "Dom Col-
lignon, a representative of the abbey of Mettach, seignior high-
justiciary and curate of Valmunster," a fine-looking man, fine
talker, and an agreeable housekeeper, avoids scandal by having
his two mistresses at his table only with a select few; he is in
other respects as little devout as possible, and much less so than
the Savoyard vicar, "finding evil only in injustice and in a lack
of charity," and considering religion merely as a political institution and for moral ends.   I might cite many others, like M. de
Grimaldi, the young and gallant bishop of Le Mans, who selects
young and gallant comrades of his own station for his grand
vicars, and who has a rendezvous for pretty women at his country
seat at Coulans.[1]   Judge of their faith by their habits.   In other
cases we have no difficulty in determining.   Scepticism is notorious with the Cardinal de Rohan, with M. de Brienne, archbishop of Sens, with M. de Talleyrand, bishop of Autun, and
with the Abbé Maury, defender of the clergy.   Rivarol,[2] himself
a sceptic, declares that at the approach of the Revolution, "the
enlightenment of the clergy equalled that of the philosophers."
"The body with the fewest prejudices," says Mercier,[3]—"who
would believe it?—is the clergy."   And the Archbishop of Narbonne, explaining the resistance of the upper class of the clergy
in 1791,[4] attributes it, not to faith but to a point of honor.   "We
conducted ourselves at that time like true gentlemen, for, with

---

[1] Merlin de Thionville, "Vie et correspondance," by Jean Raynaud.   ("La Chartreuse du
Val Saint-Pierre."   Read the entire passage).   "Souvenirs Manuscrits," by M——.
[2] Rivarol, "Mémoires," I. 344.
[3] Mercier, IV. 142.   "In Auvergne, says M. de Montlosier, I formed for myself a society
of priests, men of wit, some of whom were deists and others open atheists, with whom I
carried on a contest with my brother."   ("Mémoires," I. 37).
[4] Lafayette. "Mémoires," III. 58.

most of us, it could not be said that it was through religious feeling."

V.

The distance between the altar and the throne is a short one, and yet it requires thirty years for opinion to overcome it. No political or social attacks are yet made during the first half of the century. The irony of the " Lettres Persanes " is as cautious as it is delicate, and the " Esprit des Lois " is conservative. As to the Abbé de Saint-Pierre his reveries provoke a smile, and when he undertakes to censure Louis XIV. the Academy strikes him off its list. At last, the economists on one side and the parliamentarians on the other, give the signal. Voltaire says[1] that "about 1750 the nation, satiated with verse, tragedies, comedies, novels, operas, romantic histories, and still more romantic moralizings, and with disputes about grace and convulsions, began to discuss the question of corn." What makes bread dear ? Why is the laborer so miserable ? What constitutes the material and limits of taxation ? Ought not all land to pay taxes, and should one piece pay more than its net product ? These are the questions that find their way into drawing-rooms under the king's auspices, by means of Quesnay, his physician, "his thinker," the founder of a system which aggrandizes the sovereign to relieve the people, and which multiplies the number of tax-payers to lighten the burden of taxation. At the same time, through the opposite door, other questions enter, not less novel. " Is France[2] a mild and representative monarchy or a government of the Turkish stamp ? Are we subject to the will of an absolute master, or are we governed by a limited and regulated power? . . . The exiled parliaments are studying public rights at their sources and conferring together on these as in the academies. Through their researches, the opinion is gaining ground in the public mind that the nation is above the king, as the universal church is above the pope." The change is striking and almost immediate. " Fifty years ago," says d'Argenson, again, " the public showed no curiosity concerning matters of the State. To-day everybody reads his Gazette de Paris, even in the provinces.

---

[1] "Dict. Phil." article "Corn." The most important work of Quesnay is of the year 1758. "Tableau économique."

[2] D'Argenson, "Mémoires," IV. 141 ; VI. 320, 465; VII. 23 ; VIII. 153 (1752, 1753, 1754). Rousseau's discourse on Inequality belongs also to 1753. On this steady march of opinion consult the excellent work of d'Aubertin, "L'Esprit public au dix-huitième siècle."

People reason at random on political subjects, but nevertheless they occupy themselves with them." Conversation having once provided itself with this aliment holds fast to it, the drawing-rooms, accordingly, opening their doors to political philosophy, and, consequently, to the Social Contract, to the Encyclopedia, to the preachings of Rousseau, Mably, d'Holbach, Raynal, and Diderot. In 1759, d'Argenson, who becomes excited, already thinks the last hour has come. "We feel the breath of a philosophical anti-monarchical, free government wind; the idea is current, and possibly this form of government, already in some minds, is to be carried out the first favorable opportunity. Perhaps the *revolution* might take place with less opposition than one supposes, occurring *by acclamation."* [1]

The time is not yet come, but the seed is coming up. Bachaumont, in 1762, notices a deluge of pamphlets, tracts and political discussions, "a rage for arguing on financial and government matters." In 1765, Walpole states that the atheists, who then monopolize conversation, inveigh against kings as well as against priests. A formidable word, that of *citizen,* imported by Rousseau, has entered into common speech, and the matter is settled on the women adopting it as they would a cockade. "As a friend and a *citoyenne* could any news be more agreeable to me than that of peace and the health of my dear little one?" [2] Another word, not less significant, that of *energy,* formerly ridiculous, becomes fashionable, and is used on every occasion. [3] Along with language there is a change of sentiment, ladies of high rank passing over to the opposition. In 1771, says the scoffer Bezenval, after the exile of the Parliament "social meetings for pleasure or other purposes had become petty States-Generals in which the women, transformed into legislators, established the premisses and confidently propounded maxims of public right." The Comtesse d'Egmont, a correspondent of the King of Sweden, sends him a memorial on the fundamental law of France, favoring the Parliament, the last defender of national liberty, against the encroachments of Chancellor Maupeou. "The Chancellor," she says, [4] "within the last six months has brought people to

---

[1] This seems to be prophetic of the night of August 4, 1789.
[2] "Corresp. de Laurette de Malboissière," published by the Marquise de la Grange. (Sept. 4, 1762, November 8, 1762).
[3] Madame du Deffant in a letter to Madame de Choiseul, (quoted by Geffroy), "Gustave et la cour de France," I. 279.
[4] Geffroy, *ibid.* I. 232, 241, 245.

know the history of France who would have died without any
knowledge of it. . . . I have no doubt, sire," she adds, "that
you never will abuse the power an enraptured people have entrusted to you without limitation. . . . May your reign prove
the epoch of the re-establishment of a free and independent government, but never the source of absolute authority." Numbers
of women of the first rank, Mesdames de la Marck, de Boufflers,
de Brienne, de Mesmes, de Luxembourg, de Croy, think and
write in the same style. "Absolute power," says one of these,
"is a mortal malady which, insensibly corrupting moral qualities,
ends in the destruction of states. . . . The actions of sovereigns
are subject to the censure of their subjects as to that of the
universe. . . . France is undone if the present administration
lasts."[1] When, under Louis XVI., a new administration proposes
and withdraws feeble measures of reform, their criticism shows
the same firmness : " Childishness, weakness, constant inconsist-
ency," writes another,[2] " incessant change ; and always worse off
than we were before. Monsieur and M. le Comte d'Artois
have just made a journey through the provinces, but only as
people of that kind travel, with a frightful expenditure and
devastation along the whole road, coming back extraordinarily
fat ; Monsieur is as big as a hogshead ; as to M. le Comte
d'Artois he is bringing about order by the life he leads." An
inspiration of humanity animates these feminine breasts along
with that of liberty. They interest themselves in the poor, in
children, in the people ; Madame d'Egmont recommends Gustavus III. to plant Dalecarlia with potatoes. On the appearance
of the engraving published for the benefit of Calas[3] " all France
and even all Europe, hastens to subscribe for it, the Empress of
Russia giving 5,000 livres.[4] " Agriculture, economy, reform,
philosophy," writes Walpole, "are *bon ton*, even at the court."
President Dupaty having drawn up a memorial in behalf of
three innocent persons, sentenced " to be broken on the wheel,
everybody in society is talking about it ; " "idle conversation no
longer prevails in society," says a correspondent of Gustavus III.[5] "since it is that which forms public opinion. *Words*

---

[1] Geffroy, *ibid.* I. 267, 281. See letters by Madame de Boufflers (October, 1772, July 1774).
[2] *Ibid.* I. 285. The letters of Mme. de la March (1776, 1777, 1779).
[3] A victim of religious rancor against the protestants, whose cause, taken up by Voltaire,
excited great indignation.—Tr.
[4] Bachaumont, III. 14 (March 28, 1766. Walpole, Oct. 6, 1775).
[5] Geffroy, *ibid.* (A letter by Mme. de Staël, 1776).

have become actions.   Every sensitive heart praises with transport a memorial inspired by humanity and which appears full of talent because it is full of feeling." When Latude is released from the prison of Bicêtre Mme. de Luxembourg, Mme. de Boufflers, and Mme. de Staël dine with the grocer-woman who "for three years and a half moved heaven and earth" to set the prisoner free. It is owing to the women, to their sensibility and zeal, to a conspiracy of their sympathies, that M. de Lally succeeds in the rehabilitation of his father. When they take a fancy to a person they become infatuated with him; Madame de Lauzun, very timid, goes so far as to publicly insult a man who speaks ill of M. Necker. It must be borne in mind that, in this century, the women were queens, setting the fashion, giving the tone, leading in conversation and naturally shaping ideas and opinions.[1] When they take the lead on the political field we may be sure that the men will follow them: each one carries her drawing-room circle with her.

VI.

An aristocracy imbued with humanitarian and radical maxims, courtiers hostile to the court, privileged persons aiding in undermining privileges, presents to us a strange spectacle in the testimony of the time. A contemporary states that it is an accepted principle " to change and upset everything."[2] High and low, in assemblages, in public places, only reformers and opposing parties are encountered among the privileged classes. " In 1787, almost every prominent man of the peerage in the Parliament declared himself in favor of resistance. . . . I have seen at the dinners we then attended almost every idea put forward, which, soon afterwards, produced such startling effects."[3] Already in 1774, M. de Vaublanc, on his way to Metz, finds a diligence containing an ecclesiastic and a count, a colonel in the hussars, talking political economy constantly.[4] " It was the fashion of the day. Everybody was an economist. People conversed together only about philosophy, political economy and especially humanity, and the

---

[1] Collé, "Journal," III. 437 (1770) : "Women have got the upper hand with the French to such an extent, they have so subjugated them, that they neither feel nor think except as they do."
[2] "Correspondance," by Métra, III. 200; IV. 131.
[3] "Souvenirs Manuscrits," by M——.
[4] De Vaublanc, "Souvenirs," I. 117, 377.

means for relieving the good people, which two words were in everybody's mouth." To this must be added equality; Thomas, in a eulogy of Marshal Saxe says, "I cannot conceal it, he was of royal blood," and this phrase was admired. A few of the heads of old parliamentary or seigniorial families maintain the old patrician and monarchical standard, the new generation succumbing to novelty. "For ourselves," says one of them belonging to the youthful class of the nobility,[1] "with no regret for the past or anxiety for the future, we marched gayly along over a carpet of flowers concealing an abyss. Mocking censors of antiquated ways, of the feudal pride of our fathers and of their sober etiquette, everything antique seemed to us annoying and ridiculous. The gravity of old doctrines oppressed us. The cheerful philosophy of Voltaire amused and took possession of us. Without fathoming that of graver writers we admired it for its stamp of fearlessness and resistance to arbitrary power. . . . Liberty, whatever its language, delighted us with its spirit, and equality on account of its convenience. It is a pleasant thing to descend so long as one thinks one can ascend when one pleases; we were at once enjoying, without forethought, the advantages of the patriciate and the sweets of a plebeian philosophy. Thus, although our privileges were at stake, and the remnants of our former supremacy were undermined under our feet, this little warfare gratified us. Inexperienced in the attack, we simply admired the spectacle. Combats with the pen and with words did not appear to us capable of damaging our existing superiority, which several centuries of possession had made us regard as impregnable. The forms of the edifice remaining intact, we could not see how it could be mined from within. We laughed at the serious alarm of the old court and of the clergy which thundered against the spirit of innovation. We applauded republican scenes in the theatre,[2] philosophic discourses in our Academies, the bold publications of the literary class." If inequality still subsists in the distribution of offices and of places, "equality begins to reign in society. On many occasions literary titles obtain precedence

---

[1] De Ségur, "Mémoires," I. 17.
[2] Ibid. I. 151. "I saw the entire court at the theatre in the chateau at Versailles enthusiastically applaud Voltaire's tragedy of 'Brutus,' and especially these lines:
Je suis fils de Brutus, et je porte en mon cœur
La liberté gravée et les rois en horreur."

over titles of nobility. Courtiers and servants of the passing fashion, paid their court to Marmontel, d'Alembert and Raynal. We frequently saw in company literary men of the second and third rank greeted and receiving attentions not extended to the nobles of the provinces. . . . Institutions remained monarchical, but manners and customs became republican. A word of praise from d'Alembert or Diderot was more esteemed than the most marked favor from a prince. It was impossible to pass an evening with d'Alembert, or at the Hôtel de Larochefoucauld among the friends of Turgot, to attend a breakfast at the Abbé Raynal's, to be admitted into the society and family of M. de Malesherbes, in fine, to approach a most amiable queen and a most upright king, without believing ourselves about to enter upon a kind of golden era of which preceding centuries afforded no idea. . . . We were bewildered by the prismatic hues of fresh ideas and doctrines, radiant with hopes, ardently aglow for every sort of reputation, enthusiastic for all talents and beguiled by every seductive dream of a philosophy that was about to secure the happiness of the human species. Far from foreseeing misfortune, excess, crime, the overthrow of thrones and of principles, the future disclosed to us only the benefits which humanity was to derive from the sovereignty of reason. Free circulation was left to every reformative writing, to every project of innovation, to the most liberal ideas and to the boldest of systems. Everybody thought himself on the road to perfection without being under any embarrassment or fearing any kind of obstacle. We were proud of being Frenchmen and, yet again, Frenchmen of the eighteenth century. . . . Never was a more terrible awakening preceded by a sweeter slumber or by more seductive dreams."

They do not content themselves with dreams, with pure desires, with passive aspirations. They are active, and truly generous; a worthy cause suffices to secure their devotedness. On the news of the American rebellion, the Marquis de Lafayette, leaving his young wife pregnant, escapes, braves the orders of the court, purchases a frigate, crosses the ocean and fights by the side of Washington. "The moment the quarrel was made known to me," he says, "my heart was enlisted in it, and my only thought was to rejoin my regiment." Numbers of gentlemen follow in his footsteps. They undoubtedly love danger; "the chance of being shot is too precious to be neglected."[1]   But the main thing is to emancipate the oppressed; "we showed ourselves philosophers by becoming paladins,"[2] the chivalric sentiment enlisting in the service of liberty. Other services besides these, more sedentary and less brilliant, find no fewer zealots. The chief personages of the provinces in the provincial assemblies,[3] the bishops, archbishops, abbés, dukes, counts, and marquises, with the wealthiest and best informed of the notables in the Third-Estate, in all about a thousand persons, in short the social elect, the entire upper class convoked by the king, organize the budget, defend the tax-payer against the fisc, arrange the land-registry, equalize the *taille*, provide a substitute for the *corvée*, provide public roads, multiply charitable asylums, educate agriculturists, proposing, encouraging and directing every species of reformatory movement. I have read through the twenty volumes of their *procès-verbaux:* no better citizens, no more conscientious men, no more devoted administrators can be found, none gratuitously taking so much trouble on themselves with no object but the public welfare. Never was an aristocracy so deserving of power at the moment of losing it; the privileged class, aroused from their indolence, were again becoming public men, and, restored to their functions, were returning to their duties. In 1778, in the first assembly of Berry, the Abbé de Seguiran, the reporter, has the courage to state that "the distribution of the taxes should be a fraternal partition of public obligations."[4]   In 1780 the abbés, priors and chapters of the same province contribute 60,000 livres of their funds, and a few gentlemen, in less than twenty-four hours, contribute 17,000 livres. In 1787, in the assembly of Alençon the nobility and the clergy tax themselves 30,000 livres to relieve the indigent in each parish subject to taxation.[5] ᴸn the month of April, 1787, the king, in an assembly of the notables, speaks of "the eagerness with which archbishops and bishops

---

[1] De Lauzun, 80 (in relation to his expedition into Corsica).

[2] De Ségur, I. 87.

[3] The assemblies of Berry, Haute-Guyenne, open in 1779; those of other generalships in 1787; all are in session until 1789. (Cf. Léonce de Lavergne, "Les Assemblées provinciales").

[4] Léonce de Lavergne, *ibid.* 26, 55, 183. The tax department of the provincial assembly of Tours likewise makes its demands on the privileged class in the matter of taxation.

[5] *Procès-verbaux* of the prov. ass. of Normandy, the generalship of Alençon, 252. Cf. Archives nationales, H, 1149: in 1778 in the generality of Moulins, thirty-nine persons, mostly nobles, supply from their own funds 18,950 livres to the 60,000 livres allowed by the king for roads and asylums.

come forward claiming no exemption in their contributions to the public revenue." In the month of March, 1789, on the opening of the bailiwick assemblies, the entire clergy, nearly all the nobility, in short, the whole body of the privileged class voluntarily renounce their privileges in relation to taxation. The sacrifice is voted unanimously; they themselves offer it to the Third-Estate, and it is worth while to see their generous and sympathetic tone in the manuscript *procès-verbaux*. " The nobility of the bailiwick of Tours," says the Marquis de Lusignan,[1] "considering that they are men and citizens before being nobles, can make amends in no way more in conformity with the spirit of justice and patriotism that animates the body, for the long silence to which it has been condemned by the abuse of ministerial power, than in declaring to their fellow-citizens that, in future, they will claim none of the pecuniary advantages secured to them by custom, and that they unanimously and solemnly bind themselves to bear equally, each in proportion to his fortune, all taxes and general contributions which the nation shall prescribe." " I repeat," says the Comte de Buzançois at the meeting of the Third-Estate of Berry, "that we are all brothers, and that we are anxious to share your burdens. . . . We desire to have but one single voice go up to the assembly and thus manifest the union and harmony which should prevail there. I am directed to make the proposal to you to unite with you in one memorial." " These qualities are essential in a deputy," says the Marquis de Barbançon speaking for the nobles of Chateauroux, "integrity, firmness and knowledge; the first two are equally found among the deputies of the three orders; but knowledge will be more generally found in the Third-Estate, which is more accustomed to public affairs." " A new order of things is unfolding before us," says the Abbé Legrand in the name of the clergy of Chateauroux; "the veil of prejudice is being torn away and giving place to reason. She is possessing herself of all French hearts, attacking at the root whatever is based on former opinion and deriving her power only from herself." Not only do the privileged classes

---

[1] Archives nationales, *procès-verbaux* and memorials of the States-General, vol. XLIX. p. 712, 714 (the nobles and clergy of Dijon); t. XVI. p. 183 (the nobles of Auxerre); t. XXIX. pp. 352, 455, 458 (the clergy and nobles of Berry); t. CL. p. 266 (the clergy and nobles of Tours); t. XXIX. (the clergy and nobles of Chateauroux, January 29, 1789); pp. 572, 582. t. XIII. 765 (the nobles of Autun). See as a summary of the whole, the "Résumé des Cahiers " by Prud'homme, 3 vols.

make advances but it is no effort to them; they use the same language as the people of the Third-Estate; they are disciples of the same philosophers and seem to start from the same principles. The nobility of Clermont in Beauvoisis [1] orders its deputies "to demand, first of all, an explicit declaration of the rights belonging to all men." The nobles of Mantes and Meulan affirm "that political principles are as absolute as moral principles, since both have reason for a common basis." The nobles of Rheims demand "that the king be entreated to order the demolition of the Bastille." Frequently, after such expressions and with such a yielding disposition, the delegates of the nobles and clergy are greeted in the assemblies of the Third-Estate with the clapping of hands, "tears" and transports. On witnessing such effusions how can one avoid believing in concord? And how can one foresee strife at the first turn of the road on which they have just fraternally entered hand in hand?

Wisdom of this melancholy stamp is not theirs. They set out with the principle that man, and especially the man of the people, is good; why conjecture that he may desire evil for those who wish him well? They are conscientious in their benevolence and sympathy for him. Not only do they utter these sentiments but they give them proof. "At this moment," says a contemporary,[2] "the most active pity animates all breasts; the great dread of the opulent is to appear insensible." The archbishop of Paris, subsequently followed and stoned, is the donator of one hundred thousand crowns to the hospital of the Hôtel-Dieu. The intendant Berthier, who is to be massacred, draws up the new assessment-roll of the Ile-de-France, equalizing the *taille*, which act allows him to abate the rate, at first, an eighth, and next, a quarter.[3] The financier Beaujon constructs a hospital. Necker refuses the salary of his place and lends the treasury two millions to re-establish public credit. The Duc de Charost, from 1770 [4] down, abolishes seigniorial *corvées* on his domain and founds a hospital in his seigniory of Meillant. The Prince de

---

[1] Prud'homme, *ibid.* II. 39, 51, 59. De Lavergne, 384. In 1788, two hundred gentlemen of the first families of Dauphiny sign, conjointly with the clergy and the Third-Estate of the province, an address to the king in which occurs the following passage: "Neither time nor obligation legitimizes despotism; the rights of men derive from nature alone and are independent of their engagements."

[2] Lacretelle, "Hist. de France au dix-huitième siècle," V. 2.

[3] *Procès-verbaux* of the prov. ass. of the Ile-de-France (1787), p. 127.

[4] De Lavergne, *ibid.* 52, 369.

Beaufremont, the presidents de Vezet, de Chamolles, de Chaillot, with many seigniors beside in Franche-Comté, follow the example of the king in emancipating their serfs.[1] The bishop of Saint-Claude demands, in spite of his chapter, the enfranchisement of his mainmorts. The Marquis de Mirabeau establishes on his domain in Limousin a gratuitous bureau for the settlement of lawsuits, while daily, at Fleury, he causes nine hundred pounds of cheap bread to be made for the use of "the poor people, who fight to see who shall have it."[2] M. de Barral, bishop of Castres, directs his curates to preach and to diffuse the cultivation of potatoes. The Marquis de Guerchy himself mounts on the top of a pile of hay with Arthur Young to learn how to construct a hay-stack. The Marquis de Lasteyrie imports lithography into France. A number of grand seigniors and prelates figure in the agricultural societies, compose or translate useful books, familiarize themselves with the applications of science, study political economy, inform themselves about industries, and interest themselves, either as amateurs or promoters, in every public amelioration. "Never," says Lacretelle again, "were the French so combined together to combat the evils to which nature makes us pay tribute, and those which in a thousand ways creep into all social institutions." Can it be admitted that so many good intentions thus operating together are to end in destruction? All take courage, government as well as the higher class, in the thought of the good accomplished, or which they desire to accomplish. The king remembers that he has restored civil rights to the protestants, abolished preliminary torture, suppressed the *corvée* in kind, established the free circulation of grains, instituted provincial assemblies, built up the marine, assisted the Americans, emancipated his own serfs, diminished the expenses of his household, employed Malesherbes, Turgot and Necker, given full play to the press, and listened to public opinion.[3] No government displayed greater mildness; on the 14th of July, 1789, only seven prisoners were confined in the Bastille, of whom one was an idiot, another kept there by his family, and four

---

[1] "Le cri de la raison," by Clerget, curé d'Onans (1789), p. 258.

[2] Lucas de Montigny, "Mémoires de Mirabeau," I. 290, 368.   Théron de Montaugé, "L'agriculture et les classes rurales dans le pays Toulousain," p. 14.

[3] "Foreigners generally could scarcely form an idea of the power of public opinion at this time in France; they can with difficulty comprehend the nature of that invisible power *which commands even in the king's palace.*" (Necker, 1784, quoted by De Tocqueville).

under the charge of counterfeiting.[1]   No sovereign was more
humane, more charitable, more preoccupied with the unfortunate.
In 1784, the year of inundations and epidemics, he renders assistance to the amount of three millions.   Appeals are made to
him direct, even for personal accidents.   On the 8th of June,
1785, he sends two hundred livres to the wife of a Breton labor-
ing-man who, already having two children, brings three at once
into the world.[2]   During a severe winter he allows the poor daily
to invade his kitchen.   It is quite probable that, next to Turgot,
he is the man of his day who loved the people most.   His delegates under him conform to his views; I have read countless letters
by intendants who try to appear as little Turgots.   "One builds a
hospital, another admits artisans at his table;"[3] a certain individual undertakes the draining of a marsh.   M. de la Tour, in Provence, is so beneficent during a period of forty years that the
Tiers-Etat vote him a gold medal in spite of himself.[4]   A governor delivers a course of lectures on economical bread-making.
What possible danger is there for shepherds of this kind amidst
their flocks ?   On the king convoking the States-General nobody
had "any suspicion," nor fear of the future.   "A new State constitution is spoken of as an easy performance, and as a matter of
course."[5]   "The best and most virtuous men see in this the beginning of a new era of happiness for France and for the whole
civilized world.   The ambitious rejoice in the broad field open
to their desires.   But it would have been impossible to find the
most morose, the most timid, the most enthusiastic of men antic-
ipating any one of the extraordinary events towards which the
assembled states were drifting."

---

[1] Granier de Cassagnac, II. 236.   M. de Malesherbes, according to custom, inspected the
different state prisons, at the beginning of the reign of Louis XVI.   "He told me himself
that he had only released *two.*"   (Senac de Meilhan, "Du gouvernement, des mœurs, et
des conditions en France.")
[2] Archives nationales, II. 1418, 1149, f. 14, 2073.   Assistance rendered to various suffering
provinces and places.
[3] Aubertin, p. 484 (according to Bachaumont).
[4] De Lavergne, 472.
[5] Mathieu Dumas, "Mémoires," I. 426.   Sir Samuel Romilly, "Mémoires," I. 99.   "Confidence increased even to extravagance," (Mme. de Genlis).   On the 29th June, 1789, Necker
said at the council of the king at Marly, "What is more frivolous than the fears now
entertained concerning the organization of the assembly of the States-General ?   No law can
be passed without obtaining the king's assent."   (De Barentin, "Mémoires," p. 187).
Address of the National Assembly to its constituents, October 2, 1789.   "A great revolution
of which the idea would have appeared chimerical a few months since has been effected
amongst us."

CHAPTER III.

I.

THE new philosophy, confined to a select circle, had long served as a mere luxury for refined society. Merchants, manufacturers, shopkeepers, lawyers, attorneys, physicians, actors, professors, curates, every description of functionary, employé and clerk, the entire middle class, had been absorbed with its own cares. The horizon of each was limited, being that of the profession or occupation which each exercised, that of the corporation in which each one was comprised, of the town in which each one was born, and, at the utmost, that of the province which each one inhabited.[1] A dearth of ideas coupled with conscious diffidence restrained the bourgeois within his hereditary barriers. His eyes seldom chanced to wander outside of them into the forbidden and dangerous territory of state affairs; hardly was a furtive and rare glance bestowed on any of the public acts, on the matters which "belonged to the king." There was no

---

[1] I have verified these sentiments myself in the narration of aged people deceased twenty years ago. Cf. manuscript memoirs of Hardy the bookseller (analysed by Aubertin), and the "Travels of Arthur Young."

X

critical irritability then, except with the bar, the compulsory sat-
ellite of the Parliament, and borne along in its orbit. In 1718,
after a session of the royal court *(lit de justice)*, the lawyers
of Paris being on a strike the Regent exclaims angrily and with
astonishment, "What! those fellows meddling too!"[1]   It must
be stated furthermore that many kept themselves in the background. "My father and myself," afterwards writes the advocate
Barbier, "took no part in the uproars, among those caustic and
turbulent spirits." And he adds this significant article of faith :
"I believe that one has to fulfil his duties honorably, *without
concerning oneself with state affairs, in which one has no mission
and exercises no power.*" During the first half of the eighteenth
century I am able to discover but one centre of opposition in the
Third-Estate, the Parliament; and around it, feeding the flame,
the ancient gallican or Jansenist spirit. "The good city of
Paris," writes Barbier in 1733, "is Jansenist from top to bottom,"
and not alone the magistrates, the lawyers, the professors, the
best among the *bourgeoisie*, "but again the mass of the Parisians,
men, women and children, all upholding that doctrine, without
comprehending it, or understanding any of its distinctions and
interpretations, out of hatred to Rome and the Jesuits. Women,
the silliest, and even chambermaids, would be hacked to pieces
for it. . . ." This party is increased by the honest folks of the
kingdom who detest persecutions and injustice. Accordingly,
when the various chambers of magistrates, in conjunction with
the lawyers, tender their resignations and file out of the palace
"amidst a countless multitude, the crowd exclaims : *Behold the
true Romans, the fathers of the country !* and as the two counsel-
lors Pucelle and Menguy pass along they fling them crowns."
The quarrel between the Parliament and the Court, constantly
revived, is one of the sparks which provokes the grand final
explosion, while the Jansenist embers, smouldering in the ashes,
are to be of use in 1791 when the ecclesiastical edifice comes to
be attacked. But, within this old chimney-corner only warm
embers are now found, firebrands covered up, sometimes scatter-
ing sparks and flames, but in themselves and by themselves, not
incendiary ; the flame is kept within bounds by its nature,
and its supplies limit its heat. The Jansenist is too good a
Christian not to respect powers inaugurated from above. The

---

[1] Aubertin, *ibid.* 180, 362.

parliamentarian, conservative through his profession, would be horrified at overthrowing the established order of things. Both combat for tradition and against innovation; hence, after having defended the past against arbitrary power they are to defend it against revolutionary violence, and to fall, the one into impotency and the other into oblivion.

II.

Accordingly, the conflagration is of slow growth among the middle class, and, to ensure its spreading, a gradual transformation has to be effected beforehand to render the refractory materials combustible. In the eighteenth century a great change takes place in the condition of the Third-Estate. The bourgeois has labored, manufactured, traded, earned and saved money, and he has daily become richer and richer.[1] This great expansion of enterprises, of trade, of speculation and of fortunes dates from Law; arrested by war it reappears with more vigor and more animation at each interval of peace after the treaty of Aix-la-Chapelle in 1748, and that of Paris in 1763, and especially after the beginning of the reign of Louis XVI. The exports of France which amounted to one hundred and six millions in 1720, to one hundred and twenty-four millions in 1735, and to one hundred and ninety-two millions in 1748, amount to two hundred and fifty-seven millions in 1755, to three hundred and nine millions in 1776, and to three hundred and fifty-four millions in 1788. In 1786 St. Domingo alone sends to the metropolis one hundred and thirty-one millions of its products, and takes back fifty-four millions in merchandise. As an effect of these interchanges we see arising at Nantes, and at Bordeaux, colossal commercial houses. I consider Bordeaux, says Arthur Young, as richer and doing more business than any city in England except London; . . . of late years the progress of maritime commerce has

---

[1] Voltaire, "Siècle de Louis XV.," ch. xxxi; "Siècle de Louis XIV.," ch. xxx. "Industry increases every day. To see the private display, the prodigious number of pleasant dwellings erected in Paris and in the provinces, the numerous equipages, the conveniences, the acquisitions comprehended in the term *luxe*, one might suppose that opulence was twenty times greater than it formerly was. All this is the result of ingenuity, much more than of wealth. . . . The middle class has become wealthy by industry. Commercial gains have augmented. The opulence of the great is less than it was formerly and much larger among the middle class, the distance between men even being lessened by it. Formerly the inferior class had no resource but to serve their superiors; nowadays industry has opened up a thousand roads unknown a hundred years ago."

been more rapid in France than even in England.[1] According
to an administrator of the day, if the taxes on the consumption
of products daily increase the revenue, it is owing to various
descriptions of industry having become greatly extended since
1774.[2] And this progress is regular and constant. "We may
calculate," says Necker in 1781, "on an increase of two millions a
year on all the duties on consumption." In this great effort of
invention, labor and genius, Paris, constantly growing, is the
central workshop. It enjoys, to a much greater extent than to-
day, the monopoly of all works of intelligence and taste, books,
pictures, engravings, statues, jewelry, toilet details, carriages,
furniture, articles of fashion and rarity, whatever affords pleasure
and ornamentation for an elegant worldly society; all Europe is
thus supplied by it. In 1774 its trade in books is estimated at
forty-five millions, and that of London at only one-quarter of
that sum.[3] Many immense fortunes were accumulated, and a
still larger number of moderate fortunes, while the capital thus
increasing sought investment. The highest in the kingdom are
standing ready with outstretched hands to obtain it, nobles,
princes of the blood, provincial assemblies, assemblies of the
clergy, and, at the head of all, the king, who, the most needy,
borrows at ten per cent., and is always in quest of fresh lenders.
Already under Fleury, the debt has augmented to eighteen
millions in *rentes,* and during the Seven Years' War, to thirty-four
millions. Under Louis XVI. M. Necker borrows a capital of
five hundred and thirty millions; M. Joly de Fleury, three hundred millions; M. de Calonne, eight hundred millions; in all
sixteen hundred and thirty millions in a peroid of ten years.
The interest of the public debt, only forty-five millions in 1755,
reaches one hundred and six millions in 1776 and amounts to
two hundred and six millions in 1789.[4] What creditors are indicated by these few figures! As the Third-Estate, it must be noted,
is the sole body that makes and saves money, nearly all these
creditors belong to it. Thousands of others must be added to
these. In the first place, the financiers who make advances to

---

[1] Arthur Young, II. 360, 373.

[2] De Tocqueville, 255.

[3] Aubertin, 482.

[4] Roux and Buchez, "Histoire parlementaire." Extracted from the accounts made up by
the comptrollers-general, I. 175, 205. The report by Necker, I. 376. To the 206,000,000
must be added 15,800,000 for expenses and interest on advances.

the government, advances that are indispensable, because, from time immemorial, it has eaten the calf in the cow's belly, while the passing year is always gnawing into the product of coming years; there are eighty millions of advances in 1759, and one hundred and seventy millions in 1783. In the second place there are so many purveyors, large and small, who, on all points of the territory, keep accounts with the government for their supplies and for public works, a veritable army and increasing daily, since the government, impelled by centralization, takes sole charge of all enterprises, and, through the urgency of opinion, fosters works of public utility. Under Louis XV. the State builds six thousand leagues of roads, and under Louis XVI. in 1788, to guard against famine, it purchases grain to the amount of forty millions.

Through this increase of activity and its demands for capital it becomes the universal debtor; henceforth public affairs are no longer exclusively the king's affairs. His creditors become uneasy at his expenditures ; for it is their money he wastes, and, if he proves a bad administrator, they will be ruined. They want to know something of his budget, to examine his books ; a lender always has the right to look after his securities. We accordingly see the bourgeois raising his head and beginning to pay 'close attention to the great machine whose performances, hitherto concealed from vulgar eyes, have, up to the present time, been kept a state secret. He becomes a politician, and, at the same time, discontented. For it cannot be denied that these matters, in which he is interested, are badly conducted. Any young man of good family managing affairs in the same way would be checked. The expenses of the administration of the State are always in excess of the revenue. According to official admissions[1] the annual deficit amounted to seventy millions in 1770, and eighty millions in 1783; the attempts to reduce this consist of bankruptcies; one of two millions at the end of the reign of Louis XIV., and others almost equal to it in the time of Law, and another from a third to a half of all the *rentes* in the time of Terray, without mentioning suppressions in detail, reductions, indefinite delays in payment, and other violent and fraudulent means which a powerful debtor employs with impunity against a feeble creditor. "Fifty-six violations of public faith

---

[1] Roux and Buchez, I. 190. "Rapport," by M. de Calonne.

have occurred from Henry IV. down to the ministry of M. de Loménie inclusive,"[1] while a last bankruptcy, more frightful than the others, looms up on the horizon. Several persons, Bezenval and Linguet for instance, earnestly recommend it as a necessary and salutary amputation. Not only are there precedents for this, and in this respect the government will do no more than follow its own example, but such is its daily practice, since it lives only from day to day, by dint of expedients and delays, digging one hole to stop up another, and escaping failure only through the forced patience which it imposes on its creditors. With it, says a contemporary, people were never sure of anything, being obliged always to wait.[2] "Were their capital invested in its loans, they could never rely on a fixed epoch for the payment of interest. Were vessels reconstructed, the highways repaired, or the soldiers clothed, they remained without guarantees for their advances, without certificates of repayment, being reduced to calculating the chances of a ministerial contract as they would the risks of a bold speculation." It pays if it can and only when it can, even the members of the household, the purveyors of the table and the personal attendants of the king. In 1753 the domestics of Louis XV. had received nothing for three years. We have seen how his grooms went out to beg during the night in the streets of Versailles; how his purveyors "hid themselves;" how, under Louis XVI. in 1778, there were 792,620 francs due to the wine-merchant, and 3,467,980 francs to the purveyor of fish and meat.[3] In 1788, so great is the distress, the Minister de Loménie appropriates and expends the funds of a private subscription raised for a hospital, and, at the time of his resignation, the treasury is empty, save four hundred and fifty thousand francs, the half of which he puts in his pocket. What an administration!

In the presence of this debtor, evidently becoming insolvent, all people, far and near, interested in his business, consult together with alarm, and debtors are innumerable, consisting of bankers, merchants, manufacturers, employés, lenders of every kind and degree, and, in the front rank, the fund-holders, who

---

[1] Champfort, p. 105.
[2] De Tocqueville, 261.
[3] D'Argenson, April 12, 1752, February 11, 1752, July 24, 1753, December 7, 1753. Archives nationales, O¹, 738.

have put all their means for life into his hands, and who are to beg should he not pay them annually the forty-four millions he owes them; the industrialists and traders who have intrusted their commercial integrity to him and who would shrink with horror from failure as its issue; and after these come their creditors, their clerks, their kindred, in short, the largest portion of the laboring and peaceable class which, thus far, had obeyed without a murmur and never dreamed of bringing the established order of things under its control. Henceforth this class will exercise control attentively, distrustfully and angrily. Woe to those who are at fault, for they well know that the ruin of the State is their ruin.

III.

Meanwhile this class has climbed up the social ladder, and, through its *élite*, rejoined those in the highest position. Formerly between Dorante and M. Jourdain, between Don Juan and M. Dimanche,[1] between M. de Sotenville himself and Georges Dandin, the interval was immense; everything was different—dress, house, habits, characters, points of honor, ideas and language. On the one hand the nobles are drawn nearer to the Third-Estate and, on the other, the Third-Estate is drawn nearer to the nobles, actual equality having preceded equality as a right.

On the approach of the year 1789 it was difficult to distinguish one from the other in the street. The sword is no longer worn by gentlemen in the city; they have abandoned embroideries and laces, and walk about in plain frock-coats, or drive themselves in their cabriolets.[2] "The simplicity of English customs," and the customs of the Third Estate seem to them better adapted to ordinary life. Their prominence proves irksome to them and they grow weary of being always on parade. Henceforth they accept familiarity that they may enjoy freedom of action, and are content "to mingle with their fellow-citizens without obstacle or ostentation." It is certainly a grave sign, and the old feudal spirits have reason to tremble. The Marquis de Mirabeau, on learning that his son wishes to act as his own lawyer, consoles himself by seeing others, of still higher rank, do much worse.[3]

---

[1] Characters in Molière's comedies.—Tr.
[2] De Ségur. I. 17.
[3] Luças de Montigny, Letter of the Marquis de Mirabeau, March 23, 1783.

"Although it was difficult to accept the idea of the grandson of our grandfather, as we saw him pass by at the court, the whole crowd, little and big, raising their hats to him afar off, now about to figure at the bar of a lower tribunal, contending about matters of practice with the barking dogs of chicanery, I said to myself that Louis XIV. would be still more astonished could he see the wife of his grand-successor dressed in a peasant's frock and apron, with no attendants, not a page or any one else, running about the palace and the terraces, requesting the first scamp in a frock-coat she encountered to give her his hand, which he simply does down to the foot of the steps." An equalization of the ways and externals of life is, indeed, only a manifestation of the equalization of minds and tempers. The antique scenery being torn away indicates the disappearance of the sentiments to which it belonged. It betokened gravity, dignity, habits of self-constraint and of living in public, authority and command. It was the rigid and ostentatious parade of a social corps of staff-officers. At this time the parade is discontinued because the corps has been dissolved. If the nobles dress like the bourgeoisie it is owing to their having become bourgeois, that is to say, idlers retired from business, with nothing to do but to talk and amuse themselves. Undoubtedly they amuse themselves and converse like people of refinement; but it is not very difficult to equal them in this respect. Now that the Third-Estate has acquired its wealth a good many plebeians have become people of society. The successors of Samuel Bernard are no longer so many Turcarets, but Paris-Duverneys, Saint-Jameses, Labordes, refined men, people of culture and of feeling, possessing tact, literary and philosophical attainments, benevolent, giving fêtes and knowing how to entertain.[1] With them, with a shade of difference, we find about the same company as with a grand seignior, the same ideas and the same tone. Their sons, Messieurs de Villemer, de Francueil, d'Epinay, throw money out of the window with as much elegance as the young dukes with whom they sup. A parvenu with money and intellect soon becomes brightened, and his son, if not himself, is

---

[1] Mme. Vigée-Lebrun, I. 269, 231. The domestic establishment of two farmers-general, (M. de Verdun, at Colombes, and M. de St. James, at Neuilly). A superior type of the bourgeois and of the merchant has already been put on the stage by Sedame in "Le Philosophe sans le Savoir."

initiated: a few years' exercises in an academy, a dancing-master, and one of the four thousand public offices which confer nobility, supply him with the deficient externals. Now, in these times, as soon as one knows how to conform to the laws of good-breeding, how to bow and how to converse, one possesses a patent for admission everywhere. An Englishman [1] remarks that one of the first expressions employed in praise of a man is, "he has a very graceful address." The Maréchale de Luxembourg, so high-spirited, always selects La Harpe as her cavalier, because "he offers his arm so well." The plebeian not only enters the drawing-room, if he is fitted for it, but he stands foremost in it if he has any talent. The first place in conversation, and even in public consideration, is for Voltaire, the son of a notary, for Diderot, the son of a cutler, for Rousseau, the son of a watchmaker, for d'Alembert, a foundling brought up by a glazier; and, after the great men have disappeared, and no writers of the second grade are left, the leading duchesses are still content to have the seats at their tables occupied by Champfort, another foundling, Beaumarchais, the son of another watchmaker, La Harpe, supported and raised on charity, Marmontel, the son of a village tailor, and many others of less note, in short, every parvenu possessing any intellectual power.

The nobility, to perfect their own accomplishments, borrow their pens and aspire to their successes. " We have recovered from those old Gothic and absurd prejudices against literary culture," says the Prince de Hénin; [2] " as for myself I would compose a comedy to-morrow if I had the talent, and if I happened to be made a little angry, I would perform in it." And, in fact, " the Vicomte de Ségur, son of the minister of war, plays the part of the lover in ' Nina' on Mlle. de Guimard's stage with the actors of the Italian Comedy." [3] One of Mme. de Genlis's personages, returning to Paris after five years' absence, says that " he left men wholly devoted to play, hunting, and their small houses, and he finds them all turned authors." [4] They

---

[1] John Andrews, "A comparative view," etc., p. 58.
[2] De Tilly, "Mémoires," I. 31.
[3] Geffroy, "Gustave III," Letter of Mme. de Staël (August, 1786).
[4] Mme. de Genlis, "Adèle et Théodore" (1782), I. 312. Already in 1762, Bachaumont mentions several pieces written by grand seigniors, such as "Clytemnestre," by the Comte de Lauraguais; "Alexandre," by the Chevalier de Fénélon; "Don Carlos," by the Marquis de Ximines.

hawk about their tragedies, comedies, novels, eclogues, dissertations and treatises of all kinds from one drawing-room to
another. They strive to get their pieces played ; they previously
submit them to the judgment of actors ; they solicit a word of
praise from the *Mercure ;* they read fables at the sittings of the
Academy. They become involved in the bickerings, in the vain-
glory, in the littleness of literary life, and still worse, of the life
of the stage, inasmuch as they are themselves performers and
play in company with real actors in hundreds of private theatres.
Add to this, if you please, other petty amateur talents such as
sketching in water-colors, writing songs, and playing the flute.

After this intermixture of classes and this displacement of character what superiority rests with the nobles ? By what special
merit, through what recognized capacity are they to secure the
respect of a member of the Third-Estate ? Outside of fashionable elegance and a few points of breeding, in what respect do
they differ from him ? What superior education, what familiarity
with affairs, what experience with government, what political instruction, what local ascendancy, what moral authority can be alleged to sanction their pretensions to the highest places ? In the
way of practice, the Third-Estate already does the work, providing the qualified men, the intendants, the ministerial head-
clerks, the lay and ecclesiastical administrators, the competent
laborers of all kinds and degrees. Call to mind the Marquis of
whom we have just spoken, a former captain in the French guards,
a man of feeling and of loyalty, admitting at the elections of 1789
that " the knowledge essential to a deputy would most generally
be found in the Third-Estate, the mind there being accustomed
to business." In the way of theory: the plebeian is as well-
informed as the noble, and he thinks he is still better informed,
because, having read the same books and arrived at the same
principles, he does not, like him, stop half-way on the road to
their consequences, but plunges headlong to the very depths of
the doctrine, convinced that his logic is clairvoyance and that he
is the more enlightened because he is the least prejudiced. Consider the young men who, about twenty years of age in 1780,
born in industrious families, accustomed to effort and able to
work twelve hours a day, a Barnave, a Carnot, a Rœderer, a
Merlin de Thionville, a Robespierre, an energetic race, feeling
their strength, criticizing their rivals, aware of their weakness, com-

paring their own application and education to their levity and incompetency, and, at the moment when youthful ambition stirs within them, seeing themselves excluded in advance from any superior position, consigned for life to subaltern employment, and subjected in every career to the precedence of superiors whom they hardly recognize as their equals. At the artillery examinations where Chérin, the genealogist, refuses plebeians, and where the Abbé Bosen, a mathematician, rejects the ignorant, it is discovered that capacity is wanting among the noble pupils and nobility among the capable pupils,[1] the two qualities of gentility and intelligence seeming to exclude each other, as there are but four or five out of a hundred pupils who combine the two conditions. Now, as society at this time is mixed, such tests are frequent and easy. Whether lawyer, physician, or man of letters, a member of the Third-Estate with whom a duke converses familiarly, who sits in a diligence alongside of a count-colonel of hussars,[2] can appreciate his companion or his interlocutor, weigh his ideas, test his merit and esteem him at his just value, and I am sure that he does not overrate him. The nobility having lost a special capacity, and the Third-Estate having acquired a general capacity, they are on a par in education and in aptitudes, the inequality which separated them becoming offensive in becoming useless. Nobility being instituted by custom it is no longer sanctified by conscience ; the Third-Estate being justly excited against privileges that have no justification, whether in the capacity of the noble or in the incapacity of the bourgeois.

IV.

Distrust and wrath towards the government which compromises all fortunes, rancor and hostility against the nobility which bars all roads, are, then, the sentiments that develop themselves in the middle class solely through the advance of its wealth and culture. Acting on material of this description we can divine the effect of the new philosophy. At first, confined to the aristocratic reservoir, the doctrine filters out through all interstices like so many trickling streams, and insensibly diffuses itself among the lower class. Already, in 1727, Barbier, a bourgeois of the old stock

---

[1] Champfort, 119.
[2] De Vaublanc, I. 117. Beugnot, "Mémoires," (the first and second passages relating to society at the domiciles of M. de Brienne, and the Duc de Penthièvre.)

and having little knowledge of philosophy and philosophers except the name, thus writes in his journal: "A hundred poor families are deprived of the annuities on which they supported themselves, acquired with bonds for which the king is responsible and of which the capital is obliterated; fifty-six thousand livres are given in pensions to people who have held the best offices, where they have amassed considerable property, always at the expense of the people, and all this merely that they may rest themselves and do nothing."[1] One by one, reformative ideas penetrate to his office of consulting advocate; conversation has sufficed to propagate them, homely common sense needing no philosophy to secure their recognition. "The tax on property," said he, in 1750, "should be proportioned and equally distributed among all the king's subjects and the members of the government, in proportion to the property each really possesses in the kingdom; in England, the lands of the nobility, the clergy and the Third-Estate pay alike without distinction, and nothing is more just." In the six years which follow the flood increases. People denounce the government in the cafés, on their promenades, while the police dare not arrest malcontents "because they would have to arrest everybody." The disaffection goes on increasing up to the end of the reign. In 1744, says the bookseller Hardy, during the king's illness at Metz, private individuals cause six thousand masses to be said for his recovery and pay for them at the sacristy of Notre Dame; in 1757, after Damiens's attempt on the king's life, the number of masses demanded is only six hundred; in 1774, during the malady which carries him off, the number falls down to three. The complete discredit of the government, the immense success of Rousseau, these two events, occurring simultaneously, afford a date for the conversion of the Third-Estate to philosophy.[2] A traveller, at the beginning of the reign of Louis XVI., who returns home after some years' absence, on being asked what change he noticed in the nation, replied, "*Nothing, except that what used to be talked about*

---

[1] Barbier, II. *ibid.*; III. 255 (May, 1751). "The king is robbed by all the seigniors around him, especially on his journeys to his different chateaux, which are frequent." And September, 1750. Cf. Aubertin, 291, 415 ("Mémoires," manuscript by Hardy).

[2] Treaties of Paris and Hubersbourg, 1763. The trial of La Chalotais, 1765. Bankruptcy of Terray, 1770. Destruction of the Parliament, 1771. The first partition of Poland, 1772. Rousseau, "Discours sur l'inégalité," 1753. "Héloise," 1759. "Emile" and "Contrat Social," 1762.

in the drawing-rooms is repeated in the streets.[1] And that which is repeated in the streets is Rousseau's doctrine, the Discourse on Inequality, the Social Contract amplified, popularized and repeated by disciples in every tone and in every shape. What is more fascinating for the man of the Third-Estate? Not only is this theory in vogue, and encountered by him at the decisive moment when, for the first time, he turns his attention to general principles, but again it provides him with arms against social inequality and political absolutism, and much sharper than he needs. To people disposed to put restraints on power and to abolish privileges, what guide is more sympathetic than the writer of genius, the powerful logician, the impassioned orator, who establishes natural law, who repudiates historic law, who proclaims the equality of men, who contends for the sovereignty of the people, who denounces on every page the usurpation, the vices, the worthlessness, the malefactions of the great and of kings! And I omit the points by which he makes acceptable to a rigid and laborious *bourgeoisie*, to the new men that are working and advancing themselves, his steady earnestness, his harsh and bitter tone, his eulogy of simple habits, of domestic virtues, of personal merit, of virile energy, the plebeian addressing plebeians. It is not surprising that they should accept him for a guide and welcome his doctrines with that fervor of faith which constitutes enthusiasm, and which is always an accompaniment of the new-born idea as of the new-born affection.

A competent judge, and an eye-witness, Mallet Dupan, writes in 1799: "Rousseau had a hundred times more readers among the middle and lower classes than Voltaire. He alone inoculated the French with the doctrine of the sovereignty of the people and with its extremest consequences. It would be difficult to cite a single revolutionist who was not transported over these anarchical theories, and who did not burn with ardor to realize them. That *Contrat Social*, the disintegrator of societies, was the Koran of the pretentious talkers of 1789, of the Jacobins of 1790, of the republicans of 1791, and of the most atrocious of the madmen. . . . I heard Marat in 1788 read and comment on the *Contrat Social* in the public streets to the applause of an enthusiastic auditory." The same year, in an immense throng filling the great

---

[1] De Barante, "Tableau de la littérature française au dix-huitième siècle," 312.

hall of the Palais de Justice, Lacretelle hears the same book cited, its dogmas enforced "by members of the bar,[1] by young lawyers, by the whole lettered tribe swarming with new-fledged publicists." Hundreds of details show us that it is a catechism in every hand. In 1784[2] certain magistrates' sons, on taking their first lesson in jurisprudence of an assistant professor, M. Saveste, have the "Contrat Social" placed in their hands as a manual. Those who find this new political geometry too difficult learn at least its axioms, and if these prove unmanageable they derive from them their palpable consequences, so many convenient equivalents, the small current change of the literature in vogue, whether drama, history, or romance.[3] The dogmas of equality and liberty infiltrate and penetrate the class able to read the "Eloges" by Thomas, the pastorals of Bernardin de St. Pierre, the compilation of Raynal, the comedies of Beaumarchais and even the "Young Anarcharsis" and the literature of the resuscitated Greek and Roman antiquity.[4] "A few days ago," says Métra,[5] "a dinner of forty ecclesiastics from the country took place at the house of the curate of Orangis, five leagues from Paris. At the dessert, and in the truth which came out over their wine, they all admitted that they came to Paris to see the 'Marriage of Figaro.' . . . Up to the present time it seems as if comic authors intended to make sport for the great at the expense of the little, but here, on the contrary, it is the little who laugh at the expense of the great." Hence the success of the piece. A steward of a chateau finds a Raynal in the library, the furious declamation of which so delights him that, at the end of thirty years, he can repeat it without stumbling. A sergeant in the French guards embroiders waistcoats throughout the night to earn the wherewithal to purchase new books of this stamp. After the gallant picture of the boudoir comes the austere and patriotic picture; "Belisarius" and the "Horatii" of David indicate the new public spirit, also that of the studios.[6] The spirit is that of Rousseau, "the re-

---

[1] Lacretelle, "Dix ans d'épreuves," p. 21.

[2] "Souvenirs manuscrits," by M——.

[3] "Le Compère Mathieu," by Dulaurens (1766). "Our sufferings are due to the way in which we are brought up, namely, the state of society in which we are born. Now that state being the source of all our ills its dissolution must become that of all our good."

[4] The "Tableau de Paris," by Mercier (12 vols.), is the completest and most exact portrayal of the ideas and aspirations of the middle class from 1781 to 1788.

[5] "Correspondance," by Métra, XVII. 87 (August 20, 1784).

[6] "Belisarius," belongs to 1780, and the "Oath of the Horatii," to 1783.

publican spirit;"[1] the entire middle class, artists, employés, curates, physicians, attorneys, advocates, the lettered and the journalists, all are won over to it; and its aliment consists of the worst as well as the worthiest passions, ambition, envy, craving for liberty, zeal for the public welfare and the consciousness of right.

V.

All these passions intensify each other. There is nothing like a wrong to quicken the sentiment of justice. There is nothing like the sentiment of justice to quicken the injury proceeding from a wrong. The Third-Estate, considering itself deprived of the place to which it is entitled, finds itself uncomfortable in the place it occupies and, accordingly, suffers through a thousand petty grievances it would not, formerly, have noticed. On discovering that he is a citizen a man is irritated at being treated as a subject, no one accepting an inferior position alongside of one of whom he believes himself the equal. Hence, during a period of twenty years, the ancient régime vainly grows easier, seeming to be still more burdensome, while its scratches exasperate as if they were so many wounds. Countless instances might be quoted instead of one. At the theatre in Grenoble, Barnave,[2] a child, is with his mother in a box which the Duc de Tonnerre, governor of the province, had assigned to one of his satellites. The manager of the theatre, and next an officer of the guard, request Madame Barnave to withdraw. She refuses, whereupon the governor orders four fusileers to force her out. The pit had already taken the matter up, and violence was feared, when M. Barnave, advised of the affront, entered and led his wife away, exclaiming aloud, "I leave by order of the governor." The indignant public, all the bourgeoisie, agreed among themselves not to enter the theatre again without an apology being made; the theatre, in fact, remaining empty several months, until Madame Barnave consented to reappear there. This outrage afterwards recurred to the future deputy, and he then swore "to elevate the caste to which he belonged out of the humiliation to which it seemed

---

[1] Geffroy, "Gustave III. et la cour de France." "Paris, with *its republican spirit,* generally applauds whatever fails at Fontainebleau." (A letter by Madame de Staël, Sept. 17, 1786).

[2] Sainte-Beuve, "Causeries du Lundi," II. 24, in the article on Barnave.

condemned." In like manner Lacroix, the future member of the Convention,[1] on leaving a theatre, and jostled by a gentleman who was giving his arm to a lady, utters a loud complaint. "Who are you?" says the person. Still the provincial, he is simple enough to give his name, surname, and qualifications in full. "Very well," says the other man, "good for you—I am the Comte de Chabannes, and I am in a hurry," saying which, "laughing heartily," he jumps into his vehicle. "Ah, sir," exclaimed Lacroix, still much excited by his misadventure, "pride and prejudice establish an awful gulf between man and man!" We may rest assured that, with Marat, a veterinary surgeon in the Comte d'Artois's stables, with Robespierre, a protegé of the bishop of Arras, with Danton, an insignificant lawyer in Mery-sur-Seine, and with many others beside, self-esteem, in frequent encounters, bled in the same fashion. The concentrated bitterness with which Madame Roland's memoirs are imbued has no other cause. "She could not forgive society[2] for the inferior position she had so long occupied in it."[3] Thanks to Rousseau, vanity, so natural to man, and especially sensitive with a Frenchman, becomes still more sensitive. The slightest discrimination, a tone of the voice, seems a mark of disdain. "One day,[4] on alluding, before the minister of war, to a general officer who had obtained his rank through his merit, he exclaimed, 'Oh, yes, an officer of luck.' This expression, being repeated and commented on, does much mischief." In vain do the grandees show their condescending spirit, "welcoming with equal kindness and gen-

---

[1] De Tilly, "Mémoires," I. 243.

[2] The words of Fontanes, who knew her and admired her. (Sainte-Beuve, "Nouveaux Lundis," VIII. 221).

[3] "Mémoires de Madame Roland," *passim*. At fourteen years of age, on being introduced to Mme. de Boismorel, she is hurt at hearing her grandmother addressed "Mademoiselle." Shortly after this, she says: "I could not conceal from myself that I was of more consequence than Mlle. d'Hannaches, whose sixty years and her genealogy did not enable her to write a common-sense letter or one that was legible." About the same epoch she passes a week at Versailles with a servant of the Dauphine, and tells her mother, "'A few days more and I shall so detest these people that I shall not know how to suppress my hatred of them.' 'What injury have they done you?' she inquires. 'It is the feeling of injustice and the constant contemplation of absurdity!'" At the chateau of Fontenay where she is invited to dine, she and her mother are made to dine in the servants' room, etc. "In 1818, in a small town in the north, the Comte de —— dining with a bourgeois sub-prefect and placed by the side of the mistress of the house, says to her, on accepting the soup, 'Thanks, my dear,' (merci, ma chère). Through the Revolution the lower class bourgeoisie have full play; a moment after, she addresses him, with one of her sweetest smiles, 'Will you take some chicken, my dear?'" (It is useless to state that the sense of this anecdote is not fully conveyed by a literal translation.)—TR.

[4] De Vaublanc, I. 153.

tleness all who are presented to them." In the mansion of the Duc de Penthièvre the nobles eat at the table of the master of the house, the plebeians dine with his first gentleman and only enter the drawing-room when coffee is served. There they find "in full strength and with a high tone" the others who had the honor of dining with His Highness, and "who do not fail to salute the new arrivals with a complacency instinct with patronage."[1] This suffices; in vain the Duke "carries his attentions even to the most minute degree." Beugnot, so pliable, has no desire to return. They bear them ill-will, not only on account of their slight bows but again on account of their over-politeness. Champfort acrimoniously relates that d'Alembert, at the height of his reputation, being in Madame du Deffant's drawing-room with President Hénault and M. de Pont-de-Veyle, a physician enters named Fournier, and he, addressing Madame du Deffant, says, "Madame, I have the honor of presenting you with my very humble respects;" turning to President Hénault, "I have the honor to be your obedient servant," and then to M. de Pont-de-Veyle, "Sir, your most obedient," and to d'Alembert, "Good day, sir."[2] To a rebellious heart everything is an object of resentment. The Third-Estate, following Rousseau's example, cherishes ill-feeling against the nobles for what they do, and yet again, for what they are, for their luxury, their elegance, their insincerity, their refined and brilliant behavior. Champfort is embittered against them on account of the polite attentions with which they overwhelm him. Sieyès bears them a grudge on account of a promised abbey which he did not obtain. Each individual, besides the general grievances, has his personal grievance. Their coolness, like their familiarity, attentions and inattentions, is an offence, and, under these millions of needle-thrusts, real or imaginary, the mind gets to be full of gall.

In 1789, it is full to overflowing. "The most honorable title of the French nobility," writes Champfort, "is a direct descent from some thirty thousand helmeted, cuirassed, armletted beings

---

[1] Beugnot, "Mémoires," I. 77.

[2] Champfort, 16. "Who would believe it? Not taxation, nor *lettres-de-cachet*, nor the abuses of power, nor the vexations of intendants, and the ruinous delays of justice have provoked the ire of the nation, but their prejudices against the nobility towards which it has shown the greatest hatred. This evidently proves that the bourgeoisie, the men of letters, the financial class, in fine all who envy the nobles have excited against these the inferior class in the towns and among the rural peasantry." (Rivarol, "Mémoires.")

who, on heavy horses sheathed in armor, trod under foot eight or
ten millions of naked men, the ancestors of the actual nation.
Behold these well-established claims to the respect and affection
of their descendants! And, to complete the respectability of this
nobility, it is recruited and regenerated by the adoption of those
who have acquired fortune by plundering the cabins of the poor
who are unable to pay its impositions."[1] "Why should not the
Third-Estate send back," says Sieyès,[2] "into Franconia every
family that maintains its absurd pretension of having sprung from
the loins of a race of conquerors, and of having succeeded to
the rights of conquest? I can well imagine, were there no
police, every Cartouche firmly establishing himself on the highroad—would that give him a right to levy toll? Suppose him to
sell a monopoly of this kind, once common enough, to an honest
successor, would the right become any more respectable in the
hands of the purchaser? . . . Every privilege, in its nature, is
unjust, odious, and against the social compact. The blood boils
at the thought of its ever having been possible to legally conse-
crate down to the eighteenth century the abominable fruits of an
abominable feudal system. . . . The caste of nobles is really
a population apart, a fraudulent population, however, which, for
lack of serviceable faculties, and unable to exist alone, fastens
itself upon a living nation, like the vegetable tumors that support themselves on the sap of the plants to which they are a
burden, and which wither beneath the load. . . . They suck all,
everything being for them. . . . Every branch of the executive
power has fallen into the hands of this caste, which (formerly)
supplied the church, the robe and the sword. A sort of confra-
ternity or joint paternity leads the nobles each to prefer the other
and all to the rest of the nation. . . . The Court reigns, and
not the monarch. The Court creates and distributes offices.
And what is the Court but the head of this vast aristocracy that
covers all parts of France, and which, through its members, attains to and exercises everywhere whatever is requisite in all
branches of the public administration?"[3] Let us put an end to
"this social crime, this long parricide which one class does itself

---

[1] Champfort, 335.
[2] Sieyès, "Qu'est ce que le Tiers?" 17, 41, 139, 166.
[3] "The nobility, say the nobles, is an intermediary between the king and the people. Yes,
as the hound is an intermediary between the hunter and the hare." (Champfort).

the honor to commit daily against the others. . . . Ask no longer what place the privileged shall occupy in the social order; it is simply asking what place in a sick man's body must be assigned to a malignant ulcer that is undermining and tormenting it . . . to the loathsome disease that is consuming the living flesh." The result is apparent—let us eradicate the ulcer, or at least sweep away the vermin. The Third-Estate, in itself and by itself, is "a complete nation," requiring no organ, needing no aid to subsist or to govern itself, and which will recover its health on ridding itself of the parasites infesting its skin. "What is the Third-Estate? Everything. What, thus far, is it in the political body? Nothing. What does it demand? To become something." Not a portion but the whole. Its political ambition is as great as its social ambition, and it aspires to authority as well as to equality. If privileges are an evil that of the king is the worst for it is the greatest, and human dignity, wounded by the prerogative of the noble, perishes under the absolutism of the king. Of little consequence is it that he scarcely uses it, and that his government, deferential to public opinion, is that of a hesitating and indulgent parent. Emancipated from real despotism, the Third Estate becomes excited against possible despotism, imagining itself in slavery in consenting to remain subject. A proud spirit has recovered itself, become erect, and, the better to secure its rights, is going to claim all rights. To the man who from antiquity down has been subject to masters, it is so sweet, so intoxicating to be in their places, to say to himself, they are my mandataries, to regard himself a member of the sovereign power, king of France in his individual sphere, the sole legitimate author of all rights and of all functions! In conformity with the doctrines of Rousseau the memorials of the Third-Estate unanimously insist on a constitution for France; none exists, or at least the one she possesses is of no value. Thus far "the conditions of the social compact have been ignored;"[1] now that they have been discovered they must be written out. To say, with the nobles according to Montesquieu, that the constitution exists, that its great features need not be changed, that it is necessary only to reform abuses, that the States-General exercise only limited power, that they are incompetent to

---

[1] Prud'homme, III. 2. ("The Third-Estate of Nivernais," *passim.*) Cf., on the other hand, the memorials of the nobility of Bugey and of Alençon.

substitute another régime for the monarchy, is not true. Tacitly or expressly, the Third-Estate refuses to restrict its mandate and allows no barriers to be interposed against it. It requires its deputies accordingly to vote " not by orders but each by himself and conjointly." " In case the deputies of the clergy or of the nobility should refuse to deliberate in common and individually, the deputies of the Third-Estate, representing twenty-four millions of men, able and obliged to declare itself the National Assembly, notwithstanding the scission of the representation of four hundred thousand persons, will propose to the King in concert with those among the Clergy and the Nobility disposed to join them, their assistance in providing for the necessities of the State, and the taxes thus assented to shall be apportioned among all the subjects of the king without distinction." [1] Do not object that a people thus mutilated becomes a mere crowd, that leaders cannot be improvised, that it is difficult to dispense with natural guides, that, considering all things, this Clergy and this Nobility still form a select group, that two-fifths of the soil is in their hands, that one-half of the intelligent and cultivated class of men are in their ranks, that they are exceedingly well-disposed and that old historic bodies have always afforded to liberal constitutions their best supports. According to the principle enunciated by Rousseau we are not to value men but to count them. In politics numbers only are respectable; neither birth, nor property, nor function, nor capacity, is a title to be considered; high or low, ignorant or learned, a general, a soldier, or a hod-carrier, each individual of the social army is a unit provided with a vote; wherever a majority is found there is the right. Hence, the Third-Estate puts forth its right as incontestable, and, in its turn, it proclaims with Louis XIV., " I am the State."

This principle once admitted or enforced, all will go well. "It seemed," says an eye-witness,[2] "as if we were about to be governed by men of the golden age. This free, just and wise people, always in harmony with itself, always clear-sighted in choosing its ministers, moderate in the use of its strength and power, never could be led away, never deceived, never under the dominion of, or enslaved by, the authority which it confided. Its will would fashion the laws and the law would constitute its happiness."

---

[1] Prud'homme, *ibid.*, *Cahiers* of the Third-Estates of Dijon, Dax, Bayonne, Saint-Sévère, Rennes, etc.

[2] Marmontel, "Mémoires," II. 247.

The nation is to be *regenerated*, a phrase found in all writings and in every mouth. At Nangis, Arthur Young finds this the substance of political conversation.[1] The chaplain of a regiment, a curate in the vicinity, keeps fast hold of it; as to knowing what it means that is another matter. It is impossible to find anything out through explanations of it otherwise than "a theoretic perfection of government, questionable in its origin, hazardous in its progress, and visionary in its end." On the Englishman proposing to them the British constitution as a model they "hold it cheap in respect of liberty" and greet it with a smile; it is, especially, not in conformity with "the principles." And observe that we are at the residence of a grand seignior, in a circle of enlightened men. At Riom, at the *election* assemblies,[2] Malouet finds "persons of an ordinary stamp, practitioners, petty lawyers, with no experience of public business, quoting the 'Contrat Social,' vehemently declaiming against tyranny, and each proposing his own constitution." Most of them are without any knowledge whatever, mere traffickers in chicane; the best instructed entertain mere schoolboy ideas of politics. In the colleges of the University no history is taught.[3] "The name of Henry IV., says Lavalette, was not once uttered during my eight years of study, and, at seventeen years of age, I was still ignorant of the epoch and the mode of the establishment of the Bourbons on the throne." The stock they carry away with them consists wholly, as with Camille Desmoulins, of scraps of Latin, entering the world with brains stuffed with "re publican maxims," excited by souvenirs of Rome and Sparta, and "penetrated with profound contempt for monarchical governments." Subsequently, at the law school, they learn something about legal abstractions, or else learn nothing. In the lecture-courses at Paris there are no auditors; the professor delivers his lecture to copyists who sell their copy-books. If a pupil should attend himself and take notes he would be regarded with suspicion; he would be charged with trying to deprive the copyists of the means of earning their living. A diploma, consequently, is worthless. At Bourges one is obtainable in six months; if the young man succeeds in comprehending the law it is through

---

[1] Arthur Young, I. 222.
[2] Malouet, "Mémoires," I. 279.
[3] De Lavalette, I. 7. "Souvenirs Manuscrits," by M——.

later practice and familiarity with it.   Of foreign laws and institutions there is not the least knowledge, scarcely even a vague
or false notion of them.   Malouet himself entertains a meagre
idea of the English Parliament, while many, with respect to ceremonial, imagine it a copy of the Parliament of France.   The mechanism of free constitutions, or the conditions of effective liberty,
that is too complicated a question.   Montesquieu, save in the great
magisterial families, is antiquated for twenty years past.   Of
what avail are studies of ancient France ?   "What is the result
of so much and such profound research ?   Laborious conjecture
and reasons for doubting."[1]   It is much more convenient to
start with the rights of man and to deduce the consequences.
Schoolboy logic suffices for that to which collegiate rhetoric supplies the tirades.

In this great void of enlightenment the vague terms of liberty,
equality and the sovereignty of the people, the glowing expressions of Rousseau and his successors, all these new axioms, blaze
up like burning coals, discharging clouds of smoke and intoxicating vapor.   High-sounding and vague language is interposed
between the mind and objects around it; all outlines are confused
and the vertigo begins.   Never to the same extent have men
lost the purport of outward things.   Never have they been at
once more blind and more chimerical.   Never has their disturbed
reason rendered them more tranquil concerning real danger and
created more alarm at imaginary danger.   Strangers with cool
blood and who witness the spectacle, Mallet-Dupan, Dumont
of Geneva, Arthur Young, Jefferson, Gouverneur Morris, write
that the French are insane.   Morris, in this universal delirium,
can mention to Washington but one sane mind, that of Marmontel,
and Marmontel speaks in the same style as Morris.   At the
preliminary meetings of the clubs, and at the assemblies of
electors, he is the only one who opposes unreasonable propositions.
Surrounding him are none but the excited, the exalted about
nothing, even to grotesqueness.[2]   In every act of the established
régime, in every administrative measure, " in all police regulations,
in all financial decrees, in all the graduated authorities on which
public order and tranquillity depend, there was nought in which
they did not find an aspect of tyranny. . . . On the walls and

---

[1] Prud'homme, "Résumé des cahiers," the "preface," by J. J. Rousseau.
[2] Marmontel, II. 245.

barriers of Paris being referred to, these were denounced as enclosures for deer and derogatory to man." " I saw," says one of these orators, " at the barrier Saint-Victor, sculptured on one of the pillars—would you believe it?—an enormous lion's head, with open jaws vomiting forth chains as a menace to those who passed it. Could a more horrible emblem of slavery and of despotism be imagined!" "The orator himself imitates the roar of the lion. The listeners were all excited by it and I, who passed the barrier Saint-Victor so often, was surprised that this horrible image had not struck me. That very day I examined it closely and, on the pilaster, I found only a small buckler suspended as an ornament by a little chain attached by the sculptor to a little lion's mouth, like those we see serving as door-knockers or as water-cocks." Perverted sensations and delirious conceptions of this kind would be regarded by physicians as the symptoms of mental derangement, and we are only in the early months of the year 1789! In such excitable and over-excited brains the powerful fascination of words is about to exorcise phantoms, some of them hideous, the aristocrat and the tyrant, and others adorable, the friend of the people and the incorruptible patriot, so many disproportionate figures fashioned in dreams, but the substitutes of figures in actual life, and which the maniac is to overwhelm with his praise or pursue with his fury.

VI.

Thus does the philosophy of the eighteenth century descend among the people and propagate itself. Ideas, on the first story of the house, in handsome gilded rooms, serve only as an evening illumination, as drawing-room explosives and pleasing Bengal lights, with which people amuse themselves, and then laughingly throw from the windows into the street. Collected together in the story below and on the ground floor, transported to shops, to warehouses and into business cabinets, they find combustible material, piles of wood a long time accumulated, and here do the flames enkindle. The conflagration seems to have already begun, for the chimneys roar and a ruddy light gleams through the windows; but " No," say the people above, "those below would take care not to set the house on fire, for they live in it as we do. It is only a straw bonfire or a burning chimney, and a little water will extinguish it; and, besides, these little accidents clear the chimney and burn out the soot."

Take care! Under the vast deep arches supporting it, in the cellars of the house, there is a magazine of powder.

BOOK FIFTH.

𝕮𝖍𝖊 𝕻𝖊𝖔𝖕𝖑𝖊.

CHAPTER I.

I. Privations.—Under Louis XIV.—Under Louis XV.—Under Louis XVI.—II. The condition of the peasant during the last thirty years of the Ancient Régime.—His precarious subsistence.—State of agriculture.—Uncultivated farms.—Poor cultivation.—Inadequate wages.—Lack of comforts. —III. Aspects of the country and of the peasantry.—IV. How the peasant becomes a proprietor.—He is no better off.—Increase of taxes.—He is the "mule" of the Ancient Régime.

I.

LA BRUYÈRE wrote, just a century before 1789,[1] "Certain savage-looking beings, male and female, are seen in the country, black, livid and sunburnt, and belonging to the soil which they dig and grub with invincible stubbornness. They seem capable of articulation, and, when they stand erect, they display human lineaments. They are, in fact, men. They retire at night into their dens where they live on black bread, water and roots. They spare other human beings the trouble of sowing, ploughing and harvesting, and thus should not be in want of the bread they have planted." They continue in want of it during twenty-five years after this, and die in herds. I estimate that in 1715 more than one-third of the population, six millions, perish with hunger and of destitution. The picture, accordingly, for the first quarter of the century preceding the Revolution, far from being overdrawn, is the reverse; we shall see that, during more than half a century, up to the death of Louis XV. it is exact; perhaps instead of weakening any of its points, they should be strengthened.

---

[1] La Bruyère, edition of Destailleurs, II. 97. Addition to the fourth ed. (1689).

"In 1725," says St. Simon, "with the profuseness of Strasbourg and Chantilly, the people, in Normandy, live on the grass
of the fields. The first king in Europe is great simply by being
a king of beggars of all conditions, and by turning his kingdom
into a vast hospital of dying people of whom their all is taken
without a murmur."[1] In the most prosperous days of Fleury
and in the finest region in France, the peasant hides "his wine on
account of the excise and his bread on account of the *taille*,"[2]
convinced "that he is a lost man if any doubt exists of his dying
of starvation."[3] In 1739 d'Argenson writes in his journal:[4]
"The famine has just occasioned three insurrections in the provinces, at Ruffec, at Caen, and at Chinon. Women carrying their
bread with them have been assassinated on the highways. . . .
M. le Duc d'Orléans brought to the Council the other day a
piece of bread, and placed it on the table before the king; 'Sire,'
said he, 'there is the bread on which your subjects now feed
themselves.'" "In my own canton of Touraine men have been
eating herbage more than a year." Misery finds company on
all sides. "It is talked about at Versailles more than ever. The
king interrogated the bishop of Chartres on the condition of his
people; he replied that 'the famine and the mortality were such
that men ate grass like sheep and died like so many flies.'" In
1740,[5] Massillon, bishop of Clermont-Ferrand, writes to Fleury:
"The people of the rural districts are living in frightful destitution, without beds, without furniture; the majority, for half the
year, even lack barley and oat bread, their sole food, and which
they are compelled to take out of their own and their childrens'
mouths to pay the taxes. It pains me to see this sad spectacle
every year on my visits. The negroes of our colonies are, in this

---

[1] Oppression and misery begin about 1672. At the end of the seventeenth century (1698),
the reports made up by the intendants for the Duc de Bourgogne, state that many of the
districts and provinces have lost one-sixth, one-fifth, one-quarter, the third and even the
half of their population. (See details in the "Correspondance des contrôleurs-généraux
from 1683 to 1698," published by M. de Boislisle). According to the reports of intendants,
(Vauban, "Dîme Royale," ch. vii. § 2.), the population of France in 1698 amounted to
19,994,146 inhabitants. From 1698 to 1715 it decreases. According to Forbonnais, there
were but 16 or 17 millions under the Regency. After this epoch the population no longer
diminishes but, for forty years, it hardly increases. In 1753 (Voltaire, "Dict. Phil.," article
Population), there are 3,550,499 firesides, besides 700,000 souls in Paris, which makes from
16 to 17 millions of inhabitants if we count four and one-half persons to each fireside, and
from 18 to 19 millions if we count five persons.

[2] Floquet, "Histoire du Parlement de Normandie," VII. 402.

[3] Rousseau, "Confessions," 1st part, ch. iv. (1732).

[4] D'Argenson, 19th and 24th May, July 4, and Aug. 1, 1739.

[5] "Résumé de l'histoire d'Auvergne par un Auvergnat" (M. Tallandier), p. 313.

respect, infinitely better off, for, while working, they are fed and clothed along with their wives and children, while our peasantry, the most laborious in the kingdom, cannot, with the hardest and most devoted labor, earn bread for themselves and their families, and at the same time pay the subsidies." In 1740,[1] at Lille, the people rebel against the export of grain. "An intendant informs me that the misery increases from hour to hour, the slightest danger to the crops resulting in this for three years past. . . . Flanders, especially, is greatly embarrassed; there is nothing to live on until the harvesting, which will not take place for two months. The provinces the best off are not able to help the others. Each bourgeois in each town is obliged to feed one or two poor persons and provide them with fourteen pounds of bread per week. In the little town of Chatellerault, (of four thousand inhabitants), eighteen hundred poor, this winter, are on that footing. . . . The poor outnumber those able to live without begging . . . while prosecutions for unpaid dues are carried on with unexampled rigor. The clothes of the poor are seized, and their last measure of flour, the latches on their doors, etc. . . . The abbess of Jouarre told me yesterday that, in her canton, in Brie, most of the ground had not been planted." It is not surprising that the famine spreads even to Paris. "Fears are entertained of next Wednesday. There is no more bread in Paris, except that of the damaged flour which is brought in and which burns (when baking). The mills are working day and night at Belleville, regrinding old damaged flour. The people are ready to rebel; bread goes up a *sol* a day; no merchant dares, or is disposed, to bring in his wheat. The market on Wednesday was almost in a state of revolt, there being no bread in it after seven o'clock in the morning. . . . The poor creatures at Bicêtre were put on short allowance, three *quarterons* (twelve ounces), being reduced to only half a pound. A rebellion broke out and they forced the guards. Numbers escaped and they have inundated Paris. The watch, with the police of the neighborhood, were called out, and an attack was made on these poor wretches with bayonet and sword. About fifty of them were left on the ground; the revolt was not suppressed yesterday morning."

Ten years later the evil is greater.[2] "In the country around

---

[1] D'Argenson, 1740, Aug. 7 and 21, September 19 and 24, May 28, November 7.
[2] D'Argenson, October 4, 1749; May 20, Sept. 12, Oct. 28 Dec. 28, 1750; June 16, Dec. 22, 1751, etc.

me, ten leagues from Paris, I find increased privation and constant complaints. What must it be in our wretched provinces in the interior of the kingdom? . . . My curate tells me that eight families, supporting themselves on their labor when I left, are now begging their bread. There is no work to be had. The wealthy are economizing like the poor. And with all this the *taille* is exacted with military severity. The collectors, with their officers, accompanied by locksmiths, force open the doors and carry off and sell furniture for one-quarter of its value, the expenses exceeding the amount of the tax. . . ." "I am at this moment on my estates in Touraine. I encounter nothing but frightful privations; the melancholy sentiment of suffering no longer prevails with the poor inhabitants, but rather one of utter despair; they desire death only, and avoid increase. . . . It is estimated that one-quarter of the working-days of the year go to the *corvées*, the laborers feeding themselves, and with what? . . . I see poor people dying of destitution. They are paid fifteen sous a day, equal to a crown, for their load. Whole villages are either ruined or broken up, and none of the households recover. . . . Judging by what my neighbors tell me the inhabitants have diminished one-third. . . . The daily laborers are all leaving and taking refuge in the small towns. In many villages everybody leaves. I have several parishes in which the *taille* for three years is due, the proceedings for its collection always going on. . . . The receivers of the *taille* and of the fisc add one-half each year in expenses above the tax. . . . An assessor, on coming to the village where I have my country-house, states that the *taille* this year will be much increased; he noticed that the peasants here were fatter than elsewhere; that they had chicken feathers before their doors, and that the living here must be good, everybody doing well, etc. This is the cause of the peasant's discouragement, and likewise the cause of misfortune throughout the kingdom." "In the country where I am staying I hear that marriage is declining and that the population is decreasing on all sides. In my parish, with a few firesides, there are more than thirty single persons, male and female, old enough to marry and none of them having any idea of it. On being urged to marry they all reply alike that it is not worth while to bring unfortunate beings like themselves into the world. I have myself tried to induce some of the women to marry by offering them assistance, but they all reason in this way as if they had consulted together."[1] "One of my curates sends me word that, although he is the oldest in the province of Touraine, and has seen many things, including excessively high prices for wheat, he remembers no misery so great as that of this year, even in 1709. . . . Some of the seigniors of Touraine inform me that, being desirous of setting the inhabitants to work by the day, they found very few of them, and these so weak that they were unable to use their arms."

Those who are able to leave, emigrate. "A person from Languedoc tells me of vast numbers of peasants deserting that province and taking refuge in Piedmont, Savoy, and Spain, tormented and frightened by the measures resorted to in collecting tithes. . . . The extortioners sell everything and imprison everybody as if prisoners of war, and even with more avidity and malice, in order to gain something themselves." "I met an intendant of one of the finest provinces in the kingdom, who told me that no more farmers could be found there; that parents preferred to send their children to the towns; that living in the surrounding country was daily becoming more horrible to the inhabitants. . . . A man, well-informed in financial matters, told me that over two hundred families in Normandy had left this year, fearing the collections in their villages." At Paris, "the streets swarm with beggars. One cannot stop before a door without a dozen mendicants besetting him with their importunities. They are said to be people from the country who, unable to endure the persecutions they have to undergo, take refuge in the cities . . . preferring mendicity to labor." And yet the people of the cities are not much better off. "An officer of a company in garrison at Mesières tells me that the poverty of that place is so great that, after the officers had dined in the inns, the people rush in and pillage the remnants." "There are more than twelve thousand begging workmen in Rouen, quite as many in Tours, etc. More than twenty thousand of these workmen are estimated as having left the kingdom in three months for Spain, Germany, etc. At Lyons twenty thousand workers in silk are watched and kept in sight for fear of their going abroad." At Rouen,[2] and in Normandy, "those in easy circumstances find it difficult to get bread,

---

[1] D'Argenson, June 21, 1749; May 22, 1750; March 19, 1751; February 14, April 15, 1752, etc.

[2] Floquet, *ibid.* VII. 410 (April, 1752, an address to the Parliament of Normandy).

the bulk of the people being entirely without it, and, to ward off starvation, providing themselves with food that shocks humanity." "Even at Paris," writes d'Argenson,[1] "I learn that on the day M. le Dauphin and Mme. la Dauphine went to Notre Dame, on passing the bridge of the Tournelle, more than two thousand women assembled in that quarter crying out, 'Give us bread, or we shall die of hunger.' . . . A vicar of the parish of Saint-Marguerite affirms that over eight hundred persons died in the faubourg St. Antoine between January 20th and February 20th; that the poor expire with cold and hunger in their garrets, and that the priests, arriving too late, see them expire without any possible relief." Were I to enumerate the riots, the seditions of the famished, and the pillagings of storehouses, I should never end; these are the convulsive twitchings of exhaustion; the people have fasted as long as possible, and instinct, at last, rebels. In 1747,[2] "extensive bread-riots occur in Toulouse, and in Guyenne they take place on every market-day." In 1750, from six to seven thousand men gather in Bearn behind a river to resist the clerks; two companies of the Artois regiment fire on the rebels and kill a dozen of them. In 1752, a sedition at Rouen and in its neighborhood lasts three days; in Dauphiny and in Auvergne riotous villagers force open the grain warehouses and take away wheat at their own price; the same year, at Arles, two thousand armed peasants demand bread at the town-hall and are dispersed by the soldiers. In one province alone, that of Normandy, I find insurrections in 1725, in 1737, in 1739, in 1752, in 1764, 1765, 1766, 1767 and 1768,[3] and always on account of bread. "Entire hamlets," writes the Parliament, "being without the necessities of life, want compels them to resort to the food of brutes. . . . Two days more and Rouen will be without provisions, without grain, without bread." Accordingly, the last riot is terrible; on this occasion, the populace, again masters of the town for three days, pillage the public granaries and the stores of all the communities. Up to the last and even later, in 1770 at Rheims, in 1775 at Dijon, at Versailles, at St. Germain, at Pontoise and at Paris, in 1772 at Poitiers, in 1785 at Aix in Provence, in 1788 and 1789 in Paris and throughout France, similar eruptions are visible.[4] Undoubt-

---

[1] D'Argenson, November 26, 1751; March 15, 1753.

[2] D'Argenson, IV. 124; VI. 165; VII. 194, etc.

[3] Floquet, ibid. VI. 400–430

[4] "Correspondance," by Métra, I. 338, 341. Hippeau, "Le Gouvernement de Normandie," IV. 62, 109, 358.

edly the government under Louis XVI. is milder; the intendants are more humane, the administration is less rigid, the *taille* becomes less unequal, and the *corvée* is less onerous through its transformation, in short, misery has diminished, and yet this is greater than human nature can bear.

Examine administrative correspondence for the last thirty years preceding the Revolution. Countless statements reveal excessive suffering, even when not terminating in fury. Life to a·man of the lower class, to an artisan, or workman, subsisting on the labor of his own hands, is evidently precarious; he obtains simply enough to keep him from starvation and he does not always get that.[1] Here, in four districts, "the inhabitants live only on buckwheat," and for five years, the apple crop having failed, they drink only water. There, in a country of vineyards,[2] "the vine-dressers each year are reduced, for the most part, to begging their bread during the dull season." Elsewhere, several of the day-laborers and mechanics, obliged to sell their effects and household goods, die of the cold; insufficient and unhealthy food generates sickness, while, in two districts, thirty-five thousand persons are stated to be living on alms.[3] In a remote canton the peasants cut the grain still green and dry it in the oven, because they are too hungry to wait. The intendant of Poitiers writes that " as soon as the workhouses open, a prodigious number of the poor rush to them, in spite of the reduction of wages and of the restrictions imposed on them in behalf of the most needy." The intendant of Bourges notices that a great many métayers have sold off their furniture, and that "entire families pass two days without eating," and that in many parishes the famished stay in bed most of the day because they suffer less. The intendant of Orleans reports that "in Sologne, poor widows have burned up their wooden bedsteads and others have consumed their fruit trees," to preserve themselves from the cold, and he adds, "nothing is exaggerated in this statement; the cries of want cannot be expressed; the misery of the rural

---

[1] "Procès-verbaux de l'assemblée provinciale de Basse Normandie" (1787), p. 151.

[2] Archives nationales, G, 319. Condition of the directory of Issoudun, and H, 1149, 612, 1418.

[3] *Ibid.* The letters of M. de Crosne, intendant of Rouen (February 17, 1784); of M. de Blossac, intendant of Poitiers (May 9, 1784); of M. de Villeneuve, intendant of Bourges (March 28, 1784); of M. de Cypièrre, intendant of Orleans (May 28, 1784); of M. de Maziron, intendant of Moulins (June 28, 1786); of M. Dupont, intendant of Moulins (Nov. 16, 1779), etc.

districts must be seen with one's own eyes to obtain an idea of
it." From Rioni, from La Rochelle, from Limoges, from Lyons,
from Montauban, from Caen, from Alençon, from Flanders, from
Moulins come similar statements by other intendants. One
might call it the interruptions and repetitions of a funeral knell;
even in years not disastrous it is heard on all sides. In Burgundy, near Chatillon-sur-Seine, "taxes, seigniorial dues, the
tithes, and the expenses of cultivation, split up the productions
of the soil into thirds, leaving nothing for the unfortunate cultivators, who would have abandoned their fields, had not two
Swiss manufacturers of calicoes settled there and distributed
about the country forty thousand francs a year in cash."[1] In
Auvergne, the country is depopulated daily; many of the villages
have lost, since the beginning of the century, more than one-
third of their inhabitants.[2] "Had not steps been promptly taken
to lighten the burden of a down-trodden people," says the provincial assembly in 1787, "Auvergne would have forever lost its
population and its cultivation." In Comminges, at the outbreak
of the Revolution, certain communities threaten to abandon their
possessions, should they obtain no relief.[3] "It is a well-known
fact," says the assembly of Haute-Guyenne, in 1784, "that the lot
of the most severely taxed communities is so rigorous as to have
led their proprietors frequently to abandon their property.[4] Who
is not aware of the inhabitants of Saint-Servin having abandoned
their possessions ten times, and of their threats to resort again to
this painful proceeding in their recourse to the administration?
Only a few years ago an abandonment of the community of
Boisse took place through the combined action of the inhabitants, the seignior and the *décimateur* of that community;" and
the desertion would be still greater if the law did not forbid persons liable to the *taille* abandoning over-taxed property, except
by renouncing whatever they possessed in the community. In
the Soissonais, according to the report of the provincial assembly,[5] "misery is excessive." In Gascony the spectacle is "heart-

---

[1] Archives nationales, H, 200 (A memorial by M. Amelot, intendant at Dijon, 1786).
[2] Gautier de Bianzat, "Doléances sur les surcharges que portent les gens du Tiers-Etat,"
etc. (1789), p. 188. "Procès-verbaux de l'assemblée provinciale d'Auvergne" (1787), p. 175.
[3] Théron de Montaugé, "L'Agriculture et les chores rurales dans le Toulousain," 112.
[4] "Procès-verbaux de l'assemblée provinciale de la Haute-Guyenne," I. 47, 79.
[5] "Procès-verbaux de l'assemblée provinciale du Soissonais" (1787), p. 857; "de l'assemblée provinciale d'Auch," p. 24.

rending." In the environs of Toule, the cultivator, after paying his taxes, tithes and other dues, remains empty-handed. "Agriculture is an occupation of steady anxiety and privation, in which thousands of men are obliged to painfully vegetate."[1] In a village in Normandy, "nearly all the inhabitants, not excepting the farmers and proprietors, eat barley bread and drink water, living like the most wretched of men, so as to provide for the payment of the taxes with which they are overburdened." In the same province, at Forges, "many poor creatures eat oat bread, and others bread of soaked bran, this nourishment causing many deaths among infants."[2] People evidently live from day to day; whenever the crop proves poor they lack bread. Let a frost come, a hailstorm, an inundation, and an entire province is incapable of supporting itself until the coming year; in many places even an ordinary winter suffices to bring on distress. On all sides hands are seen outstretched to the king, who is the universal almoner. The people may be said to resemble a man attempting to wade through a pool with the water up to his chin, and who, losing his footing at the slightest depression, sinks down and drowns. Existent charity and the fresh spirit of humanity vainly strive to rescue them; the water has risen too high. It must subside to a lower level, and the pool be drawn off through some adequate outlet. Thus far the poor man catches breath only at intervals, running the risk of drowning at every moment.

II.

Between 1750 and 1760,[3] the idlers who eat suppers begin to regard with compassion and alarm the laborers who go without dinners. Why are the latter so impoverished; and by what mischance, on a soil as rich as that of France, do those lack bread who grow the grain? In the first place many farms remain uncultivated, and, what is worse, many are deserted. According to the best observers "one-quarter of the soil is absolutely lying waste. . . . Hundreds and hundreds of *arpents* of heath and moor form extensive deserts."[4] "Let a person traverse Anjou,

---

[1] "Résumé des cahiers," by Prud'homme, III. 271.
[2] Hippeau, *ibid*. VI. 74, 243 (Complaints drawn up by the Chevalier de Bertin).
[3] See the article "Fermiers et Grains," in the Encyclopedia, by Quesnay, 1756.
[4] Théron de Montaugé, p. 25. "Ephémérides du citoyen," III. 190 (1766); IX. 15 (an article by M. de Butré, 1767).

Maine, Brittany, Poitou, Limousin, la Marche, Berry, Nivernais, Bourbonnais and Auvergne, and he finds one-half of these provinces in heaths, forming immense plains, all of which might be cultivated." In Touraine, in Poitou and in Berry they form solitary expanses of thirty thousand *arpents.* In one canton alone, near Preuilly, forty thousand *arpents* of good soil consist of heath. The agricultural society of Rennes declares that two-thirds of Brittany is lying waste. This is not sterility but decadence. The régime invented by Louis XIV. has produced its effect; the soil for a century past has been reverting to a wild state. "We see only abandoned and ruinous chateaux; the principal towns of the fiefs, in which the nobility formerly lived at their ease, are all now occupied by poor métayer herdsmen whose scanty labor hardly suffices for their subsistence, and a remnant of tax ready to disappear through the ruin of the proprietors and the desertion of the settlers." In the election district of Confolens a piece of property rented for 2,956 livres in 1665, brings in only 900 livres in 1747. On the confines of la Marche and of Berry a domain which, in 1660, honorably supported two seigniorial families is now simply a small unproductive métayer-farm; "the traces of the furrows once made by the ploughshare being still visible on the surrounding heaths." Sologne, once flourishing,[1] becomes a marsh and a forest; a hundred years earlier it produced three times the quantity of grain; two-thirds of its mills are gone; not a vestige of its vineyards remains; "grapes have given way to the heath." Thus abandoned by the spade and the plough, a vast portion of the soil ceases to feed man, while the rest, poorly cultivated, scarcely provides the simplest necessities.[2]

In the first place, on the failure of a crop, this portion remains untilled; its occupant is too poor to purchase seed; the intendant is often obliged to distribute seed, without which the disaster of the current year would be followed by sterility the following year.[3] Every calamity, accordingly, in these days affects the future as

---

[1] "Procès-verbaux de l'assemblée provinciale de l'Orléanais" (1787), in a memoir by M. d'Autroche.

[2] One is surprised to see so many supported where one-half, or one-quarter of the arable ground is sterile wastes.—ARTHUR YOUNG.

[3] Archives nationales, H, 1149. A letter of the Comtesse de Saint-Georges (1772) on the effects of frost. "The ground this year will remain uncultivated, there being already much land in this condition, and especially in our parish." Théron de Montaugé, *ibid.* 45, 80.

well as the present; during the two years of 1784 and 1785, around Toulouse, the drought having caused the loss of all draft animals, many of the cultivators are obliged to let their fields lie fallow. In the second place, cultivation, when it does take place, is carried on according to mediæval modes. Arthur Young, in 1789, considers that French agriculture has not progressed beyond that of the tenth century.[1] Except in Flanders and on the plains of Alsace, the fields lie fallow one year out of three, and oftentimes one year out of two. The implements are poor; there are no ploughs made of iron; in many places the plough of Virgil's time is still in use. Cart-axles and wheel-tires are made of wood, while a harrow often consists of the trestle of a cart. There are few animals and but little manure; the capital bestowed on cultivation is three times less than that of the present day. The yield is slight: "our ordinary farms," says a good observer, "taking one with another return about six times the seed sown."[2] In 1778, on the rich soil around Toulouse, wheat returns about five for one, while at the present day it yields eight to one and more. Arthur Young estimates that, in his day, the English acre produces twenty-eight bushels of grain, and the French acre eighteen bushels, and that the value of the total product of the same area for a given length of time is thirty-six pounds sterling in England and only twenty-five in France. As the parish roads are frightful, and transportation often impracticable, it is clear that, in remote cantons, where poor soil yields scarcely three times the seed sown, food is not always obtainable. How do they manage to live until the next crop? This is the question always under consideration previous to, and during, the Revolution. I find, in manuscript correspondence, the syndics and mayors of villages estimating the quantities for local subsistence at so many bushels in the granaries, so many sheaves in the barns, so many mouths to be filled, so many days to wait until the August wheat comes in, and concluding on short supplies for two, three and four months. Such a state of inter-communication and of agriculture condemns a country to periodical famines, and I venture to state that, alongside of the small-pox which out of eight deaths causes one, another endemic disease exists, as prevalent and as destructive, and this disease is starvation.

---

[1] Arthur Young, II. 112, 115. Théron de Montaugé, 52, 61.
[2] The Marquis de Mirabeau, "Traité de la population," p. 29.

We can easily imagine the people as sufferers by it, and, especially, the peasant. An advance in the price of bread prevents him from getting any, and even without that advance, he obtains it with difficulty. Wheat bread cost, as at the present day, three *sous* per pound,[1] but as the average day's work brought only nineteen *sous* instead of forty, the day-laborer, working the same time, could buy only the half of a loaf instead of a full loaf.[2] Taking everything into account, and wages being estimated according to the price of grain, we find that the husbandman's manual labor then procured him 959 *litres* of wheat, while nowadays it gives him 1,851 *litres*; his well-being, accordingly, has advanced ninety-three per cent., which suffices to show to what extent his predecessors suffered privations. And these privations are peculiar to France. Through analogous observations and estimates Arthur Young shows that in France those who lived on field labor, and they constituted the great majority, are seventy-six per cent. less comfortable than the same laborers in England, while they are seventy-six per cent. less well fed and well clothed, besides being worse treated in sickness and in health. The result is that, in seven-eighths of the kingdom, there are no farmers, but simply métayers.[3] The peasant is too poor to undertake cultivation on his own account, possessing no agricultural capital.[4] "The proprietor, desirous of improving his land, finds no one to cultivate it but miserable creatures possessing only a pair of hands; he is obliged to advance everything for its cultivation at his own expense, animals, implements and seed, and even to advance the wherewithal to this métayer to feed him until the first crop comes in." "At Vatan, for example, in Berry, the métayers, almost every year, borrow bread of the proprietor in order to await the harvesting." "Very rarely is one found who is not indebted to his master at least one hundred livres a year." Frequently the latter proposes to abandon the entire crop to them on condition that they demand nothing of him during the year; "these miserable creatures" have refused;

---

[1] Cf. Galiani, "Dialogues sur le commerce des blés" (1770), p. 193. Wheat bread at this time cost four *sous* per pound.

[2] Arthur Young, II. 200, 201, 260–265. Théron de Montaugé, 59, 68, 75, 79, 81, 84.

[3] "The poor people who cultivate the soil here are *métayers*, that is, men who hire the land without ability to stock it; the proprietor is forced to provide cattle and seed and he and his tenants divide the produce."—ARTHUR YOUNG.

[4] "Ephémérides du citoyen," VI. 81–94 (1767), and IX. 99 (1767).

left to themselves, they would not be sure of keeping themselves alive. In Limousin and in Angoumois their poverty is so great [1] " that, deducting the taxes to which they are subject, they have no more than from twenty-five to thirty livres each person per annum to spend; and not in money, it must be stated, but counting whatever they consume in kind out of the crops they produce. Frequently they have less, and when they cannot possibly make a living the master is obliged to support them. . . . The métayer is always reduced to just what is absolutely necessary to keep him from starving." As to the small proprietor, the villager who ploughs his land himself, his condition is but little better. " Agriculture,[2] as our peasants practise it, is a veritable drudgery; they die by thousands in childhood, and in maturity they seek places everywhere but where they should be." In 1783, throughout the plain of the Toulousain they eat only maize, a mixture of flour, common seeds and very little wheat; those on the mountains feed, a part of the year, on chestnuts; the potato is hardly known, and, according to Arthur Young, ninety-nine out of a hundred peasants would refuse to eat it. According to the reports of intendants, the basis of food, in Normandy, is oats; in the election-district of Troyes, buckwheat; in the Marche and in Limousin, buckwheat with chestnuts and radishes; in Auvergne, buckwheat, chestnuts, milk-curds and a little salted goat's meat; in Beauce, a mixture of barley and rye; in Berry, a mixture of barley and oats. There is no wheat bread; the peasant consumes inferior flour only because he is unable to pay two sous a pound for his bread. There is no butcher's meat; at best he kills one pig a year. His dwelling is built of clay *(pisé)*, roofed with thatch, without windows, and the floor is the beaten ground. Even when the soil furnishes good building materials, stone, slate and tile, the windows have no sashes. In a parish in Normandy, in 1789, " most of the dwellings consist of four posts." They are often mere stables or barns " to which a chimney has been added made of four poles and some mud." Their clothes are rags, and often in winter these are muslin rags. In Quercy and elsewhere, they have no stockings, or shoes or *sabots* (wooden shoes). " It is not in the power of an English imagination," says Arthur Young, "to figure

---

[1] Turgot, "Collections des économistes," I. 544, 549.

[2] Marquis de Mirabeau, "Traité de la population," 83.

the animals that waited on us here at the *Chapeau Rouge*,
—creatures that were called by courtesy Souillac women, but
in reality walking dung-hills. But a neatly dressed, clean
waiting-girl at an inn, will be looked for in vain in France."
On reading descriptions made on the spot we see in France a
similar aspect of country and of peasantry as in Ireland, at least
in its broad outlines.

III.

In the most fertile regions, for instance, in Limagne, both cottages and faces denote " misery and privation."[1] " The peasants
are generally feeble, emaciated and of slight stature." Nearly all derive wheat and wine from their homesteads, but they are forced to sell
this to pay their rents and imposts; they eat black bread, made
of rye and barley, and their sole beverage is water poured on the
lees and the husks. " An Englishman[2] who has not travelled can
not imagine the figure made by infinitely the greater part of the
countrywomen in France." Arthur Young, who stops to talk
with one of these in Champagne, says that " this woman, at no
great distance, might have been taken for sixty or seventy, her figure was so bent and her face so hardened and furrowed by labor,—
but she said she was only twenty-eight." This woman, her husband and her household, afford a sufficiently accurate example of
the condition of the small proprietary husbandmen. Their property
consists simply of a patch of ground, with a cow and a poor little
horse; their seven children consume the whole of the cow's milk.
They owe to one seignior a *franchard* (forty-two pounds) of flour,
and three chickens; to another three *franchards* of oats, one chicken
and one *sou*, to which must be added the *taille* and other imposts.
" God keep us! " she said, " for the *tailles* and the dues crush us."
What must it be in districts where the soil is poor !   " From Ormes,
(near Chatellerault), as far as Poitiers," writes a lady,[3] " there is a
good deal of ground which brings in nothing, and from Poitiers
to my residence (in Limousin) twenty-five thousand *arpents* of
ground consist wholly of heath and sea-grass.   The peasantry live
on rye, of which they do not remove the bran, and which is as black
and heavy as lead.   In Poitou, and here, they plough up only the

---

[1] Dulaure, "Description de l'Auvergne," 1789.
[2] Arthur Young, I. 235.
[3] "Ephémérides du citoyen," XX. 146, a letter of the Marquis de ——, August 17, 1767.

skin of the ground with a miserable little plough without wheels. . . .
From Poitiers to Montmorillon it is nine leagues, equal to sixteen
of Paris, and I assure you that I have seen but four men on the
road, and, between Montmorillon and my own house, which is
four leagues, but three; and then only at a distance, not having
met one on the road.   You need not be surprised at this in such
a country. . . . Marriage takes place as early as with the grand
seigniors," doubtless for fear of the militia.   " But the population of
the country is no greater because almost every infant dies.   Mothers
having scarcely any milk, their infants eat the bread of which I
spoke, the stomach of a girl of four years being as big as that of a pregnant woman. . . . The rye crop this year was ruined by the frost
on Easter day; flour is scarce; of the twelve *métairies* owned by
my mother, four of them may, perhaps, have some on hand.
There has been no rain since Easter; no hay, no pasture, no vegetables, no fruit.   You see the lot of the poor peasant.   There is
no manure, and there are no cattle. . . . My mother, whose granaries used to be always full, has not a grain of wheat in them,
because, for two years past, she has fed all her métayers and the
poor."

" The peasant is assisted," says a seignior of the same province, " protected, and rarely maltreated, but he is looked upon
with disdain.   If kindly and pliable he is made subservient, but
if ill-disposed he becomes soured and irritable. . . . He is kept
in misery, in an abject state, by men who are not at all inhuman
but whose prejudices, especially among the nobles, lead them to
regard him as of a different species of being. . . . The proprietor gets all he can out of him; in any event, looking upon him
and his oxen as domestic animals, he puts them into harness and
employs them in all weathers for every kind of journey, and for
every species of carting and transport.   On the other hand, this
métayer thinks of living with as little labor as possible, converting as much ground as he can into pasturage, for the reason that
the product arising from the increase of stock costs him no labor.
The little ploughing he does is for the purpose of raising
low-priced provisions suitable for his own nourishment, such as
buckwheat, radishes, etc.   His enjoyment consists only of his
own idleness and sluggishness, hoping for a good chestnut year
and doing nothing voluntarily but procreate;" unable to hire
farming hands he begets children.   The rest, ordinary laborers,

have small supplies, " living on the herbage, and on a few goats
which devour everything." Often again, these, by order of Parliament, are killed by the keepers.   A woman, with two children
in swaddling clothes, having no milk, "and without an inch of
ground," whose two goats, her sole resource, had thus been slain,
and another, with one goat slain in the same way, and who begs
along with her boy, present themselves at the gate of the chateau ;
one receives twelve livres, while the other is admitted as a domestic, and henceforth, "this village is all bows and smiling faces."
In short, they are not accustomed to benefactions; the lot of
all these poor people is to endure.   " As with rain and hail, they regard as inevitable the necessity of being oppressed by the strongest, the richest, the most skilful, the most in repute," and this
stamps on them, "if one may be allowed to say so, an air of painful suffering."

In Auvergne, a feudal country, covered with extensive ecclesiastic and seigniorial domains, the misery is the same.   At
Clermont-Ferrand,[1] "there are many streets that can for blackness, dirt and scents only be represented by narrow channels cut in a night dunghill."   In the inns of the largest bourgs,
"closeness, misery, dirtiness and darkness."   That of Pradelles
is "one of the worst in France."   That of Aubenas, says Young,
" would be a purgatory for one of my pigs."   The senses, in
short, are paralysed.   The primitive man is content so long as he
can sleep and get something to eat.   He gets something to eat,
but what kind of food ?   To put up with the indigestible mess a
peasant here requires a still tougher stomach than in Limousin ;
in certain villages where, ten years later, every year twenty or
twenty-five hogs are to be slaughtered, they now slaughter but
three.[2]   On contemplating this temperament, rude and intact
since Vercingetorix, and, moreover, rendered more savage by
suffering, one cannot avoid being somewhat alarmed.   The Marquis de Mirabeau describes "the votive festival of Mont-Dore:
savages descending from the mountain in torrents,[3] the curate
with stole and surplice, the justice in his wig, the police corps
with sabres drawn, all guarding the open square before letting
the bagpipers play ; the dance interrupted in a quarter of an hour

---

[1] Arthur Young, I. 280, 289, 294.
[2] Lafayette, " Mémoires," V. 533.
[3] Lucas de Montigny, *ibid.* (a letter of August 18, 1777).

by a fight; the hootings and cries of children, of the feeble and other spectators, urging them on as the rabble urge on so many fighting dogs; frightful-looking men, or rather wild beasts covered with coats of coarse wool, wearing wide leather belts pierced with copper nails, gigantic in stature, which is increased by high *sabots*, and making themselves still taller by standing on tiptoe to see the battle, stamping with their feet as it progresses and rubbing each other's flanks with their elbows, their faces haggard and covered with long matted hair, the upper portion pallid, and the lower distended, indicative of cruel delight and a sort of ferocious impatience. And these folks pay the *taille*! And now they want to take away their salt! And they know nothing of those they despoil, of those whom they think they govern, believing that, by a few strokes of a cowardly and careless pen, they may starve them with impunity up to the final catastrophe! Poor Jean-Jacques, I said to myself, had any one despatched you, with your system, to copy music amongst these folks, he would have had some sharp replies to make to your discourses!" Prophetic warning and admirable foresight in one whom an excess of evil does not blind to the evil of the remedy! Enlightened by his feudal and rural instincts, the old man at once judges both the government and the philosophers, the Ancient Régime and the Revolution.

IV.

Misery begets bitterness in a man; but ownership coupled with misery renders him still more bitter. He may have submitted to indigence but not to spoliation—which is the situation of the peasant in 1789, for, during the eighteenth century, he had become the possessor of land. But how could he maintain himself in such destitution? The fact is almost incredible, but it is nevertheless true. We can only explain it by the character of the French peasant, by his sobriety, his tenacity, his rigor with himself, his dissimulation, his hereditary passion for property and especially for that of the soil. He had lived on privations, and economized *sou* after *sou*. Every year a few pieces of silver are added to his little store of crowns buried in the most secret recess of his cellar; Rousseau's peasant, concealing his wine and bread in a pit, assuredly had a yet more secret hiding-place; a little money in a woollen stocking or in a jug escapes, more readily than elsewhere, the search of the clerks.   Dressed in rags, going barefoot, eating nothing but coarse black bread, but cherishing the little treasure in his breast on which he builds so many hopes, he watches for the opportunity which never fails to come.   "In spite of privileges," writes a gentleman in 1755, "the nobles are daily being ruined and reduced, the Third-Estate making all the fortunes."   A number of domains, through forced or voluntary sales, thus pass into the hands of financiers, of men of the quill, of merchants, and of the well-to-do bourgeois.   Before undergoing this total dispossession, however, the seignior, involved in debt, is evidently resigned to partial alienations of his property.   The peasant who has bribed the steward is at hand with his hoard.   "It is poor property, my lord, and it costs you more than you get from it." This may refer to an isolated patch, one end of a field or meadow, sometimes a farm whose farmer pays nothing, and generally worked by a métayer whose wants and indolence make him an annual expense to his master.   The latter may say to himself that the alienated parcel is not lost, since, some day or other, through his right of repurchase, he may take it back, while, in the meantime, he enjoys a *cens*, drawbacks, and the lord's dues. Moreover, there is on his domain and around him, extensive open spaces which the decline of cultivation and depopulation have left a desert.   To restore the value of this he must surrender its proprietorship.   There is no other way by which to attach man permanently to the soil.   And the government helps him along in this matter.   Obtaining no revenue from the abandoned soil, it assents to a provisional withdrawal of its too weighty hand.   By the edict of 1766, a piece of cleared waste land remains free of the *taille* for fifteen years, and, thereupon, in twenty-eight provinces four hundred thousand *arpents* are cleared in three years.[1]

This is the mode by which the seigniorial domain gradually crumbles away and decreases.   Towards the last, in many places, with the exception of the chateau and the small adjoining farm which brings in two or three thousand francs a year, nothing is left to the seignior but his feudal dues;[2] the rest of the soil

---

[1] "Procès-verbaux de l'assemblée provinciale de Basse Normandie" (1787), p. 205.

[2] Léonce de Lavergne, p. 26 (according to the tables of indemnity granted to the *emigrés* in 1825).   In the estate of Blet (see note 2 at the end of the volume), twenty-two parcels are alienated in 1760.   Arthur Young, I. 308 (the domain of Tour-d'Aigues, in Provence), and II. 198, 214.   Doniol, "Histoire des classes rurales," p. 450.   De Tocqueville, p. 36.

belongs to the peasantry. Forbonnais already remarks, towards 1750, that many of the nobles and of the ennobled "reduced to extreme poverty but with titles to immense possessions," have sold off portions to small cultivators at low prices, and often for the amount of the *taille*. Towards 1760, one-quarter of the soil is said to have already passed into the hands of agriculturalists. In 1772, in relation to the *vingtième*, which is levied on the net revenue of real property, the intendant of Caen, having completed the statement of his quota, estimates that out of one hundred and fifty thousand "there are perhaps fifty thousand whose liabilities did not exceed five *sous*, and perhaps still as many more not exceeding twenty *sous*." [1] Contemporary observers authenticate this passion of the peasant for real property. "The savings of the lower classes, which elsewhere are invested with individuals and in the public funds, are wholly destined in France to the purchase of land." "Accordingly the number of small rural holdings is always on the increase. Necker says that there is an *immensity* of them." Arthur Young, in 1789, is astonished at their great number and "inclines to think that they form a third of the kingdom." This already would be our actual estimate, and we still find, approximatively, the actual figures, on estimating the number of proprietors in comparison with the number of inhabitants.

The small cultivator, however, in becoming a possessor of the soil assumed its charges. Simply as day-laborer, and with his arms alone, he was only partially affected by the taxes; "where there is nothing the king loses his dues." But now, vainly is he poor and declaring himself still poorer; the fisc has a hold on him and on every portion of his new possessions. The collectors, peasants like himself, and jealous, by virtue of being his

---

[1] Archives nationales, H, 1463 (a letter by M. de Fontette, November 16, 1772). Cf. Cochut, "Revue des Deux Mondes," September, 1848. The sale of the national property seems not to have sensibly increased small properties nor sensibly diminished the number of the large ones. The Revolution developed moderate sized properties. In 1848, the large estates numbered 183,000 (23,000 families paying 300 francs taxes, and more, and possessing on the average 260 *hectares* of land, and 160,000 families paying from 250 to 500 francs taxes and possessing on the average 75 *hectares*). These 183,000 families possess 18,000,000 *hectares*. There are besides 700,000 medium sized estates (paying from 50 to 250 francs tax), and comprising 15,000,000 *hectares*. And finally 3,900,000 small properties comprising 15,000,000 *hectares* (900,000 paying from 25 to 50 francs tax, averaging five and one-half *hectares* each, and 3,000,000 paying less than 25 francs, averaging three and one-ninth *hectares* each). According to the partial statements of De Tocqueville the number of holders of real property had increased, on the average, to five-twelfths ; the population, at the same time, having increased five-thirteenths (from 26 to 36 millions).

neighbors, know how much his property, exposed to view, brings in; hence they take all they can lay their hands on. Vainly has he labored with renewed energy; his hands remain as empty, and, at the end of the year, he discovers that his field has produced him nothing. The more he acquires and produces the more burdensome do the taxes become. In 1715, the *taille* and the poll-tax, which he alone pays, or nearly alone, amounts to sixty-six millions of livres; the amount is ninety-three millions in 1759 and one hundred and ten millions in 1789.[1] In 1757, the imposts amount to 283,156,000 livres; in 1789 to 476,294,000 livres.

Theoretically, through humanity and through good sense, there is, doubtless, a desire to relieve the peasant, and pity is felt for him. But, in practice, through necessity and routine, he is treated according to Cardinal Richelieu's precept, as a beast of burden to which oats are measured out for fear that he may become too strong and kick, "a mule which, accustomed to his load, is spoiled more by long repose than by work."

---

[1] "Compte-général des revenus et dépenses fixes au 1er Mai, 1789 (Imprimerie Royale, 1789). De Luynes, XVI. 49. Roux and Buchez, I. 206, 374. (This relates only to the countries of *election ;* in the provinces, with assemblies, the increase is no less great). Archives nationales, H², 1610 (the parish of Bourget, in Anjou). Extracts from the *taille* rolls of three *métayer*-farms belonging to M. de Ruillé. The imposts in 1762 are 334 *livres*, 3 *sous ;* in 1783, 372 *livres*, 15 *sous.*

CHAPTER II.

TAXATION THE PRINCIPAL CAUSE OF MISERY.—I. Direct taxes.—State of different domains at the end of the reign of Louis XV.—Levies of the tithe-owner and of the fisc.—What remains to the proprietor.—II. State of certain provinces on the outbreak of the Revolution.—The *taille*, and other imposts.—The proportion of these taxes in relation to income.—The sum total immense.—III. Four direct taxes on the common laborer.—IV. Collections and seizures.—V. Indirect taxes.—The salt-tax and the excise.—VI. Why taxation is so burdensome.—Exemptions and privileges.—VII. The *octrois* of towns.—The poor the greatest sufferers.—VIII. Complaints in the memorials.

I.

LET us closely examine the extortions he has to endure, which are very great, much beyond any that we can imagine. Economists had long prepared the budget of a farm and shown by statistics the excess of charges with which the cultivator is overwhelmed. If he continues to cultivate, they say, he must have his share in the crops, an inviolable portion, equal to one-half of the entire production, and from which nothing can be deducted without ruining him. This portion, in short, accurately represents, and not a *sou* too much, in the first place, the interest of the capital first expended on the farm in cattle, furniture, and implements of husbandry; in the second place, the maintenance of this capital, every year depreciated by wear and tear; in the third place, the advances made during the current year for seed, wages, and food for men and animals; and, in the last place, the compensation due him for the risks he takes and his losses. Here is a first lien which must be satisfied beforehand, taking precedence of all others, superior to that of the seignior, to that of the tithe-owner *(décimateur)*, to even that of the king, for it is an indebtedness due to the soil.[1] After this is paid back, then, and only then,

---

4 "Collection des économistes," II. 832. See a tabular statement by Beaudan.

that which remains, the *net product*, can be touched.   Now, in the then state of agriculture, the tithe-owner and the king appropriate one-half of this net product, when the estate is large, and the whole, if the estate is a small one.[1]   A certain large farm in Picardy, worth to its owner 3,600 livres, pays 1,800 livres to the king, and 1,311 livres to the tithe owner; another, in the Soissonnais, rented for 4,500 livres, pays 2,200 livres taxes and more than 1,000 livres to the tithes.   An ordinary métayer-farm near Nevers pays into the treasury 138 livres, 121 livres to the church, and 114 livres to the proprietor.   On another, in Poitou, the fisc absorbs 348 livres, and the proprietor receives only 238.   In general, in the regions of large farms, the proprietor obtains ten livres the *arpent* if the cultivation is very good, and three livres when ordinary.   In the regions of small farms, and of the métayer system, he gets fifteen sous the *arpent*, eight sous and even six sous. The entire net profit may be said to go to the church and into the State treasury.

Hired labor, meantime, is no less costly.   On this métayer-farm in Poitou, which brings in eight sous the *arpent*, thirty-six laborers consume each twenty-six francs per annum in rye, two francs respectively in vegetables, oil and milk preparations, and two francs ten sous in pork, amounting to a sum total, each year, for each person, of sixteen pounds of meat at an expense of thirty-six francs.   In fact they drink water only, use rape-seed oil for soup and for light, never taste butter, and dress themselves in materials made of the wool and hair of the sheep and goats they raise.   They purchase nothing save the tools necessary to make the fabrics of which these provide the material.   On another métayer-farm, on the confines of la Marche and Berry, forty-six laborers cost a smaller sum, each one consuming only the value of twenty-five francs per annum.   We can judge by this of the exorbitant share appropriated to themselves by the Church and State, since, at so small a cost of cultivation, the proprietor finds in his pocket, at the end of the year, six or eight sous per *arpent*, out of which, if plebeian, he must still pay the dues to his seignior, contribute to the common purse for the militia, buy his taxed salt and work out his *corvée* and the rest. Towards the end of the reign of Louis XV. in Limousin, says

---

1 "Ephémérides du citoyen," IX. 15; an article by M. de Butré, 1767.

Turgot,[1] the king derives for himself alone " about as much from the soil as the proprietor." In a certain election-district, that of Tulle, where he abstracts fifty-six and one-half per cent. of the product, there remains to the latter forty-three and one-half per cent. thus accounting for "a multitude of domains being abandoned."

It must not be supposed that time renders the tax less onerous or that, in other provinces, the cultivator is better treated. In this respect the documents are authentic and almost up to the latest hour. We have only to take up the official statements of the provincial assemblies held in 1787, to learn by official figures to what extent the fisc may abuse the men who labor, and take bread out of the mouths of those who have earned it by the sweat of their brows.

II.

Direct taxation alone is here concerned, the *tailles*, collateral imposts, poll-tax, *vingtièmes*, and the pecuniary tax substituted for the *corvée*.[2] In Champagne, the tax-payer pays on 100 livres income fifty-four livres fifteen sous, on the average, and in many parishes,[3] seventy-one livres thirteen sous. In the Ile-de-France, "if a taxable inhabitant of a village, the proprietor of twenty *arpents* of land which he himself works, and the income of which is estimated at ten livres per *arpent*, it is supposed that he is likewise the owner of the house he occupies, the site being valued at forty livres."[4] This tax-payer pays for his real *taille*, personal and industrial, thirty-five livres fourteen sous, for collateral taxes seventeen livres seventeen sous, for the poll-tax twenty one livres eight sous, for the *vingtièmes* twenty-four livres four sous, in all ninety-nine livres three sous, to which must be added about five livres as the substitution for the *corvée*, in all 104 livres on a piece of property which he rents for 240 ivres, a tax amounting to five-twelfths of his income.

It is much worse on making the same calculation for the

---

[1] "Collection des économistes," I. 551, 562.

[2] "Procès-verbaux de l'assemblée provinciale de Champagne " (1787), p. 240.

[3] Cf. "Notice historique sur la Révolution dans le département de l'Eure," by Boivin-Champeaux, p. 37. A memorial of the parish of Epreville; on 100 francs income the Treasury takes 22 for the *taille*, 16 for collaterals, 15 for the poll-tax, 11 for the *vingtièmes*, otal 67 livres.

[4] "Procès-verbaux de l'assemblée provinciale de l'Ile-de-France " (1787), p. 131.

poorer generalities. In Haute-Guyenne,[1] "all property in land is taxed for the *taille*, the collateral imposts, and the *vingtièmes*, more than one-quarter of its revenue, the only deduction being the expenses of cultivation; also dwellings, one-third of their revenue, deducting only the cost of repairs and of maintenance; to which must be added the poll-tax, which takes about one-tenth of the revenue; the tithe, which absorbs one-seventh; the seigniorial rents which take another seventh; the tax substituted for the *corvée;* the costs of compulsory collections, seizures, sequestrations and constraints, and all ordinary and extraordinary local charges. This being subtracted, it is evident that, in communities moderately taxed, the proprietor does not enjoy a third of his income, and that, in the communities wronged by the assessments, the proprietors are reduced to the status of simple farmers scarcely able to get enough to restore the expenses of cultivation." In Auvergne,[2] the *taille* amounts to four sous on the livre net profit; the collateral imposts and the poll-tax take off four sous three deniers more; the *vingtièmes*, two sous and three deniers; the contribution to the royal roads, to the free gift, to local charges and the cost of levying, take again one sou one denier, the total being eleven sous and seven deniers on the livre income, without counting seigniorial dues and the tithe. "The bureau, moreover, recognizes with regret, that several of the collections pay at the rate of seventeen sous, sixteen sous, and the most moderate at the rate of fourteen sous the livre. The evidence of this is in the bureau; it is on file in the registry of the court of excise, and of the election-districts. It is still more apparent in parishes where an infinite number of assessments are found, laid on property that has been abandoned, which the collectors lease, and the product of which is often inadequate to pay the tax." Statistics of this kind are terribly eloquent. They may be summed up in one word. Putting together Normandy, the Orleans region, that of Soissons, Champagne, Ile-de-France, Berry, Poitou, Auvergne, the Lyons region, Gascony, and Haute-Guyenne, in brief the principal *election* sections, we find that out of every hundred francs of revenue the direct tax on the tax-payer is fifty-three francs, or more than one-half.[3] This is about five times as much as at the present day.

---

[1] "Procès-verbaux de l'ass. prov. de la Haute-Guyenne" (1784), II. 17, 40, 47.

[2] " Procès-verbaux de l'ass. prov. d'Auvergne" (1787), p. 253.

[3] See note 5 at the end of the volume.

III.

The fisc, however, in thus bearing down on taxable property has not released the taxable person without property. In the absence of land it seizes on men. In default of an income it taxes a man's wages. With the exception of the *vingtièmes*, the preceding imposts not only bore on those who possessed something but, again, on those who possessed nothing. In the Toulousain,[1] at St. Pierre de Barjouville, the poorest day-laborer, with nothing but his hands by which to earn his support, and getting ten sous a day, pays eight, nine and ten livres poll-tax. "In Burgundy[2] it is common to see a poor mechanic, without any property, taxed eighteen and twenty livres for his poll-tax and the *taille*." In Limousin,[3] all the money brought back by the masons in winter serves "to pay the imposts charged to their families." As to the rural day-laborers and the settlers *(colons)* the proprietor, even when privileged, who employs them, is obliged to take upon himself a part of their quota, otherwise, being without anything to eat, they cannot work,[4] even in the interest of the master; man must have his ration of bread the same as an ox his ration of hay. "In Brittany,[5] it is notorious that nine-tenths of the artisans, though poorly fed and poorly clothed, have not a crown free of debt at the end of the year," the poll-tax and others carrying off this only and last crown. At Paris[6] "the dealer in ashes, the buyer of old bottles, the gleaner of the gutters, the peddlers of old iron and old hats," the moment they obtain a shelter pay the poll-tax of three livres and ten sous each. To ensure its payment the occupant of a house who sub-lets to them is made responsible. Moreover, in case of delay, a "blue man," a bailiff's subordinate, is sent who installs himself on the spot and whose time they have to pay for. Mercier cites a mechanic, named Quatremain, who, with four small children, lodged in the sixth story, where he had arranged a chimney as a sort of alcove in which he and his family slept.

---

[1] "Théron de Montaugé," p. 109 (1763). Wages at this time are from 7 to 12 sous a day in summer.

[2] Archives nationales, procès-verbaux and memorials of the States-General, v. LIX. p. 6. A memorial to M. Necker, by M. d'Orgeux, honorary counsellor to the Parliament of Burgundy, Oct 25, 1788.

[3] *Ibid.* H, 1418. A letter of the intendant of Limoges, Feb. 26, 1784.

[4] Turgot, II. 259.

[5] Archives nationales, H, 426 (remonstrances of the Parliament of Brittany, Feb. 1783;.

[6] Mercier, XI. 59; X. 262.

"One day I opened his door, fastened with a latch only, the room presenting to view nothing but the walls and a vice; the man, coming out from under his chimney, half sick, says to me, 'I thought it was the blue man for the poll-tax.'" Thus, whatever the condition of the person subject to taxation, however stripped and destitute, the dexterous hands of the fisc take hold of him. Mistakes cannot possibly occur : it puts on no disguise, it comes on the appointed day and rudely lays its hand on his shoulder. The garret and the hut, as well as the farm and the farm-house know the collector, the constable and the bailiff; no hovel escapes the detestable brood. The people sow, harvest their crops, work and undergo privation for their benefit; and, should the farthings so painfully saved each week amount, at the end of the year, to a piece of silver, the mouth of their pouch closes over it.

IV.

Observe the system actually at work. It is a sort of shearing machine, clumsy and badly put together, of which the action is about as mischievous as it is serviceable. The worst feature is, that, with its creaking gear, the taxable, those employed as its final instruments, are equally shorn and flayed. Each parish contains two, three, five, or seven individuals who, under the title of collectors, and under the authority of the *election* tribunal, apportion and assess the taxes. "No duty is more onerous;"[1] everybody, through patronage or favor, tries to get rid of it. The communities are constantly pleading against the refractory, and, that nobody may escape under the pretext of ignorance, the table of future collectors is made up for ten and fifteen years in advance. In parishes of the second class these consist of "small proprietors, each of whom becomes a collector about every six years." In many of the villages the artisans, day-laborers, and métayer-farmers perform the service, although requiring all their time to earn their own living. In Auvergne, where the able-bodied men expatriate themselves in winter to find work, the women are taken;[2] in the election-district of Saint-Flour, a cer-

---

[1] Archives nationales, H, 1422, a letter by M. d'Aine, intendant of Limoges (February 17, 1782); one by the intendant of Moulins (April, 1779); the trial of the community of Mollon (Bordelais), and the tables of its collectors.

[2] "Procès-verbaux de l'ass. prov. d'Auvergne," p. 266.

tain village has four collectors in petticoats. They are responsible for all claims entrusted to them, their property, their furniture and their persons; and, up to the time of Turgot, each is bound for the others. We can judge of their risks and sufferings. In 1785,[1] in one single district in Champagne, eighty-five are imprisoned and two hundred of them are on the road every year. "The collector, says the provincial assembly of Berry,[2] usually passes one-half of the day for two years running from door to door to see delinquent tax-payers." "This service," writes Turgot,[3] "is the despair and almost always the ruin of those obliged to perform it; all families in easy circumstances in a village are thus successively reduced to want." In short, there is no collector who is not forced to act and who has not each year "eight or ten writs" served on him.[4] Sometimes he is imprisoned at the expense of the parish. Sometimes proceedings are instituted against him and the tax-contributors by the installation of "'blue men' and seizures, seizures under arrest, seizures in execution and sales of furniture." "In the single district of Villefranche," says the provincial Assembly of Haute-Guyenne, "a hundred and six warrant officers and other agents of the bailiff are counted always on the road."

The thing becomes customary and the parish suffers in vain, for it would suffer yet more were it to do otherwise. "Near Aurillac," says the Marquis de Mirabeau,[5] "there is industry, application and economy without which there would be only misery and want. This produces a partially insolvent people with timorous rich ones who, for fear of overcharge, produce the impoverished. The *taille* once assessed, everybody groans and complains and nobody pays it. The term having expired, at the hour and minute, constraint begins, the collectors, although able, taking no trouble to arrest this by making a settlement, notwithstanding the installation of the bailiff's men is costly. But this kind of expense is habitual and people expect it instead of fearing it, for, if it were less rigorous, they would be sure to be additionally burdened the following year." The receiver, indeed, who

[1] Albert Babeau, "Histoire de Troyes," I. 72.
[2] "Procès-verbaux de l'ass. prov. de Berry" (1778), I. pp. 72, 80.
[3] De Tocqueville, 187.
[4] Archives nationales, H, 1417. (A letter of M. de Cypièrre, intendant at Orleans, April 17, 1765).
[5] "Traité de Population," 2d part, p. 26.

pays the bailiff's officers a franc a day, makes them pay two francs and appropriates the difference. Hence " if certain parishes venture to pay promptly, without awaiting constraint, the receiver, who sees himself deprived of the best portion of his gains, becomes ill-humored, and, at the next department (meeting), an arrangement is made between himself, messieurs the elected, the subdelegate and other shavers of this species, for the parish to bear a double load, to teach it how to behave itself."

A population of administrative blood-suckers thus lives on the peasant. " Lately," says an intendant, "in the district of Romorantin,[1] the collectors received nothing from a sale of furniture amounting to six hundred livres, because the proceeds were absorbed by the expenses. In the district of Chateaudun the same thing occurred at a sale amounting to nine hundred livres and there are other transactions of the same kind of which we have no information, however flagrant." Besides this, the fisc itself is pitiless. The same intendant writes, in 1784, a year of famine:[2] " People have seen, with horror, the collector, in the country, disputing with heads of families over the costs of a sale of furniture which had been appropriated to stopping their children's cry of want." Were the collectors not to make seizures they would themselves be seized. Urged on by the receiver we see them, in the documents, soliciting, prosecuting and persecuting the tax-payers. Every Sunday and every fête-day they are posted at the church door to warn delinquents; and then, during the week they go from door to door to obtain their dues. " Commonly they cannot write, and take a scribe with them." Out of six hundred and six traversing the district of Saint-Flour not ten of them are able to read the official summons and sign a receipt; hence innumerable mistakes and frauds. Besides a scribe they take along the bailiff's subordinates, persons of the lowest class, laborers without work, conscious of being hated and who act accordingly. " Whatever orders may be given them not to take anything, not to make the inhabitants feed them, or to enter taverns with collectors," habit is too strong " and the abuse continues."[3] But, burdensome as the bailiff's

[1] Archives nationales, H, 1417. (A letter of M. de Cypièrre, intendant at Orleans, April, 17. 1765).

[2] *Ibid.* H, 1418. (Letter of May 28, 1784).

[3] *Ibid.* (Letter of the intendant of Tours, June 15, 1765.)

men may be, care is taken not to evade them. In this respect, writes an intendant, "their obduracy is strange." "No person," a receiver reports,[1] "pays the collector until he sees the bailiff's man in his house." The peasant resembles his ass, refusing to go without being beaten, and, although in this he may appear stupid, he is politic. For the collector, being responsible, "naturally inclines to an increase of the assessment on prompt payers to the advantage of the negligent. Hence the prompt payer becomes, in his turn, negligent and, although with money in his chest, he allows the process to go on."[2] Summing all up, he calculates that the process, even if expensive, costs less than extra taxation, and of the two evils he chooses the least. He has but one resource against the collector and receiver, his simulated or actual poverty, voluntary or involuntary. "Every one subject to the *taille*," says, again, the provincial assembly of Berry, "dreads to expose his resources; he avoids any display of these in his furniture, in his dress, in his food, and in everything open to another's observation." "M. de Choiseul-Gouffier,[3] willing to roof his peasants' houses, liable to take fire, with tiles, they thanked him for his kindness but begged him to leave them as they were, telling him that if these were covered with tiles, instead of with thatch, the subdelegates would increase their taxation." "People work, but merely to satisfy their prime necessities. . . . The fear of paying an extra crown makes an average man neglect a profit of four times the amount."[4] ". . . Accordingly, lean cattle, poor implements, and bad manure-heaps when they might have others."[5] "If I earned any more," says a peasant, "it would be for the collector." Annual and illimitable spoliation "takes away even the desire for comforts." The majority, pusillanimous, distrustful, stupefied, "debased," "differing little from the old serfs,"[6] resemble Egyptian fellahs and Hindoo pariahs. The fisc, indeed, through the absolutism and enormity of its indebtedness, renders property of all kinds precarious, every acquisition vain, every accumulation delusive ; in fact, proprietors are possessors only of that which they can sequestrate from it.

[1] Archives Nationales, H, 1417. A report by Raudon, receiver of *tailles* in the *election* of Laon, January, 1764.

[2] "Procès-verbaux de l'ass. prov. de Berry" (1778), I. p. 72.

[3] Champfort, 93.

[4] "Procès-verbaux de l'ass. prov. de Berry," I. 77.

[5] Arthur Young, II. 205.

[6] "Procès-verbaux of the ass. prov. of the generalship of Rouen" (1787), p. 271.

V.

The fisc, in every country, has two hands, one which visibly and directly searches the coffers of tax-payers, and the other which covertly employs the hand of an intermediary so as not to incur the odium of fresh extortions. Here, no precaution of this kind is taken, the claws of the latter being as visible as those of the former; according to its structure and the complaints made of it, I am tempted to believe it more offensive than the other.

In the first place, the salt-tax, the excises and the customs are annually estimated and sold to adjudicators who, purely as a business matter, make as much profit as they can by their bargain. In relation to the tax-payer they are not administrators but speculators; they have bought him up. He belongs to them by the terms of their contract; they will squeeze out of him, not merely their advances and the interest on their advances, but, again, every possible benefit. This suffices to indicate the mode of levying indirect imposts. In the second place, by means of the salt-tax and the excises, the inquisition enters each household. In the provinces where these are levied, in Ile-de-France, Maine, Anjou, Touraine, Orléanais, Berry, Bourbonnais, Burgogne, Champagne, Perche, Normandy and Picardy, salt costs thirteen sous a pound, four times as much as at the present day, and, considering the standard of money, eight times as much.[1] And, furthermore, by virtue of the ordinance of 1680, each person over seven years of age is expected to purchase seven pounds per annum, which, with four persons to a family, makes eighteen francs a year, and equal to nineteen days' work: a new direct tax, which, like the *taille*, is a fiscal hand in the pockets of the tax-payers, and compelling them, like the *taille*, to torment each other. Many of them, in fact, are officially appointed to assess this obligatory use of salt and, like the collectors of the *taille*, these are "corporately responsible for the price of the salt." Others below them, ever following the same course as in collecting the *taille*, are likewise responsible. "After the former have been distrained in their persons and property, the speculator *fermier* is authorized to commence action, under the principle of

---

[1] Letrosne (1779). "De l'administration provinciale et de la reforme de l'impôt," pp. 39, 262 and 138. Archives nationales, H. 138 (1782). Cahier de Bugey, "Salt costs the countryman purchasing it of the retailers from 15 to 17 sous a pound, according to the way of measuring it."

mutual responsibility, against the principal inhabitants of the parish." The effects of this system have just been described. Accordingly, "in Normandy," says the Rouen parliament,[1] "unfortunates without bread are daily objects of seizure, sale and execution."

But if the rigor is as great as in the matter of the *taille*, the vexations are ten times greater, for these are domestic, minute and of daily occurrence. It is forbidden to divert an ounce of the seven obligatory pounds to any use but that of the "pot and the salt-cellar." If a villager should economize the salt of his soup to make brine for a piece of pork, with a view to winter consumption, let him look out for the collecting-clerks! His pork is confiscated and the fine is three hundred livres. The man must come to the warehouse and purchase other salt, make a declaration, carry off a certificate and show this at every visit of inspection. So much the worse for him if he has not the wherewithal to pay for this supplementary salt; he has only to sell his pig and abstain from meat at Christmas. This is the more frequent case, and I dare say that, for the métayers who pay twenty-five francs per annum, it is the usual case. It is forbidden to make use of any other salt for the pot and salt-cellar than that of the seven pounds. "I am able to cite," says Letrosne, "two sisters residing one league from a town in which the warehouse is open only on Saturday. Their supply was exhausted. To pass three or four days until Saturday comes they boil a remnant of brine from which they extract a few ounces of salt. A visit from the clerk ensues and a *procès-verbal.* Having friends and protectors this costs them only forty-eight livres." It is forbidden to take water from the ocean and from other saline sources, under a penalty of from twenty to forty livres fine. It is forbidden to water cattle in marshes and other places containing salt, under penalty of confiscation and a fine of three hundred livres. It is forbidden to put salt into the bellies of mackerel on returning from fishing, or between their superposed layers. An order prescribes one pound and a half to a barrel. Another order prescribes the destruction annually of the natural salt formed in certain cantons in Provence. Judges are prohibited from moderating or reducing the penalties imposed in salt

---

[1] Floquet, VI. 367 (May 10, 1760).

cases, under penalty of accountability and of deposition. I pass over quantities of orders and prohibitions, existing by hundreds. This legislation encompasses tax-payers like a net with a thousand meshes, while the official who casts it is interested in finding them at fault. We see the fisherman, accordingly, unpacking his barrel, the housewife seeking a certificate for her hams, the exciseman inspecting the buffet, testing the brine, peering into the salt-box and, if it is of good quality, declaring it contraband because that of the *ferme*, the only legitimate salt, is usually adulterated and mixed with plaster.

Meanwhile, other officials, those of the excise, descend into the cellar. None are more formidable, nor who more eagerly seize on pretexts for delinquency.[1] "Let a citizen charitably bestow a bottle of wine on a poor feeble creature and he is liable to prosecution and to excessive penalties. . . . The poor invalid that may interest his curate in the begging of a bottle of wine for him will undergo a trial, ruining not alone the unfortunate man that obtains it, but again the benefactor who gave it to him. This is not a fancied story." By virtue of the right of deficient revenue the clerks may, at any hour, take an inventory of wine on hand, even the stores of a vineyard proprietor, indicate what he may consume, tax him for the rest and for the surplus quantity already drunk, the *ferme* thus associating itself with the wine-producer and claiming its portion of his production. In a vineyard at Epernay[2] on four casks of wine, the average product of one *arpent*, and worth six hundred francs, it levies, at first, thirty francs, and then, after the sale of the four casks, seventy-five francs additionally. Naturally, "the inhabitants resort to the shrewdest and best planned artifices to escape" such potent rights.[3] But the clerks are alert, watchful, and well-informed, and they pounce down unexpectedly on every suspected domicile; their instructions prescribe frequent inspections and exact registries "enabling them to see at a glance the condition of the cellar of each inhabitant."[4] The manufacturer having paid up, the merchant now has his turn. The latter, on sending the four casks to the consumer again pays seventy-five francs to the *ferme*.

---

[1] Boivin-Champeaux, p. 44. (Cahiers of Bray and of Gamaches).

[2] Arthur Young, II. 175–178.

[3] Archives nationales, G, 300; G, 319.   (Memorials and instructions of various local directors of the Excise to their successors).

[4] Letrosne, *ibid.* 523.

The wine is despatched and the *ferme* prescribes the roads by which it must go; should others be taken it is confiscated, and at every step on the way some payment must be made. "A boat laden with wine from Languedoc, Dauphiny or Roussillon, ascending the Rhone and descending the Loire to reach Paris, through the Briare canal, pays on the way, leaving out charges on the Rhone, from thirty-five to forty kinds of duty, not comprising the charges on entering Paris." It pays these "at fifteen or sixteen places, the multiplied payments obliging the carriers to devote twelve or fifteen days more to the passage than they otherwise would if their duties could be paid at one bureau." The charges on the routes by water are particularly heavy. "From Pontarlier to Lyons there are twenty-five or thirty tolls; from Lyons to Aigues-Mortes there are others, so that whatever costs ten sous in Burgundy, amounts to fifteen and eighteen sous at Lyons, and to over twenty-five sous at Aigues-Mortes." The wine at last reaches the barriers of the city where it is to be drunk. Here it pays an *octroi* of forty-seven francs per hogshead. Entering Paris it goes into the tapster's or innkeeper's cellar where it again pays from thirty to forty francs for the duty on selling it at retail; at Rethel the duty is from fifty to sixty francs per puncheon, Rheims gauge. The total is exorbitant. "At Rennes,[1] the dues and duties on a barrel of Bordeaux wine, together with a fifth over and above the tax, local charges, eight sous per pound and the *octroi*, amount to more than seventy-two livres exclusive of the purchase money; to which must be added the expenses and duties advanced by the Rennes merchant and which he recovers from the purchaser, Bordeaux drayage, freight, insurance, tolls of the flood-gate, entrance duty into the town, hospital dues, fees of gaugers, brokers and inspectors. The total outlay for the tapster who sells a barrel of wine amounts to two hundred livres." We may imagine whether, at this price, the people of Rennes drink it, while these charges fall on the wine-grower, since, if consumers do not purchase, he is unable to sell.

Accordingly, among the small growers, he is the most to be pitied; according to the testimony of Arthur Young, wine-grower and misery are two synonymous terms. The crop often fails, "every doubtful crop ruining the man without capital." In

---

[1] Archives nationales, H, 426 (Papers of the Parliament of Brittany, February, 1783).

Burgundy, in Berry, in Soisonnais, in the Trois-Evêchés, in Champagne,[1] I find in every report that he lacks bread and lives on alms. In Champagne, the syndics of Bar-sur-Aube write[2] that the inhabitants, to escape duties, have more than once emptied their wine into the river, the provincial assembly declaring that "in the greater portion of the province the slightest augmentation of duties would cause the cultivators to desert the soil." Such is the history of wine under the ancient régime. From the producer who grows to the tapster who sells, what extortions and what vexations! As to the salt-tax, according to the comptroller-general,[3] this annually produces four thousand domiciliary seizures, three thousand four hundred imprisonments, five hundred sentences to flogging, exile and the galleys. If ever two imposts were well combined, not only to despoil, but to irritate the peasantry, the poor and the people, here they are.

VI.

Evidently the burden of taxation forms the chief cause of misery; hence an accumulated, deep-seated hatred against the fisc and its agents, receivers, store-house keepers, excise officials, customs officers and clerks. But why is taxation so burdensome? The answer is not doubtful, the communes which annually plead against certain persons to subject them to the *taille* writing it out fully in their demands. What renders the charge overwhelming is the fact that the strongest and those best able to bear taxation succeed in evading it, the prime cause of misery being their exemption.

Let us follow up the matter impost after impost. In the first place, not only are nobles and ecclesiastics exempt from the personal *taille* but again, as we have already seen, they are exempt from the cultivator's *taille*, through cultivating their domains themselves or by a steward. In Auvergne,[4] in the single election-district of Clermont, fifty parishes are enumerated in

---

[1] "Procès-verbaux de l'ass. prov. de Soissonnais" (1787), p. 45. Archives nationales, H, 1515 (Remonstrances of the Parliament of Metz, 1768). "The class of indigents form more than twelve-thirteenths of the whole number of villages of laborers and generally those of the wine-growers." *Ibid*. G, 319 (Tableau des directions of Chateaudun and Issoudun).

[2] Albert Babeau, I. 89. p. 21.

[3] "Mémoires," presented to the Assembly of Notables, by M. de Calonne (1787), p. 67.

[4] Gautier de Bianzat, "Doléances," 193, 225. "Procès-verbaux de l'ass. prov. de Poitou" (1787), p. 99.

which, owing to this arrangement, every estate of a privileged person is exempt, the *taille* falling wholly on those subject to it. Furthermore, it suffices for a privileged person to maintain that his farmer is only a steward, which is the case in Poitou in several parishes, the subdelegate and the *élu* not daring to look into the matter too closely. In this way the privileged classes escape the *taille*, they and their property, including their farms. Now, the *taille*, ever augmenting, is that which provides, through its special delegations, such a vast number of new offices. A man of the Third-Estate has merely to run through the history of its period-ical increase to see how it alone, or almost alone, paid and is pay-ing[1] for the construction of bridges, roads, canals and courts of jus-tice, for the purchase of offices, for the establishment and support of houses of refuge, insane asylums, nurseries, post-houses for horses, fencing and riding schools, for paving and sweeping Paris, for salaries of lieutenants-general, governors, and provincial com-manders, for the fees of bailiffs, seneschals and vice-bailiffs, for the salaries of financial and election officials and of commission-ers despatched to the provinces, for those of the police of the watch and I know not how many other purposes. In the prov-inces which hold assemblies, where the *taille* would seem to be more justly apportioned, the like inequality is found. In Bur-gundy[2] the expenses of the police, of public festivities, of keep-ing horses, all sums appropriated to the courses of lectures on chemistry, botany, anatomy and parturition, to the encourage-ment of the arts, to subscriptions to the chancellorship, to frank-ing letters, to presents given to the chiefs and subalterns of com-mands, to salaries of officials of the provincial assemblies, to the ministerial secretaryship, to expenses of levying taxes and even alms, in short, 1,800,000 livres are spent in the public service at the charge of the Third-Estate, the two higher orders not paying a cent.

In the second place, with respect to the poll-tax, originally dis-tributed among twenty-two classes and intended to bear equally on all according to fortunes, we know that, from the first, the clergy buy themselves off, and, as to the nobles, they manage

---

[1] Gautier de Bianzat, *ibid.*

[2] Archives nationales, the procès-verbaux and cahiers of the States-General, V. 59. p. 6. (Letter of M. Orgeux to M. Necker), t. 27. p. 560–573. (Cahiers of the Third-Estate of Arnay-le-Duc).

so well as to have their tax reduced proportionately with its increase at the expense of the Third-Estate. A count or a marquis,
an intendant or a master of requests, with 40,000 livres income,
who, according to the tariff of 1695,[1] should pay from 1,700 to
2,500 livres, pays only 400 livres, while a bourgeois with 6,000
livres income, and who, according to the same tariff, should pay
70 livres, pays 720. The poll-tax of the privileged individual is
thus diminished three-quarters or five-sixths, while that of the
taille-payer has increased tenfold. In the Ile-de-France,[2] on an
income of 240 livres, the *taille*-payer pays twenty-one livres eight
sous, and the nobles three livres, and the intendant himself states
that he taxes the nobles only an eighteenth of their revenue; that
of Orléanais taxes them only a hundredth, while, on the other
hand, those subject to the *taille* are assessed one-eleventh. If
other privileged parties are added to the nobles, such as officers
of justice, employés of the *fermes*, and exempted townsmen,
a group is formed embracing nearly everybody rich or well-off
and whose revenue certainly greatly surpasses that of those who
are subject to the *taille*. Now, the budgets of the provincial assemblies inform us how much each province levies on each of
the two groups: in the Lyonnais district those subject to the
taille pay 898,000 livres, the privileged, 190,000; in the Ile-de-
France, the former pay 2,689,000 livres and the latter 232,000;
in the generalship of Alençon, the former pay 1,067,000 livres
and the latter 122,000; in Champagne, the former pay 1,377,000
livres, and the latter 199,000; in Haute-Guyenne, the former pay
1,268,000 livres, and the latter 61,000; in the generalship of
Auch, the former pay 797,000 livres, the privileged 21,000; in
Auvergne the former pay 1,753,000 livres and the latter 86,000;
in short, summing up the total of ten provinces, 11,636,000 livres
paid by the poor group and 1,450,000 livres by the rich group,
the latter paying eight times less than it ought to pay.

   With respect to the *vingtièmes*, the disproportion is less, the precise amounts not being attainable; we may nevertheless assume
that the assessment of the privileged class is about one-half of

---

[1] In these figures the rise of the money standard has been kept in mind, the silver "marc,"
worth 29 francs in 1695, being worth 49 francs during the last half of the eighteenth century.
[2] "Procès-verbaux de l'ass. prov. de l'Ile-de-France," 132, 158; "—— de l'Orléanais,"
96, 367.

what it should be. "In 1772," says[1] M. de Calonne, "it was admitted that the *vingtièmes* were not carried to their full value. False declarations, counterfeit leases, too favorable conditions granted to almost all the wealthy proprietors gave rise to inequalities and countless errors. A verification of 4,902 parishes shows that the product of the two *vingtièmes* amounting to 54,000,000 should have amounted to 81,000,000." A seigniorial domain which, according to its own return of income, should pay 2,400 livres, pays only 1,216. The case is much worse with the princes of the blood; we have seen that their domains are exempt and pay only 188,000 livres instead of 2,400,000. Under this system, which crushes the weak to relieve the strong, the more capable one is of contributing, the less one contributes. The same story characterizes the fourth and last direct impost, namely, the tax substituted for the *corvée.* This tax, attached, at first, to the *vingtièmes* and consequently extending to all proprietors, through an act of the Council is attached to the *taille* and, consequently, bears on those the most burdened.[2] Now this tax amounts to an extra of one-quarter added to the principal of the *taille*, of which one example may be cited, that of Champagne, where, on every 100 livres income the sum of six livres five sous devolves on the *taille*-payer. "Thus," says the provincial assembly, "every road impaired by active commerce, by the multiplied coursings of the rich, is repaired wholly by the contributions of the poor."

As these figures spread out before the eye we involuntarily recur to the two animals in the fable, the horse and the mule travelling together on the same road; the horse, by right, may prance along as he pleases; hence his load is gradually transferred to the mule, the beast of burden, which finally sinks beneath the extra load.

Not only, in the corps of tax-payers, are the privileged disburdened to the detriment of the taxable, but again, in the corps of the taxable, the rich are relieved to the injury of the poor, to such an extent that the heaviest portion of the load finally falls on the most indigent and most laborious class, on the small proprietor

---

[1] "Mémoire," presented to the Assembly of Notables (1787), p. 1. See note 2 at the end of the volume, on the domain of Blet.

[2] "Procès-verbaux de l'ass. prov. d'Alsace" (1787), p. 116; "—— of Champagne," 192. (According to a declaration of June 2, 1787, the tax substituted for the *corvée* may be extended to one-sixth of the *taille*, with accessory taxes and the poll-tax combined). "De la généralité d'Alençon," 179; "—— du Berry," I. 218.

cultivating his own field, on the simple artisan with nothing but his tools and his hands, and, in general, on the inhabitants of villages. In the first place, in the matter of imposts, a number of the towns are " abonnées," or free. Compiègne, for the *taille* and its accessories, with 1,671 firesides, pays only 8,000 francs, whilst one of the villages in its neighborhood, Canly, with 148 firesides, pays 4,475 francs.[1] In the poll-tax, Versailles, Saint-Germain, Beauvais, Etampes, Pontoise, Saint-Denis, Compiègne, Fontaine-bleau, taxed in the aggregate at 169,000 livres, are two-thirds exempt, contributing but little more than one franc, instead of three francs ten sous, per head of the population; at Versailles it is still less, since for 70,000 inhabitants the poll-tax amounts to only 51,600 francs.[2] Besides, in any event, on the apportionment of a tax, the bourgeois of the town is favored above his rural neighbors. Accordingly, " the inhabitants of the country, who depend on the town and are comprehended in its functions, are treated with a rigor of which it would be difficult to form an idea. . . . Town influence is constantly throwing the burden on those who are trying to be relieved of it, the richest of citizens paying less *taille* than the most miserable of the peasant farmers." Hence, " a horror of the *taille* depopulates the rural districts, concentrating in the towns both capacity and capital."[3] Outside of the towns there is the same inequality. Each year, the *élus* and their collectors, exercising arbitrary power, fix the *taille* of the parish and of each inhabitant. In these ignorant and partial hands the scales are not held by equity but by self-interest, local hatreds, the desire for revenge, the necessity of favoring some friend, relative, neighbor, protector, or patron, some powerful or some dangerous person. The intendant of Moulins, on visiting his generalship, finds " people of influence paying nothing, while the poor are over-charged." That of Dijon writes that " the basis of apportionment is arbitrary, to such an extent that the people of the province must not be allowed to suffer any longer." In the generalship of Rouen " some parishes pay over four sous the livre and others scarcely one sou."[4] " For three years past that I have lived in the coun-

---

[1] Archives nationales, G, 322 (Memoir on the excise dues of Compiègne and its neighborhood, 1786).

[2] " Procès-verbaux de l'ass. prov. de l'Ile-de-France," p. 104.

[3] " Procès-verbaux de l'ass. prov. de Berry, I. 85, II. 91. "——— de l'Orléanais, p. 225." " Arbitrariness, injustice, inequality, are inseparable from the *taille* when any change of collector takes place."

[4] " Procès-verbaux de l'ass. prov. de la généralité de Rouen," p. 91.

try," writes a lady of the same district, "I have remarked that most of the wealthy proprietors are the least pressed; they are selected to make the apportionment, and the people are always abused."[1] "I live on an estate ten leagues from Paris," wrote d'Argenson, "where an effort is made to assess the *taille* proportionately, but only injustice has prevailed; the seigniors have succeeded in relieving their farmers."[2] Besides those who, through favor, diminish their *taille*, others buy themselves off entirely. An intendant, visiting the subdelegation of Bar-sur-Seine, observes "that the rich cultivators succeed in obtaining petty commissions in connection with the king's household and enjoy the privileges attached to these, which throws the burden of taxation on the others."[3] "One of the leading causes of our prodigious taxation," says the provincial assembly of Auvergne, "is the inconceivable number of the privileged, which daily increases through traffic in and the assignment of offices; cases occur in which these have ennobled six families in less than twenty years." Should this abuse continue, "in a hundred years every tax-payer the most capable of supporting taxation will be ennobled."[4] Observe, moreover, that an infinity of offices and functions, without conferring nobility, exempt their titularies from the personal *taille* and reduce their poll-tax to the fortieth of their income; at first, all public functionaries, administrative or judicial, and next all employments in the salt-department, in the customs, in the post-office, in the royal domains, and in the excise.[5] "There are few parishes," writes an intendant, "in which these employés are not found, while several contain as many as two or three."[6] A postmaster is exempt from the *taille*, in all his possessions and offices, and even on his farms to the extent of a hundred *arpents*. The notaries of Angoulême are exempt from the *corvée*, from collections, and the lodging of soldiers, while neither their sons or chief clerks can be drafted in the militia. On closely examining the great fiscal net in administrative correspondence, we detect at every step some

[1] Hippeau, VI. 22 (1788).
[2] D'Argenson, VI. 37.
[3] Archives nationales, H. 200 (Memoir of M. Amelot, 1785).
[4] "Procès-verbaux de l'ass. prov. d'Auvergne," 253.
[5] Boivin-Champeaux, "Doléances de la parvisse de Tilleul-Lambert" (Eure). "Numbers of privileged characters, Messieurs of the elections, Messieurs the post-masters, Messieurs the presidents and other attachés of the salt-warehouse, every individual possessing extensive property pays but a third or a half of the taxes they ought to pay."
[6] De Tocqueville, 385. "Procès-verbaux de l'ass. prov. de Lyonnais," p. 56.

meshes by which, with slight effort and industry, all the big and average-sized fish escape; the small fry alone remain at the bottom of the scoop.   A surgeon not an apothecary, a man of good family forty-five years old, in commerce, but living with his parent and in a province with a written code, escapes the collector. The same immunity is extended to the begging agents of the monks of "la Merci" and "L'Etroite Observance."   Throughout the South and the East individuals in easy circumstances purchase this commission of beggar for a "*louis*," or for ten crowns, and, putting three livres in a cup, go about presenting it in this or that parish:[1] ten of the inhabitants of a small mountain village and five inhabitants in the little village of Treignac obtain their discharge in this fashion.   Consequently, "the collections fall on the poor, always powerless and often insolvent," the privileged who effect the ruin of the tax-payer causing the deficiencies of the treasury.

VII.

One word more to complete the picture.   People take refuge in the towns and, indeed, compared with the country, the towns are a refuge.   But misery accompanies the poor, for, on the one hand, they are involved in debt, and, on the other, the coterie administering municipal affairs imposes taxation on the indigent. The towns being oppressed by the fisc, they oppress the people by throwing on these the load which the king imposes on them.   Seven times in twenty-eight years[2] he withdraws and re-sells the right of appointing their municipal officers, and, to get rid of "this enormous financial burden," the towns double their *octrois*.   At present, although liberated, they still make payment; the annual charge has become a perpetual charge; never does the fisc release its hold; once beginning to suck it continues to suck.   "Hence, in Brittany," says an intendant, "not a town is there whose expenses are not greater than its revenue."[3]   They are unable to mend their pavements, and repair their streets, "the approaches to them being almost impracticable."   What could

[1] Archives nationales, H, 1422.   (Letters of M. d'Aine, intendant, also of the receiver for the *election* of Tulle, February 23, 1783).
[2] De Tocqueville, 64, 363.
[3] Archives nationales, H, 612, 614.   (Letters of M. de la Bove, September 11, and Dec. 2, 1774; June 28, 1777).

they do for self-support, obliged, as they are, to pay over again after having already paid ? Their augmented *octrois*, in 1748, ought to furnish in eleven years the 606,000 livres agreed upon ; but, the eleven years having lapsed, the satisfied fisc still maintains its exigencies, and to such an extent that, in 1774, they have contributed 2,071,052 livres, the provisional *octroi* being still maintained. Now, this exorbitant *octroi* bears heavily every-where on the most indispensable necessities, the artisan being more heavily burdened than the bourgeois. In Paris, as we have seen above, wine pays forty-seven livres a puncheon entrance duty which, at the present standard of value, must be doubled. "A turbot, taken on the coast at Harfleur and brought by post, pays an entrance duty of eleven times its value, the people of the capital therefore being condemned to dispense with fish from the sea."[1] At the gates of Paris, in the little parish of Aubervilliers, I find "excessive duties on hay, straw, seeds, tallow, candles, eggs, sugar, fish, faggots and firewood."[2] Compiègne pays the whole amount of its *taille* by means of a tax on beverages and cattle.[3] "In Toul and in Verdun the taxes are so onerous that but few consent to remain in the town, except those kept there by their offices and by old habits."[4] At Coulommiers, "the merchants and the people are so severely taxed they dread undertaking any enterprise." Popular hatred everywhere is profound against *octroi*, barrier and clerk. The bourgeois oligarchy everywhere first cares for itself before caring for those it governs. At Nevers and at Moulins,[5] "all rich persons find means to escape the col-lections by different commissions, or through their influence with the *élus*, to such an extent that the collectors of Nevers, of the present and preceding year, would be considered true beggars : there are no small villages whose collectors are solvent, since the métayers have to be taken." At Angers, "independent of pres-ents and candles, which annually consume 2,172 livres, the public pence are employed and wasted in clandestine outlays according to the fancy of the municipal officers." In Provence, where the communities are free to tax themselves and where they ought, apparently, to consider the poor, "most of the towns, and notably

---

[1] Mercier, II. 62.

[2] "Doléances" of the parish of Aubervilliers.

[3] Archives nationales, G, 300; G, 322 (" Mémoires " on the excise duties).

[4] "Procès-verbaux de l'ass. prov. des Trois-Evêchés," p. 442.

[5] Archives nationales, H, 1422 (Letter of the intendant of Moulins, April 1779).

Aix, Marseilles and Toulon,[1] pay their impositions," local and general, "only by the duty of *piquet.*" This is a tax "on all species of flour belonging to and consumed on the territory;" for example, of 254,897 livres, which Toulon expends, the *piquet* furnishes 233,405. Thus the taxation falls wholly on the people, while the bishop, the marquis, the president, the merchant of importance pay less on their dinner of delicate fish and becaficos than the caulker or porter on his two pounds of bread rubbed with a piece of garlic! Bread in this country is already too dear! And the quality is so poor that Malouet, the intendant of the marine, refuses to let his workmen eat it! "Sire," said M. de la Fare, bishop of Nancy, from his pulpit, May 4th, 1789, "Sire, the people over which you reign has given unmistakable proofs of its patience. . . . They are martyrs in whom life seems to have been allowed to remain to enable them to suffer the longer."

VIII.

"I am miserable because too much is taken from me. Too much is taken from me because not enough is taken from the privileged. Not only do the privileged force me to pay in their place, but, again, they previously deduct from my earnings their ecclesiastic and feudal dues. When, out of my income of 100 francs, I have parted with fifty-three francs, and more, to the collector, I am obliged again to give fourteen francs to the seignior, also more than fourteen for tithes,[2] and, out of the remaining eighteen or nineteen francs, I have additionally to satisfy the excisemen. I alone, a poor man, pay two governments, one the old government, local and now absent, useless, inconvenient and humiliating, and active only through annoyances, exemptions and taxes; and the other, recent, centralized, everywhere present, which, taking upon itself all functions, has vast needs, and makes my meagre shoulders support its enormous weight." These, in precise terms, are the vague ideas beginning to ferment in the popular brain

---

[1] Archives nationales, H, 1312 (Letters of M. d'Antheman procureur-général of the excise court (May 19, 1783), and of the Archbishop of Aix (June 15, 1783).) Provence produced wheat only sufficient for seven and a half months' consumption.

[2] The feudal dues may be estimated at a seventh of the net income and the *dîme* also at a seventh. These are the figures given by the ass. prov. of Haute-Guyenne (Procès-verbaux, p. 47). Isolated instances, in other provinces, indicate similar results. The *dîme* ranges from a tenth to the thirteenth of the gross product, and commonly the tenth. I regard the average as about the fourteenth, and as one-half of the gross product must be deducted for expenses of cultivation, it amounts to one-seventh. Letrosne says a fifth and even a quarter.

and encountered on every page of the records of the States-General. "Would to God," says a Normandy village,[1] "the monarch might take into his own hands the defence of the miserable citizen pelted and oppressed by clerks, seigniors, justiciary and clergy!" "Sire," writes a village in Champagne,[2] "the only message to us on your part is a demand for money. We were led to believe that this might cease, but every year the demand comes for more. We do not hold you responsible for this because we love you, but those whom you employ, who better know how to manage their own affairs than yours. We believed that you were deceived by them and we, in our chagrin, said to ourselves, If our good king only knew of this! . . . We are crushed down with every species of taxation; thus far we have given you a part of our bread, and, should this continue, we shall be in want. . . . Could you see the miserable tenements in which we live, the poor food we eat, you would feel for us; this would prove to you better than words that we can support this no longer and that it must be lessened. . . . That which grieves us is that those who possess the most, pay the least. We pay the *tailles* and for our implements, while the ecclesiastics and nobles who own the best land pay nothing. Why do the rich pay the least and the poor the most? Should not each pay according to his ability? Sire, we entreat that things may be so arranged, for that is just. . . . Did we dare, we should undertake to plant the slopes with vines; but we are so persecuted by the clerks of the excise we would rather pull up those already planted; the wine that we could make would all go to them, scarcely any of it remaining for ourselves. These exactions are a great scourge and, to escape them, we would rather let the ground lie waste. . . . Relieve us of all these extortions and of the excisemen; we are great sufferers through all these devices; now is the time to change them; never shall we be happy as long as these last. We entreat all this of you, Sire, along with others of your subjects as wearied as ourselves. . . . We would entreat yet more but you cannot do all at one time." Imposts and privileges, in the really popular memorials, are the two enemies against which complaints everywhere arise.[3] " We are overwhelmed by

---

[1] Boivin-Champeaux, 72.

[2] Grievances of the community of Culmon (Election de Langres.)

[3] Boivin-Champeaux, 34, 36, 41, 48. Périn ("Doléances de sparoisses rurales de l'Artois," 301, 308). Archives nationales, procès-verbaux and cahiers of the States-Généraux, v. XVII. p. 12 (Letter of the inhabitants of Darcy-de-Viteux).

demands for subsidies, . . . we are burdened with taxes beyond our strength, . . . we do not feel able to support any more, . . . we perish, overpowered by the sacrifices demanded of us. . . . Labor is taxed while indolence is exempt. . . . Feudalism is the most disastrous of abuses, the evils it causes surpassing those of hail and lightning. . . . Subsistence is impossible if three-quarters of the crops are to be taken for field-rents, *terrage*, etc. . . . The proprietor has a fourth part, the *décimateur* a twelfth, the harvester a twelfth, taxation a tenth, not counting the depredations of vast quantities of game which devour the growing crops : nothing is left for the poor cultivator but pain and sorrow." Why should the Third-Estate alone pay for roads on which the nobles and the clergy drive in their carriages ? Why are the poor alone subject to militia draftings ? Why does "the subdelegate cause only the defenceless and the unprotected to be drafted ? " Why does it suffice to be the servant of a privileged person to escape this service ? Destroy those dove-cotes, formerly only small pigeon-pens and which now contain as many as five thousand pairs. Abolish the barbarous rights of " *motte, quevaise* and *domaine congéable* [1] under which more than five hundred thousand persons still suffer in Lower Brittany." "You have in your armies, Sire, more than thirty thousand Franche-Comté serfs ; " should one of these become an officer and be pensioned out of the service he would be obliged to return to and live in the hut in which he was born, otherwise; at his death, the seignior will take his pittance. Let there be no more absentee prelates, nor abbés-commendatory. "The present deficit is not to be paid by us but by the bishops and beneficiaries; deprive the princes of the church of two-thirds of their revenues." "Let feudalism be abolished. Man, the peasant especially, is tyrannically bowed down to the impoverished ground on which he lies exhausted. . . . There is no freedom, no prosperity, no happiness where the soil is enthralled. . . . Let the lord's dues, and other odious taxes not feudal, be abolished, a thousand times returned to the privileged. Let feudalism content itself with its iron sceptre without adding the poniard of the revenue speculator." [2]   Here,

---

[1] *Motte :* a mound indicative of seigniorial dominion ; *quevaise :* the right of forcing a resident to remain on his property under penalty of forfeiture ; *domaine congéable :* property held subject to capricious ejection.

[2] Prud'homme, " Résumé des cahiers," III. *passim.*, and especially from 317 to 340.

and for some time before this, it is not the countryman who speaks but the *procureur*, the lawyer, who places professional metaphors and theories at his service.   But the lawyer has simply translated the countryman's sentiments into literary dialect.

CHAPTER III.

INTELLECTUAL STATE OF THE PEOPLE.—I. Intellectual incapacity.—How ideas are transformed into marvellous stories.—II. Political incapacity.—Interpretation of political rumors and of government action.—III. Destructive impulses.—The object of blind rage.—Distrust of natural leaders.—Suspicion of them changed into hatred.—Disposition of the people in 1789.—IV. Insurrectionary leaders and recruits.—Poachers.—Smugglers and dealers in contraband salt.—Banditti.—Beggars and vagabonds.—Advent of brigands.—The people of Paris.

I.

To comprehend their actions we ought now to look into the condition of their minds, to know the current train of their ideas, their mode of thinking. But, is it really essential to draw this portrait, and are not the details of their mental condition we have just presented sufficient? We shall obtain a knowledge of them later, and through their actions, when, in Touraine, they come to bestowing kicks with their *sabots* on a mayor and his assistant chosen by themselves, because, in obeying the National Assembly, these two unfortunate men prepared a table of imposts; or when, at Troyes, they drag through the streets and tear to pieces the venerable magistrate who was nourishing them at that very moment, and who had just dictated his testament in their favor. Take the still rude brain of a contemporary peasant and deprive it of the ideas which, for eighty years past, have entered it by so many channels, through the primary school of each village, through the return home of the conscript after his seven years' service, through the prodigious multiplication of books, newspapers, roads, railroads, foreign travel and every other species of communication.[1] Try to imagine the peasant of that epoch,

---

[1] Théron de Montaugé, 102, 113. In the Toulousain ten parishes out of fifty have schools. In Gascony, says the ass. prov. of Auch (p. 24), "most of the rural districts are without schoolmasters or parsonages." In 1778, the post between Paris and Toulouse runs only three

penned and shut up from father to son in his hamlet, without parish highways, deprived of news, with no instruction but the Sunday sermon, solicitous only for his daily bread and the imposts, " with his wretched, dried-up aspect,"[1] not daring to repair his house, always persecuted, distrustful, his mind contracted and stinted, so to say, by misery.   His condition is almost that of his ox or his ass, while his ideas are those of his condition.   He has been a long time stolid ; " he lacks even instinct,"[2] mechanically and fixedly regarding the ground on which he drags along his hereditary plough.   In 1751, d'Argenson wrote in his journal : " nothing in the news from the court affects them ; the reign is indifferent to them. . . . The distance between the capital and the province daily widens. . . . Here they are ignorant of the striking occurrences that most impressed us at Paris. . . . The inhabitants of the country are merely poverty-stricken slaves, draft cattle under a yoke, moving on as they are goaded, caring for nothing and embarrassed by nothing, provided they can eat and sleep at regular hours."   They make no complaints, " they do not even dream of complaining ;"[3] their wretchedness seems to them natural like winter or hail.   Their minds, like their agriculture, still belong to the middle ages.   In the Toulousain,[4] to ascertain who committed a robbery, to cure a man or a sick animal, they resort to a sorcerer, who divines this by means of a sieve.   The countryman fully believes in ghosts and, on All Saints' eve, he lays the cloth for the dead.   In Auvergne, at the outbreak of the Revolution, on a contagious fever making its appearance, M. de Montlosier, declared to be a sorcerer, is the cause of it, and two hundred men assemble together to demolish his dwelling.   Their religious belief is on the same level.[5]   " Their priests drink with them and sell them absolution.   On Sundays, at the sermon, they put up lieutenancies and sub-lieutenancies (among the saints) for sale : so much for a lieutenant's place under St. Peter !   If the peasant hesitates in his bid, a eulogy of

---

times a week ; that of Toulouse by way of Alby, Rodez, etc., twice a week ; for Beaumont, Saint-Girons, etc., once a week.   "In the country," says Théron de Montaugé, "one may be said to live in solitude and exile."   In 1789 the Paris post reaches Besançon three times a week.   (Arthur Young, I. 257).

[1] One of the Marquis de Mirabeau's expressions.

[2] Archives nationales, G, 300, letter of an excise director at Coulommiers, Aug. 13, 1781.

[3] D'Argenson, VI. 425 (June 16, 1751).

[4] De Montlosier, I. 102, 146.

[5] Théron de Montaugé, 102.

St. Peter at once begins, and then our peasants run it up fast enough." To intellects in a primitive state, barren of ideas and crowded with images, idols on earth are as essential as idols in heaven. " No doubt whatever existed in my mind," says Rétit de la Bretonne,[1] " of the power of the king to compel any man to bestow his wife or daughter on me, and my village (Sacy, in Burgundy) thought as I did."[2] There is no room in minds of this description for abstract conceptions, for any idea of social order; they are submissive to it and that is all. " The mass of the people," writes Gouverneur Morris in 1789, " have no religion but that of their priests, no law but that of those above them, no morality but that of self-interest; these are the beings who, led on by drunken curates, are now on the high road to liberty, and the first use they make of it is to rebel on all sides because there is a dearth."[3]

How could things be otherwise? Every idea, previous to taking root in their brain, must possess a legendary form, as absurd as it is simple, adapted to their experiences, their faculties, their fears and their aspirations. Once planted in this uncultivated and fertile soil it vegetates and becomes transformed, developing into gross excrescences, sombre foliage and poisonous fruit. The more monstrous the greater its vigor, clinging to the slightest of probabilities and tenacious against the most certain of demonstrations. Under Louis XV., in an arrest of vagabonds, a few children having been carried off wilfully or by mistake, the rumor spreads that the king takes baths in blood to restore his exhausted functions, and, so true does this seem to be, the women, horrified through their maternal instincts, join in the riot; a policeman is seized and knocked down, and, on his demanding a confessor, a woman in the crowd, picking up a stone, cries out that he must not have time to go to heaven, and smashes his head with it, believing that she is performing an act of justice.[4] Under Louis XVI. evidence is presented to the people that there is no scarcity: in 1789,[5] an officer, listening to the conversation of his soldiers, hears them state "with full belief that the princes

[1] Monsieur Nicolas, I. 448.
[2] "Tableaux de la Révolution," by Schmidt, II. 7 (Report by the agent Perriere who lived in Auvergne.)
[3] Gouverneur Morris, II. 69, April 29, 1789.
[4] Mercier, "Tableau de Paris," XII. 83.
[5] De Vaublanc, 209.

and courtiers, with a view to starve Paris out, are throwing flour into the Seine." Turning to a quarter-master he asks him how he can possibly believe such an absurd story. "Lieutenant," he replies, "'tis time—the bags were tied with *blue strings (cordons bleus)*." To them this is a sufficent reason, and no argument could convince them to the contrary. Thus, among the dregs of society, foul and horrible romances are forged, in connection with famine and the Bastille, in which Louis XVI., the queen Marie Antoinette, the Comte d'Artois, Madame de Lamballe, the Polignacs, the revenue farmers, the seigniors and ladies of high rank are portrayed as vampires and ghouls. I have seen many editions of these in the pamphlets of the day, in the engravings not exhibited, and among popular prints and illustrations, the latter the most efficacious, since they appeal to the eye. They surpass the stories of Mandrin and Cartouche, being exactly suitable for men whose literature consists of the complaints of Mandrin and Cartouche.

II.

By this we can judge of their political intelligence. Every object appears to them in a false light; they are like children who, at each turn of the road, see in each tree or bush some frightful hobgoblin. Arthur Young, on visiting the springs near Clermont, is arrested,[1] and the people want to imprison a woman, his guide, some of the bystanders regarding him as "an agent of the Queen, who intended to blow the town up with a mine, and send all that escaped to the galleys." Six days after this, beyond Puy, and notwithstanding his passport, the village guard come and take him out of bed at eleven o'clock at night, declaring that "I was undoubtedly a conspirator with the Queen, the Count d'Artois and the Count d'Entragues (who has property here), who had employed me as *arpenteur* to measure their fields in order to double their taxes." We here take the unconscious, apprehensive, popular imagination in the act; a slight indication, a word, prompting the construction of either airy castles or fantastic dungeons, and seeing these as plainly as if they were so many substantial realities. They have not the inward resources that render them capable of separating and discerning; their

[1] Arthur Young, I. 283 (Aug. 13, 1789); I. 289 (Aug. 19, 1789).

conceptions are formed *in a lump ;* both object and fancy appear
together and are united in one single perception. At the moment of electing deputies the report is current in Provence [1] that
"the best of kings desires perfect equality, that there are to be
no more bishops, nor seigniors, nor tithes, nor seigniorial dues,
no more titles or distinctions, no more hunting or fishing rights,
. . . that the people are to be wholly relieved of taxation, and
that the first two orders alone are to provide the expenses of the
government." Whereupon forty or fifty riots take place in one
day. "Several communities refuse to make any payments to
their treasurer outside of royal requisitions." Others do better:
"on pillaging the strong-box of the receiver of the tax on leather
at Brignolles, they shout out *Vive le Roi !* " "The peasant constantly asserts his pillage and destruction to be in conformity
with the king's will." A little later, in Auvergne, the peasants
who burn castles are to display "much repugnance" in thus mal-
treating "such kind seigniors," but they allege "imperative orders, having been advised that the king wished it." [2] At Lyons,
when the tapsters of the town and the peasants of the neighborhood pass over the bodies of the customs officials they believe
that the king has suspended all customs dues for three days.[3]
The scope of their imagination is proportionate to their short-
sightedness. " Bread, no more rents, no more taxes!" is the sole
cry, the cry of want, while exasperated want plunges ahead like
a famished bull. Down with the monopolist!—storehouses are
forced open, convoys of grain are stopped, markets are pillaged,
bakers are hung, and the price of bread is fixed so that none is
to be had or is concealed. Down with the *octroi !*—barriers are
demolished, clerks are beaten, money is wanting in the towns for
urgent expenses. Burn tax registries, account-books, municipal
archives, seigniors' charter-safes, convent parchments, every detestable document creative of debtors and sufferers! The village
itself is no longer able to preserve its parish property. The rage
against any written document, against public officers, against any

---

[1] Archives nationales, H, 274. Letters respectively of M. de Caraman (March 18 and
April 12, 1789); M. d'Eymar de Montmegran (April 2); M. de la Tour (March 30). "The
sovereign's greatest benefit is interpreted in the strangest manner by an ignorant populace."
[2] Doniol, "Hist. des classes rurales," 495. (Letter of Aug. 3, 1789, to M. de Clermont-
Tonnerre).
[3] Archives nationales, H, 1453. (Letter of Imbert Colonnès, prévôt des marchands, dated
July 5, 1789).

man more or less connected with grain, is blind and determined. The furious animal destroys all, although wounding himself, driving and roaring against the obstacle that ought to be outflanked.

III.

This is owing to the absence of leaders and to the absence of organization, a multitude being simply a herd. Its mistrust of its natural leaders, of the great, of the wealthy, of persons in office and clothed with authority, is inveterate and incurable. Vainly do these wish it well and do it good; it has no faith in their humanity or disinterestedness. It has been too down-trodden; it entertains prejudices against every measure proceeding from them, even the most liberal and the most beneficial. "At the mere mention of the new assemblies," says a provincial commission in 1787,[1] "we heard a workman exclaim, 'What, more new extortioners!'" Superiors of every kind are suspected, and from suspicion to hostility the road is not long. In 1788[2] Mercier declares that "insubordination has been manifest for some years, especially among the trades. . . . Formerly, on entering a printing-office the men took off their hats. Now they content themselves with staring and leering at you; scarcely have you crossed the threshold when you hear yourself more lightly spoken of than if you were one of them." The same attitude is taken by the peasants in the environs of Paris; Madame Vigée-Lebrun,[3] on going to Romainville to visit Marshal de Ségur, remarks: "Not only do they not remove their hats but they regard us insolently; some of them even threatened us with clubs." In March and April following this, her guests arrive at her concert in consternation. "In the morning, at the promenade of Longchamps, the populace, assembled at the barrier of l'Etoile, insulted the people passing by in carriages in the grossest manner; some of these wretches jumped on the footsteps exclaiming: 'Next year you shall be behind the carriage and we inside.'" At the close of the year 1788, the stream becomes a torrent and the torrent a cataract. An intendant[4] writes that, in his province, the government must decide, and

---

[1] "Procès-verbaux de l'ass. prov. de l'Orléanais," p. 296. "Distrust still prevails throughout the rural districts. . . . Your first orders for departmental assemblies only awakened suspicion in certain quarters."

[2] "Tableau de Paris," XII. 186.

[3] Mme. Vigée-Lebrun, I. 158 (1788); I. 183 (1789).

[4] Archives nationales, H, 723. (Letter of M. de Caumartin, intendant at Besançon, Dec. 5, 1788).

in the popular sense, to separate from privileged classes, abandon old forms and give the Third-Estate a double vote. The clergy and the nobles are detested, and their supremacy is a yoke. "Last July," he says, "the old States-General would have been received with transport and there would have been few obstacles to its formation. During the past five months minds have become enlightened; respective interests have been discussed, and leagues formed. You have been kept in ignorance of the fermentation which is at its height among all classes of the Third-Estate, and a spark will kindle the conflagration. If the king's decision should be favorable to the first two orders a general insurrection will occur throughout the province, 600,000 men in arms and the horrors of the Jacquerie." The word is spoken and the reality is coming. An insurrectionary multitude rejecting its natural leaders must elect or submit to others. It is like an army which, entering on a campaign, should depose its officers; the new grades are for the boldest, most violent, most oppressed, for those who, putting themselves ahead, cry out "march" and thus form advanced bands. In 1789, the bands are ready; for, below the mass that suffers another suffers yet more, with which the insurrection is permanent, and which, repressed, persecuted, and obscure, only awaits an opportunity to issue from its hiding-place and ravage in the open daylight.

IV.

Vagrants, every species of refractory spirit, victims of the law and of the police, mendicants, deformities, foul, filthy, haggard and savage, are engendered by the abuses of the system, and, around every one of the social wounds these swarm like vermin. Four hundred leagues of guarded captainries and the security enjoyed by vast quantities of game feeding on crops under their owners' eyes, give rise to thousands of poachers, the more dangerous that they are armed, and defy the most terrible laws. Already in 1752 [1] are seen around Paris "gatherings of fifty or sixty, all fully armed and acting as if on regular foraging campaigns, with the infantry at the centre and the cavalry on the wings. . . . They live in the forests behind retired and guarded entrenchments, paying exactly for what they take to

---

[1] D'Argenson, March 13, 1752.

live on." In 1777, at Sens in Burgundy, the procureur-général, M. Terray, hunting on his own property with two officers, meets a gang of poachers who fire on the game under his own eye, and soon afterwards fire on them. M. Terray is wounded and one of the officers has his coat pierced; guards arrive, but the poachers stand firm and repel them; dragoons are sent for, at Provins, and the poachers kill one of these, along with three horses, and are attacked with sabres; four of them are brought to the ground and seven are captured. Reports of the States-General show that every year, in each extensive forest, murders occur, sometimes at the hands of a poacher, and again, and the most frequently, by the shot of a gamekeeper. Domestic warfare is organized; every vast domain thus harbors its rebels, provided with powder and ball and knowing how to use them.

Other recruits for turbulence are found in smugglers and in dealers in contraband salt.[1] A tax, as soon as it becomes exorbitant, invites fraud, and raises up a population of delinquents against its army of clerks. The number of defrauders of this species may be estimated by the number of their supervisors: twelve hundred leagues of interior custom districts are guarded by 50,000 men, of which 23,000 are soldiers not in uniform.[2] "In the chief provinces of the salt-tax and in the provinces of the five great *fermes*, four leagues one way and another along the line of defence," cultivation is abandoned; everybody is either a customs official or a smuggler.[3] The more excessive the tax the higher the premium offered to the violators of the law; at every place on the boundaries of Brittany with Normandy, Maine and Anjou, four *sous* per pound added to the salt-tax multiplies beyond any conception the already enormous number of contraband dealers. "Numerous bands of men,[4] armed with *frettes*, or long sticks pointed with iron, and often with pistols or guns, attempt to force a passage. A multitude of women and of children, quite young, cross the lines of the brigades while, on the

---

[1] Beugnot, I. 142. "No inhabitant of the barony of Choiseul mingled with any of the bands composed of the patriots of Montigny, smugglers and outcasts of the neighborhood." See, on the poachers of the day, "Les deux amis de Bourbonne," by Diderot.

[2] De Calonne, "Mémoires presentés à l'ass. des notables," No. 8. Necker, "De l'Ad ministration des Finances," I. 195.

[3] Letrosne, "De l'Administration des Finances," 59.

[4] Archives nationales, H. 426. (Memorials of the farmers-general, Jan. 13, 1781; Sept. 15, 1782). H, 614. (Letter of M. de Coetlosquet, April 25, 1777). H, 1431. Report by the farmers-general, March 9, 1787.

other hand, troops of dogs brought upon the free soil and kept
there a certain time without food, are loaded with salt, and this,
urged by their hunger, they immediately transport to their masters."
Vagabonds, outlaws, the famished, sniff this lucrative occupation
from afar and run to it like so many packs of hounds. "The
outskirts of Brittany are filled with a population of emigrants,
mostly outcasts from their own districts, and who, after a year's
sojourn here in domicile, enjoy the privileges of the Bretons:
their occupation is limited to collecting piles of salt to re-sell to
the contraband dealers." We obtain a glimpse, as in a flash of
lightning, of this long line of restless, hunted, midnight rovers, a
male and female population of savage wanderers, accustomed to
blows, hardened to the inclemencies of the weather, ragged,
"almost all with an obstinate itch;" and I find similar bodies in
the vicinity of Morlaix, Lorient, and other ports on the frontiers
of other provinces and on the frontiers of the kingdom. From
1783 to 1787, in Quercy, two allied bands of smugglers, sixty
and eighty each, defraud the revenue of forty thousands of
tobacco, kill two customs officers, and, with their guns, defend
their magazine in the mountains; to suppress them soldiers are
requisite, which their military commander will not furnish. In
1789,[1] a large troop of smugglers carry on operations permanently
on the frontiers of Maine and Anjou; the military commander
writes that "their chief is an intelligent and formidable bandit,
that he already has under him fifty-five men, that he will soon
have a corps, embarrassing through misery and through the disposition of minds;" it would be well, possibly, to corrupt some of
his men so as to have him betrayed, since they cannot capture
him. These are the means resorted to in regions where brigandage is endemic. Here, indeed, as in Calabria, the people are on
the side of the brigands against the gendarmes. The exploits
of Mandrin in 1754,[2] may be remembered: his company of sixty
men who bring in contraband goods and ransom only the clerks,
his expedition, lasting nearly a year, across Franche-Comté, Lyonnais, Bourbonnais, Auvergne and Burgundy, the twenty-seven
towns he enters making no resistance, delivering prisoners and
making sale of his merchandise; to overcome him a camp had
to be formed at Valence and two thousand men sent against him;

---

[1] Archives nationales, H, 1453. Letter of the Baron de Bezenval, June 19, 1789.
[2] "Mandrin," by Paul Simian, passim. "Histoire de Bearme," by Rossègnol, p. 453.

he was taken through treachery, and still at the present day certain families are proud of their relationship to him, declaring him a liberator. No symptom is more alarming: on the enemies of the law being preferred by the people to its defenders, society disintegrates and the worms begin to work. Add to these the veritable brigands, assassins and robbers. "In 1782,[1] the provost's court of Montargis is engaged on the trial of Hulin and two hundred of his accomplices who, for ten years, by means of joint enterprises, have desolated a portion of the kingdom." Mercier enumerates in France "an army of more than 10,000 brigands and vagabonds" against which the police, composed of 3,756 men, is always on the march. "Complaints are daily made," says the provincial assembly of Haute-Guyenne, "that there is no police in the country." The absentee seignior pays no attention to this matter; his judges and officials take good care not to operate gratuitously against an insolvent criminal, while "his estates become the refuge of all the rascals of the canton."[2] Every abuse thus engenders a danger, ill-placed neglect equally with excessive rigor, relaxed feudalism equally with a too-exacting monarchy. All institutions seem under agreement to multiply or tolerate the abettors of disorder, and to prepare, outside the social pale, the executive agents who are to carry it by storm.

But the total effect of all this is yet more pernicious, for, out of the vast numbers of laborers it ruins it forms mendicants unwilling to work, dangerous sluggards going about begging and extorting bread from peasants who have not too much for themselves. "The vagabonds about the country," says Letrosne,[3] "are a terrible pest; they are like an enemy's force which, distributed over the territory, obtains a living as it pleases, levying veritable contributions. . . . They are constantly roving around the country, examining the approaches to houses, and informing themselves about their inmates and of their habits. Woe to those supposed to have money! . . . What numbers of highway robberies and what burglaries! What numbers of travellers assassinated, and houses and doors broken into! What assassinations of curates, farmers and widows, tormented to discover money and afterwards killed!" Twenty-five years anterior

---

[1] Mercier, XI. 116.
[2] See *ante*, book I. p. 55.
[3] Letrosne, *ibid.* (1779), p. 539.

to the Revolution it was not infrequent to see fifteen or twenty of these "invade a farm-house to sleep there, intimidating the farmers and exacting whatever they pleased." In 1764, the government takes measures against them which indicate the magnitude of the evil.[1] "Are held to be vagabonds and vagrants, and condemned as such, those who, for a preceding term of six months, shall have exercised no trade or profession, and who, having no occupation or means of subsistence, can procure no persons worthy of confidence to attest and verify their habits and mode of life. . . . The intent of His Majesty is not merely to arrest vagabonds traversing the country but, again, all mendicants whatsoever who, without occupations, may be regarded as suspected of vagabondage." The penalty for able-bodied men is three years in the galleys; in case of a second conviction, nine years; in case of a third conviction, the galleys for life. For invalid culprits, three years imprisonment; in case of a second conviction, nine years, and for a third, imprisonment for life. Under the age of sixteen, they are put in a hospital. "A mendicant who has made himself liable to arrest by the police," says the circular, "is not to be released except under the most positive assurance that he will no longer beg; this course will be followed only in case of persons worthy of confidence and *solvent* guaranteeing the mendicant, and engaging to provide him with employment or to support him, and they shall indicate the means by which they are to prevent him from begging." This being furnished, the special authorization of the intendant must be obtained in addition. By virtue of this law, 50,000 beggars are said to have been arrested at once, and, as the ordinary hospitals and prisons were not large enough to contain them, jails had to be constructed. Up to the end of the ancient régime this measure is carried out with occasional intermissions: in Languedoc, in 1768, arrests were still made of 433 in six months, and, in 1785, 205 in four months.[2] About the same epoch 300 were confined in the depot of Besançon, 500 in that of Rennes and 650 in that of St. Denis. It cost the king a million a year to support them, and God knows how they were supported! Water, straw, bread, and two ounces of

[1] Archives nationales, F16, 965, and H, 892. (Ordinance of August 4, 1764; a circular of instructions of July 20, 1767; a letter of a police lieutenant of Toulouse, September 21, 1787).

[2] Archives nationales, H, 724; H, 554; F4, 2397; F16, 965. Letters of the jail-keepers of Carcassonne (June 22, 1789); of Béziers (July 19, 1786); of Nimes (July 1, 1786); of the intendant, M d'Aine (March 19, 1786).

salted grease, the whole at an expense of five *sous* a day; and, as the price of provisions for twenty years back had increased more than a third, the keeper who had them in charge was obliged to make them fast or ruin himself. With respect to the mode of filling the depots, the police are Turks in their treatment of the lower class; they strike into the heap, their broom bruising as many as they sweep out. According to the ordinance of 1778, writes an intendant,[1] "the police must arrest not only beggars and vagabonds whom they encounter but, again, those denounced as such or as suspected persons. The citizen, the most irreproachable in his conduct and the least open to suspicion of vagabondage, is not sure of not being shut up in the depot, as his freedom depends on a policeman who is constantly liable to be deceived by false denunciation or corrupted by a bribe. I have seen in the depot at Rennes several husbands arrested solely through the denunciation of their wives, and as many women through that of their husbands; several children by the first wife at the solicitation of their step-mothers; many female domestics pregnant by the masters they served, shut up at their instigation, and girls in the same situation at the instance of their seducers; children denounced by their fathers, and fathers denounced by their children; all without the slightest evidence of vagabondage or mendicity. . . . No decision of the provost's court exists restoring the incarcerated to their liberty, notwithstanding the infinite number arrested unjustly." Suppose that a humane intendant, like this one, sets them at liberty : there they are in the streets, mendicants through the action of the law which proscribes mendicity and which adds to the wretched it prosecutes the wretched it creates, still more embittered and corrupt in body and in soul. " It nearly always happens," says the same intendant, "that the prisoners, arrested twenty-five or thirty leagues from the depot, are not confined there until three or four months after their arrest, and sometimes longer. Meanwhile, they are transferred from brigade to brigade, in the prisons found along the road, where they remain until the number increases sufficiently to form a convoy. Men and women are confined in the same prison, the result of which is, the females not pregnant on entering it are always so on their arrival at the depot. The prisons are

---

[1] Archives nationales, H, 554. (Letter of M. de Bertrand, intendant of Rennes, August 7, 1785).

2 C

generally unhealthy; frequently, the majority of the prisoners are sick on leaving it; " and many become rascals on coming in contact with rascals. Moral contagion and physical contagion, the ulcer thus increasing through the remedy, centres of repression becoming centres of corruption.

And yet with all its rigors the law does not attain its ends. "Our towns," says the parliament of Brittany,[1] "are so filled with beggars it seems as if the measures taken to suppress mendicity only increase it." "The principal highways," writes the intendant, "are infested with dangerous vagabonds and vagrants, actual beggars, which the police do not arrest, either through negligence or because their interference is not provoked by special solicitations." What would be done with them if they were arrested? There are too many, and there is no place to put them. And, moreover, how prevent people who live on alms from demanding alms? The effect, undoubtedly, is lamentable but inevitable. Poverty, to a certain extent, is a slow gangrene in which the morbid parts consume the healthy parts, the man scarcely able to subsist being eaten up alive by the man who has nothing to live on. "The peasant is ruined, perishing, the victim of oppression by the multitude of the poor that lay waste the country and take refuge in the towns. Hence the mobs so prejudicial to public safety, that crowd of smugglers and vagrants, that large body of men who have become robbers and assassins, solely because they lack bread. This gives but a faint idea of the disorders I have seen with my own eyes.[2] The poverty of the rural districts, excessive in itself, becomes yet more so through the disturbances it engenders; we have not to seek elsewhere for frightful sources of mendicity and for all the vices." [3] Of what avail are palliatives or violent proceedings against an evil which is in the blood, and which belongs to the very constitution of the social organism? What police force could effect anything in a parish in which one-quarter or one-third of its inhabitants have nothing to eat but that which they beg from door to door? At Argentré,[4] in Brittany, "a town without trade or

[1] Archives nationales, H, 426. (Remonstrance, Feb. 4, 1783). H, 554. (Letter of M. de Bertrand, Aug. 17, 1785).

[2] *Ibid.* H, 614. (Memorial by René de Hauteville, parliamentary advocate, St. Brieuc, Dec. 25, 1776).

[3] "Procès-verbaux de l'ass. prov. de Soissonnais" (1787), p. 457.

[4] Archives nationales, H, 616. (A letter of M. de Boves, intendant of Rennes, April 1774).

industry, out of 2,300 inhabitants, more than one-half are anything else but well-off, and over 500 are reduced to beggary."
At Dainville, in Artois, " out of 130 houses sixty are on the poor-
list." [1] In Normandy, according to statements made by the
curates, "of 900 parishioners in Saint-Malo, three-quarters can
barely live and the rest are in poverty." "Of 1,500 inhabitants
in Saint-Patrice, 400 live on alms; of 500 inhabitants in Saint-
Laurent three-quarters live on alms. " At Marbœuf, says a report,
"of 500 persons inhabiting our parish, 100 are reduced to mendicity, and besides these, thirty and forty a day come to us from
neighboring parishes." [2] At Bolbone in Languedoc [3] daily at the
convent gate is "general alms-giving to 300 or 400 poor people,
independent of that for the aged and the sick, which is more
numerously attended." At Lyons, in 1787, "30,000 workmen
depend on public charity for subsistence;" at Rennes, in 1788,
after an inundation, "two-thirds of the inhabitants are in a state
of destitution;" [4] at Paris, out of 650,000 inhabitants, the census
of 1791 enumerates 118,784 as indigent. [5] Let frost or hail come,
as in 1788, let a crop fail, let bread cost four *sous* a pound, and
let a workman in the charity-workshops earn only twelve *sous*
a day, [6] can one imagine that people will resign themselves to
death by starvation ? Around Rouen, during the winter of 1788,
the forests are pillaged in open day, the woods at Baguères are
wholly cut away, the fallen trees are publicly sold by the marauders. [7] Both the famished and the marauders go together,
necessity making itself the accomplice of crime. From province
to province we can follow up their tracks : four months later, in
the vicinity of Etampes, fifteen brigands break into four farm-
houses during the night, while the farmers, threatened by incen-
diaries, are obliged to give, one three hundred francs, another
five hundred, all the money, probably, they have in their coffers. [8]

---

[1] Périn, "La Jeunesse de Robespierre," 301. (Doléances des parvisses rurales in 1789).

[2] Théron de Montaugé, p. 87. (Letter of the prior of the convent, March, 1789).

[3] Hippeau, "Le Gouvern. de Normandie," VII. 147–177 (1789). Boivin-Champeaux,
"Notice hist. sur la Révolution dans le département de l'Eure," p. 83 (1789).

[4] "Procès-verbaux de l'ass. prov. de Lyonnais," p. 57. Archives nationales, F⁴, 2073.
Memorial of Jan. 24, 1788. "Charitable assistance is very limited, the provincial authorities
providing no resources for such accidents."

[5] Levasseur, "La France industrielle," 119. In 1862, the population being almost triple
(1,696,000), there are but 90,000.

[6] Albert Babeau, "Hist. de Troyes," I. 91. (Letter of the mayor Huez, July 30, 1788).

[7] Floquet, VII. 506.

[8] Archives nationales, H, 1453. (Letter of M. de Saint-Suzanne, April 29, 1789).

"Robbers, convicts, the worthless of every species," are to form the advance guard of insurrections and lead the peasantry to the extreme of violence.[1] After the sack of the Reveillon house in Paris it is remarked that "of the forty ringleaders arrested, there was scarcely one who was not an old offender, and either flogged or branded."[2] In every revolution the lees of society come to the surface. Never had these been visible before; like badgers in the woods, or rats in the sewers, they had remained in their burrows or in their holes. They issue from these in swarms, while, in Paris, what figures suddenly come to light![3] "Never had any like them been seen in open day. . . . Where do they come from? who has brought them out of their obscure hiding-places? . . . Foreigners from every country, armed with clubs, ragged, . . . some almost naked, others oddly dressed" in incongruous patches and "frightful to look at," constitute the riotous chiefs or their subordinates, at six francs per head, behind which the people are to march.

"In Paris," says Mercier,[4] "the people are weak, pallid, diminutive, stunted," maltreated, "and, apparently, a class apart from other classes in the State. The rich and the great who possess equipages, enjoy the privilege of crushing them or of mutilating them in the streets. . . . There is no convenience for foot-passengers, no sidewalks. Hundreds of victims die annually under the carriage wheels." "I saw," says Arthur Young, "a poor child run over and probably killed, and have been myself many times blackened with the mud of the kennels. . . . If young noblemen in London were to drive their chaises in streets without foot-ways, as their brethren do at Paris, they would speedily and justly get very well thrashed or rolled in the kennel." Mercier grows uneasy in the face of the immense populace. "In Paris there are, probably, two hundred thousand individuals with no property intrinsically worth fifty crowns, and yet the city subsists!" Order, consequently, is maintained only through fear and by force, owing to the soldiery of the watch who are called

---

[1] Arthur Young, I. 256.

[2] "Corresp. secrète inédite," from 1777 to 1792, published by M. de Lescure, II. 351 (May 8, 1789). Cf. C. Desmoulins, "La Lanterne," of 100 rioters arrested at Lyons 96 were *branded.*

[3] De Bezenval, II. 344, 350. Dussault, "La Prise de la Bastille," 352. Marmontel, II. ch. xiv. 249. Mme. Vigée-Lebrun, I. 177, 188.

[4] Mercier, I. 32; VI. 15; X. 179; XI. 59; XII. 83. Arthur Young, I. 122.

tristes-à-patte by the masses. "This appellation excites the rage of this species of militia, who then deal heavier blows around them, wounding indiscriminately all they encounter. The low class is always ready to make war on them because it has never been fairly treated by them." In fact, "a squad of the guard often scatters, with no trouble, platoons of five or six hundred men, at first greatly excited, but melting away in the twinkling of an eye, after the soldiery have distributed a few blows and handcuffed two or three of the ringleaders." Nevertheless, "were the people of Paris abandoned to their first transports, did they not feel the horse and foot guards behind them, the commissary and policeman, they would set no limits to their disorder. The populace, delivered from its accustomed restraint, would give itself up to violence of so cruel a stamp as not to know when to stop. . . . As long as white bread[1] lasts, the commotion will not prove general ; the flour market[2] must interest itself in the matter, if the women are to remain tranquil. . . . Should white bread be wanting for two market days in succession, the uprising would be universal, and it is impossible to foresee the lengths this mul titude at bay will go to escape famine, they and their children." In 1789 white bread proves to be wanting throughout France.

---

[1] In the original, *pain de Gonesse,* —bread, made in a village of this name near Paris, and renowned for its whiteness.—TR.

[2] "Dialogues sur le commerce des blés," by Galiani (1770). "If the powerful of the markets are content, no misfortune will happen to the administration. The great conspire and rebel ; the bourgeois murmurs and lives a celibate; peasants and artisans despair and go away; porters get up riots."

CHAPTER IV.

I. Military force declines.—How the army is recruited.—How the soldier is treated.—II. The social organization is dissolved.—No central rallying-point.—Inertia of the provinces.—Ascendancy of Paris.—III. Direction of the current.—The people led by lawyers.—Theories and piques the sole surviving forces.

I.

AGAINST universal sedition where is force? In the hundred and fifty thousand men who maintain order dispositions are the same as in the twenty-six millions of men who are subject to it, while abuses, disaffection, and all the causes that dissolve the nation, dissolve the army. Of the ninety millions of pay[1] which the army annually costs the treasury, forty-six millions are for officers and only forty-four millions for soldiers, and we are already aware that a new ordinance reserves ranks of all kinds for verified nobles. In no direction is this inequality, against which public opinion rebels so vigorously, more apparent; on the one hand, authority, honors, money, leisure, good-living, social enjoyments, and plays in private, for the minority; on the other hand, for the majority, subjection, dejection, fatigue, a forced or betrayed enlistment, no hope of promotion, pay at six *sous* a day, a narrow cot for two, bread fit for dogs, and, for several years, kicks like those bestowed on a dog;[2] on the one hand, a nobility of high estate, and, on the other, the lowest of the populace. One might say that this was specially designed for contrasts and to intensify irritation. "The insignificant pay of the soldier," says an economist, "the way in which he is dressed, lodged and fed, his utter dependence, would render it cruelty to take any other than a man of the lower class."[3]

---

[1] Necker, "De l'Administration des Finances," II. 422, 435.
[2] Aubertin, 345. Letter of the Comte de St. Germain (during the Seven Years War). "The soldier's hardships make one's heart bleed; he passes his days in a state of abject misery, despised and living like a fighting dog in chains."
[3] De Tocqueville, 190, 191.

Indeed, he is sought for only in the very lowest stages. Not only are nobles and the bourgeoisie exempt from conscription, but again the employés of the administration, of the *fermes* and of public works, " all gamekeepers and forest-rangers, the hired domestics and valets of ecclesiastics, of communities, of religious establishments, of the gentry and of nobles," [1] and even of the bourgeoisie living in grand style, and still better, the sons of cultivators in easy circumstances, and, in general, all possessing influence or any species of protector. There remains, accordingly, for the militia none but the poorest class, and they do not willingly enter it. On the contrary, the service is hateful to them ; they conceal themselves in the forests where they have to be pursued with arms in the hand : in a certain canton which, three years later, furnishes in one day from fifty to one hundred volunteers, the young men cut off their thumbs to escape the draft.[2] To this scum of society is added the sweepings of the depots and of the jails. Among the vagabonds that fill these, after winnowing out those able to make their families known or to obtain sponsors, " there are none left," says an intendant, " but those who are entirely unknown and dangerous, out of which those regarded as the least vicious are selected and efforts are made to place these in the army." [3] The last of its affluents is the half-forced, half-voluntary enlistment by which the ranks are for the most part filled, the offscourings of large towns, like adventurers, discharged apprentices, young reprobates turned out of doors, and people without homes or steady occupation. The recruiting agent who is paid so much a head for his recruits and so much an inch on their stature above five feet, " holds his court in a tavern, treats" and fashions the article: " Come, boys, soup, fish, meat and salad is what you get to eat in the regiment;" that is all, " I don't deceive you—pie and Arbois wine are the extras." [4] He pushes around the glass, pays accordingly and, if need be, yields his mistress. " After a few days debauchery, the young

---

[1] Archives nationales, H, 1591.

[2] De Rochambeau, "Mémoires," I. 427. D'Argenson, Decem. 24, 1752: "30,000 men have been punished for desertion since the peace of 1748; this extensive desertion is attributed to the new drill which fatigues and disheartens the soldier, and especially the veterans." Voltaire, "Dict. Phil.," article "Punishments." "I was amazed one day on seeing the list of deserters, for eight years amounting to 60,000."

[3] Archives nationales, H, 554. (Letter of M. de Bertrand, intendant of Rennes, August 17, 1785).

[4] Mercier, XI. 121.

libertine, with no money to pay his score, is obliged to sell himself, while the laborer, transformed to a soldier, begins to drill under the lash." Strange recruits these, for the protection of society, all selected from the attacking class, down-trodden peasants, imprisoned vagabonds, social outcasts, poor fellows in debt, disheartened, excited and easily tempted, who, according to circumstances, become at one time rioters, and at another soldiers.

Which lot is preferable? The bread the soldier eats is not more abundant than that of the prisoner, while poorer in quality · for the bran is taken out of the bread which the locked-up vagabond eats, and left in the bread which is eaten by the soldier who locks him up. In this state of things the soldier ought not to meditate on his lot, and yet this is just what his officers incite him to do. They also have become politicians and fault-finders. Some years before the Revolution [1] "disputes occurred" in the army, "discussions and complaints, and, the new ideas fermenting in their heads, a correspondence was established between two regiments. Written information was obtained from Paris, authorized by the Minister of War, which cost, I believe, twelve louis per annum. It soon took a philosophic turn, embracing dissertations, criticisms of the ministry, and of the government, desirable changes and, therefore, the more diffused." Sergeants like Hoche, and fencing-masters like Augereau, certainly often read this news, carelessly left lying on the tables, and commented on it during the evening in their soldier quarters. Discontent is of ancient date, and already, at the end of the late reign, grievous words are heard. At a banquet given by a prince of the blood,[2] with a table set for a hundred guests under an immense tent and served by grenadiers, the odor these diffused offended the prince's delicate olfactories. "These worthy fellows," said he, a little too loud, "smell strong of the stocking." One of the grenadiers bluntly responded, "Because we haven't got any," which "was followed by profound silence." During the ensuing years irritation smoulders and augments; the soldiers of Rochambeau have fought side by side with the free militia of America, and they keep this in mind. In 1788,[3] Marshal de Vaux, previous to the

---

[1] De Vaublanc, 149.
[2] De Ségur, I. 20 (1767).
[3] Augeard "Mémoires," 165.

insurrection in Dauphiny, writes to the minister that " it is impossible to rely on the troops," while four months after the opening of the States-General sixteen thousand deserters roaming around Paris lead the revolts instead of suppressing them.[1]

II.

This dyke once carried away no other remains, the inundation overspreading France like an immense plain. With other nations in like circumstances, some obstacles have been encountered; elevations have existed, centres of refuge, old constructions in which, in the universal fright, a portion of the population could find shelter. Here, the first crisis sweeps away all that remains, each individual of the twenty-six scattered millions standing alone by himself. The administrations of Richelieu and Louis XIV. had been a long time at work insensibly destroying the natural groupings which, when suddenly dissolved, unite and form over again of their own accord. Except in Vendée, I find no place, nor any class, in which a good many men, having confidence in a few men, are able, in the hour of danger, to rally around these and form a compact body. Neither provincial nor municipal patriotism any longer exists. The inferior clergy are hostile to the prelates, the gentry of the province to the nobility of the court, the vassal to the seignior, the peasant to the townsman, the urban population to the municipal oligarchy, corporation to corporation, parish to parish, neighbor to neighbor. All are separated by their privileges and their jealousies, by the consciousness of having been imposed on, or frustrated, for the advantage of another. The journeyman tailor is embittered against his foreman for preventing him from doing a day's work in private houses, hairdressers against their employers for the like reason, the pastrycook against the baker who prevents him from baking the pies of housekeepers, the village spinner against the town spinners who wish to break him up, the rural wine-growers against the bourgeois who, in the circle of seven leagues, strives to have their vines pulled up,[2] the village against the neighboring village whose reduction of taxation has ruined it, the overtaxed peasant against the undertaxed peasant, one-half of a par-

---

[1] Horace Walpole, September 5, 1789.

[2] Laboulaye, " De l'Administration française sous Louis XVI." (Revue des Cours littéraires, IV. 743). Albert Babeau, I. iii. (Doléances et vœux des corporations de Troyes).

ish against its collectors, who, to its detriment, have favored the other half. "The nation," says Turgot, mournfully,[1] " is a society composed of different orders badly united and of a people whose members have few mutual liens, *nobody, consequently, caring for any interest but his own. Nowhere is there any sign of an interest in common.* Towns and villages maintain no more relation with each other than the districts to which they are attached ; they are even unable to agree together with a view to carry out public improvements of great importance to them." The central power for a hundred and fifty years rules through its division of power. Men have been kept separate, prevented from acting in concert, the work being so successful that they no longer understand each other, each class ignoring the other class, each forming of the other a chimerical picture, each bestowing on the other the hues of its own imagination, one composing an idyl, the other framing a melodrama, one imagining peasants as sentimental swains, the other convinced that the nobles are horrible tyrants.

Through this mutual misconception and this secular isolation, the French lose the habit, the art and the faculty for acting in an entire body. They are no longer capable of spontaneous agreement and collective action. No one, in the moment of danger, dares rely on his neighbors or on his equals. No one knows where to turn to obtain a guide. "A man willing to be responsible for the smallest district cannot be found ; and, more than this, one man able to answer for another man."[2] Utter confusion exists and there is no remedy. The theoretical Utopia is brought to perfection and the savage condition has recommenced. Individuals now stand in juxtaposition ; every man reverts back to his original feebleness, while his possessions and his life are at the mercy of the first band that comes along. He has nothing within him to control him but the sheep-like habit of being led, of awaiting an impulsion, of turning towards the accustomed centre, towards Paris, from which his orders have always arrived. Arthur Young is struck with this mechanical movement.[3] Political ignorance and docility are everywhere complete. He, a foreigner, conveys the news of Alsace into Burgundy : the insurrec-

---

[1] De Tocqueville, 158.

[2] *Ibid.* 304 (The words of Burke).

[3] Travels in France, I. 240, 263.

tion there had been terrible, the populace having sacked the city-hall at Strasbourg, of which not a word was known at Dijon; "yet it is nine days since it happened; had it been nineteen I question if they would more than have received the intelligence." There are no newspapers in the cafés; no local centres of information, of resolution, of action. The province submits to events at the capital; "people dare not move; they dare not even form an opinion before Paris speaks." Monarchical centralization thus culminates. Groups are deprived of their cohesiveness and individuals of their springs of action. Only human dust remains, and this, whirling about and gathered together in massive force, is blindly driven along by the wind.

III.

We are all well aware from which side the gale comes, and, to assure ourselves, we have merely to see how the reports of the Third-Estate are made up. The peasant is led by the man of the law, the petty attorney of the rural districts, the envious advocate and theorist. He insists, in the report, on a statement being made in writing and at length of his local and personal grievances, his protest against taxes and deductions, his request to have his dog free of the clog, and his desire to own a gun to use against the wolves.[1] The latter, who suggests and directs, envelopes all this in the language of the Rights of Man and that of the circular of Sieyès. "For two months," writes a commandant in the South,[2] "inferior judges and lawyers, with which both town and country swarm, with a view to their election to the States-General, have been racing after the members of the Third-Estate, under the pretext of standing by them and of giving them information. . . . They have striven to make them believe that, in the States-General, they alone would be masters and regulate all the affairs of the kingdom; that the Third-Estate, in selecting its deputies among men of the robe, would secure the might and the right to take the lead, to abolish nobility and to cancel all its rights and privileges; that nobility would no longer be hereditary; that all citizens, in deserving it, would be entitled to claim it; that, if the people deputed them, they would have accorded

---

[1] Beugnot, I. 115, 116.
[2] Archives nationales, procès-verbaux and cahiers of the States-General, XIII. p. 405. (Letter of the Marquis de Fodoas, commandant of Armagnac, to M. Necker, May 29, 1789.)

to the Third-Estate whatever it desired, because the curates, belonging to the Third-Estate, having agreed to separate from the
higher clergy and unite with them, the nobles and the clergy,
united together, would have but one vote against two of the
Third-Estate. . . . If the Third-Estate had chosen sensible
townspeople or merchants they would have combined without
difficulty with the other two orders. But the assemblies of the
bailiwicks and other districts were stuffed with men of the robe
who have absorbed all opinions and striven to take precedence
of the others, each, in his own behalf, intriguing and conspiring to
be appointed a deputy." "In Touraine," writes the intendant,
"most of the votes have been bespoken or begged for. Trusty
agents, at the moment of voting, placed ready-prepared ballots in
the hands of the voters, and put in their way, on reaching the
taverns, every document and suggestion calculated to excite
their imaginations and determine their choice for the gentry of
the bar." "In the *sénéchaussée* of Lectoure, a number of parishes have not been designated or notified to send their reports or
deputies to the district assembly. In those which were notified
the lawyers, attorneys and notaries of the small neighboring
towns have made up the list of grievances themselves without
summoning the community. . . . Exact copies of this single
rough draft were made and sold at a high price to the councils of
each country parish." This is an alarming symptom, one marking
out in advance the road the Revolution is to take: the man of
the people is indoctrinated by the advocate, the pikeman allowing
himself to be led by the spokesman.

The effect of their combination is apparent the first year. In
Franche-Comté [1] after consultation with a person named Rouget,
the peasants of the Marquis de Chaila " determine to make no
further payments to him, and to divide amongst themselves the
product of the wood-cuttings." In his paper " the lawyer states
that all the communities of the province have decided to do the
same thing. . . . His consultation is diffused to such an extent
around the country that many of the communities are satisfied
that they owe nothing more to the king nor to the seigniors. M.
de Marnésia, deputy to the (National) Assembly, has arrived (here)
to pass a few days at home on account of his health. He has

---

[1] Archives nationales, H, 784. (Letters of M. de Langeron, military commandant at
Besançon, October 16 and 18, 1789). The consultation is annexed.

been treated in the rudest and most scandalous manner; it was even proposed to conduct him back to Paris under guard. After his departure his chateau was attacked, the doors burst open and the walls of his garden pulled down. (And yet) no gentleman has done more for the people on his domain than M. le Marquis de Marnésia. . . . Excesses of every kind are on the increase; I have constant complaints of the abuse which the national militia make of their arms, and which I cannot remedy." According to an utterance in the National Assembly the police imagines that it is to be disbanded and has therefore no desire to make enemies for itself. " The *baillages* are as timid as the police-forces; I send them business constantly, but no culprit is punished." " No nation enjoys liberty so indefinite and so disastrous to honest people; it is absolutely against the rights of man to see oneself constantly liable to have his throat cut by the scoundrels who daily confound liberty with license." In other words, the passions, to obtain a sanction, have recourse to theory, and theory, to secure its application, has recourse to the passions. For example, near Liancourt, the Duc de Larochefoucauld possessed an uncultivated area of ground; "at the commencement of the revolution, the poor of the town declare that, as they form a part of the nation, untilled lands being national property, this belongs to them," and " with no other formality " they take possession of it, divide it up, plant hedges and clear it off. "This, says Arthur Young, shows the general disposition. . . . Pushed a little farther the consequences would not be slight for properties in this kingdom." Already, in the preceding year, near Rouen, the marauders, who cut down and sell the forests, declare that " the people have the right to take whatever they require for their necessities." They have had the doctrine preached to them that they are sovereign, and they act as sovereigns. The condition of their intellects being given, nothing is more natural than their conduct. Several millions of savages are thus let loose by a few thousand declaimers, the politics of the café finding an interpreter and ministrants in the mob of the streets. On the one hand brute force is at the service of the radical dogma. On the other hand radical dogma is at the service of brute force. And here, in disintegrated France, do the two powers appear together erect on the general ruin.

CHAPTER V.

I.

THEY are the successors and executors of the ancient régime, and, on contemplating the way in which this engendered, brought forth, nourished, installed and stimulated them we cannot avoid considering its history as one long suicide, like that of a man who, having mounted to the top of an immense ladder, cuts away from under his feet the support which has kept him up. In a case of this kind good intentions are not sufficient; to be liberal and even generous, to enter upon a few semi-reforms, is of no avail. On the contrary, through both their qualities and defects, through both their virtues and their vices, the privileged wrought their own destruction, their merits contributing to their ruin as well as their faults.—Founders of society, formerly entitled to their advantages through their services, they have preserved their rank without fulfilling their duties; their position in the local as in the central government is a sinecure, and their privileges have become abuses. At their head, the king. creating France by devoting himself to her as if his own property, ended by sacrificing her as if his own property; the public purse is his private purse, while passions, vanities, personal weaknesses, luxurious habits, family solicitudes, the intrigues of a mistress and the caprices of a wife, govern a state of twenty-six millions of men with an arbitrariness, a heedlessness, a prodigality, an unskilfulness, an absence of consistency that would scarcely be overlooked in the management of a private domain.—The king and the privileged excel in one direction, in good-breeding, in good taste, in fashion, in the talent for self-display and in entertaining, in the gift of graceful conversation, in finesse and in gaiety, in the art of converting life into a brilliant and ingenious festivity, regarding the world as a drawing-room of refined idlers in which it suffices to be amiable and witty, whilst, actually, it is an arena where one must be strong for combats, and a laboratory in which one must work in order to be useful.—Through the habit, perfection and sway of polished intercourse they stamped on the French intellect a classic form, which, combined with recent scientific acquisitions, produced the philosophy of the eighteenth century, the ill-repute of tradition, the ambition of recasting all human institutions according to the sole dictates of reason, the appliance of mathematical methods to politics and morals, the catechism of the rights of man, and other dogmas of anarchical and despotic character in the *Contrat Social.*—Once this chimera is born they welcome it as a drawing-room fancy; they use the little monster as a plaything, as yet innocent and decked with ribbons like a pastoral lambkin; they never dream of its becoming a raging, formidable brute; they nourish it, and caress it, and then, opening their doors, they let it descend into the streets. —Here, amongst a middle class which the government has rendered ill-disposed by compromising its fortunes, which the privileged have offended by restricting its ambition, which is wounded by inequality through injured self-esteem, the revolutionary theory gains rapid accessions, a sudden asperity, and, in a few years, it finds itself undisputed master of public opinion.— At this moment and at its summons, another colossal monster rises up, a monster with millions of heads, a blind, startled animal, an entire people pressed down, exasperated and suddenly loosed against the government whose exactions have despoiled it, against the privileged whose rights have reduced it to starvation, without, in these rural districts abandoned by their natural protectors, encountering any surviving authority; without, in these provinces subject to the yoke of mechanical centralization, a single independent group being left; without, in this society disaggregated by despotism, the possibility of forming any centres of initiation and resistance; without, in this upper class disarmed by its very humanity, any statesman being found exempt from illusion and capable of action; without these good intentions and fine intellects being able to protect themselves against the two enemies of all liberty and of all order, against the contagion of the democratic nightmare which disturbs the ablest heads and against the irruptions of the popular brutishness which perverts the best of laws. At the moment of opening the States-General the course of ideas and events is not only fixed but, again, apparent. Each generation, beforehand and unconsciously, bears

within itself its future and its history long before the issue the
destinies of this one could be anticipated; and, if the details fell
within our comprehension as well as the completed whole, we
could readily accept the following fiction which La Harpe composed at the end of the Directory, recurring to his souvenirs.

II.

"It seems to me," he says, "as if it were but yesterday, and yet
it is at the beginning of the year 1788. We were dining with
one of our confrères of the Academy, a grand seignior and a
man of intelligence. The company was numerous and of every
profession, courtiers, advocates, men of letters and academicians;
all had feasted luxuriously according to custom. At the dessert,
the wines of Malvoisie and of Constance contributed to the social
gaiety a sort of freedom not always kept within decorous
limits. At that time society had reached the point at which
everything may be expressed that excites laughter. Champfort
had read to us his impious and libertine stories, and great ladies
had listened to these without recourse to their fans. Hence a
deluge of witticisms against religion, one quoting a tirade from
'La Pucelle,' another bringing forward certain philosophical
stanzas by Diderot. . . . and with unbounded applause. . . . The
conversation becomes more serious; admiration is expressed at
the revolution accomplished by Voltaire, and all agree in its being
the first title to his fame. 'He gave the tone to his century,
finding readers in the antechambers as well as in the drawing-
room.' One of the guests narrates, bursting with laughter,
what a hairdresser said to him while powdering his hair: 'You
see, sir, although I am a miserable scrub, I have no more religion
than any one else.' They conclude that the Revolution will
soon be consummated, that superstition and fanaticism must
wholly give way to philosophy, and they thus calculate the probabilities of the epoch and those of the future society which will
see the reign of reason. The most aged lament not being able
to flatter themselves that they will see it; the young rejoice
in a reasonable prospect of seeing it, and especially do they
congratulate the Academy on having paved the way for
the great work, and on having been the headquarters, the centre,
the inspirer of freedom of thought.

"One of the guests had taken no part in this gay conversation,

. . . a person named Cazotte, an amiable and original man, but, unfortunately, infatuated with the reveries of the illuminati. In the most serious tone he begins: 'Gentlemen,' says he, 'be content; you will witness this great revolution that you so much desire. You know that I am something of a prophet, and I repeat it, you will witness it. . . . Do you know the result of this revolution, for all of you, so long as you remain here?'—'Ah!' exclaims Condorcet with his shrewd, simple air and smile, 'let us see, a philosopher is not sorry to encounter a prophet.'—'You, Monsieur de Condorcet, will expire stretched on the floor of a dungeon; you will die of the poison you take to escape the executioner, of the poison which the felicity of that era will compel you always to carry about your person!' At first, great astonishment was manifested, and then came an outburst of laughter. 'What has all this in common with philosophy and the reign of reason?'—'Precisely what I have just remarked to you; in the name of philosophy, of humanity, of freedom, under the reign of reason, you will thus reach your end; and, evidently, the reign of reason will arrive, for there will be temples of reason, and, in those days, in all France, the temples will be those alone of reason. . . . You, Monsieur de Champfort, you will sever your veins with twenty-two strokes of a razor and yet you will not die for months afterwards. You, Monsieur Vicq-d'Azir, you will not open your own veins but you will have them opened six times in one day, in the agonies of gout, so as to be more certain of success, and you will die that night. You, Monsieur de Nicolai, on the scaffold; you, Monsieur Bailly, on the scaffold; you, Monsieur de Malesherbes, on the scaffold; . . . you, Monsieur Roucher, also on the scaffold.'— 'But then we shall have been overcome by Turks or Tartars?'— 'By no means; you will be governed, as I have already told you, solely by philosophy and reason. Those who are to treat you in this manner will all be philosophers, will all, at every moment, have on their lips the phrases you have uttered within the hour, will repeat your maxims, will quote, like yourselves, the stanzas of Diderot and of "La Pucelle."'—'And when will all this happen?'—'Six years will not pass before what I tell you will be accomplished.'—'Well, these are miracles,' exclaims La Harpe, 'and you leave me out?'—'You will be no less a miracle, for you will then be a Christian.'—'Ah,' interposes Champfort, 'I breathe

2 D

again; if we are to die only when La Harpe becomes a Christian
we are immortals.'—'As to that, we women,' says the Duchesse
de Gramont, 'are extremely fortunate in being of no consequence
in revolutions.   It is understood that we are not to blame, and
our sex . . .'—'Your sex, ladies, will not protect you this time.
. . . You will be treated precisely as men, with no difference
whatever. . . . You, Madame la Duchesse, will be led to the
scaffold, you and many ladies besides yourself, in a cart with your
hands tied behind your back.'—'Ah, in that event, I hope to have
at least a carriage covered with black.'—'No, Madame, greater
ladies than yourself will go, like yourself, in a cart and with their
hands tied like yours.' 'Greater ladies! What, princesses of the
blood!'—'Still greater ladies than those . . .' They began to
think the jest carried too far.   Madame de Gramont, to dispel
the gloom, did not insist on a reply to her last exclamation, con-
tenting herself by saying in the lightest tone, 'And they will not
even leave one a confessor!'—'No, Madame, neither you nor
any other person will be allowed a confessor; the last of the condemned that will have one, as an act of grace, will be . . .'   He
stopped a moment.   'Tell me, now, who is the fortunate mortal
enjoying this prerogative?'—'It is the last that will remain to
him, and it will be the King of France.'"

NOTES.

Note 1.

On the number of ecclesiastics and nobles.

These approximative estimates are arrived at in the following manner:

1. The number of nobles in 1789 was unknown. The genealogist Chérin, in his "Abrégé chronologique des Edits, etc." (1789), states that he is ignorant of the number. Moheau, to whom Lavoisier refers in his report, 1791, is equally ignorant in this respect. ("Recherches sur la population de la France," 1778, p. 105); Lavoisier states the number as 83,000, while the Marquis de Bouillé ("Mémoires," p. 50), states 80,000 families; neither of these authorities advancing proofs of their statements. I find in the "Catalogue nominatif des gentilshommes en 1789," by Laroque and De Barthélemy, the number of nobles voting, directly or by proxy, in the elections of 1789, in Provence, Languedoc, Lyonnais, Forez, Beaujolais, Touraine, Normandy, and Ile-de-France, as 9,167. According to the census of 1790, given by Arthur Young in his "Travels in France," the population of these provinces was 7,757,000, which gives a proportion of 30,000 nobles voting in a population of 26,000,000. On examining the law and on summing up the lists, we find that each noble represents somewhat less than a family, inasmuch as the son of the owner of a fief votes if he is twenty-five years of age; I think, accordingly, that we are not far out of the way in estimating the number of noble families at 26,000 or 28,000, which number, at five individuals to the family, gives 130,000 or 140,000 nobles. The territory of France in 1789 being 27,000 square leagues, and the population 26,000,000, we may assign one noble family to every square league of territory and to every 1,000 inhabitants.

2. Concerning the clergy I find in the National Archives, among the ecclesiastical records, the following enumeration of monks belonging to 28 orders: Grand Augustins 694, Petits-Pères 250, Barnabites 90, English Benedictines 52, Benedictines of Cluny 298, of Vannes 612, of Saint-Maur 1,672, Citeaux 1,806, Récollets 2,238, Prémontrés 399, Prémontrés Réformés 394, Capucins 3,720, Carmes déchaussés 555, Grands-Carmes 853, Hospitaliers de Saint-Jean de Dieu 218, Chartreux 1,144, Cordeliers 2,018, Dominicans 1,172, Feuillants 148, Genovéfains 570, Mathurins 310, Minimes 684, Notre-Dame de la Merci 31, Notre-Saveur 203, Tiers-Ordre de St. Francis 365, Saint-Jean ès Vignes de Soissons 31, Théatins 25, abbaye de Saint-Victor 21, Maisons soumises à l'ordinaire 305. Total 20,745 monks in 2,489 convents. To this

must be added the Pères de l'Oratoire, de la Mission, de la Doctrine chrétienne and some others; the total of monks being about 23,000. As to nuns, I have a catalogue from the National Archives of twelve dioceses, comprising according to "France ecclésiastique" 1788, 5,576 parishes: the dioceses respectively of Perpignan, Tulle, Marseilles, Rhodes, Saint-Flour, Toulouse, le Mans, Limoges, Lisieux, Rouen, Reims, and Noyon, in all, 5,394 nuns in 198 establishments. The proportion is 37,000 nuns in 1,500 establishments for the 38,000 parishes of France. The total of regular clergy thus amounts to 60,000 persons. The secular clergy may be estimated at 70,000: curates and vicars 60,000 ("Histoire de l'Eglise de France," XII. 142, by the Abbé Guettée); prelates, vicars-general, canons of chapters, 2,800; collegiate canons, 5,600; ecclesiastics without livings, 3,000 (Sieyès). Moheau, a clear-headed and cautious statistician, writes in 1778 ("Recherches," p. 100): "Perhaps, to-day, there are 130,000 ecclesiastics in the kingdom." The enumeration of 1866 ("Statistique de la France," population), gives 51,100 members of the secular clergy, 18,500 monks, 86,300 nuns; total, 155,900 in a population of 38,000,000 inhabitants.

Note 2.

On feudal rights and on the state of feudal dominion in 1783.

The following information, for which I am indebted to M. de Boislisle, is derived from an act of partition drawn up September 6, 1783.

It relates to the estates of Blet and Brosses. The barony and estate of Blet lies in Bourbonnais, two leagues from Dun-le-Roi. Blet, says a memorial of an administrator of the Excise, is a "good parish; the soil is excellent, mostly in wood and pasture, the surplus being in tillable land for wheat, rye and oats. . . . The roads are bad, especially in winter. The trade consists principally of horned cattle and embraces grain; the woods rot away on account of their remoteness from the towns and the difficulty of turning them to account." [1]

"This estate," says the act of valuation, "is in royal tenure on account of the king's chateau and fortress of Ainay, under the designation of the town of Blet." The town was formerly fortified and its castle still remains. Its population was once large, "but the civil wars of the sixteenth century, and especially the emigration of the protestants caused it to be deserted to such an extent that out of its former population of 3,000 scarcely 300 remain,[2] which is the fate of nearly all the towns in this country." The estate of Blet, for many centuries in the possession of the Sully family, passed, on the marriage of the heiress in 1363, to the house of Saint-Quentin, and was then transmitted in direct line down to 1748, the date of the death of Alexander II. of Saint-Quentins, Count of Blet, governor of Berg-op-Zoom, and father of three daughters from whom the actual heirs descend. These heirs are the Count de Simiane, the Chevalier de Simiane, and the minors of Bercy,

---

[1] Archives nationales, G, 319 ("Etat actuel de la Direction de Bourges au point de vue des aides," 1774).

[2] Blet, at the present day, contains 1,629 inhabitants.

_ach party owning one-third, represented by 97,667 livres in the Blet estate, and 20,408 livres in the Brosses estate. The eldest, Comte de Simiane, enjoys, besides, a *préciput* (according to custom in the Bourbonnais), worth 15,000 livres, comprising the castle with the adjoining farm and the seigniorial rights, honorary as well as profitable.

The entire domain, comprising both estates, is valued at 369,227 livres. The estate of Blet, comprises 1,437 *arpents*, worked by seven farmers and furnished, by the proprietor, with cattle valued at 13,781 livres. They pay together to the proprietor 12,060 livres rent (besides claims for poultry and *corvées*). One, only, has a large farm, paying 7,800 livres per annum, the others paying rents of 1,300, 740, 640, and 240 livres per annum. The Brosses estate comprises 515 *arpents*, worked by two farmers to whom the proprietor furnishes cattle estimated at 3,750 livres, and these together return to the proprietor 2,240 livres.[1] These *métairies* are all poor; only one of them has two rooms with fire-places; two or three, one room with a fire-place; the others consist of a kitchen with an oven outside, and stables and barns. Repairs on the tenements are essential on all the farms except three, "having been neglected for thirty years." "The mill-flume requires to be cleaned out, and the stream whose inundations injure the large meadow; also repairs are necessary on the banks of the two ponds; on the church, which is the seignior's duty, the roof being in a sad state, the rain penetrating through the arch;" and the roads require mending, these being in a deplorable condition during the winter. "The restoration and repairs of these roads seem never to have been thought of." The soil of the Blet estate is excellent, but it requires draining and ditching to carry off the water, otherwise the low lands will continue to produce nothing but weeds. Signs of neglect and desertion are everywhere visible. The chateau of Blet has remained unoccupied since 1748; the furniture, accordingly, is almost all decayed and useless; in 1748 this was worth 7,612 livres, and now it is estimated at 1,000 livres. "The water-power costs nearly as much to maintain as the income derived from it. The use of plaster as manure is unknown," and yet "in the land of plaster it costs almost nothing." The ground, moist and very good, would grow excellent live hedges; and yet the fields are enclosed with bare fences against the cattle, "which expense, say the farmers, is equal to a third of the net income." This domain, as just described, is valued as follows:

1. The estate of Blet, according to the custom of the country for noble estates, is valued at rate twenty-five, namely, 373,000 livres, from which must be deducted a capital of 65,056 livres, representing the annual charges (the fixed salary of the curate, repairs, etc.), not including personal charges like the *vingtièmes*. Its net revenue per annum is 12,300 livres, and is worth, net, 308,003 livres.

2. The estate of Brosses is estimated at rate twenty-two, ceasing to be noble through the transfer of judicial and fief rights to that of Blet. Thus rated it is worth 73,583 livres, from which must be deducted a capital of

---

[1] The farms of Blet and Brosses really produce nothing for the proprietor, inasmuch as the tithes and the *champart* (field-rents), (articles 22 and 23), are comprehended in the rate of the leases.

12,359 livres for actual charges, the estate bringing in 3,140 livres per annum
and worth, net, 61,224 livres.

These revenues are derived from the following sources:

1. Rights of the high, low and middle courts of justice over the entire
territory of Blet and other villages, Brosses and Jalay. The upper courts,
according to an act passed at the Châtelet, April 29, 1702, "take cognizance
of all actions, real and personal, civil and criminal, even actions between
nobles and ecclesiastics, relating to seals and inventories of movable effects,
tutelages, curacies, the administration of the property of minors, of domains,
and of the customary dues and revenues of the seigniory, etc."

2. Rights of the forests, edict of 1707. The seignior's warden decides
in all cases concerning waters, and woods, and customs, and crimes relating
to fishing and hunting.

3. Right of *voirie*, or the police of the highways, streets, and buildings
(excepting the great main roads). The seignior appoints a bailly, warden
and road overseer, one M. Theurault (at Sagonne), a fiscal attorney, Baujard
(at Blet); he may remove them "in case they make no returns." "The
rights of the *greffe* were formerly secured to the seignior, but as it is now
very difficult to find intelligent persons in the country able to fulfil its
functions, the seignior abandons his rights to those whom it may concern."
(The seignior pays forty-eight livres per annum to the bailly to hold his
court once a month, and twenty-four livres per annum to the fiscal attorney
to attend them).

He receives the fines and confiscations of cattle awarded by his officers.
The profit therefrom, an average year, is eight livres.

He must maintain a jail and a jailer. (It is not stated whether there was
one). No sign of a gibbet is found in the seigniory.

He may appoint twelve notaries; only one, in fact, is appointed at Blet
"and he has nothing to do," a M. Baujard, fiscal attorney. This commission is assigned him gratuitously, to keep up the privilege, "otherwise it
would be impossible to find any one sufficiently intelligent to perform its
functions."

He appoints a sergeant, but, for a long time, this sergeant pays no rent or
anything for his lodging.

4. Personal and real *taille*. In Bourbonnais the *taille* was formerly
serf, and the serfs mainmortable. "Seigniors still possessing rights of
bordelage, well established throughout their fiefs and courts, at the present
time, enjoy rights of succession to their vassals in all cases, even to the
prejudice of their children if non-resident and no longer dwelling under their
roofs." But in 1255, Hodes de Sully, having granted a charter, renounced
this right of real and personal *taille* for a right of bourgeoisie, still maintained, (see further on).

5. Right to unclaimed property, cattle, furniture, effects, stray swarms of
bees, treasure-trove; (no profits from this for twenty years past).

6. Right to property of deceased persons without heirs, to that of
deceased bastards, the possessions of condemned criminals either to death,
to the galleys or to exile, etc., (no profit).

7. Right of the chase and of fishing, the latter worth fifteen livres per
annum.

8. Right of *bourgeoisie* (see article 4), according to the charter of 1255, and the court-roll of 1484. The wealthiest pay annually twelve bushels of oats at forty livres and twelve deniers *parasis ;* the less wealthy nine bushels and nine deniers; all others six bushels and six deniers. "These rights of *bourgeoisie* are well established, set forth in all court-rolls and acknowledgments rendered to the king and perpetuated by numerous admissions; the motives that have led former stewards and *fermiers* to interrupt the collection of these cannot be divined. Many of the seigniors in Bourbonnais have the benefit of and exact these taxes of their vassals by virtue of titles much more open to question than those of the seigniors of Blet."

9. Rights of protection of the chateau of Blet. The royal edict of 1497, fixing this charge for the inhabitants of Blet and all those dwelling within the jurisdiction of its tribunals, those of Charly, Boismarvier, etc., at five sous per fire per annum, which has been carried out. "Only lately has the collection of this been suspended, notwithstanding its recognition at no late date, the inhabitants all admitting themselves to be subject to the said *guet et garde* of the chateau.

10. Right of toll on all merchandise and provisions passing through the town of Blet, except grain, flour and vegetables. (A trial pending before the Council of State since 1727 and not terminated in 1745; "the collection thereof, meanwhile, being suspended").

11. Right of *potage* on wines sold at retail in Blet, ensuring to the seignior nine pints of wine per cask, leased in 1782 for six years, at sixty livres per annum.

12. Right of *boucherie* or of taking the tongues of all animals slaughtered in the town, with, additionally, the heads and feet of all calves. No slaughter-house at Blet, and yet "during the harvesting of each year about twelve head of cattle are slaughtered." This tax is collected by the steward and is valued at three livres per annum.

13. Right of fairs and markets, *aunage*, weight and measures. Five fairs per annum and one market-day each week, but little frequented; no grain-market. This right is valued at twenty-four livres per annum.

14. *Corvées* of teams and manual labor, through seigniorial right, on ninety-seven persons at Blet (twenty-two *corvées* of teams and seventy-five of manual labor), twenty-six persons at Brosses (five teams and twenty-one hands). The seignior pays six sous for food, each *corvée*, on men, and twelve sous on each *corvée* of four oxen. "Among those subject to this *corvée* the larger number are reduced almost to beggary and have large families, which often induces the seignior not to exact this right rigorously." The reduced value of the *corvées* is forty-nine livres fifteen sols.

15. *Banalité* (socome), of the mill, (a sentence of 1736 condemning Roy, a laborer, to have his grain ground in the mill of Blet, and to pay a fine for having ceased to have grain ground there during three years). The miller reserves a sixteenth of the flour ground. The district-mill, as well as the windmill, with six *arpents* adjoining, are leased at 600 livres per annum.

16. *Banalité* of the oven. Agreement of 1537 between the seignior and his vassals: he allows them the privilege of a small oven in their domicile of three squares, six inches each, to bake pies, biscuits and cakes; in other

respects subject to the district oven. He is entitled to one-sixteenth of the dough ; this right might produce 150 livres annually, but, for several years, the oven has been dilapidated.

17. Right of the *colombier*, dove-cot. The chateau park contains one.

18. Right of *bordelage*. (The seignior is heir-at-law, except when the children of the deceased live with their parents at the time of his death). This right covers an area of forty-eight *arpents*. For twenty years, through neglect or from other causes, he has derived nothing from this.

19. Right over waste and abandoned ground and to alluvial accumulations.

20. Right, purely honorary, of seat and burial in the choir, of incense and of special prayer, of funeral hangings outside and inside the church.

21. Rights of *lods et ventes* on copyholders, due by the purchaser of property liable to this lien, in forty days. "In Bourbonnais, the *lods et ventes* are collected at a third, a quarter, at the sixth, eighth and twelfth rate." The seignior of Blet and Brosses collects at rate six. It is estimated that sales are made once in eighty years ; these rights bear on 1,356 *arpents* which are worth, the best, 192 livres per *arpent*, the second best, 110 livres, the poorest, 75 livres. At this rate the 1,350 *arpents* are worth 162,750 livres. A discount of one-quarter of the *lods et ventes* is allowed to purchasers. Annual revenue of this right 254 livres.

22. Right of tithe and of *charnage*. The seignior has obtained all tithe rights, save a few belonging to the canons of Dun-le-Roi and to the prior of Chaumont. The tithes are levied on the thirteenth shcaf. They are comprised in the leases.

23. Right of *terrage* or *champart:* the right of collecting, after the tithes, a portion of the produce of the ground. "In Bourbonnais, the *terrage* is collected in various ways, on the third sheaf, on the fifth, sixth, seventh, and commonly one-quarter; at Blet it is the twelfth." The seignior of Blet collects *terrage* only on a certain number of the farms of his seigniory; "in relation to Brosses, it appears that all domains possessed by copyholders are subject to the right." These rights of *terrage* are comprised in the leases of the farms of Blet and of Brosses.

24. *Cens, surcens* and *rentes* due on real property of different kinds, houses, fields, meadows, etc., situated in the territory of the seigniory. In the seigniory of Blet, 810 *arpents*, divided into 511 portions, in the hands of 120 copyholders, are in this condition, and their *cens* annually consists of 137 francs in money, sixty-seven bushels of wheat, three of barley, 159 of oats, sixteen hens, 130 chickens, six cocks and capons ; the total valued at 575 francs. On the Brosses estate, eighty-five *arpents*, divided into 112 parcels, in the hands of twenty copyholders, are in this condition, and their total *cens* is fourteen francs money, seventeen bushels of wheat, thirty-two of barley, twenty-six hens, three chickens and one capon ; the whole valued at 126 francs.

25. Rights over the commons (124 *arpents* in Blet and 164 *arpents* in Brosses).

The vassals have on these only the right of use. "Almost the whole of the land, on which they exercise this right of pasturage, belongs to the seigniors, save this right with which they are burdened: it is granted only to a few individuals."

26. Rights over the *fiefs mouvants* of the barony of Blet. Some are situated in Bourbonnais, nineteen being in this condition. In Bourbonnais, the fiefs, even when owned by plebeians, simply owe *la bouche et les mains* to the seignior at each mutation. Formerly the seignior of Blet enforced, in this case, the right of redemption which has been allowed to fall into desuetude. Others are situated in Berry where the right of redemption is exercised. One fief in Berry, that of Cormesse held by the archbishop of Bourges, comprising eighty-five *arpents*, besides a portion of the tithes, and producing 2,100 livres per annum, admitting a *mutation* every twenty years, annually brings to the seignior of Blet 105 livres.

Besides the charges indicated there are the following:

1. To the curate of Blet, his fixed salary. According to royal enactment in 1686, this should be 300 livres. According to arrangement in 1692, the curate, desirous of assuring himself of this fixed salary, yielded to the seignior all the *dimes*, *novales*, etc. The edict of 1768 having fixed the curate's salary at 500 livres, the curate claimed this sum through writs. The canons of Dun-le-Roi and the prior of Chaumont, possessing tithes on the territory of Blet, were obliged to pay a portion of it. At present it is at the charge of the seignior of Blet.

2. To the guard, besides his lodging, warming and the use of three *arpents*, 200 livres.

3. To the steward or registrar, to preserve the archives, look after repairs, collect *lods et ventes*, and fines, 432 livres, besides the use of ten *arpents*.

4. To the king, the *vingtièmes*. Formerly the estates of Blet and Brosses paid 810 livres for the two *vingtièmes* and the two sous per livre. After the establishment of the third *vingtième* they paid 1,216 livres.

Note 3.

Difference between the actual and nominal revenues of ecclesiastical dignities and benefices.

According to Raudot ("La France avant la Revolution," p. 84), one-half extra must be added to the official valuation; according to Boiteau ("Etat de la France en 1789," p. 195), this must be tripled and even quadrupled. I think that, for the episcopal sees, one-half extra should be added and, for the abbeys and priories, double, and sometimes triple and even quadruple the amount. The following facts show the variation between official and actual sums.

1. In the "Almanach Royal," the bishopric of Troyes is valued at 14,000 livres; in "France Ecclésiastique of 1788," at 50,000. According to Albert Babeau ("Histoire de la Révolution dans le département de l'Aube"), it brings in 70,000 livres. In "France Ecclésiastique," the bishopric of Strasbourg is put down at 400,000 livres. According to the Duc de Lévis ("Souvenirs," p. 156) it brings in at least 600,000 livres income.

2. In the same work, the abbey of Jumièges is assigned for 23,000 livres. I find, in the papers of the ecclesiastic committee, it brings to the abbé 50,000 livres. In this work the abbey of Bèze is estimated at 8,000 livres. I find it bringing to the monks alone 30,000, while the abbé's portion is at

least as large. (" De l'Etat religieux, par les abbés de Bonnefoi et Bernard," 1784). The abbé thus receives 30,000 livres. Bernay (Eure), is officially reported at 16,000. The "Doléances" of the *cahiers* estimate it at 57,000. Saint-Amand is put down as bringing to the Cardinal of York 6,000 livres and actually brings him 100,000. (De Luynes, XIII. 215).

Clairvaux, in the same work, is put down at 9,000, and in Warroquier ("Etat Général de la France en 1789,") at 60,000. According to Beugnot, who belongs to the country, and a practical man, the abbé has from 300,000 to 400,000 livres income.

Saint-Faron, says Boiteau, set down at 18,000 livres, is worth 120,000 livres.

The abbey of Saint-Germain des Près (in the stewardships), is put down at 100,000 livres. The Comte de Clermont, who formerly had it, leased it at 160,000 livres, "not including reserved fields and all that the farmers furnished in straw and oats for his horses." (Jules Cousin, "Comte de Clermont and his court.")

Saint-Waas d'Arras, according to "La France Ecclésiastique," brings 40,000 livres. Cardinal de Rohan refused 1,000 livres per month for his portion offered to him by the monks. (Duc de Lévis, "Souvenirs," p. 156). Its value thus is about 300,000 livres.

Remiremont, the abbess always being a royal princess, one of the most powerful monasteries, the richest and best endowed, is officially valued at the ridiculous sum of 15,000 livres.

Note 4.

On the education of princes and princesses.

An entire chapter might be devoted to this subject; I shall cite but a few texts.

(Barbier, "Journal," October, 1670). The Dauphine has just given birth to an infant.

"La jeune princesse en est à sa quatrième nourrice. . . . J'ai appris à cette occasion que tout se fait par forme à la cour, suivant un protocole de médecin, en sorte que c'est un miracle d'élever un prince et une princesse. La nourrice n'a d'autres fonctions que de donner à têter à l'enfant quand on le lui apporte; elle ne peut pas lui toucher. Il y a des remueuses et femmes préposées pour cela, mais qui n'ont point d'ordre à recevoir de la nourrice. Il y a des heures pour remuer l'enfant, trois ou quatre fois dans la journée. Si l'enfant dort, on le réveille pour le remuer. Si, après avoir été changé, il fait dans ses langes, il reste ainsi trois ou quatre heures dans son ordure. Si une épingle le pique, la nourrice ne doit pas l'ôter; il faut chercher et attendre une autre femme; l'enfant crie dans tous ces cas, il se tourmente et s'échauffe, en sorte que c'est une vraie misère que toutes ces cérémonies."

(Madame de Genlis, "Souvenirs de Félicie," p. 74. Conversation with Madame Louise, daughter of Louis XV., and recently become a Carmelite).

" I should like to know what troubled you most in getting accustomed to your new profession ? "

" You could never imagine," she replied, smiling. " It was the descent of a small flight of steps alone by myself. At first it seemed to me a dreadful precipice, and I was obliged to sit down on the steps and slide down in that attitude." "A princess, indeed, who had never descended any but the grand staircase at Versailles, leaning on the arm of her cavalier in waiting and surrounded by pages, necessarily trembled on finding herself alone on the brink of steep winding steps. (Such is) the education, so absurd in many respects, generally bestowed on persons of this rank ; always watched from infancy, followed, assisted, escorted and everything anticipated, (they) are thus, in great part, deprived of the faculties with which nature has endowed them."

Madame Campan, "Mémoires," I. 18, 28.

"Madame Louise often told me that, although twelve years of age, she had not fully learned the alphabet. . . .

"It was necessary to decide absolutely whether a certain water-bird was fat or lean. Madame Victoire consulted a bishop. . . . He replied that, in a doubt of this kind, after having the bird cooked it would be necessary to puncture in on a very cold silver dish and, if the juice coagulated in one-quarter of an hour, the bird might be considered fat. Madame Victoire immediately put it to test; the juice did not coagulate. The princess was highly delighted, as she was very fond of this species of game. Fasting (on religious grounds), to which Madame Victoire was addicted, put her to inconvenience ; accordingly she awaited the midnight stroke of Holy Saturday impatiently. A dish of chicken and rice and other succulent dishes were then at once served up."

("Journal de Dumont d'Urville," commanding the vessel on which Charles X. left France in 1830. Quoted by Vaulabelle, History of the Restoration, VIII. p. 465).

"The king and the Duc d'Angoulême questioned me on my various campaigns, but especially on my voyage around the world in the 'Astrolabe.' My narrative seemed to interest them very much, their interruptions consisting of questions of remarkable naïveté, showing that they possessed no notions whatever, even the most superficial, on the sciences or on voyages, being as ignorant on these points as any of the old *rentiers* of the Marais."

Note 5.

On the rate of direct taxation.

The following figures are extracted from the *procès-verbaux* of the provincial assemblies (1778–1787).

	Taille.	Accessiores de la taille.	Capitation taillable.	Impôt des routes.	Total en multiples de la taille.
Ile-de-France, ...	4,296,040	2,207,826	2,689,287	519,989	2,23
Lyonnais,............	1,356,954	903,653	898,089	315,869	2,61
Généralité de Rouen,.	2,671,939	1,595,051	1,715,592	598,258[1]	2,46
Généralité de Caen,..	1,939,665	1,212,429	1,187,823	659,034	2,56
Berry, ...	821,921	448,431	464,955	236,900	2,50
Poitou, ...	2,309,681	1,113,766	1,403,402	520,000	2,30
Soissonnais,.........	1,062,392	911,883	734,899	462,883	2,94
Orléanais,..........	2,353,892	1,256,125	1,485,720	586,385	2,34
Champagne,.........	1,783,850	1,459,780	1,377,371	807,280	3
Généralité d'Alençon,	1,742,655	1,120,041	1,067,849	435,637	2,47
Auvergne, ...	1,999,040	1,399,678	1,753,026	310,468	2,70
Généralité d'Auch,...	1,440,533	931,261	797,268	316,909[2]	2,35
Haute-Guyenne, ...	2,131,314	1,267,619	1,268,855	308,993[3]	2,47

The principal of the *taille* being one, the figures in the last column represent, for each province, the total of the four taxes in relation to the *taille*. The average of all these is 2.53. The accessories of the *taille*, the poll-tax and the tax for roads, are fixed for each assessable party, pro rata to his *taille*. Multiply the sum representing the portion of the *taille* deducted from a net income by 2.53, to know the sum of the four taxes put together and deducted from this income.

This part varies from province to province, from parish to parish, and even from individual to individual. Nevertheless we may estimate that the *taille*, on the average, especially when bearing on a small peasant proprietor, without protector or influence, abstracts one-sixth of his net income, say 16 fr. 66 c. on 100 francs. For example, according to the declarations of the provincial assemblies, in Champagne, it deducts 3 sous and ⅔ of a denier per livre, or 15 fr. 28 c. on 100 francs; in the Ile-de-France, 35 livres 14 sous on 240 livres, or 14 fr. 87 c. on 100; in Auvergne, 4 sous per livre of the net income, that is to say, 20 per 100. Finally, in the generalship of Auch, the provincial assembly estimates that the *taille* and accessories absorb three-tenths of the net revenue, by which it is evident that, taking the amounts of the provincial budget, the *taille* alone absorbs eighteen fr. ten c. on 100 francs of revenue.

Thus stated, if the *taille* as principal absorbs one-sixth of the net income of the subject of the *taille*, that is to say, 16 fr. 66 c. on 100, the total of

---

[1] This amount is not given by the provincial assembly; to fill up this blank I have taken the tenth of the *taille*, of the accessories and of the assessable poll-tax, this being the mode followed by the provincial assembly of Lyonnais. By the declaration of June 2, 1787, the tax on roads may be carried to one-sixth of the three preceding imposts; it is commonly one-tenth or, in relation to the principal of the *taille*, one-quarter.—[2] Same remark.—[3] The provincial assembly carries this amount to one-eleventh of the *taille* and accessories combined.

the four imposts above mentioned, takes 16 fr. 66 c. × 2,53 = 42 fr. 15 c. on 100 fr. income. To which must be added 11 fr. for the two *vingtièmes* and 4 sous per livre added to the first *vingtième*, total 53 fr. 15 c. direct tax on 100 livres income subject to the *taille.*

The *dime,* tithe, being estimated at a seventh of the net income, abstracts in addition 14 fr. 28 c. The feudal dues being valued at the same sum also take off 14 fr. 28 c., total 28 fr. 56 c.

Sum total of deductions of the direct royal tax, of the ecclesiastic tithes, and of feudal dues, 81 fr. 71 c. on 100 fr. income. There remain to the tax- payer 18 fr. 29 c.

INDEX.

THE END.

C58002